Balanced Scorecards and Operational Dashboards with Microsoft® Excel®

Ron Person

WILEY

Wiley Publishing, Inc.

Balanced Scorecards and Operational Dashboards with Microsoft® Excel®

Published by
Wiley Publishing, Inc.
10475 Crosspoint Boulevard
Indianapolis, IN 46256
www.wiley.com

Copyright © 2009 by Tor Consulting, Inc., Santa Rosa, California
Published by Wiley Publishing, Inc., Indianapolis, Indiana
Published simultaneously in Canada

ISBN: 978-0-470-38681-1

Manufactured in the United States of America

10 9 8 7 6 5

Library of Congress Cataloging-in-Publication Data is available from the publisher.

For general information on our other products and services, please contact our Customer Care Department within the United States at (877) 762-2974 and outside the United States at (317) 572-3993, fax (317) 572-4002.

Wiley also publishes its books in a variety of electronic formats. Some content that appears in print may not be available in electronic books.

Balanced Scorecards and Operational Dashboards with Microsoft® Excel®

About the Author

Ron Person helps his clients create a competitive advantage in strategic execution and a culture of high-performance.

Ron's firm, Tor Consulting, works with small- to mid-sized organizations with revenues of $25 to $500 million. His clients in the United States and internationally include hospitals, banks, biotech companies, medical device manufacturers, and financial services firms, spanning a diversity of organizations such as:

- Medtronic CardioVascular
- Bethanie Group (Western Australia's largest elder care and hospital system)
- Wells Fargo Center for the Arts
- Palladeo (retail strategy, design, and construction)
- U.S. Army Corps of Engineers
- U.S. Naval Undersea Warfare Center

Prior to founding Tor Consulting, Ron has been:

- A manager of competitive analysis for a Fortune 500 corporation
- One of Microsoft's first twelve consulting partners
- The founder or co-founder of four companies, two of them high-tech
- The author of more than 20 business and computer books, including four international bestsellers with almost 4 million copies in print

He has personally conducted workshops for thousands of businesspeople and has spoken before conferences and groups such as Vistage (the world's leading Chief Executive organization), Microsoft technical conferences, the American Society for Quality, APICS (the Association for Operations Managers), the Project Management Institute, PIHRA (the Professionals in Human Resources Association), and the American Association of Homes and Services for the Aging.

Ron's education and credentials include:

- Certification by the Balanced Scorecard Collaborative, the educational division of the founders of Balanced Scorecard, Drs. Kaplan and Norton. Only a few independent consultants each year pass this rigorous training and examination.

- Member of the California Awards for Performance Excellence™ Board of Examiners, 2008 (California's Malcolm Baldridge award for excellence in organizational performance)

- A Six Sigma Black Belt

- An M.B.A. in marketing and finance with highest honors

- An M.S. in physics

- Training as a facilitator for strategic planning by the Institute for Cultural Affairs and the Center for Strategic Facilitation

For additional information on how your organization can create a competitive advantage through strategic execution and accelerated performance, contact Ron Person at:

ron@torconsulting.com
(707) 568-6976
www.torconsulting.com

About the Technical Editor

Doug Holland, a "blue-badge" software engineer at Intel Corporation since March 2007, holds a master's degree in software engineering from Oxford University, has received the Microsoft MVP award within the Visual C# category, and is also an Intel Black Belt Software Developer. Outside work, Doug enjoys spending time with his wife and four children and is an officer and aircrew member in the Civil Air Patrol/U.S. Air Force Auxiliary.

Credits

Acquisitions Editor
Katie Mohr

Development Editor
Adaobi Obi Tulton

Technical Editor
Doug Holland

Production Editor
Melissa Lopez

Copy Editor
Publication Services, Inc.

Editorial Manager
Mary Beth Wakefield

Production Manager
Tim Tate

**Vice President and Executive
Group Publisher**
Richard Swadley

**Vice President and
Executive Publisher**
Joseph B. Wikert

Compositor
Craig Johnson,
Happenstance Type-O-Rama

Proofreaders
Corina Copp and Josh Chase,
WordOne

Indexer
Jack Lewis

Cover Image
© Jupiter Images/Goodshoot

Cover Designer
Michael E. Trent

Acknowledgments

Having been a consultant for more than 20 years, I realize that one of the responsibilities of a consultant is collecting and filtering ideas that help clients, then putting the best ones into practice in ways that make them productive and beneficial. There are many people and sources who have built the foundation of the ideas presented in this book. Here are a few I would like to thank.

First, thank you to my past and future clients. I truly enjoy meeting and working with each new team to help create a competitive and performance advantage.

Thank you to Drs. Kaplan and Norton of the Palladium Group for furthering the advancement of management science with Balanced Scorecards and Strategy Maps.

Each year, a few consultants complete the Balanced Scorecard certification program delivered through the Balanced Scorecard Collaborative, the educational division of the Palladium Group. Thank you to Edward A. Barrows, Jr., Vice President of Balanced Scorecard Collaborative, a Palladium company, and Karen A. DiMartino, Manager, Advisory Services, for conducting an excellent Balanced Scorecard certification program.

The consulting profession can often be lonely, and the opportunities to develop our professional skills are neglected as we help clients and spend time with family. Many people have committed extra time to developing the professional skills of consultants, and we consultants owe them a debt of gratitude. A few of these people in northern California are:

> Harry Chapman, Bay Area Consulting Group, founder of the Bay Area Consultants Network

> Rogene Baxter, the Bridgewater Group, former president of the Institute of Management Consultants, Northern California Chapter

Gary White, Pacific Crest Marketing, board member of the Bay Area Consultants Network

Sanford Friedman, Mapping2Success, board member of the Bay Area Consultants Network

Gloria Dunn, President, Wiser Ways to Work

Jane Stallman, Center for Strategic Facilitation

Thank you to Cathy Webber, Senior Lead, CAPE, for introducing me to California Awards for Excellence™, California's Malcolm Baldridge award for organizational excellence. And thank you for the time and skills imparted by

Diane Akers, 2008 California Awards for Excellence™, Board of Judges

Ruth Miller, Senior Lead, California Awards for Excellence™

After having written more than 20 books, I wasn't sure I wanted to write again, but working with a great team from Wiley Publishing has made it easy to get back in the saddle. Thanks to:

Nancy Muir, software entrepreneur and author of innumerable books, for giving me the nudge that pushed me back into writing

Adaobi Obi Tulton, Senior Development Editor, for being a soft-spoken "velvet hammer" who asked me the right questions, found answers to my queries, and kept reminding me of deadlines

Thanks also to those who trust authors to produce the best book that will serve their readers:

Katie Mohr, Acquisitions Editor

Greg Croy, Acquisitions Editor

Jim Minatel, Acquisitions Director

The multitude of editors for this book have worked hard; if errors have slipped by their well-trained eyes, those errors are mine.

Finally, and most importantly, my thanks to my family for their loving support and understanding. I missed you during the time spent on this book. My love to Barb, Annika, Rohan, Marjorie, and Anne.

Contents

Introduction

This book is a guide to how your organization can create a competitive advantage by successfully executing strategy and accelerating performance. You must begin with a vision that is held and communicated through leadership to every employee. That vision is achieved when employees work in concert knowing how they contribute to strategic success and operational performance. A Strategy Map and Balanced Scorecard are the map and measures to how you can achieve strategic success. Operational maps and operational dashboards are the maps and measures that show you how to accelerate operational success.

When I work with truly high-performance teams I see in their eyes a fire and focus that builds energy and intensity throughout the team. That energy comes in two phases. The first phase is the initial excitement of the vision — what the team can build in the future. The second phase, which sustains and builds their energy, comes when they translate their vision into action. Seeing that energy and fire in a team's eyes is what gives me a passion for my work.

One of my reasons for writing this book is to give organizations of all sizes tools for creating their own execution advantage and building a culture of high performance. This book isn't just for large multinational organizations. Small- to mid-sized organizations need strategy management, decision-making, and performance management tools as much as or more than multinational corporations. But they don't have the hundreds of thousands of dollars necessary for Business Intelligence software and long strategic planning processes. And the limited resources of small- and mid-sized organizations require them to have even greater focus and alignment.

Success through Strategic Execution and Accelerating Operational Performance

Business horror stories repeat themselves. We've all seen the numbers that define the stories:

- 90% of corporate strategies fail to achieve their expected results
- 80% of projects are late or over budget
- 70% of mergers fail to exceed the value of the original companies

Those are pretty uncomfortable statistics. However, some organizations succeed well beyond expectations. One famous bank merger achieved a nineteen fold profit increase in three years. One hotel chain increased its profit margin 3 percent over industry average in 3 years. What is the difference between the terrible failures and the huge successes?

Whether at the macro level of executing your strategy and aligning your company or at the micro level of creating a project team that meets deadlines, there are a few core principles that remain the same:

- Create a "burning platform" that moves people away from business as usual.
- Identify the objectives most critical to success.
- Define the initiatives that will make those objectives succeed.
- Select the "critical few" metrics to track performance and alignment.
- Create a culture of measurable high performance while breaking down silos.
- Maintain and sustain the high performance culture.

Some of my clients who have been through the processes described in this book have said,

- "Our leadership team had the best strategic discussions they have ever had."
- "The budget process was significantly easier than in any previous year."
- "This process is changing our entire culture to keep up with our high growth."

Who This Book Will Help

This book is built to be a practical guide. It doesn't have much theory in it. There are already many books with theory and case studies about Balanced Scorecards, Six Sigma, Lean, and other performance improvement methods. Rather, this book is intended to be a guide for the people who make it happen. It will help you map your future, identify the critical few metrics, implement the Balanced Scorecard and create operational dashboards.

There are three different audiences for this book: the Executive Sponsor or operations manager, facilitators and consultants, and software developers.

Executive Sponsor

Balanced Scorecards and performance improvement programs don't succeed without an executive sponsor. Members of the executive leadership team and the senior managers who are team leaders should scan Parts I and II of this book to understand the timeframes and commitments involved in creating success.

Members of the executive leadership team who have heard the term Balanced Scorecard may not know what it takes to drives strategic success with a Balanced Scorecard. They can scan Part I to see what is involved. It takes time and commitment from the executive leadership team.

Two telephone calls from senior managers remind me that many do not know what is involved in creating a Balanced Scorecard or how it affects an organization when correctly implemented. In one telephone call, the manager asked me, "We're having a two-day corporate retreat for the executive leadership team. Could you do a Balanced Scorecard for us in two hours?"

Another call illustrated the business buzz-word effect. A manager, whose division executive had heard about a Balanced Scorecard being used at a pharmaceutical competitor called. He had been tasked to "Go put together a Balanced Scorecard for the division in the next week."

Neither of these cases had executive commitment or the timeframes necessary to create a Balanced Scorecard that drives success and creates a culture of high performance.

Facilitators and Consultants

Facilitators and consultants are vital to creating a Balanced Scorecard or operational dashboard. They are the guides who help the executive leadership team and managers through sticky spots. When discussions get too easy because no one is asking the hard questions, the facilitator has to be able to step in and ask the probing question that puts a tough issue in the spotlight, so it will be addressed. It is imperative, especially in the case of strategic Balanced Scorecards, to have a consultant who has no agenda and who is politically impartial.

Software Developers

The majority of Balanced Scorecards and operational dashboards are created in Microsoft Excel. You don't need to be an Excel Visual Basic guru to build them when you know the correct combination of worksheet functions. Part III contains most of the building blocks for creating and maintaining powerful scorecards and dashboards.

Note: Build a Scorecard or Dashboard You Can Maintain

Part III contains the methods and tools necessary for building powerful decision making aids in Excel. But there is more to building them than just a few techniques. Make sure your Excel developer knows how to build systems that can be easily maintained and updated. Whether you use an internal or external developer, make sure he documents the system and shows others how to maintain it.

Additional skills the software developer needs are the abilities to interview users to discover their needs, understand what is critical in a business process, design user interfaces, build maintainable architectures, and integrate live data.

How This Book Is Organized

Balanced Scorecards and Operational Dashboards in Excel has three parts. Part I covers the steps and processes required for building a Balanced Scorecard to execute strategy. Part II introduces the basics of mapping operational processes and identifying critical metrics. Part III shows intermediate-to-advanced Excel users techniques specific to creating dashboards.

Part I

Part I describes the journey of building and rolling out the Strategy Map and Balanced Scorecard that is used by over 50 percent of Fortune 1000 companies and more than 70 percent of international corporations. It begins with an overview of the tools commonly used to develop organizational strategy. A chapter is devoted to building the Strategy Map, the diagram that visually defines the strategic themes on which the organization will focus and the objectives that will drive success. The next chapter describes how the Strategy Map must be converted to an action plan that details the initiatives to reach success, and the metrics required to keep those initiatives on track and on time. Once the metrics are defined, then the Balanced Scorecard can be developed and used — not just as a dashboard for strategic progress, but as a core mechanism to guide ongoing strategy meetings. The last chapter describes some of the communication and rollout processes necessary to communicate the change.

Part II

Part II is only three chapters long, but it describes a few methods of mapping operations, such as process maps and economic value maps, and how to use them to identify the critical few metrics that drive an operation and measure its success.

Part III

Part III gives many specific examples of how to use Excel to build Balanced Scorecards and operational dashboards. Excel is the most widely used business analysis and graphics tool in the world; the majority of Balanced Scorecards and operational dashboards in the world are built using it. Scorecards and dashboards in Excel do not need to use Visual Basic for Applications, but they do need a good architecture, and they require a few little-known worksheet functions.

Free Resources That Extend This Book

There is much more to executing strategy and creating high performance than will fit in this book. Newsletters, articles, tools, video demonstrations, and software are available free of charge at www.torconsulting.com.

Download Free Excel Sample Files

The Excel training examples and operational dashboards featured in Part III are available for free download by going to the author's web site or the publisher's web site:

```
www.torconsulting.com
www.wiley.com/go/scorecardsanddashboardswithexcel
```

Free Balanced Scorecard and Operational Dashboard Resources

Staying ahead of the competition and keeping your organization performing at its highest level is an ongoing process. To get a jump start on improving your execution advantage and performance advantage, go to www.torconsulting.com for additional:

- Whitepapers on improving performance
- Balanced Scorecard and dashboard demonstrations
- Video demonstrations
- Excel sample files
- Templates

To stay ahead of your competition and to get performance tune-ups, sign up for *The newsletter*, the newsletter for improving organizational performance. *The newsletter* contains practical tips on building a high performance in small- and mid-sized businesses and strategic business units. Sign up at www.torconsulting.com.

Consulting and In-House Workshops

No book can convey all the lessons learned through years of experience. And books certainly can't build the dynamic interaction that creates valuable insights among leaders and buy-in among employees. In today's fast-moving, competitive environment, you need timely solutions that work right the first time.

We work with executive leadership teams, executive sponsors, implementation teams, and IT developers to build and roll out Balanced Scorecards and operational dashboards. We can help you with all the processes and software described in this book, and more — and we can transfer that knowledge to your people through workshops and mentoring.

USE A BALANCED SCORECARD CONSULTANT CERTIFIED BY THE FOUNDERS OF THE BALANCED SCORECARD

Your organization's success may depend upon the validity and the implementation of your Balanced Scorecard. Only a few independent consultants are certified each year through the Balanced Scorecard Collaborative, the educational division of Drs. Kaplan and Norton consulting firm. To learn more about how a certified Balanced Scorecard consultant can help you, call Ron Person at Tor Consulting.

(The consultative and facilitative methods described in this book are those developed by the author and have not been certified or vetted by the Palladium Group or the Balanced Scorecard Collaborative.)

Balanced Scorecard Consulting and Workshops

Our purpose is to help your organization execute its strategy. We can help you do that with:

- Consulting through the entire Balanced Scorecard or operational dashboard process
- Mentoring for Balanced Scorecard sponsors and facilitators
- Customized on site workshops
- Executive briefings
- Excel developer training

We work with clients in-house or via telephone and web-based support. Our clients are both U.S. and international.

We can guide you through all the processes in this book and more. We can help you to:

- Clarify mission, vision, values, and strategic destination statement
- Inform and motivate the executive leadership team
- Build the case for change
- Guide the executive leadership team to build a Strategy Map
- Guide the implementation teams to build a Tactical Action Plans
- Guide the implementation teams and metrics teams to define critical metrics
- Plan the communication and rollup
- Develop a fully functional Excel-based Balanced Scorecard that uses manual updates or database integration

CLIENTS RECEIVE A FULL-FEATURED EXCEL-BASED BALANCED SCORECARD OR OPERATIONAL DASHBOARD

Our consulting engagements usually include a fully functioning Balanced Scorecard or operational dashboard. These systems can either use manually updated data or be integrated with your data sources.

Balanced Scorecard Audits and Updates

It may have been two years ago that you developed a Balanced Scorecard — perhaps you need to bring it up to date. Or maybe your organization has attempted to develop a Balanced Scorecard but has had less than satisfactory results. If your organization faces a situation similar to these, you may benefit from an audit of your Balanced Scorecard.

Operational Dashboard Consulting and Workshops

If you need to improve operational performance, we conduct in-house workshops to train teams on operational mapping methods, defining the "critical few" metrics, and developing Excel dashboards. These workshops commonly work on the actual business issues you need to resolve.

Contact Us

For consulting and workshops in Balanced Scorecards and operational dashboards, contact Ron Person at Tor Consulting:

Ron Person
ron@torconsulting.com
(707) 568-6976

Strategic Performance with Balanced Scorecards

In This Part

Accelerating Strategic Performance

The essence of strategy is choosing what not to do.
Michael Porter

The rate of change in the business world is accelerating. To get ahead — in fact, to just keep up — organizations of all types must accelerate their strategic performance.

They have to work with higher performance, more precise focus, and better strategic alignment. For this to happen, all parts of the organization must clearly understand and be firmly aligned with strategic goals.

In the last two decades, a strategic management system has been developed that enables organizations to achieve the clarity and alignment necessary to accelerate strategic performance. That system is the Balanced Scorecard.

Managing with a 500-Year-Old System

Until recently organizations have used the same accounting system to track assets and value production that was used 500 years ago in Venice, Italy. In 1494 Fra Luca Pacioli, Franciscan monk and friend of Leonardo da Vinci, wrote *Everything about Arithmetic, Geometry, and Proportions* (see Figure 1.1). It was the first best-selling business book to come off of Gutenberg's printing press.

Luca Pacioli's Portrait, Gallery of Museum of Capodimonte, Naples

Figure 1.1: Over 500 years ago, Fra Luca Pacioli, on the left, documented the double-entry accounting system we still use today.

What made his book such a best-seller throughout Europe was that it contained detailed instructions on how the merchants of Venice kept their accounts using double-entry accounting. His book included sections on:

- Modern accounting cycles
- Double-entry accounting
- Journals and ledgers
- Assets, liabilities, capital, income, and expenses
- Closing
- Trial balances

The reason his book blazed through the halls of commerce in Europe was because for the first time it gave businesspeople a way to value their tangible assets and measure how they were producing value. But what is surprising is that we still use the same accounting system used by the merchants of Venice 500 years ago.

The Failure of Modern Management Systems

Research by Margaret Blair of the Brookings Institute into the market value of corporations listed in the Compustat database shows that the market value of U.S. corporations has shifted significantly from tangible to intangible assets. In the ten years from 1982 to 1992, the contribution of intangible assets to market value has risen from 32 percent to 68 percent. As shown in Table 1.1, subsequent studies from multiple sources estimate that since 1998, intangible assets' contribution to corporate value is approximately 85 percent.[1]

Table 1.1: The growth of intangible asset contribution to corporate value

	INTANGIBLE	TANGIBLE
1982	32%	68%
1992	68%	32%
1998	85%	15%

How can intangible assets such as people, processes, patents, and data be monitored and managed effectively using a 500-year old system designed for use with tangible assets?

Ram Charan, international consultant and co-author of *Execution*,[2] wrote an article in *Fortune* magazine titled "Why CEOs Fail." In writing about highly experienced, well-known CEOs who lead their companies into failure, he said, "In the majority of cases — we estimate 70% — the real problem isn't the high-concept boners the boffins love to talk about. It's bad execution."[3]

Charan goes on to write how most CEOs are hard-working, experienced, brilliant people. His research found one problem common to all the failures:

"Yes, strategy matters. A good, clear strategy is necessary for success — but not sufficient for survival. So look again at all those derailed CEOs on the cover [of the magazine]. They're smart people who worried deeply about a lot of things. They just weren't worrying enough about the right things: execution, decisiveness, follow-through, delivering on commitments."

So executives and managers face two serious problems. First, the source of value production has switched from tangible assets that can be monitored with current accounting systems to intangible assets that are difficult to manage. Second, most corporations fail at executing their strategy.

A Modern Strategic Management System

In 1992 Harvard professor Robert Kaplan and consultant David Norton published the article, "The Balanced Scorecard — Measures That Drive Performance," in the *Harvard Business Review*.[4] The ideas in this article sowed the seeds of a strategic management system to translate strategy into action, to monitor strategic execution, and to align organizations around strategy.

Initial attempts to use the Balanced Scorecard seemed to either propel organizations to success or burden them with administrative overhead and dismal results. The difference between failure and success was often in the selection of metrics used to measure strategic execution. In 2000 Kaplan and Norton published another article in the *Harvard Business Review* titled, "Having Trouble with Your Strategy? Then Map It."[5] This article outlined how to build a visual map that shows the objectives and causal links necessary to execute a strategy. It was these causal links that enabled executives to identify the key metrics that drive success. The combination of these two ideas, the Strategy Map and the Balanced Scorecard, combined with more recent developments, has built a strategic management system that is an important part of modern business management.

The Strategy Map is a visual map of how an organization will execute its strategy. The Strategy Map shows the objectives needed to execute the strategy and the causal links between objectives. The Strategy Map is a tool for clear communication and helps identify the "critical few" metrics to monitor strategic execution. You can learn more about Strategy Maps in Chapter 4, "Step-by-Step to Building Your Strategy Map."

The Balanced Scorecard is part of a system that translates strategy into action. The Balanced Scorecard gives a balanced view in four perspectives of how well an organization is driving execution and how successful the results are. The four perspectives in the Balanced Scorecard and Strategy Map give executives a more balanced view of their organizations, going beyond financial measures to include finance, customer and marketplace, internal operations, and learning and growth — which includes people, culture, intellectual property, and IT infrastructure.

The Strategy Map and Balanced Scorecard can take one to three years to implement in an organization, but the results can be impressive. The effects of a Balanced Scorecard are:

- **Clarifying Strategy.** The discussions and thought that go into developing the Strategy Map bring clarity and understanding to the executive team in terms of the strategy and interplay between departmental silos. The graphical Strategy Map pinpoints for employees how they contribute to strategic success.

- **Translating Strategy into Action and Executing It.** The Strategy Map, combined with a Tactical Action Plan and Implementation Plan, give a clear roadmap to everyone showing how the strategy will be translated into action. The Balanced Scorecard is used to stay on track and to monitor execution.

■ **Aligning Business Units around the Strategy.** Most organizations develop "silos," functional departments or divisions that are more concerned with their own success than they are with achieving success for the entire organization. But developing the Strategy Map and Tactical Action Plan requires that the walls between silos come down. Focusing on Strategic Themes forces departments to work together, breaking down silos even more.

■ **Communicating the Strategy to All Levels.** The process of cascading the Balanced Scorecard through the organization gives each level the opportunity to contribute to organizational success. It gives executives the ability to communicate with functional managers about how to achieve strategic goals. It gives functional managers the ability to provide feedback to executives about capability and capacity.

■ **Monitoring and Managing Strategic Execution.** Research has shown that most executive staff spend less than 10 percent of their time monitoring strategy and execution. Instead of leading through strategy, executive staff often become embroiled in operational performance, something better left to managers. Using the Balanced Scorecard as an agenda gives executive meetings a central focus on strategic leadership.

Why Use a Balanced Scorecard?

Building a Strategy Map and Balanced Scorecard for an organization follows much the same process as taking a trip to a specific location. To take a trip you need to:

■ Select a destination

■ Agree on the type of trip

■ Agree on the route

■ Map the route

■ Plan time and resources

■ Travel

■ Stay on course

Leading a business in our high-speed world isn't that different from flying a high-speed jet. Imagine boarding a small jet, pausing at the entry, and asking the pilot a few questions:

You: "What is our destination?"

Pilot: "The crew got together and talked about a destination. We couldn't come to an exact agreement, so we decided to go somewhere out West. If something better comes up while we're en route, we might change direction."

You: "What route will we be taking?" (Maybe I'll still go. It sounds adventurous, although it could be a waste of time and fuel. It shouldn't be too dangerous.)

Pilot: "Well, we aren't sure about the exact route, but I've been that general direction before, so I don't need maps. I'm experienced."

You: "I notice that your cockpit dashboard seems a bit sparse. There aren't any flight instruments — just stacks of paper. How will you monitor the flight?" (This is starting to sound a bit iffy. The pilot may be experienced, but how will she communicate her experience to the copilot, the flight engineer, the steward, the ground crew, other aircraft, and the Federal Aviation Administration?)

Pilot: "Well, we're comfortable with the detail of printed reports. While we're in flight, I can request a short stack of printed reports that give me airspeed, altitude, attitude, and heading. The copilot gets a larger stack with operational data about radio settings, fuel, hydraulics, and technical details. We have to ask for the data, but it only takes a few minutes to get new reports — so we're in pretty good shape as long as everything stays stable and we don't have mechanical, weather, or crew problems."

You: "Sounds like quite an adventure you're about to embark on. Sorry I won't be able to go with you."

The metaphor isn't that far from how some organizations manage. Many startups and high-tech companies make their strategy going after any opportunity. Although the idea of a pilot flying with reference only to printed reports seems outlandish, consider how many organizations manage while looking only at financial reports. Financials show only lagging results from efforts that may date months before. Doing this is almost the same as flying by printed reports alone.

We know, and recent research confirms, that executives and managers with over ten years' experience in an industry can have a good "gut instinct" for making decisions, but how can they communicate that "gut instinct" to the hundreds or thousands of people they must lead and manage? How can employees and managers without such experience understand the strategy and make good decisions?

The Strategy Map gives an organization an excellent visual tool to explain what is important for strategic success and how and where in the strategy each employee contributes. Executives and managers at multiple levels can use the Balanced Scorecard to monitor whether they are actually driving strategic success. If the results aren't happening as planned, then the Strategy Map, Strategic Objectives, and Balanced Scorecard need to be revised until the organization has a valid model of what works.

Building a Balanced Scorecard

The trip activities listed in the scenario in the previous section correspond to similar activities in building a Strategy Map and Balanced Scorecard, as shown in Table 1.2.

Table 1.2: Building a Balanced Scorecard is a journey.

TRAVEL	BALANCED SCORECARD	INTENT
Select a destination	Destination Statement	State in one page what your organization wants to be at the end of your strategic horizon.
Agree on the type of trip	Strategic Themes	Your trip's journey might have a theme of speed or low cost. Your Balanced Scorecard might have Strategic Themes such as customer intimacy or operational excellence. How you execute your Strategic Themes differentiates you from your competitors.
Agree on the route	Executive and Division Alignment	Leaders, managers, and employees must all be going in the same direction.
Map the route	Strategy Map	Identify the route and objectives that will get you to your destination.
Plan time and resources	Tactical Action Plan and Implementation Plan	Identify the measures, metrics, and initiatives, and who is accountable.
Travel	Prioritize, budget, and act	Execute the strategy.
Stay on track	Balanced Scorecard	Monitor your Balanced Scorecard to make sure your organization is on track.

Does the Balanced Scorecard Guarantee Business Success?

There is no killer methodology that guarantees success in business. The Strategy Map and Balanced Scorecard do not guarantee success. Organizations can still fail by having the wrong strategy, by having a poorly built Strategy Map and Balanced Scorecard, by failing to use the Balanced Scorecard once it is implemented, or by failing to modify the Balanced Scorecard if their hypothesis of what works is wrong.

I occasionally meet consultants and executives who proclaim, "We tried a Balanced Scorecard and it didn't work." Their perception may be true — some research shows that approximately 30 percent of Balanced Scorecard attempts fail.

There are many reasons for failure, and the Balanced Scorecard fails in companies for a variety of reasons. Some of the most common are:

- **Lack of senior executive commitment.** An executive at the highest level in the strategic business unit must sponsor the Balanced Scorecard. Without the commitment of the senior executive, managers and employees feel that the Balanced Scorecard is just another "management fad of the month." The senior executive must make a case for change in the organization that will light a fire under everyone.

- **Lack of a case for change.** Organizations are difficult to change. The Balanced Scorecard is used to create a culture of high performance, translating strategy into action. Without a driving need for change, and an organization-wide awareness of the need, the Balanced Scorecard will become just another performance management system that will fade.

- **Lack of an experienced consultant or facilitator.** Developing and implementing a Balanced Scorecard is difficult. It is critical to use an experienced facilitator or consultant to guide initial development and to train internal facilitators and managers who can carry on the work. You are betting the strategic success of your organization on this effort. You don't want to use a general business consultant who has read a book or *Harvard Business Review* article on Balanced Scorecards. There are many bear traps to avoid, and you want someone who knows how to avoid them.

- **Too many metrics.** Too many metrics can create a confusing model of what drives strategic success. The Balanced Scorecard becomes an Operational Dashboard.

- **Wrong metrics.** Using the wrong metrics drives performance in the wrong direction.

- **Too long to develop.** Taking too long drains motivation and loses key resources.

- **Cultural mismatch.** Organizations with a cultural norm of low performance or organizations with dictatorial executives require a major cultural change before implementing a Balanced Scorecard.

Some executives and consultants have asked me if the Balanced Scorecard replaces Six Sigma, if it's more productive than LEAN, or if it coordinates projects better than a Project Management Office. A Balanced Scorecard does not replace any of these. It works as a strategic management system that acts as an envelope to keep Six Sigma and LEAN projects aligned with strategy. It works with accounting, budgeting, and the Project Management Office to optimize them for the organization, rather than just for individual silos.

Some organizational cultures just don't work well with a Balanced Scorecard. For example, some nonprofits, such as hospitals, work well with Balanced Scorecards and can use them to significantly increase their efficiency and performance. Other nonprofits, such as social service organizations, seem to have a great deal of difficulty working with measures and metrics. Some for-profit high-tech companies, especially startups, feel that their business changes too rapidly for a well-thought-out strategy. As mentioned, their strategy is "Go after any opportunity." Other for-profit high-tech companies, such as medical device manufacturers, have a focus that benefits greatly from a Balanced Scorecard.

I've seen organizations that have a cultural mismatch with a Balanced Scorecard and have no desire to change. Some of these organizations seem to have a culture of self-inflicted low performance. In particular, one director of an umbrella social services organization comes to mind. As part of a group of pro bono senior consultants, I volunteered to help the organization increase productivity and manage staffing problems. When our pro bono group presented our findings, along with numerous no-cost and low-cost solutions, the director scolded us with: "We are here to help people. We are not your Silicon Valley corporation concerned with measuring, planning, and performance." Those of us on the consulting team who gathered later for an After-Action Review felt a lot of sadness for the organization's clients. The director had the attitude that her organization couldn't increase performance and care for people at the same time. By enabling low performance under her management she was abandoning many children that might have had a head start on education. Low performance with no desire to change meant that many low-income families weren't being served by the health clinic under her control.

Does the Balanced Scorecard Really Work?

The now famous quote, "What gets measured gets done," is most often attributed to the management guru Peter Drucker. Although it seems to be an obvious truth, a more direct proof of the value of Balanced Scorecards is its acceptance and use among corporations worldwide. Bain & Company, an international consulting firm, does an annual survey on management tools among its 6,200-plus large corporate clients. The results of Bain's 2006 survey show that Balanced Scorecards are used by 70 percent of their clients with a 3.5/5.0 satisfaction level. This makes the Balanced Scorecard one of the most widely used strategic tools and places it within the cluster of tools that garner high levels of satisfaction.

Although the Bain & Company survey shows the pervasive use of the Balanced Scorecard, many organizations don't talk much about their success to the press. But successes that have been published cover a wide range of industries.

- Duke Children's Hospital reduced costs by $30 million and increased net margin by $50 million in two to three years while increasing patient and staff satisfaction.[6]

- Delta Dental of Kansas, the largest dental benefits provider in Kansas, is a 90-employee company that saw its revenues jump from $63 million in 2001 to $172 million in 2006 (a 173 percent increase) while increasing employees' satisfaction and understanding of their job.[7]

- Crown Castle International, the world's largest owner of telecom infrastructure, needed a strategic shift from its acquisition strategy in 2001 to a strategy of operational excellence in 2003. Even as its competitors faced meltdown, it saw cash flow rise from negative $300 million to positive $100 million and its stock price beat market indices by more than 300 percent.[8]

- Keycorp, one of the nation's largest bank financial services organizations, has cascaded its four strategic themes through all 19,000 employees.[9] The Key Corporate and Investment Banking Group (KCIB) improved its ROE by 28.8 percent from 2002 to 2005, and its vendor satisfaction ratings also improved. In three years, its ratings went from 45–74 percent to 86–93 percent.[10]

Do Small and Medium-Sized Businesses Benefit from the Balanced Scorecard?

Executives of small and medium-sized businesses (SMBs) may have the impression that the Strategy Map and Balanced Scorecard are just for large corporations. Actually, small and medium-sized businesses may find that Balanced Scorecards are easier for them to implement, and that the payoff comes quicker. Of the Balanced Scorecard Hall of Fame winners, 20 percent are small and medium-sized businesses.

SMBs may have even more to gain from Strategy Maps and Balanced Scorecards than large organizations, because of the limited resources that SMBs have. SMBs in particular have to make sure that they focus their efforts, provide better services, and drop projects that aren't aligned with strategy. The Balanced Scorecard is designed to align an organization around a focus and to make it easier to identify projects that aren't within that focus.

Communication and decision-making within SMBs can improve as well. Strategy Maps, freed by fewer layers of management and fewer employees, make communication easier and faster. Strategic issues can come to light faster when the Balanced Scorecard is incorporated into normal executive team meetings.

Many SMBs are opportunity-driven. SMBs providing high value in growing niches will see opportunity everywhere. Maintaining a focused strategic direction can be just as difficult as walking a kid in a straight line through a toy store. This is where a Balanced Scorecard can help. In the article "Why the BSC Is Just as Effective for Small and Medium-Sized Firms," Tom Lefebvre, director of Strategic Planning for the Alaska Native Tribal Health Consortium (ANTHC), says that the Balanced Scorecard "has provided a framework that has created absolute clarity of our strategy and ultimate vision." Because of the Balanced Scorecard, ANTHC has increased its cash flow and has seen an 80 percent drop in nursing turnover.[11]

Strategic plans in all organizations usually become far too complex to implement. This is where the Balanced Scorecard can help. By working through the Balanced Scorecard process, from Strategy Map to Balanced Scorecard to Tactical Action Plan to Implementation Plan, it becomes obvious which initiatives and projects contribute to strategy and how they must be scheduled and budgeted over time.

The work of developing a Balanced Scorecard is intense in an SMB in which everyone wears multiple hats. This is where an experienced consultant can help facilitators and managers get up to speed quickly and reduce the burden. Writeups from the Balanced Scorecard Hall of Fame winners show that the first year of development is hard work, that the second year gets easier, and that the third year is even easier — with benefits coming in.

Is the Balanced Scorecard Worth Developing?

Is the Balanced Scorecard worth developing in your organization? It takes dedication and work, but ask yourself these questions:

- Would we be more successful if the executive team focused more on strategic leadership and less on operational problems?
- Would we be more successful if our executives and managers used Strategy Maps as a forum to constructively breach the walls between silos?
- Would our managers be more knowledgeable about what drives their business if they had to define the "critical few" metrics that drive and measure success?
- Would our employees be more proactive and satisfied if they understood how they affect strategic success?

If your answers to these questions are yes — if changes such as these would increase the success of your organization and its people — then you should find out how you can implement your Balanced Scorecard.

Summary

The rate of change in the world of business is accelerating. The only way for organizations to succeed is to execute their strategy. If your organization wants to succeed, you have to translate your strategy into action, aligning your organization with strategic objectives and making sure that every employee knows how he or she contributes to strategic success. The most powerful tools you can find for building a culture of high performance are the Strategy Map and Balanced Scorecard. Creating them and building a high-performance culture isn't easy, but it is a journey that can lead to organizational success.

Notes

1. M. Blair, *Ownership and Control: Rethinking Corporate Governance for the Twenty-First Century* (Washington, D.C.: Brookings Institution, 1995).

2. M. Bognanno, "Why the BSC Is Just as Effective for Small and Medium-Sized Firms," *Balanced Scorecard Report*, January–February 2008.

3. L. Bossidy and R. Charan, *Execution: The Discipline of Getting Things Done* (New York, New York, Crown Business, 2002).

4. Crown Castle International, "The Balanced Scorecard Hall of Fame Profile Series," *Harvard Business School Publishing and Balanced Scorecard Collaborative*, 2005.

5. Delta Dental of Kansas, "Balanced Scorecard Hall of Fame Report 2007," *Harvard Business School Publishing and Balanced Scorecard Collaborative*, 2007: 17.

6. R. Kaplan, *Alignment* (Boston, Massachusetts, Harvard Business School Press 2006), 273–277.

7. Kaplan, *The Strategy Focused Organization* (Boston, Massachusetts, Harvard Business School Press, 2001), 20.

8. R. Kaplan and D. Norton, "Having Trouble with Your Strategy? Then Map It," *Harvard Business Review*, September 2000.

9. R. Kaplan and D. Norton, "The Balanced Scorecard — Measures That Drive Performance," *Harvard Business Review*, July 2005.

10. "KeyCorp Honors Its Top Technology Suppliers," Actuate Corporation, February 26, 2004, www.actuate.com/company/news.

11. C. Ram, "Why CEOs Fail," *Fortune* 139, no. 12 (June 21, 1999).

Developing Your Strategic Foundation

Plans are nothing; planning is everything.
Dwight D. Eisenhower

The most widely used management tool is strategic planning. Bain & Company, an international consulting firm, does an annual survey of more than 8,000 international clients. Since the early 1990s, this survey has shown strategic planning to be one of the most frequently used and highly rated management tools.

Before you can begin developing a Balanced Scorecard, you must have a strategic foundation to start from. For most organizations this foundation has the following components:

- Mission, vision, and values
- Assessment of internal and external environment
- Strategy formulation
- Strategic destination statement
- Strategy Map

Any search of Amazon.com will point you to many books on business strategy. There are at least 10 schools of thought on business strategy, and most business executives have their own preferences and opinions that guide their development of strategy. With such a broad field for strategic planning, this chapter won't attempt to describe how to formulate your own business strategy, but it may give you some background on the basic tools needed for developing strategy in preparation for your Balanced Scorecard.

You must remember one thing as you develop your strategy. What differentiates you from your competition is how well you execute your strategy. You may develop a great strategy, but it will fail if you can't, or don't, execute it. The Balanced Scorecard is your tool for strategic execution.

Note: Balanced Scorecards as a Management Tool

Bain & Company's survey of management tools reports that Balanced Scorecards had an adoption and satisfaction rate of approximately 70 percent in 2006. Interestingly, the survey also showed that those users who claimed the highest success rates with the Balanced Scorecard were those that reported that they required the greatest effort.

Developing Your Strategic Foundation

The members of the executive leadership team are the leaders of your organization. The leadership team should lay the basic foundation for the company by defining its mission, vision, and values.

Most businesspeople recognize the need for an organization to have a mission, a vision, and values, but there is often confusion about what these elements are. You can tell that there is confusion when it is hard to tell the difference between the three. Descriptions about beliefs and values show up in a vision statement, and descriptions of an organization's future appear in a mission statement.

Without clarity in your mission, vision, and values, it will be very difficult for you to create a successful strategy. Alice and the Cheshire Cat discussed the reasons for knowing where you want to go in Lewis Carroll's *Alice's Adventures in Wonderland*:

'Would you tell me, please, which way I ought to go from here?'

'That depends a good deal on where you want to get to,' said the Cat.

'I don't much care where–' said Alice.

'Then it doesn't matter which way you go,' said the Cat.

'–so long as I get SOMEWHERE,' Alice added as an explanation.

'Oh, you're sure to do that,' said the Cat.

If you want your organization to achieve a specific future goal, create clear and concise mission, vision, and value statements. You will also need a clear, concise, and precisely quantified Strategic Destination Statement, something described at the end of this chapter.

To keep your mission, vision, and values clear and concise, use these questions as clarifiers:

Mission	What do we do? Why do we exist?
Vision	What do we want to be? (Notice that this is not about doing. It is about being in the future.)
Values	What do we believe in? How do we act?

The Strategic Destination Statement, described at the end of this chapter, is similar to the vision statement, but it details the specifics of what the organization will be, who its customers will be, what the timeframe is for accomplishing these things, and how it will get there.

Values

Values are the things that the people in the organization believe in. Values determine how people act, what their ethics are, and what their behaviors are as they go about their business. Value statements come from the people and from what their leadership values. Values exist in the culture and are promoted by the leaders. It is rare that values can be instilled through training classes and workshops.

On returning from business flights I sometimes go out of my way to stop at a Nordstrom here in northern California. On one side-trip last year I stopped to look for a tie and ended up buying a pair of dress pants, a couple of shirts, and a tie that wasn't the one I'd originally wanted. The pants needed some alteration and were shipped to my home. The whole process took about 30 minutes, and I enjoyed the conversation with the young clerk who helped me.

Almost two months later, I stopped in at the same Nordstrom, hoping to find the tie I had originally been looking for. As I walked toward the men's department, the same young clerk stepped forward and greeted me by name. It had been two months since we had talked for a scant 30 minutes — yet he remembered my name. This type of caring for people — not "customers" — isn't learned through a vision statement. It is in the culture of the organization, and the culture recreates itself as the organization hires new people that fit the culture. The vision statement comes from the culture and what its leaders value.

It isn't hard to find examples of vision statements on the Web. Some examples from famous organizations are:

- Unequivocal excellence in all aspects of the company
- Science-based innovation

- Profit, but profit from work that benefits humanity
- No cynicism
- Nurturing and promulgation of "wholesome American values"
- Fanatical attention to consistency and detail

Examine your vision statement to make sure that it talks about what your beliefs are and how you act.

Mission

The mission statement says what you do as an organization — why you exist. The most memorable mission statements are short and inspiring.

I remember walking with a senior engineer through one high-tech plant. As we walked the halls, I asked him about the company's mission and vision statement. He stopped and pulled from his shirt pocket a three-fold laminated card. There were the company's mission, vision, and values, in all their 12-paragraph, nine-point glory. Putting on his glasses, he began to read. He only had to read through the first three paragraphs with a smile before I got his message. Everyone was expected to carry the mission, vision, and values with them, but they were so large, cumbersome, and convoluted that they couldn't be remembered.

Compare that to a mission statement attributed to Disney:

We make people happy.

One of my clients, Palladeo, envisions, creates, and constructs retail environments. It supplies a total solution to its retail clients, from customer research to creating and installing fixtures, to building the building. Its mission statement?

We increase sales for our customers.

It isn't easy creating a concise mission statement. I am told that it took many meetings before one of the executive team said the phrase and everyone grabbed it.

To see examples of both good and bad mission statements, go to www.missionstatements.com.

Vision

Vision statements inspire an organization to be more than what they are now. Vision statements are all about what they will be in the future, not about what the organization will do to get there. We'll leave the doing and the details to the Strategic Destination Statement, described later.

The timeframe for your vision statement will depend upon the speed of change in your industry. If you are in a rapidly changing industry, your vision statement may have a very short strategic horizon of a few years. If you are in a stable industry, your strategic horizon may be 10 years. Most organizations use a strategic horizon of three to five years.

Vision statements should inspire their audience with a big, glorious picture of what could be. Those big glorious pictures are BHAGs — Big, Hairy, Audacious Goals. BHAGs were first described by best-selling authors James Collins and Jerry Porras, who wrote about them in the article "Building Your Company's Vision" in a 1996 article for *Harvard Business Review*.[1] They later expanded on the concept in their book *Built to Last: Successful Habits of Visionary Companies* (Collins Business, 2004).[2]

In "Built to Last," Collins and Porras illustrate how a clear and compelling vision serves as a catalyst to inspire people to reach new heights. Their book describes the differences between 18 companies inspired by BHAGs and 18 other companies.

This same big vision is described by Jon Katzenbach and Douglas Smith in *The Wisdom of Teams*[3] as the catalytic force necessary to create a high-performance team. They show how high performance and exceptional effort don't happen in organizations or in teams until there is a "timely crisis." Teams and companies have to have a big, almost insurmountable goal that is only achievable through extraordinary effort.

Developing Your Vision

One thing I use to help an organization imagine their BHAG or vision is guided imagery. Guided imagery helps people relax, letting their imagination go beyond its normal limits. Counselors, meditators, and therapists have used it for decades.

Before initiating this process, consider the culture of the company and your own experience. Using this process with a group of English barristers might be completely different from using it with a group in a California organic foods grocery chain. Individuals who are uncomfortable relaxing into this process can participate at whatever level they are comfortable with. For participants who are practiced in meditation or self-hypnosis, it can be as relaxing and invigorating as a minivacation.

In this process, you will lead your "visionary" group on a trip into the future. On that trip, they will experience and see how the organization "is" in the future. Upon returning to the present, each person will write down the four or five most important new "ways of being" they saw in the future. These can then be used as the source for a vision statement.

Before you begin, you must know what your strategic horizon is. How far out will this vision be? Most organizations use three to five years for the horizon.

Choose a room with comfortable chairs and tables for writing. You will need to dim the light slightly in the room by pulling any shades and turning down overhead lights. One wall will need a smooth surface or large whiteboard on which you will capture the vision with a giant notepad of the sort typically used for group meetings.

The visioneering team should be six to eight senior executives with cross-functional positions and 10 years' experience in the industry or more. The whole process will take two to three hours.

Before you begin, remind everyone that the vision is not "what we are going to do," but rather "what we will be in x years."

Begin with a warm-up discussion about envisioning the future and BHAGs. You may want to use examples from experience or from books such as *Built to Last* or *Good to Great*. In one instance, a group started with a movie on how near-impossible visions have become realities. The movie included clips from John F. Kennedy's speech about putting a man on the moon and clips from Martin Luther King's "I Have A Dream" speech.

Guided imagery involves relaxing the group, dimming the light to remove distraction, helping the group move to a state of relaxation, and then guiding the group through an experience using nonjudgmental statements.

One client's visioneering session took place in the headquarters on an upper floor of a large office building. I dimmed the lights, had everyone put down their pens, and gave people the option of closing their eyes if they felt comfortable doing so. I then proceeded to guide them on a bus trip to see their company, PerformCo., in the future. Clients have told me later that they referred to this as the "Magic Bus."

Remember to leave time between statements as you guide people with your voice. It is very uncomfortable to participate in a guided imagery session that feels rushed because the guide is moving on to the next scene before the participants are ready to. You must think about what will work for the person seeing the guided images.

My soft "tour guide" voice follows a script something like this:

"We are going on a trip into the future to see what PerformCo. has become. While you are on this trip, watch and listen for important points you want to remember.

"We will be traveling through offices and seeing presentations. You will have a chance to read important items on white boards. You may even see a newspaper headline or overhear a conversation. Remember what is important to you about PerformCo's future. Now, let's take a trip.

"Imagine that you are in front of the elevator and that we are going down to a bus that will take us to PerformCo in x years.

"The elevator doors open. You step in, and the doors swoosh close behind you. You feel the elevator sway slightly as it moves down. You look up and see the floor numbers count down to the bottom floor. As it goes down each floor, you feel more and more relaxed and comfortable, yet your mind feels awake. 10, 9, 8, . . ." (Do this slowly and in a soft voice.)

"We're on the bottom floor. The doors open, and there's a bus waiting for us outside. The bus opens its doors, and we get on." (Wait for a moment as people get on the bus in their mind.)

"As the bus starts, the driver says, "We're going x years into the future. We will be stopping at a couple of locations, including the PerformCo office, and… I will be here to take you back when you're ready."

"You feel the bus move rapidly, and the windows fog. It stops.

"You are at one of PerformCo's newest locations.

"The doors swoosh open. As you step off the bus, the wind blows against the side of your face. You hear the crunch of small stones under your feet.

"You stand outside and look at the facility. What is your impression?

"Look around. Notice the building. Notice the people. Can you form an impression about how they feel being here?

"You walk to the reception door, open it, and walk inside.

"There's a directory board in the reception area. Notice the divisions and departments and departments on the board. Has the organizational structure changed?

"Walk down the hall.

"There's a group of customers in the hallway. They don't notice you. You overhear them talking about PerformCo. What are they saying?

"You continue walking. Looking into a lounge area, you see PerformCo employees and customers in the same room around a table. What are they doing? What is their position toward each other?

"You've walked full circle and are coming back to reception. There's a *Wall Street Journal* lying open. The special interest story is about PerformCo. What does it say?

"*Beep. Beep.* The bus is outside waiting.

"You walk out to the bus.

"The driver says, "Now, we're going to one of our premiere sites. It's a real model for the industry.

"The windows fog, the bus rumbles, and then the windows clear. And the bus stops.

"You exit and walk directly into the facility. As you enter, you see a hallway leading to offices, so you walk down it.

"You wander the hallways, remembering how things look.

"You come across two employees in the hallway. They are talking about why they work here. You overhear what they are saying.

"As you continue walking, you see an open room with someone talking about slides showing on a screen.

"The speaker says, 'These are the three accomplishments that have driven our success in the last *x* years.' You watch as a slide comes up with three bulleted items. Read what the slide says. Remember it.

"*Beep. Beep.* The bus is waiting outside.

"You hurry to the exit.

"The bus driver says, 'I hope you've enjoyed your trip. You are a lucky group of people. Not many get to take this trip. But now it's time to return.

"The bus begins moving. The windows fog, and then they clear.

"You are back at your building. You know you will remember the most important things you saw and heard.

"The bus doors open. You step forward. As you step down from the bus, a cool breeze brushes your face. You feel energized and refreshed. You enter the elevator and watch the floor numbers count up. As the elevator goes up you feel more and more refreshed and energized. 1, 2, 3 … 10. The memories from your trip are very clear."

Quietly and individually, have everyone write on a notepad the most important things he or she saw or heard on the trip. This is just a personal list. Later, the participants will select the most important of their recollections.

Pass out large 8″X6″ note cards. You'll want about 40 cards total from the group. Write one idea per card, using only five to seven words.

As the facilitator, you should now use an affinity grouping process to get dynamic discussions going about the content of the cards as you post them on the wall. Let the team group and regroup the cards into affinity groups with common intent. The intent of each of these groups will form your vision statement.

The names for each of these groups will become the core for your vision statement. The actual construction of a final statement is best left to a small group of two or three people who are good wordsmiths. If you attempt to "wordsmith" a strategy statement with a group of more than three people you will be in for a long, tedious process that will devolve your vision statement into nothing more than a boring platitude.

Developing a vision statement in this way may not create a vision statement with quantitative, finely defined goals. But it can capture the BHAG and create an inspirational vision.

You will use the work here to move forward to a Strategic Destination Statement like that described at the end of this chapter. It is the Strategic Destination Statement that precisely defines what your organization will be at a specific time in the future, who your customers will be; and not only what your value proposition for them will be, but how you will deliver it. Getting to a precise Strategic Destination Statement is critical, because it is your springboard to your Strategy Map and Balanced Scorecard.

Developing Your Strategic Assessment

Strategic assessment is the evaluation of how and where your organization fits in its environment. This is a Darwinian "fit." Your strategy must find the fit that will enable your organization to prosper and grow while fending off voracious competitors.

In your strategic assessment, you must evaluate external opportunities and threats. Define how you can take advantage of those external opportunities and neutralize or side-step the threats. Large-scope external threats are evaluated with a PESTEL analysis. Porter's 5 Forces model is widely used to assess near-scope industry and competitive threats. A SWOT analysis evaluates your organization's strengths, weaknesses, opportunities, and threats from an internal perspective.

This section briefly describes these tools. More information on these tools is available in strategic planning books and on the Web. Additional references and whitepapers are available at www.torconsulting.com.

Defining Your External Environment by Using PESTEL

Use PESTEL (also referred to as PEST or STEP) with groups to assess the external environment, pressures, and threats that may affect your organization's business. It is a good process for shifting from an inward to an outward focus. PESTEL reminds people of the external forces outside their control that they must plan for. You should use a PESTEL analysis along with an industry analysis such as Porter's 5 Forces and an internally focused analysis such as SWOT.

PESTEL considers the external influences of the following environments:

- Political
- Economic
- Social
- Technological
- Environmental
- Legal

Examples of the subtopics within PESTEL are:

- **Political.** Election changes, public policy shifts, war, tax changes, terrorism
- **Economic.** Consumer confidence, inflation, economic growth and trends (regional, national, and international), government funding, new business formation rates, job growth, unemployment, exchange rates, foreign competition, tariff changes

- **Social.** Demographics of workforce and the target customer, fashion and lifestyle shifts, population movements, immigration and emigration, occupational trends and needs, economic profiles, health shifts

- **Technical.** New production methods, new fuels and energy sources, communication methods and channels, increased obsolescence rates, production equipment and processes, outsourcing

- **Environmental.** Environmental regulations, public opinion, environmental risk/accidents, recycling

- **Legal.** Employment law, industry law and lawsuits, consumer protection law, international law and regulations

There are advantages and disadvantages to using PESTEL. A team of informed managers or analysts can quickly complete a PESTEL using little more than an online search through the *Wall Street Journal*, trade magazines, and business archives, such as EBSCOhost. But the results so garnered are general impressions of external influences. For small and mid-sized businesses, this is probably sufficient; to do an in-depth, quantitative external market analysis requires dedicated market analysts and can take weeks or longer — and cost a lot.

In surging markets that have raised the prosperity of all companies in an industry, a PESTEL analysis can help the team realize that their fortunes will change when the environment changes. For example, a change in the governing political party may result in a tax policy change that will affect their client's ability to purchase.

PESTEL is also useful in quickly evaluating a new market your organization is considering. Although you may not be worried about competitors or functional replacements, other external conditions may be revealed by PESTEL.

To perform a PESTEL, gather an informed, experience group and then:

1. Brainstorm the factors that could impact your organization.

2. Identify how these factors might affect your business.

3. Specify the probability and level of effect for those factors.

Your result might be a one- or two-page table of considerations with weighting.

Defining Your Industry Environment with Porter's 5 Forces

I still remember the first time I read Michael Porter's seminal book *Competitive Strategy: Techniques for Analyzing Industries and Competitors.*[4] Like Balanced Scorecards, it was one of those slap-your-forehead types of experiences. Porter's models used framework and structure to make competitive analysis and strategic positioning easy to understand.

Note: What Is Strategy?

Michael Porter's 2000 article "What Is Strategy?", available from *Harvard Business Review* through Amazon, is a must for anyone needing a base in strategy.[5]

Porter's 5 Forces model analyzes the industry and competition surrounding a business. It helps in understanding how consumers and competitors affect each other in the market. Unlike PESTEL, which looks at the large external environment, 5 Forces looks only at those internal and marketplace factors that directly affect an organization.

The 5 Forces and some of their factors that affect businesses are:

- **Substitute Products**

  How much power can your consumers exert by switching?

  Products that can easily be substituted affect your ability to raise prices. Switching is affected by how easily buyers switch, the perceived differences between products, and product quality or features. When there are more products "close" to you, there is less ability for you to raise prices.

- **Entry of New Competitors**

  How likely are new competitors to enter the market?

  If you receive a high margin on your products, competitors are more likely to move into your area. Prevent new entrants by raising barriers to entry via methods such as registering patents or controlling distribution channels.

- **Competitive Rivalry**

  How much power do you have compared to your rivals?

  Each industry has its own model of competition. Some resort to intense price cutting; others expand advertising and promotion.

- **Consumer Bargaining Power**

  How easily can consumers lower prices?

  Consumers can affect pricing when they have competitive pricing information, when there are few consumers and many competitors (switching costs), and when they can easily find substitute products.

- **Supplier Bargaining Power**

  How easily can suppliers raise prices?

  Suppliers can affect pricing when the product they supply is rare or unique, when supplier switching costs are high, and when there are few suppliers and many competitors.

Defining Your Strengths and Weaknesses with the Balanced Scorecard SWOT

Whereas the PESTEL and Porter's 5 Forces look outside your organization, the SWOT looks within your organization. SWOT is the tool most businesspeople are familiar with for strategic analysis.

SWOT stands for:

- **Strengths**

  Where your organization is strong

- **Weaknesses**

  Where your organization is weak

- **Opportunities**

  Where your organization has great potential

- **Threats**

  Where your organization could be at risk

A very important point to remember is that a SWOT must be done with one specific strategy in mind. It is against this strategy that you are comparing your strengths, weaknesses, opportunities, and threats. This may mean that you may have to use a process of defining a "straw strategy," developing a SWOT, revising the "straw strategy," reanalyzing the SWOT, and so forth until you create a viable strategy.

Many consultants do a SWOT with just four columns — one for each letter — and a long bullet list under each letter. You can add greater depth and insight to your SWOT by building a SWOT around the four perspectives used in a Balanced Scorecard. Using the following method also generates a lot of discussion among the executive team. The four perspectives are:

- Financial
- Customer
- Internal Operations
- Learning and Growth

These perspectives are described in detail in Chapter 4, "Step-by-Step to Building Your Strategy Map."

Begin your SWOT session by creating a grid on a wall. Use large 8″X6″ 3M Post-it® Super Sticky Notes for table headers. Build your grid with large cell areas and arrange headers like this:

	STRENGTHS	WEAKNESSES	OPPORTUNITIES	THREATS
Financial				
Customer				
Internal Operations				
Learning & Growth				

Guide the executive team through individual brainstorming and have them write down their individual thoughts on sticky notes. Allow the executive team to decide where they want to put notes, but limit the number of notes per individual so that they must set priorities; this also keeps the table from becoming too crowded. The group should discuss each note and decide where to place it.

When this is done correctly, you should end up with a lot of discussion, new understanding, and a color "Heat Map" that identifies areas you should focus on or avoid.

Developing Your Strategic Destination Statement

The very useful Harvard Business Review article "Can You Say What Your Strategy Is?" by David Collis and Michael Rukstad (April 2008),[6] outlines multiple strategy tools. One of these tools illustrates a way of building a Strategic Destination Statement. The Strategic Destination Statement is like a vision statement with specific details of what will be achieved in a specific timeframe with specific offerings to specific customer profiles. The Strategic Destination Statement is essential to developing a well-constructed Strategy Map.

With mission, vision, and values as a base, and having completed the external and internal analysis previously described in this chapter, your executive leadership team should be ready to develop its Strategic Destination Statement.

Begin by showing your team a sample Strategic Destination Statement. A finished one might look like this:

"PerformCo will expand to offices in the top 10 markets in California and remain in the top quartile of private investment firms by 20xx by offering a portfolio of green technology for clients with net worths of $1 to $10M who want environmental contribution, better-than-average returns, and moderate risk through our close contacts and expertise in green technology."

A good, experienced facilitator will be able to use the following structure to bring the executive leadership team to agreement around a structured statement. It is critical that you get agreement on and commitment to the Destination Statement. Going forward at this point without a solid Destination Statement can be a waste of time and endanger your strategic success. Make sure you use a facilitator who is experienced at leading executive teams and building agreement.

PerformCo Strategic Destination Statement

PerformCo will (action)	expand
to (result)	offices in the top 10 markets in California, and
	be in the top quartile of investment banks
by (timeframe)	20xx
by (method)	offering a portfolio of green technology
for (customer)	clients with net worths of $1 to $10M who want environmental contribution, better-than-average returns, and moderate risk
through (means)	our close contacts and expertise in green technology

At the end of facilitation, you should have a structure similar to this with notes that focus on the most important concepts. There will usually be too much to fit in a single paragraph, but a few wordsmiths can use this to craft a Strategic Destination Statement.

Summary

Developing a winning strategy requires external, industry, and internal assessments. Leaving one of these assessments out could be costly and might result in a flawed strategy dangerous to the organization's future. All the methods described in this chapter can be used in a short amount of time by an experienced facilitator working with the executive leadership team. These methods are very appropriate for small to mid-sized organizations that do not have the time or resources needed to conduct in-depth, lengthy market and competitive analyses.

The Strategic Destination Statement that you develop after your assessments is the destination for your Strategy Map. The next chapter will guide you through developing your Strategy Map.

Notes

1. J. Collins and J. Porras, *Built to Last: Successful Habits of Visionary Companies,* New York, New York: Collins Business, 2004)

2. J. Collins and J. Porras, "Building Your Company's Vision," *Harvard Business Review*, September, 1996.

3. D. Collis and M. Rukstad, "Can You Say What Your Strategy Is?" *Harvard Business Review*, April 2008.

4. J. Katzenback and D. Smith, *The Wisdom of Teams,* New York, New York: Collins Business, 1994

5. M. Porter, "What Is Strategy?" *Harvard Business Review*, February, 2000.

6. M. Porter, *Competitive Strategy: Techniques for Analyzing Industries and Competitors,* New York, New York: Free Press, 1980), 4.

CHAPTER 3

Preparing to Build Your Balanced Scorecard

If I had six hours to chop down a tree, I'd spend the first hour sharpening the ax.
Abraham Lincoln

The Balanced Scorecard is how you manage the execution of your strategic plan. The level of your organization's success depends upon how well you implement it. For good implementation, you have to have a good foundation, and that foundation depends both upon your Balanced Scorecard's purpose and upon your levels of planning and commitment.

Why Do You Want to Use a Balanced Scorecard?

You need to know your organization's purpose for implementing a Balanced Scorecard before you begin developing one. It takes intense, hard work to develop a Balanced Scorecard that becomes a part of your organization's culture. If the Balanced Scorecard isn't driven by the organization's core purpose, its power to guide your organization will move to a lower priority, and people will lose commitment as they face daily crises.

The Balanced Scorecard is not a tool of performance management. It is a tool to translate strategy into action, to remove silos, and to promote a culture of high performance. A lot happens during the development and implementation of a Balanced Scorecard: Extra work is required of executives and managers, the walls between silos are reduced or eliminated, new channels of communication are opened, the value placed on performance changes, and much, much more.

Organizations don't change easily. In a cultural version of Newton's first law, they are bound by their inertia. I've seen small organizations of less than a hundred people have as much difficulty changing as large organizations. So why go through all the work, intensity, and effort that the Balanced Scorecard requires? Because the Balanced Scorecard has proven itself to be one of the most effective tools for translating strategy into action, aligning the entire organization around that strategy, and monitoring the execution of strategy.

Before you begin developing a Balanced Scorecard, you must know the purpose for doing that in your organization. You must clearly understand why the CEO and executive sponsor want to implement a Balanced Scorecard. The purpose could be driven by internal or external pressures. Some reasons might be:

- Internal:
  - A new CEO wants to implement a new strategy and align the culture with that strategy
  - Two organizations are merging and need to create common cultures, visions, and processes
  - Silos in the organization are so strong and pervasive that they are pulling the organization apart
  - The Board of Directors and stockholders demand increased performance
- External:
  - Demographic changes threaten to detrimentally affect the workforce
  - Competitors are releasing new products that threaten your position
  - Customer needs and buying patterns are changing

Be clear on the purpose of the Balanced Scorecard so that you know what to emphasize and where to spend your resources. For example, if you believe that the purposes of the Balanced Scorecard are to significantly increase performance at all levels and to build a permanent culture change of high performance, then you would incorporate in your Balanced Scorecard implementation:

- Development of a culture of high performance
- Development of an HR plan for Strategic Job Analysis
- Development of performance methods such as Six Sigma or Lean
- Cascading scorecards down to the personal level
- Expectations of significant high-performance results in one to three years

If, instead, your CEO and executive sponsor want to use the Balanced Scorecard as a vehicle to reduce department silos and increase horizontal and vertical communication, you would focus on:

- Creating an easy-to-understand Strategy Map posted in communal areas

- Hosting ongoing "Town Hall" meetings to communicate and gather feedback

- Building interdepartmental teams that optimize results for the organization, not for silos

- Near-term results

One of my recent clients exactly fits this last profile. As a large nonprofit center for the performing arts, it was faced with developing a strategy to easily communicate to donors, employees, and the community. It faced serious strategic issues — highly profitable Indian casinos were bringing in big-time entertainment but making no social contribution to the community, and there was the possibility of a new facility. We used the Balanced Scorecard, coupled with group facilitation methods, to capture needs and capabilities from employees, to involve multiple levels of management in participative strategic planning, and to develop an easily communicable strategic plan, Strategy Map, and Implementation Plan. The organization's purpose was involvement, clarity, and communication, and it felt that its purpose was met without needing to develop detailed metrics.

Is Your Organization Ready for the Balanced Scorecard Journey?

Not all organizations are capable of developing and implementing a Balanced Scorecard. Certain things are critical to success. If your organization is lacking these key elements, you will find it significantly more difficult for you to succeed.

Senior Executive Commitment

Commitment from the senior executive for the business unit implementing the Balanced Scorecard is paramount. Without that commitment, the Balanced Scorecard will almost certainly fail.

It shouldn't be surprising that this is of topmost importance. The Standish Group's research into 23,000 IT projects from 1994 to 1998 found that the highest single cause of project management failure was lack of executive commitment.

And the Balanced Scorecard is not a one-off project; it requires ongoing commitment. Implementing a Balanced Scorecard requires an organizational culture change. That requires vision and leadership at the highest level. Without it, you are almost guaranteed to fail.

Experienced Facilitator or Consultant

When talking with many executives and other consultants I sometimes hear them claim that they tried building a Balanced Scorecard but dropped it partway in, or that it failed shortly after launch. On closer examination, what I usually discover is that there was no high-level executive commitment, or that the Balanced Scorecard was done as a "project" by someone with no experience.

To develop and implement a Balanced Scorecard, you need an internal or external consultant and facilitator who has experience in numerous areas, including knowledge of:

- Facilitation skills with senior executives
- Strategic planning
- The Balanced Scorecard, Strategy Map, and Implementation Plans
- Process mapping skills
- Business metrics
- Working with IT to develop software
- Training your managers and facilitators in how to continue developing the Balanced Scorecard

You may want to use a consultant or facilitator from outside your organization. Consultants or facilitators from outside your organization have the added advantage of:

- Bringing cross-industry knowledge and metrics
- Asking questions about the elephant in the room, the major issue no one wants to address
- Having no internal agendas

Executive Sponsor Commitment

A Balanced Scorecard must have an executive sponsor who will take responsibility for bringing it to fruition. The executive sponsor works with the consultant or facilitator to motivate her peers and make resources available to the consultant, facilitator, and development teams.

Executive Time and Commitment

Senior executives must devote time upfront to developing the Strategy Map and Tactical Action Plan. They must also be able to motivate and commit an experienced manager to the core team that will turn those initiatives into action.

The Balanced Scorecard also acts as an agenda for frequent executive reviews of strategy. In too many organizations the executive team reviews strategy annually. Organizations driven by the Balanced Scorecard do partial strategic assessments monthly and in-depth reviews quarterly. These more frequent assessments take from one to three hours rather than a "too late" annual review that takes days.

Participative Culture with Open Communication

A viable Balanced Scorecard can only exist in a culture of communication and participation. A Balanced Scorecard that is developed in isolation and sent "down the hill" becomes just another top-down directive that won't last.

"The Silent Killers of Strategy Implementation," an article in the summer 2000 edition of SLOAN Management Review,[1] describes six things that can kill the execution of strategy. Three of those six killers are brought about by failure to openly communicate and participate.

A Balanced Scorecard has a greater chance of success when built in a participative environment with a flow of communication between executives, managers, and employees. Without feedback from employees, the strategic initiatives won't be built on a realistic foundation of capacity and capabilities. Using group facilitation and feedback provided by representatives of all employees concerning methods of accomplishing initiatives and projects builds commitment.

You Must Make Your Case for Change

The Balanced Scorecard will create change in your organization, and few organizations change easily. To make that change happen, and to keep the organization from reverting back to old ways, the CEO and executive team must make a strong case for change and then communicate it and live it continually.

Building a case for change has the greatest effect when the executive team members build the case themselves. You can guide them in filling out a change state table like the one shown in Table 3.1. Begin with the current state, then ask the executives what they think the future state and impact will be if the organization doesn't change.

Table 3.1: A Sample Change State Table

CURRENT STATE	FUTURE STATE	IMPACT
Few available skilled banking officers	Predation on current employees; higher salaries required; more training needed for existing officers	Limits expansion plans; increases salary costs; loss of private clients
Loss of high-net-worth clients	Increased loss with flux in bank officers; lack of personal knowledge about clients	Increased loss of high-net-worth clients to banks with experienced and stable staff; pressure for closer customer relationships
Competitor's web sites easier to use for customer data access	Clients will migrate to private banks with better communication and data access that give timely information and integration with personal investment tools	Increased loss of high-net-worth clients

Guiding the executive team through the current and future states and letting them state their own conclusions about the impact can light the fires that create a "burning platform" for change.

Jon Katzenbach and Douglas Smith write in their best-seller *The Wisdom of Teams* (HarperBusiness, 1994)[2] that high-performance teams arise in the face of timely critical issues. The same is true when adopting the Balanced Scorecard to change your own organization.

Even if you don't face a "timely critical issue," you need to develop one in order to prepare and protect yourself. Your business may be stable now, but with the pressures and changing currents of global markets, global competition, financial instability, and Internet speed, you won't have to wait long for a timely critical issue.

One of my clients had been growing at over 20 percent per year. It was at the top of its industry and felt in control. It had completed a well-done risk map of the current state. Going through the change state exercise and pinpointing the impact let all executives feel in their gut what they intellectually saw in the risk map. They were facing a perfect storm in the near future. Although they were in a calm spot at that moment, they foresaw that:

- Government funding, a major source of revenue, was at a change point. A change in government policy would severely detract from revenue.

- Real estate values were skyrocketing, and they had used that to their advantage, but now building contractor rates were also skyrocketing. If the real estate market collapsed, their clients wouldn't have the liquidity to buy products and services.

- Skilled staff members were growing hard to find. The industry sector had the lowest unemployment rates in history. They depended on licensed professionals, people difficult to find and retain. The future looked even worse.

Within months after completing this exercise, they were hit by two of the three weather fronts in their perfect storm. The federal policies came under review, which could affect their revenue sources. Then the new HR director revealed that employee retention was much worse than previously thought — and that the latest demographics research showed that hiring problems would significantly worsen. The client's work on its change state table, Strategy Map, and Implementation Plans gave it months of advance preparation for its perfect storm.

Motivating Executives

The CEO and the executive team need to know the results the Balanced Scorecard can produce, how it can change their culture, and the roles they must play to make it work. Although the Balanced Scorecard gives everyone in the organization a common direction and understanding, it is the leadership from executives and the daily empowerment from managers that give staff and employees the confidence and power to make their own decisions and actions leading to strategic success.

Mid-level managers and employees need lasting commitment and vision from their leaders. Leaders need to continually emphasize that the Balanced Scorecard is the tool that will be used to manage strategic execution.

Perhaps this is best illustrated by the following story. I was enjoying an early morning breakfast with eight project managers employed by one of the largest insurance companies in the United States. The topic of conversation turned to managing and sustaining change. At that point, the head of the Project Management Office stopped the conversation cold when she said, "I wish we could get the executives to stop flying on planes."

A non sequitur like that made everyone turn to find out where she was going next. She paused, took a sip of coffee, and said, "Don't you see? Every time an executive flies on a plane, they read the latest business book. When they get back, we change direction again." We all grimaced at the painful truth and laughed loud enough to be heard throughout the restaurant.

So how do you motivate the executive staff? How do you get them committed to stay the course? Here are some seed ideas:

- Results are the voice executives hear and believe. You need to show results from similar companies. You need to show results from companies facing similar perfect storms.

- Let executives hear it from other executives. As a consultant certified by Kaplan and Norton on Balanced Scorecard consulting, I show video testimonies from CEOs and senior executives who have used and implemented the Balanced Scorecard.

- Gather quotes and testimonials from CEOs and senior executives. Don't just proclaim that the Balanced Scorecard is wonderful — also reveal how much work it takes, and how the culture will change.

- Reveal how the Balanced Scorecard can fail. About 30 to 50 percent of organizations that start a Balanced Scorecard don't successfully implement it. They may end up with an executive dashboard or may drop it completely. There are many reasons for failure, and you must address them.

- Educate executives in the overall process of how their organization will be affected.

- Let executives know the initial and ongoing time and resource commitments required of themselves and the people they commit to the Balanced Scorecard.

The job of the CEO and senior executives is to lead with vision. The people who follow them need to see a level of commitment in the actions of their leaders that demonstrates that the Balanced Scorecard will remain and be used. Such actions need to be seen and communicated continually to be believed and to create change in the culture.

One of the most important jobs for the CEO, executive sponsor, and Balanced Scorecard consultant is creating the case for change and motivation so that the majority of the members of the executive leadership team will work for a successful Balanced Scorecard.

Building Balanced Scorecard Teams

A single knowledgeable individual can build a Balanced Scorecard, but it is rare that a Balanced Scorecard built like this will succeed. Without the insights and commitment of executives, mid-level managers, and line personnel, the Balanced Scorecard is viewed as an "executive-level" directive that loses momentum over time. At best, it becomes an executive dashboard — and does not drive culture change or successful execution of strategy.

Building and rolling out a Balanced Scorecard requires at least three levels of teams. The executive team is composed of senior executives, who translate the strategy into a Strategy Map with its strategic objectives and causal links between objectives. They begin developing the Tactical Action Plan that defines how those objectives will be measured and what Strategic Initiatives are necessary to reach the objectives. The Strategic Theme Team then works with what the executive team has developed and creates a plan for making it happen. The

Strategic Theme Team further develops the Tactical Action Plan, completing the metrics and Strategic Initiatives and working with managers to define what projects are necessary in the initiatives. An experienced Balanced Scorecard consultant should guide each of the teams, gathering feedback, facilitating meetings, and helping in the rollout and with communication.

Actual composition of team numbers of participants and participants' roles will vary between organizations. Large organizations with multiple divisions will replicate the team structures throughout their divisions. Small to mid-sized businesses may build a Balanced Scorecard with just two teams and two facilitators.

A breakdown of the teams and their participants, roles, and products when developing the Balanced Scorecard looks like this:

Executive Team

Participants

Six to eight senior executives in the strategic business unit or their designated representative

Role

Translate strategy into objectives

Define what drives the business model

Act as Strategic Theme sponsors to monitor Core Team results

Output

Strategy Map

Tactical Action Plan

Leadership for the Strategic Theme Team

Commitment

Education session

Three half-day workshops

If an executive becomes a strategic theme sponsor, she chairs a monthly meeting with her Strategic Theme Team

Strategic Theme Teams

Participants

Strategic Theme Managers

One manager for each Strategic Theme. There are usually three to five Strategic Themes.

This is a good role for executives or managers being groomed for higher and broader experience.

Team members

> Composed of two to five members with wide cross-functional experience. Beware of overloading in one functional area. Usually this occurs in the area of finance. Experienced with managing initiatives and projects across the company.

Role and Output

> Complete Tactical Action Plan that defines initiatives
>
> Complete metric definitions that define measures and metrics
>
> Develop projects to accomplish initiatives
>
> Report to Strategic Theme sponsor
>
> Compare existing projects and budgets to the new Strategic Initiatives, projects, and budgets

Commitment

> Education session
>
> Bi-weekly or monthly meetings to coordinate development within the Strategic Team
>
> Project development meetings with managers

Facilitators and Consultants

Participants

Consultant

> Experienced in guiding strategy process and developing the Balanced Scorecard
>
> Experienced in developing executive motivation
>
> Trained in using the Balanced Scorecard
>
> Able to train facilitators in Balanced Scorecard development

Facilitators and trainers

> Experience in facilitating
>
> Trained to teach the Balanced Scorecard
>
> Trained in using the Balanced Scorecard as an agenda for operational meetings

Role and Output

Consultant

> Guide executives through Strategy Map and Balanced Scorecard development

Guide Strategic Theme Team through Tactical Action Plan development

Access to a large library of background resources

Propose and develop metrics

Work with IT for the selection or development of software

Facilitate

Gathering of feedback from managers and employees

Brainstorming of ideas

Process mapping

Planning

Facilitate and host the rollout and communication plan

Commitment

Available to aid Strategy Theme Teams, project planning teams, communication rollout, front-line feedback, and capability assessments

Background Research

Before starting work on the Balanced Scorecard, before doing interviews, and before the first meeting, the consultant or facilitator leading the Balanced Scorecard process must have a 30,000-foot knowledge of all aspects of the organization and its environment. Part of the consultant or facilitator's job is to act as the "outsider" who asks questions probing accepted industry "truths" and revealing the elephants in the room. Asking these questions is sometimes easier and more acceptable if done by an outsider who isn't expected to have a detailed knowledge of the organization and industry. The consultant or facilitator should not be "drinking the Kool-Aid" in the corporate punch bowl.

There are many sources where you can get broad industry knowledge as well as internal knowledge of a company. I usually schedule a couple of weeks to do reading and research before beginning interviews and workshops.

Critical sources for review are:

- Mission, vision, and value statements
- Strategic plans
- Operational plans
- Annual and quarterly reports
- High-level financial reports

- Key financial metrics
- Key operational metrics
- SWOT analysis, if separate from strategic plans
- Risk analyses or heat maps
- Organization charts with names and contact information of key participants
- Expansion plans

Additional materials for review are:

- Morningstar analysis on public companies
- Consultant's reports or surveys
- HR and employee surveys
- Hiring demographics and environment
- Customer satisfaction surveys
- Competitive analysis
- Industry analyst reports
- Trade journals for environmental conditions
- Benchmark reports
- Trade Web sites
- Key competitors' web sites

Interviewing Executives

Executive interviews are your opportunity to get input from individual executives about their views of the future, what they understand to be the key objectives for the organization and their divisions, and where barriers in the existing organization exist. It is your chance to identify ways in which divisions may not be aligned toward common goals. This can also reveal how silos are creating sub-optimal successes, stopping the larger organization short of success.

The executive interview is also your chance to learn what metrics and criteria executives watch and use when making strategic and tactical decisions. These metrics and how they are analyzed and compared will help you later in selecting metrics and designing dashboards.

One test I frequently use at an interview is asking to see the reports or metrics that are most important to a particular executive's decision-making. Often these can be reduced to a few critical pages — those pages or data that the executive wants to see first thing each morning.

In one of my first jobs as a product manager fresh out of business school, I was put on a "Tiger Team" to reduce the paper glut filling the corners in offices throughout the Fortune 500 company I worked for. Reams of computer print-outs were stacked from reports generated weekly. After interviewing executives and managers, the team learned that most managers used only a few key numbers — and, at most, a few pages — from the two- or three-inch stack of paper they received weekly. We reduced wasted time, increased the speed of decision-making, and saved many trees by rebuilding reports around the few pieces of data important to each manager. All new ad hoc reports had a sunset date that, when reached, stopped the report.

Most interviews will take about one hour. Always schedule at least an hour between interviews to give yourself time to rewrite notes and refresh your brain. If I don't schedule time between interviews, I can lose facts and forget insights.

Some interviewers work in a two-person team: One person is the interviewer and maintains eye contact and rapport; the other person takes the quiet role of scribe.

I usually do my interviews on-site and solo, although doing phone interviews is sometimes a necessity. I prepare a list of about eight questions and keep it in front of me while taking just a few notes that will jog my memory later in case my voice recorder fails. Immediately after the interview, I rewrite my notes. Of course, I let the executive being interviewed know ahead of time that I will be asking her about which key metrics she uses for decision-making. This usually results in her showing me how she uses a couple of key pages containing metrics and charts. I always ask for copies.

Instead of a scribe to back up my memory, I use a portable digital voice recorder. The one I use records over 100 hours of interviews and runs on one AAA battery. When an interview is over, I plug it into my laptop and download the recording as an MP3 file that makes it easy to play back the interview while I transcribe it on my laptop. A digital recorder with these capabilities costs between $100 and $200 and is well worth the expense.

Make sure that any recorder you get has a microphone plug size that will fit a telephone adaptor. For about $30, you can go to Radio Shack or another retail electronic store and buy a phone adaptor that enables you to connect to a land-line (though not portable) phone. Of course, the law requires you to notify the other person that you are recording the interview.

Be sure to take a few memory reminder notes even if you are using a voice recorder. A journalist told me a nightmarish story of a time when she conducted a long and hard-to-get interview. Wanting to pay close attention, she took no notes, depending solely on her trusty cassette recorder. When she left the interview, she found that her recorder had failed. She panicked and forgot some of what happened during the interview.

You will probably only get through six to eight questions in an hour, so make sure that you have the most important ones at hand. Keep the interview brisk and on target.

This is an interview that could be important to the future of the company so, while being friendly, don't open with questions about the desktop picture of the family at Disneyland or get into a discussion about why there is a mounted halibut tail on the wall.

Have your most important questions thought out and well rehearsed beforehand. Although you will only have time for six or eight questions, you have many to choose from. Some of the questions you might ask are:

- Have you had experience with the Balanced Scorecard before?
- What are your organization's most important strategic objectives?
- How does your division contribute to those objectives?
- Where has your division been most successful?
- What has made your division successful in that objective?
- What is your vision for increasing your success in the next three to five years?
- Do you see large trends or shifts changing your industry?
- Where are the barriers to the organization's success?
- Which competitor is most dangerous over the long term, and why?
- Which metrics do you watch that show success or drive success?
- Are there sets of metrics that you compare when making decisions?
- Is there a metric or an alert you watch that signals a future problem?
- What in the business keeps you awake at night?
- Because I know your time is tight, is there someone in your organization I can talk to if I need additional clarification?

Summary

The Balanced Scorecard has an impressive record of helping organizations execute their strategy, but without a burning case for change you may not be able to sustain momentum.

The most important factors for success are:

- Commitment from the senior executive
- Guidance by a consultant experienced in Balanced Scorecards (not just an executive consultant)
- A burning case for change — one that makes everyone in the organization understand why change is necessary

Notes

1. M. Beer and R. Eisenstat, "The Silent Killers of Strategy Implementation," *SLOAN Management Review* 41, no. 4 (summer 2000): pp 29–40.

2. J. Katzenbach and D. Smith, *The Wisdom of Teams,* New York, New York: Collins Business, 1994).

Step-by-Step to Building Your Strategy Map

Change is the law of life. And those who look only to the past or present are certain to miss the future.

John F. Kennedy
U.S. President, 1917–1963

You know where you want to go. You've got your vision and Strategic Destination Statement completed, and now you face translating your strategy into action. The first step in translating strategy into action is to create a Strategy Map.

Without a Strategy Map, your Balanced Scorecard will be an executive scorecard. It will report on measures important to the executive, but it will not give you an accurate view of how the entire organization is driving and succeeding at its Strategic Objectives.

There are four reasons you need to create a Strategy Map, even if you never build a Balanced Scorecard. First, early versions of Balanced Scorecards had a low success rate because the metrics they monitored were often chosen from the metrics currently in use, which may not have been the metrics that drove strategy. Second, in most organizations few managers and employees have a clear and concise concept of their organization's strategy. In fact, research shows that less than 10 percent of employees have a clear understanding of their organization's strategy, and 50 percent of executives spend virtually no time on strategic discussion.[1] Third, without a clear, concise model of what drives your strategy, you have no feedback about which drivers are working and which are not. And finally, when the objectives on the Strategy Map are broken down into initiatives and projects, it makes it easy to identify strategic funding during the budget process.

What Is a Strategy Map?

A Strategy Map is a visual representation of what your executive team believes will drive your strategy. Just as a road map shows the path to a destination, the Strategy Maps show which chain of objectives will lead to successfully executing your strategy.

Figure 4.1 shows a Strategy Map for a medical device manufacturer. Like the Balanced Scorecard, which it reinforces, most Strategy Maps have four perspectives. Perspectives are described in more detail in a later section. From the top of the map down these perspectives are:

- Financial
- Customer and marketplace
- Internal operations
- Learning and growth (composed of human capital, culture, and IT infrastructure)

These perspectives appear as horizontal bands on the map.

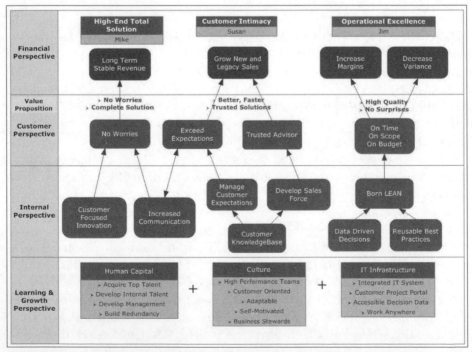

Figure 4.1: A Strategy Map shows four perspectives, Strategic Themes, and the objectives used to execute those Strategic Themes.

A good strategy has to focus itself on thrusts that satisfy customer needs. It must be able to defend them against competitors. These focused efforts are Strategic Themes. They appear on the Strategy Map as vertical columns. These are also described in more detail in a later section.

Within this grid of perspectives and Strategic Themes are ovals that represent Strategic Objectives. Accomplishing these objectives is what drives the success of the Strategic Theme. The causal links between objectives, where one objective drives another, are shown as arrows.

> *The Strategy Map is your executive team's hypothesis of how to drive success.*

It's a one-page description that shows every employee how the organization will reach its Strategic Destination.

Strategy Maps are not static. Like a chemistry experiment from school, you make a hypothesis, or educated guess, about what drives success. Some parts of this chain of causal links may succeed, and others may fail. When a hypothesis is wrong, you modify that part of your strategy and the map to try to get it right. Over time a learning organization will modify its Strategy Map, Balanced Scorecard, and Implementation Plan until it has a map showing the objectives and drivers that accurately reflect the business. How well you execute that strategy is the subject of Chapter 5, "Step-by-Step to Building Your Tactical Action Plan," Chapter 6, "Step-by-Step to Selecting Metrics and Setting Targets," and Chapter 7, "Step-by-Step to Developing Your Implementation Plan."

Leveraging Your Strategy Map

Earlier in this chapter, I listed four reasons why Strategy Maps are fundamental to strategic success. First, a Strategy Map makes it easier to identify the critical few metrics that drive your model. These are measures of driving force or success on the causal links.

Second, communicating a strategy to everyone in an organization helps get everyone aligned and onboard. The Strategy Map is a great "talking tool" that can be used in town hall meetings to talk through where the organization is placing its emphasis.

Third, by using the critical few metrics to monitor your Strategic Objectives, you can learn what does or does not drive success. Instead of managing by instinct, you have data to back up decisions.

Finally, clients tell me how taking the Strategy Map through to the Implementation Plan phase makes their budgeting processes easier. Prioritizing and time-phasing initiatives and projects is visibly easier when you know what's necessary to support Strategic Objectives.

Perspectives: Monitoring Your Strategy from Different Points of View

Since the time of 4,000-year-old Sumerian records written on clay tablets, businesses have continued to rely on finance and accounting as the primary measurement tools of business. While financial measures are essential, they only show the results of what happened in prior months. They are not predictive and cannot help you drive the business.

The Balanced Scorecard takes its name from the fact that it uses balanced perspectives of what drives business and strategy. Balanced Scorecards in for-profit businesses use the four perspectives described earlier in this chapter — financial, customer and marketplace, internal operations, and learning and growth. Learning and growth includes the people, culture, intellectual capital, and IT infrastructure within a company. You can see these four perspectives in Figure 4.1.

You can understand why the perspectives are in this order by asking a series of questions about for-profit businesses. Starting at the top, in the financial perspective, we ask the question, "What do our financial results have to be to satisfy our stakeholders?" In the customer and marketplace perspective we ask, "What must we achieve with our customers and marketplace to successfully reach our financial results?" In the internal operations we ask, "What must we achieve with our internal operations for success with our customers and marketplace?" Finally, in the learning and growth perspective we ask, "What must our people, culture, intellectual capital, and IT be to succeed with our internal operations?"

Even though these four perspectives appear in nearly every Strategy Map, they may not be in this specific order, and there may be an additional perspective. For example, most nonprofits put the mission perspective at the top instead of finance. Nonprofits with fixed funding may move the finance perspective to the bottom. Other nonprofits, such as nonprofit hospitals earning revenue, don't want the appearance of driving for higher revenue, so they put customer and finance perspectives on the second level underneath the mission perspective.

RENAME PERSPECTIVES TO FIT YOUR CULTURE

The names for the four perspectives may not fit your culture, especially if you are a nonprofit with employees and volunteers who are not motivated by the for-profit business model. One of my clients, a nonprofit healthcare provider, was concerned about communicating the importance of sound finances to their employees, who were primarily motivated by service to others. They renamed the financial perspective Financial Stewardship. Their caregivers found this name and its intention easier to understand and accept.

Other perspectives may also be included. In industries where leading-edge products are critical for survival, such as pharmaceuticals, "leading-edge products" may be a Strategic Theme, and there may be a "leading-edge" perspective across all themes.

Strategic Themes: Concentrating Resources and Momentum along Specific Themes

There is one big strategic lesson that crosses history: Spreading your resources across too wide a front almost certainly spells defeat. Focus is the key to success.

Strategy Maps use Strategic Themes to focus strategy on specific points. Strategic Themes appear as columns of objectives in a Strategy Map. Limit yourself to three to five Strategic Themes. In fact, going beyond three themes magnifies the number of initiatives and projects geometrically, making success that much harder. Figure 4.1 shows three Strategic Themes: Total Solution, Customer Intimacy, and Operational Excellence. Notice in Figure 4.1 that the learning and growth perspective, at the bottom, spans all three Strategic Themes. It is not uncommon for the learning and growth perspective to span more than one theme.

We are all familiar with Strategic Themes; we just may not know them as such. When you think of most great companies, you probably are instantly aware of their predominant Strategic Themes. Table 4.1 shows some examples.

Table 4.1: Examples of Strategic Themes Used by Organizations

THEME	ORGANIZATION
Operational Excellence	Toyota Toyota uses Six Sigma and Lean to create a high-performance operation, eliminating variance and waste while satisfying customers' most important needs.
Total Solution	IBM Selling against IBM is tough because it provides a total solution involving hardware, software, consulting, and support.
Leading-Edge Products/ Service	Apple Apple has a cult-like following because of its delivery of products and services (iTunes) that are on the leading edge.
System Lock-In	Microsoft Once you start using its software products, the cost of switching is too high to consider the competition.
Quality	Lexus Their employees have told me, "We produce the highest-quality production cars in the United States."

Selecting Strategic Themes is a combination of art and science. My clients and I review their business environment by looking at the PESTEL, 5 Forces, and SWOT. Then we examine their Strategic Destination Statement. The gap between their current state and their future vision is what the Strategic Themes must fill.

After reviewing all of this, I guide my clients through a list of 14 Strategic Themes that recur throughout for-profit strategies. At this point the top two Strategic Themes are usually obvious.

TIPS ON SELECTING STRATEGIC THEMES

Here are a few tips on selecting strategic themes:

■ **Select no more than three to five Strategic Themes**

■ **Give them memorable and motivational names of three to five words beginning with a verb; select themes that complement each other**

■ **Avoid themes "owned" by a major competitor**

■ **Select themes that will bridge the strategic gap to your destination**

■ **Select themes you can defend with good execution**

It is important to select Strategic Themes that are complementary and that are achievable within the organization's resources and timeframe.

In some cases, Strategic Themes target an impending gap in the PESTEL analysis. For example, the aging worldwide population presents many businesses with a serious problem: finding qualified, highly skilled people. The U.S. Bureau of Labor Statistics has reported that in the next few years, the jobs in greatest need will be medical technicians, caregivers, and skilled construction workers.

A frequently found objective to support many themes is "Developing Internal Talent" or "Acquiring Highly Skilled Talent." But two recent clients designated an entire Strategic Theme as "Acquiring, Developing, and Retaining High-Skill Employees." If they cannot succeed at this theme, their strategies may fail.

Objectives and Causal Links: Modeling What Drives Your Business Success

You now have a grid on which to build your Strategy Map. It should have four (or more) perspectives down the left side and three to five Strategic Themes across the top.

The interior of this grid contains Strategic Objectives and the causal links between them. Strategic Objectives are goals that will help you accomplish the Strategic Theme. The causal links are the effects that one objective has on another. For example, succeeding at an internal operations objective may drive a result in a customer objective. The book *Strategy Maps*, by David Kaplan and Peter Norton, has many examples of Strategy Maps in many different industries.[2]

Developing a Strategy Map shouldn't be a long process, but it is something that most people, including executives, find difficult at first. This is where executives must have a big picture vision. I've found that most managers find this difficult because they are too used to thinking from a project point of view, rather than from a high-level, strategic point of view. If you begin building your Strategy Map by focusing on projects or narrow goals, you will limit the scope of alternatives and solutions as you drill down to turn your strategy into action.

The objectives, shown as ovals or rectangles within the Strategy Map, are what will make a Strategic Theme succeed. The causal links between objectives show your hypothesis of how success in one objective drives success in another. These causal links are important because if you get them right, it makes it very easy to select the critical few metrics for your Balanced Scorecard.

Selecting a Strategy Map Facilitator

A facilitator or consultant is important in leading the Strategy Map process. A facilitator who has developed successful Strategy Maps will know when to ask probing questions, when to point out that some Strategic Objectives are too tactical, and when to guide the discussion to conclusion.

It is difficult to use a member of the executive team as the facilitator. It is difficult, if not impossible, to switch between being a contributor and being an objective facilitator for any length of time. This is especially true when CEOs attempt to facilitate.

Even company employees who are experienced facilitators may find facilitating Strategy Map sessions difficult. They must be able to shake off the accepted "truths" in the organization and see an objective reality. They must be able to ask blunt questions about the "elephant on the table" that people are unwilling to acknowledge. An experienced, independent Balanced Scorecard consultant can work with those situations.

A good facilitator will know how and when to ask probing questions that spark deeper and animated discussion. An experienced facilitator will have a basket of business stories from other industries that can be interjected to illustrate different scenarios.

Finally, a good facilitator will have a broad knowledge of all business areas, so the facilitator can ask those probing questions about the relations between objectives in finance, sales and marketing, operations, IT, and human capital.

> ### USE A BALANCED SCORECARD CONSULTANT CERTIFIED BY KAPLAN AND NORTON
>
> Your organization's strategy, performance, and possibly its ultimate success depend upon how well you develop and implement your Balanced Scorecard. That is a lot of responsibility to put on a general or executive consultant who is inexperienced and untrained in the development of a Balanced Scorecard. Only a few independent consultants are certified each year by the Palladium Group, the consulting firm of Drs. Kaplan and Norton. Their certification process includes intensive training and examination. To learn more about finding a Balanced Scorecard consultant, please refer to the Introduction. (The consultative and facilitative methods described in this book have not been certified or vetted by the Palladium Group.)

Step-by-Step to Creating Your Strategy Map

Two methods of developing Strategy Maps work effectively with executive leadership teams or their appointed strategic team. Each of these two methods works in different situations.

The Straw Dog Approach

In the straw dog approach, you present the executive leadership team or their appointed strategic team with a Strategy Map you have built. This is used as a structure for discussion, to tear down, and to rebuild.

Advantages:

- Less executive time required. This method can be quicker, requiring a single meeting of 3–4 hours.
- By being able to review the straw dog Strategy Map prior to the meeting, executives have time to do in-depth thinking about the objectives and causal links.

Disadvantages:

- If it is a lack of time for executives or their designated manager that drives this method, then the executive team may be too operational and not have a strategic orientation. Lack of CEO commitment is a key cause of failure.

- There may be less buy-in from executives since they are just signing off on the Strategy Map rather than building it themselves.

- The team that builds the straw dog Strategy Map exposes their lack of knowledge if they don't have a very thorough understanding of the business and its strategy.

The steps to using the straw dog approach are these:

1. Educate and motivate the executive leadership team on the Balanced Scorecard.

2. Interview executive leadership team members for themes and objectives (see discussions in earlier chapters).

3. Use a small team of three senior, cross-functional managers and the executive sponsor to build a straw dog Strategy Map. Focus on:

   - What will get us to our Strategic Destination?

   - What will fill the strategic gap we face?

   - What are defensible Strategic Themes we can own?

4. Send out the straw dog Strategy Map and Destination Statement with the question, "Is this the best set of objectives and causal links to get us to our Strategic Destination?"

5. Convene a Strategy Map review with the executive leadership team.

6. Review the Destination Statement.

7. Walk through the straw dog Strategy Map. Use a white board and large sticky notes to create an interactive Strategy Map you can present and rebuild.

8. Discuss and rebuild it on the fly. Plan at least three hours minimum.

9. Redraw the map using one of the tools described in Chapter 13, "Drawing Strategy and Process Maps," and redistribute it, asking for comments.

10. Stay open to future revisions.

The Intensive Discussion Approach

In this method the facilitator must be well schooled in the possible outcomes, but the map begins with a blank wall. Intense brainstorming and discussion result in generating new ideas, cracking silo walls, and achieving greater buy-in.

Advantages:

- This is a good but intense method to use, where a single culture needs to be created.

- This method opens communication and begins to crack silo walls.

- There is a greater opportunity for cross-functional and synergistic solutions.

- There is a better chance for breakthrough thinking.

- This method allows all voices to be heard.

- The ideas generated by brainstorming and affinity groupings produce excellent source notes to feed into the Initiatives and Projects steps that follow Strategy Maps.

CEOS SAY INTENSIVE METHOD GENERATES GREAT DISCUSSION

This method, when done correctly, opens up a lot of intense discussion on topics that are either not faced in day-to-day meetings or are topics the leadership team normally does not discuss. It is an opportunity for operationally oriented executive teams to really immerse themselves in strategic thinking. CEOs have told me that the discussions resulting from this method have been some of the most valuable they have heard from their teams.

Disadvantages:

- This method works best if the same executive team goes through the PESTEL and SWOT processes before building the Strategy Map. This gives them a common background.

- This takes more executive time, usually two, 3-hour meetings.

- This method requires a facilitator who is experienced with executives and who has strong business experience, a collection of "business stories" about alternative objectives and themes, and an understanding of the dynamics of "crucial conversations."

The steps for this approach are these:

1. Educate and motivate the executive leadership team on the Balanced Scorecard and strategic themes.

2. Research the business and interview executive leadership team members for themes and objectives.

3. Consider building a straw dog Strategy Map to understand possible outcomes and develop probing questions. This is a practice aid to help the facilitator develop insight. This is not to distribute to the leadership team.

4. Send short whitepapers and industry-related Strategy Maps to bring the executive leadership team up to speed.

5. Convene Strategy Map building sessions with the executive leadership team.

6. Use brainstorming, affinity mapping, and process mapping processes to build a Strategy Map on the fly with the executive leadership team.

7. Redraw the map using one of the tools described in Chapter 13 and redistribute.

8. Solicit comments and stay open to future modifications.

Note: Capture Information with a High-Resolution Camera

A lot of high-value thinking goes into a Strategy Map. Don't lose it. Once the sticky notes are taken down from an affinity group exercise, they could easily be mistaken for trash and discarded or mixed-up, and the causal links would be lost.

I don't know if it's the Boy Scout in me or just knowing how much effort goes into a map, but I use a high-resolution digital camera to capture the map while it is on the board at different points in the process. At the end I also sketch a map. I upload the digital photos to my PC, and that evening in my hotel room or on the plane, I'm able to view the magnified pictures and convert them into a Strategy Map and affinity maps.

Conducting Strategy Map Sessions

Here are some tips on working with a team to build the Strategy Map:

- Use a team of executives who are familiar with strategic visions and thinking; otherwise the process can be mired in tactics and operations.

- These processes usually take two or three, 3-hour meetings after the PESTEL, 5 Forces, and SWOT are complete.

- The team should include six to ten cross-functional members.

- Use large sticky notes to post repositionable objectives on the wall. This beats PowerPoints any day for interactive idea generation. I find the large 3M Post-it® Super Sticky Notes work best.

- Write the Strategic Objectives in large, bold block letters so everyone can read them from a distance.

- Phrase objectives in three to seven words.

- When possible, use this syntax: verb, adjective, noun. For example,

  Manage Customer Expectations, or

  Grow Legacy Sales

When you are finished with a draft Strategy Map, review it by starting at the top of each perspective and working your way down each theme. Ask these questions:

- Will the objective above be driven by the success of the objective below?

- Is this the best objective at this point?

- Is there an objective missing?

- Is this a maintenance or operational objective that is done regardless of strategy?

- Will these objectives accomplish success for this Strategic Theme?

LIMIT A MAP TO 24 OBJECTIVES

Research on best practices by the Palladium Group and Kaplan and Norton's consultancy show the best success comes with Strategy Maps that have fewer than 24 objectives. If you have too many objectives it is difficult to form a clear and concise mental model of what drives your strategy. Some large multinational organizations use only 10 to 15 objectives in their Strategy Map.

Let the team know that the Strategy Map they have built will change. It is not static. Usually insights will drive change in the first week or two as it is reviewed and given more thought. After a map has been in use for 6 months to a year, it will need to change again as you learn what drives success or as the business environment changes. The Strategy Map is a living document that needs to be adjusted as the business environment changes and as objectives are met.

Before you close the session, ask the following probing questions:

- Can we identify the top two or three objectives that are the organization's defensible barrier against competitors?

- If successfully executed, will this strategy hold off competitors?

- Can competitors easily duplicate this strategy?

- Which of these objectives must be executed first? (This is important information as a first step in prioritizing initiatives.)

Questions you may want to ask in closing are these:

- Will this get us to the Strategic Destination?

- Will everyone in your organization understand this map?

- How do you feel about this map and what it will do when executed?

Selecting Strategic Theme Sponsors

Strategic Theme Sponsors take executive responsibility for leading a Strategic Theme. Strategic Themes require cross-functional thinking and teamwork to execute successfully. Usually a Theme Team of cross-functional directors or senior managers works to develop and manage the Strategic Theme. The Theme Team reports to the Strategic Theme Sponsor monthly to insure they are on track.

During the Strategy Map process it usually becomes evident which executives have energy, enthusiasm, and knowledge regarding specific themes. Executive sponsors often self-select by the time the Strategy Map is built.

Summary

The Strategy Map is the foundation for your strategy. Done correctly it is a one-page strategic summary that clearly communicates to everyone in the organization how they can contribute to success. The objectives and causal links in the Strategy Map make it straightforward, although still not easy, to select the critical few metrics for the Balanced Scorecard.

Once you have drafted the Strategy Map it's time to complete a Tactical Action Plan and Implementation Plan. The Tactical Action Plan identifies the metrics that measure each theme and its initiatives. The Implementation Plan creates a breakdown of the projects in each initiative, which objectives are impacted, and how projects should be phased over time. This is covered in the following two chapters.

Notes

1. R. Kaplan and D. Norton, *The Execution Premium: Linking Strategy to Operations for Competitive Advantage,* Boston, Massachusetts: Harvard Business Press, 2008.

2. R. Kaplan and D. Norton, *Strategy Maps: Converting Intangible Assets into Tangible Outcomes,* Boston, Massachusetts: Harvard Business Press, 2004.

CHAPTER 5

Step-by-Step from Strategy to Action

… the essence of strategy is in the activities — to perform activities differently or to perform different activities than rivals.

Michael Porter

Your Strategy Map gives you a clear illustration of your strategy. Now you must translate that strategy into action, for it is only in the execution of your strategy that you win. Your Strategy Map has multiple perspectives into your organization — Strategic Themes that focus energy and resources, and objectives designed to close the gaps between your present and future. This chapter will guide you through translating the Strategic Objectives on the Strategy Map into initiatives. In later chapters, these initiatives will become the actions you use to execute your strategy.

Turning Your Strategy Map into Measurable Action

In Robert Kaplan and Peter Norton's *Harvard Business Review* article, "Using the Balanced Scorecard as a Strategic Management System," they describe a simple table that makes the translation from Strategic Objectives into action a process that is straightforward, although not without effort.[1] Figure 5.1 shows a Tactical Action Plan that converts the objectives of one Strategic Theme into measures, metrics, targets, and initiatives.

The first column of the Tactical Action Plan is the Strategy Map for one Strategic Theme. The name under the Strategic Theme at the top of the first column is the executive sponsor for this theme.

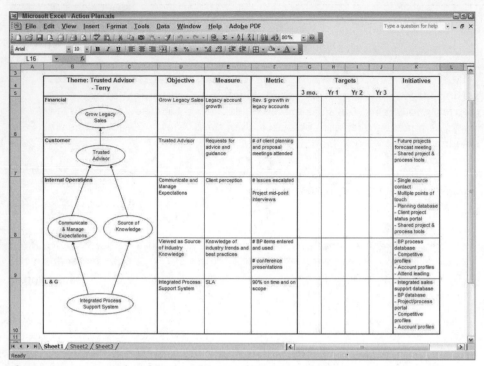

Figure 5.1: Convert the objectives from each Strategic Theme in your Strategy Map into measures, targets, and initiatives.

The other columns in the table are described in Table 5.1:

Table 5.1: A Tactical Action Plan

COLUMN	DESCRIPTION
Strategic Theme Map	This map segment shows the Strategic Objectives and causal links for one Strategic Theme.
Objectives	Listing the objectives as bulleted text makes it easier to align measurements and initiatives in the table.
Measure	This is the unit by which progress to the objective will be evaluated. An objective may have multiple measurements. The Measure is usually selected by the executive leadership team during their Strategy Mapping workshop.
Metric	The metric is a quantifiable evaluation of the measure. A measure may have many different metrics. Metrics may be lead or lag and are defined in detail by the Strategic Theme Team.
Target	Targets are the quantitative value at a given point in time needed to achieve the objectives.
Initiatives	Initiatives are collections of actions or projects designed to achieve the Strategic Objective.

Note: Selecting Measures

The executive leadership team selects the measurements for each objective near the end of their Strategy Map workshop, described in Chapter 4, "Step-by-Step to Building Your Strategy Map." Chapter 6, "Selecting Metrics and Setting Targets," talks in detail about selecting and defining measurements, metrics, and targets. Once the executive leadership team has defined what it wants as a measure for each objective, then the Strategic Theme Teams will develop the metrics and their definitions.

Strategic Theme Teams

After the executive leadership team has developed a Strategy Map and selected measurements, it needs to select members for the Strategic Theme Teams. The Strategic Theme Teams will translate the Strategy Map into the Tactical Action Plan, similar to that shown in Figure 5.1, incorporating metrics, targets, and initiatives.

There is one Strategic Theme Team per Strategic Theme. The Strategic Theme Team reports to the Strategic Theme's executive sponsor, but each team will have its own leader. Each Strategic Theme Team is composed of four to six people. If there are three Strategic Themes, then there will be a total of 12 to 18 people for all the Strategic Theme Teams. The members of these teams:

- Are highly experienced managers or directors who may be on a development track as future executives

- Have cross-functional knowledge and responsibilities supporting the Strategic Theme's objectives. Because Strategic Themes are cross-functional, it is critical that each team have experience in areas of operations, marketing, finance, human capital, and so on.

- Have the ability to dedicate time to analyzing and developing metrics and initiatives

- Have the power and ability necessary for leading initiatives

- Have experience planning and executing initiatives and projects

Motivating and Educating the Strategic Theme Teams

It is as important to educate and motivate the directors and managers who compose your Strategic Theme Teams as it is to educate and motivate the executive leadership team. In preparation for the first meeting, which is focused on motivation and education, I usually send short articles that concisely describe the concepts of the Strategy Map and the Balanced Scorecard. It is important to also include articles and whitepapers about Balanced Scorecard successes by their competitors or within their industry. Keeping these articles short ensures that they will be read.

The first meeting with Strategic Theme Team members has three parts. The meeting begins with the CEO, Strategic Theme sponsors, and the facilitator guiding the Theme Team through the case for change. They must feel the need for change. Next, the facilitator explains the Balanced Scorecard process and its successful use in related businesses. The last hour-and-a-half is used to begin brainstorming new initiatives and to develop commitment to specific themes.

I recommend that the CEO and each of the Strategic Theme Team leaders be at this first meeting. The CEO should open the meeting with the case for change, explaining how the executive leadership team has developed a Strategy Map to articulate the organization's strategy. She should explain that the members of this meeting will be looked on to translate the strategy and Strategy Map into initiatives that will drive the organization to its objectives.

After the CEO presents the case for change, the facilitator should illustrate how the Balanced Scorecard has worked successfully in the same or similar industries. At that point, each of the executive theme sponsors should explain the objectives and causal links in their Strategic Themes and the cross-functional responsibility they have in ensuring that the themes are successfully executed.

The facilitator and executive sponsor can then begin the education process to inform the Strategic Theme Team members about the Balanced Scorecard and the duties of the Strategic Theme Team members.

After the education and motivation process is complete, and before continuing, ensure that everyone understands the definitions of perspectives, Strategic Themes, objectives, and initiatives. People often confuse Strategic Initiatives with projects. Let them know that initiatives are collections of projects designed to reach a Strategic Objective. Your organization may have its own definition for these terms, so use terms everyone in your organization understands.

Brainstorming Initiatives

Before the meeting, you should have prepared sets of partially completed Tactical Action Plans. You should have copies of each Strategic Theme that have the Strategic Theme Map, Objectives, and Measurement columns completed. These templates will be used by team members as guides for later work.

You should also have examples of completed Tactical Action Plans. People learn more easily from examples than from long-winded explanations. A variety of examples of Balanced Scorecards and Tactical Action Plans related to your industry can help team members see the syntax of initiative as well as how the Tactical Action Plan is completed.

Note: CEOs and Sponsors Should Leave During Brainstorming

Executive sponsors should leave the room before brainstorming sessions, because their political and referential weight can limit new ideas.

There are many ways to brainstorm and develop ideas. Here is one way that allows you to capture the voice of quiet members as well as to get team members committed to specific Strategic Themes:

1. Tell the group that they will be brainstorming initiatives that will help the organization reach the Strategic Objectives. Let them know they will be working in groups focused on one Strategic Theme.

    It is important to let the Strategic Theme Teams know from the very beginning that they are developing ideas and proposals for initiatives, not developing the actual strategy. The Strategic Theme Team's proposals must still be made consistent with existing initiatives and projects and go to the executive leadership team for alignment, modification, and approval.

AN INEXPERIENCED FACILITATOR CAN CAUSE DISTRESS

In one situation, a city government staff nearly mutinied after they went through a process to develop initiatives. An inexperienced facilitator did not make it clear to the staff that the purpose of the meetings was to develop proposals for initiatives. The staff thought they were actually developing strategy. It wasn't until late in the action planning process that the facilitator and general manager finally clarified to the staff that they were brainstorming proposals that would then be rationalized, aligned, and approved. This shocking turn of events left the Strategy Theme Teams feeling disempowered, and much ill will developed. But when a process of this sort is guided by an experienced strategic facilitator, it can generate new ideas, develop enthusiasm for new directions, and be an energizing, expansive, and fun experience.

---

2. Give the Strategy Theme Teams a written set of rules for their brainstorming:

    ▪ Any initiative can be proposed. These are proposals, not final initiatives.

    ▪ Current initiatives and initiatives already in the general plan will be rationalized later with new proposed initiatives.

- Brainstorming will be done individually and in silence until everyone is complete. Repeat this! Research has shown the best idea generation begins with silent generation, followed later by group work.

- Don't discuss ideas until everyone in the Strategic Theme Team is finished with their individual ideas.

3. Give the Strategic Theme Teams a written set of rules for writing their brainstorming notes:

   - Use the large-sized 3M Post-it® Super Sticky Notes to capture ideas

   - Write one idea per note

   - Write three to five words per note

   - Write in **bold** letters

   - Write initiatives in a syntax such as:

     Cross-sell marketing

     Single source data system

     High-value customer retention program

   A Strategic Theme Team will usually generate 30 to 40 initiative ideas.

4. Demonstrate to the entire group the affinity grouping process used to consolidate ideas into initiatives:

   - Post all notes on the wall. Discuss the meaning and intent of each note as it is posted.

   - Group notes with similar intent. Some groups may have a large number of notes; others may have just one or two.

   - Write a name for this group on a note, and post it over each group. These names will be the names of initiatives.

   - Keep all the notes. They can be used as ideas for projects to support the initiatives.

   - Select a Strategic Theme Team leader to report back on the named initiatives that the Strategic Theme Team develops.

5. Let the group know that they need to divide into Strategic Theme Teams, with four to six people working on each Strategic Theme.

6. Dismiss the Strategic Theme Teams to break-out rooms. Give them about one hour to work on brainstorming and initiative naming. Let them know that their ideas will be integrated with appropriate current initiatives.

7. While the Strategic Theme Teams are in their break-out areas, create on the walls a large version of the Tactical Action Plan for each Strategic Theme. Use 3M Post-it® Super Sticky Notes to create the map column of each theme. Leave room to the right of each theme's map for the initiatives developed by the Strategic Theme Teams.

8. Go around to each group and help them with their brainstorming processes.

9. Reconvene all the Strategic Theme Teams.

10. By turns, ask each team leader to post and explain their initiatives next to each objective on the wall.

11. Ask the Strategic Theme Teams for feedback about how they feel concerning their work, and whether they think the initiatives will accomplish the objective.

12. Let the Strategic Theme Teams know that prior to the next meeting there will be individual teamwork to further develop the initiatives. The work they have done here will be rationalized with existing initiatives and sent forward as a proposal to the executive leadership team.

This first meeting may or may not develop many new initiatives, depending upon how much prior work has been done and whether these same team members were involved. What I have found is that if this is the organization's first attempt at a structured strategy and execution plan, there will be a lot of new ideas, excitement, and enthusiasm. However, if the organization has had multiple false starts or has failed previously with a strategic plan or Balanced Scorecard, there may be more of a "wait and see" attitude. In the latter case, I can usually build positive enthusiasm by showing teams what happens next:

- Initiatives are rationalized and prioritized.
- Initiatives are divided into projects.
- Projects are phased and funded over time.
- Progress is monitored using the Balanced Scorecard.

When people see that there is a structured way to reach these long-term goals, their optimism returns.

At the end of this first meeting, people have usually self-selected the Strategic Theme Team they want to work in. This is a good point at which to ask Strategic Theme Teams to enter the initiatives they have brainstormed into a Tactical Action Plan. They also need to enter all the brainstorming notes from their team — these notes may aid in developing ideas for projects within each initiative.

Developing a Robust List of Initiatives

After the initial brainstorming meeting, each Strategic Theme Team will usually need one or two more meetings to fully develop a proposal of initiatives that support the Strategic Objectives. In the second meeting, Strategic Theme Team members should look through current and planned initiatives and note those that support their team's Strategic Objectives. These current initiatives should then be added to the Action Plan.

A tool that helps at this point is a spreadsheet, like the one in Figure 5.2. This sheet has Strategic Objectives listed down the left side and current initiatives across the top. Dots within the cells indicate where a current initiative supports a Strategic Objective.

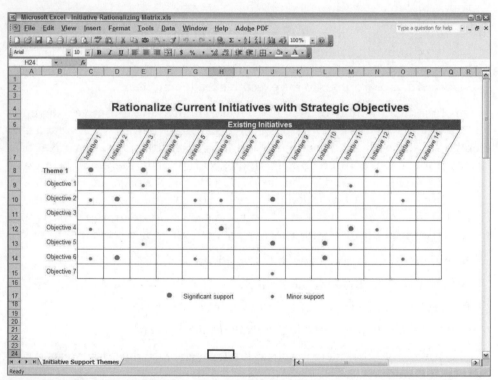

Figure 5.2: Check which of your existing initiatives support your Strategic Objectives.

Notice in this figure that Strategic Objective 3 is not supported by any current initiative. Initiatives 7, 9, and 14 do not support any Strategic Objective. Unless these initiatives are needed for normal operation and maintenance, they might need to be eliminated.

A short description should be given of how any initiative with a dot supports its related Strategic Objective. Those initiatives that do not support a Strategic Objective may be candidates to be phased out. The Strategic Theme Teams should then sit down with their executive sponsors and review their initiatives and Action Plan, making any modifications necessary.

Prioritizing Initiatives

Organizations that face a crisis will find it easy to prioritize initiatives. Their selection of initiatives is driven by the need to surmount their crisis.

Complex organizations with a large number of initiatives need a structured approach to selecting and prioritizing initiatives. One way to do this is to use a spreadsheet that prioritizes initiatives by weighting factors. Figure 5.3 shows a spreadsheet for prioritizing initiatives.

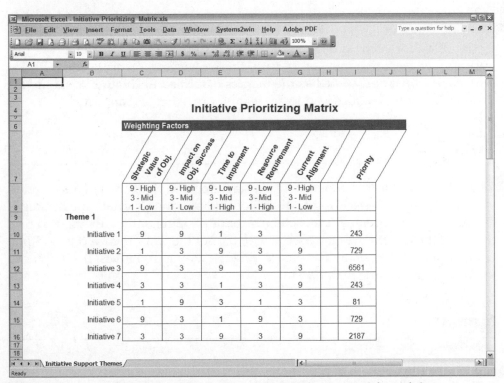

Figure 5.3: Prioritize initiatives using a spreadsheet with exponential weighting.

Weighting values are often chosen from 1 to 5. However, I find that this produces a narrow distribution between weighted initiatives. Using weights of 1, 3, and 9 gives a wider distribution:

1 Lowest-level

3 Mid-level

9 Highest-level

In Figure 5.3, the weighting factors are

- Strategic Value
- Initiative's Impact on Objective's Success
- Time Required for Implementation
- Resources Required for Implementation
- Current Alignment with Initiative Definition

The weighting factors you use will depend upon your business priorities. After developing a prioritized list of initiatives and completing the Tactical Action Plan for each Strategic Theme, the result should be presented to the appropriate executive sponsor. In turn, these reviewed Tactical Action Plans, with their initiatives, as well as the metrics described in Chapter 6, should be proposed to the executive leadership team for revision and approval.

Summary

Your strategic success depends upon selecting the right initiatives — ones you are capable of executing well and ones that strongly affect the Strategic Objective. The processes in this chapter for developing, rationalizing, and prioritizing these initiatives may seem tedious, but the work involved is nothing compared to the wastefulness of selecting the wrong initiatives. In Chapter 6, you will complete the Action Plan.

Notes

1. R. Kaplan and D. Norton, "Using the Balanced Scorecard as a Strategic Management System," *Harvard Business Review*, July 2007.

Step-by-Step to Selecting Metrics and Setting Targets

Get the data first! Then distort it with your judgment.
Mark Twain
Satirist, Author; 1835–1910

There are two reasons for measures and targets. One is to drive change in behavior, and the other is to drive change in processes. It is that simple!

It is also that important! If you pick the wrong measure, you drive change in the wrong direction. If you pick a target that's too easy, you don't motivate people with enough challenge, and you may leave unrealized gains on the table. If you pick a target that's too difficult, you overwhelm people. You need to get the right metric with a target that is a stretch, but is achievable.

Don't expect to get all your objectives and measures right the first time; few organizations do. Objectives and measures usually evolve as you test your model of what drives your organization.

Your Strategy Map is a map of where you want to go in the future. As you achieve one strategic objective and it becomes a maintenance initiative, you will need to reevaluate your Strategy Map and add new objectives and measures to keep up your momentum and direction toward the goal described in your Strategic Destination Statement.

Achieving Balance in Your Balanced Scorecard

Most Balanced Scorecards are not balanced when first developed. In fact, if they are developed by in-house executives or facilitators inexperienced with Balanced Scorecards, they will usually be heavily weighted toward the financial perspective. That's because the executive team is familiar with that perspective: their minds are used to analyzing these numbers, and all the financial data are available. Finding the "critical few" measures for the financial perspective is usually quick and obvious.

It's important when you develop your Strategy Map that the team be cross-functional and have an awareness of all parts of the organization. This will help you develop an even balance in your objectives and measures.

What I find usually happens is that as soon as everyone lets go of financial objectives and starts working on a balanced viewpoint, there is a rush to operational objectives and measures — again because these are familiar.

When you have completed your initial Strategy Map, it is important that your consultant or facilitator guide you through each perspective from the top down. Test to ensure that the objectives and measures in one perspective actually drive the objective in the next higher layer.

Some of the most difficult measures to develop are in learning and growth. The measures of culture, employee attitude, and employee engagement can be difficult to quantify. Excellent books on this topic include:

- *The ROI of Human Capital: Measuring the Economic Value of Employee Performance* by Jac Fitz-enz (New York, New York: AMACOM, 2000)

- *How to Measure Human Resource Management*, 3rd ed., by Jac Fitz-enz (New York, New York: McGraw-Hill, 2001)

- *The Workforce Scorecard: Managing Human Capital to Execute Strategy* by Richard Beatty, Brian Becker, and Mark Huselid (Boston, Massachusetts: Harvard Business School Press, 2005)

- *The HR Scorecard: Linking People, Strategy, and Performance* by Brian Becker, Mark Huselid, and David Ulrich (Boston, Massachusetts: Harvard Business School Press, 2001)

The Workforce Scorecard and *The HR Scorecard* have correlated a "critical few" human capital metrics to high-performing companies. Some of their findings are real eye-openers. Implementing a critical few human capital programs that are measured with a critical few metrics produces a magnitude of difference.

The Right Number of Measures

Well-developed, usable Balanced Scorecards seem to have 12 to 24 metrics, with the number being more on the lower side. Many global corporations have 10 to 15 metrics.

The more metrics you have, the harder it will be for you to form a clear picture of your Strategic Model's drivers and interactions. The Balanced Scorecards I've seen with more than 20 metrics usually have had operational metrics creep in. This happens when an executive leadership team is used to digging in and helping with operational issues. The executives feel a need to monitor those operational issues in the Balanced Scorecard. Remember, the Balanced Scorecard is for strategic alignment and focus. Operational Dashboards can be used to handle operational issues and troubleshoot operational concerns.

In an article titled "Swamped," in *CFO Europe* magazine (November 16, 2004), Janet Kersnar[5] reported that the Hackett Group completed a survey of 2,400 European and U.S. companies. In that survey the Hackett Group found 70 percent of the Balanced Scorecards were failing to help their companies as much as they should have. The conclusion was that these Balanced Scorecards were not providing "concise, predictive and actionable information about how a company is performing and may perform in the future." Notice the words "concise" and "actionable." One reason is that senior executives in the survey were inundated with 132 metrics, the large majority of them financial, which they reviewed every month. When Hackett compared the surveyed companies with best practice companies in Hackett's extensive database, the researchers found that managers in best practice companies used one-ninth the metrics of the companies noted above.

If You Have More Than the "Critical Few," You Lose

One of the leading reasons for failure in Balanced Scorecards is too many metrics. The results are illustrated by a call I got last year from the quality control manager for a large telecom company. The company faced a deadly situation: if the windows on the top floor of their skyscraper had not been bolted shut, people would have been jumping to the streets below rather than attending their monthly management review. The division VP was reviewing about 100 metrics in a 2-hour, death-by-PowerPoint meeting. The results were mind numbing. No one knew which metrics were important. No one knew which metrics drove the business. No one knew which metrics signaled success. They needed help identifying the "critical few" metrics.

We scheduled a meeting for two weeks out, but before we could have our first meeting, the entire organization was acquired by a larger telecom. I still wonder if the 2-hour, all-hands PowerPoint meeting wasn't just one symptom of the larger problem that forced the company into being acquired. Clarity, alignment, and focus on what was important might have prevented their problems.

Lead and Lag Metrics: Drivers and Results

Metrics on a Balanced Scorecard can be divided into two large categories: leading and lagging. Leading measures drive an objective. They are the arrowhead on the causal link. Lagging measures are the results of an objective.

Well-built Balanced Scorecards have a good mix of leading and lagging metrics so the leadership team can form a mental model of what are the most important drivers for each Strategic Theme, and what are the most important results to be expected for a Strategic Theme.

It's obvious from the causal links on a Strategy Map that the lagging (result) metric from one objective will be the leading (driver) metric into another metric.

As Table 6.1 shows, measures in the financial perspective are all going to be lagging. A good, general rule of thumb in a for-profit Balanced Scorecard is that any measure in dollars is lagging. Conversely, measures in the learning and growth perspective are almost all leading. They drive change in internal operations and customer perspectives.

Internal operations and customer measures are a mix of both lead and lag metrics. These perspectives usually have multiple objectives in one perspective layer that feed each other.

Table 6.1: Each Perspective Has a Different Mix of Lead and Lag Measures

PERSPECTIVE	TYPE OF MEASURE
Financial	100% lag (result)
Customer	Mix of lead and lag
Internal Operations	Mix of lead and lag
Learning and Growth	100% lead (driver)

MOTIVATING WITH METRICS

Being measured can be intimidating or it can be motivating. It depends on whether you feel the goal is achievable, your level of empowerment, and whether you have a way of learning the skills you will need to reach a higher level. Following is a personal, not a business, story, but I think it illustrates my point.

My six-year old son entered first grade almost halfway through the year through no fault of his own. Through the work of two great teachers at his public school and his mom's mentoring, he finished the year slightly below average on reading tests. The principal sent a letter to all students saying any student who read 800 pages over the summer would get to have an ice cream cone with her. Any student who read 1,200 pages would get to have a banana split with her.

The ice cream and the time with the principal were motivators, but the motivation only lasted a day for my son (we walk to the ice cream store about every other week). I thought about what his motivators were and how to get him engaged. He and I talked through ideas and came up with the following plan:

■ **Visual indicator:** We put a thermometer chart on the kitchen door that showed how many pages had been read, with a picture of the reward at each major point.

■ **Awareness of progress:** It was up to him to color the thermometer and write the name of the book (with some prodding) each time he finished a book.

■ **Personal empowerment and decision making within a defined scope:** He got to pick about half the books to read from the Level 1 to Level 3 readers at the library.

■ **Modeling by mentors:** Either his mom, his GoGo (Zulu for grandma), or I read the book to him, with lots of emphasis and enunciation; then he read it sometime that day. This gave him good modeling.

■ **Short-term rewards:** Whenever there was a jump in proficiency, we had an impromptu "parade" around the house to acknowledge how much he had improved.

■ **Rewards:** At 800 pages, he got the science kit he had been craving. At 1,200 pages, he and I went to lunch at the kids' fun center in town and played games.

The results have been amazing. In the first five days, he read over 500 pages without prompting (he got his science kit shortly after). It's been two weeks now and he's slowed down a little, but he still reads over 50 pages a day, and he's closing in on that lunch at the kids' fun center (I've got my earplugs ready for when I take him).

There is a marked difference in his fluency and attitude. He got bored the other day while watching his hour of TV, picked up a book, and started reading to himself, ignoring the TV.

Our next steps will be to help him internalize his feelings of reward and power so he doesn't need to depend upon us.

Sample Objectives and Metrics

There are many good books available on defining new metrics as well as lists of industry standard metrics. Industry consultants, performance consultants, and Balanced Scorecard consultants will have lists of metrics that are standard for your industry or similar business models.

Although a list may cut down on your need for brainstorming, choosing the correct metric for your objective and situation is critical. Table 6.2 shows a sample of objective/measure pairs from a few of my clients. There may be many metrics possible for one objective. The one you select depends upon your unique situation.

Table 6.2: Sample Pairs of Objectives and Measures

PERSPECTIVE	OBJECTIVE	MEASURE
Finance	Increase new product sales	% revenue from products less than 3 years old
Finance	Balanced revenue portfolio	Ratio of revenue by product line and segment
Finance	Stabilize cash flow	Reduce variance from budget
Finance	Increase account penetration	% of the total contract
Customer	Customer delight	% on survey saying they would refer a friend
Customer	On time; on budget; on scope	Project time, budget, and scope variance
Customer	Make it easy	Greater than 4/5 on satisfaction surveys given at intermediate stage gates
Customer	Trusted advisor relationship	# of "C" level meetings and client design meetings invited to
Internal Operations	Be Lean	$$$ saved due to top X Lean projects
Internal Operations	Hassle-free delivery of transactions	% claims paid in 30 days
Internal Operations	Close contact client engagement	Index of engagement scores
Internal Operations	Manufacturing performance	Cycle times, unit cost, waste
Learning & Growth	Management/supervisor development	% of management/supervisor training completed
Learning & Growth	Employee development	% of employees with current 360 evaluation
Learning & Growth	Managerial loyalty	Management positions filled through internal promotion
Learning & Growth	Strategic readiness	% of strategic employee positions with qualified successor

> **WHY A CONSULTANT CAN HELP SELECT METRICS**
>
> There are many good books on metrics, measures, and Key Performance Indicators (KPIs). Those books are in addition to all the internal experience you already have about measures in your organization. A consultant can help you get a different perspective on your measures by recommending alternatives used in similar industries; questioning the validity of assumptions; and proposing proxies, indexes, or countermeasures for balance. Balanced Scorecard consultants should be able to give you many alternatives.

Step-by-Step to Selecting Your Metrics

Developing measures and metrics seems to be either very easy or pretty tough. In some cases there are no clear answers as to which is the best metric to use.

Compose your metrics teams of each Strategic Theme team and subject matter experts (SMEs) in the areas you need to measure. As much as possible your team should have depth in the metric, but also have cross-functional knowledge.

I usually do this by having as many members as possible, usually three or four, of the Strategic Theme team meet and then augment them with SMEs for the specific metric being defined. You may also need to include someone from IT or human resources/human capital (HR/HC) when you talk about what data are available and who is responsible for them.

Here is a general outline for the steps to follow:

1. Quickly review the Strategy Map.

2. Review the objective you are focusing on.

3. Review the measure selected by the executive leadership team. You may need to redefine this if the SME has a constructive alternative.

4. Discuss the "intent" of the measure: What behavior is it intended to change? What actions or processes are it intended to change?

5. Brainstorm individually which quantitative metrics will work.

6. Reduce these to a single metric or two counterbalancing metrics:

    ■ Does it measure the intent?

    ■ Does this measure strategic or operational change?

    ■ Is it "actionable"?

    ■ Are the data available or can they be captured cost/time effectively?

7. While this information is fresh in everyone's mind, use a Metric Definition sheet described in the next section to capture a definition of the metric. One or two individuals can complete these at a later time.

One of the things I observe in working with small- and mid-sized businesses on their Balanced Scorecards is the difference between strategic thinkers and operational doers. These two types have different ways of thinking, analyzing, and communicating. A good facilitator will help you smooth out these differences and keep the discussion moving at a strategic level while satisfying the SMEs' need for detail by capturing detailed ideas that may be valuable during implementation.

EXPAND YOUR METRIC BRAINSTORMING WITH LISTS OF METRICS

After you brainstorm metrics, it's a good idea to look through lists of metrics for examples or categories you might have missed. To see lists of metrics, look in the resource area at Tor Consulting Inc. on the Web at www.torconsulting.com.

Defining the Metric with a Metric Definition

Once you have selected a metric, the Strategic Theme team and its SMEs need to create a written description of that metric, the targets, and the alert values.

Many clients create a Metric Definition table that includes the following items:

- Metric name
- Strategic Theme
- Objective measured
- Theme Team leader and members
- Rational for this metric
- What it drives or measures
- How it is calculated
- Data sources and where they are located
- Alert levels over time
- Target levels over time

In my experience it is difficult to get team members to complete the Metric Definition, so we usually do it interactively on a laptop as we are defining and selecting metrics. That leaves just clean-up work later.

Some of the items from the Metric Definition should be put in the Briefing Book of your Balanced Scorecard. The Briefing Book is a one-screen form linked to each Balanced Scorecard chart so the leadership team can see for which Strategic Theme and objective the metric is used, who the owner is, and what current actions are being taken. The Briefing Book is described in more detail in Chapter 27, "Finishing Touches."

Look Out! What You Measure Is What You Get!

The old saying, "What you measure is what you get" has a corollary from the dark side: "If you measure the wrong thing, you'll get the wrong result." Make sure you select metrics that drive the behaviors and process changes you want.

In their book *The HR Scorecard: Linking People, Strategy, and Performance*, Huselid, Becker, and Ulrich reveal the results of their research into how HR/HC creates a high-performance work system (HPWS). Their findings for 429 firms in 1998 reveal a striking difference between corporations in the top and bottom 10 percent of financial performance. They found specific HR metrics that pinpoint the difference between top- and bottom-performing corporations. They said, "The most striking attribute of these comparisons is not any one HR management practice — it is not recruiting or training or compensation. Rather, the differences are much more comprehensive — and systemic." It wasn't one or two specific measures that made a difference. It was an entire system of specific metrics that seemed to make the difference between winners and losers. If you measure the right HR metrics, doing so can help make your organization a winner. If you measure the wrong HR metrics, at best you waste your time and money.

Another example showing the relationship between well-chosen metrics and strategic success is exemplified by the turnaround in Sears, Roebuck and Company in the 1990s. In a *Harvard Business Review* article written by Rucci, Kirn, and Quinn entitled "The Employee-Customer-Profit Chain at Sears," Sears developed and communicated a set of metrics that saved the company. In one year, 1992–93, the merchandising group went from a loss of $3 billion to a net income of $752 million. They produced this dramatic change by building an *employee-customer-profit* model that defined the causal links that drove their business success. In one area they found that a 5 percent improvement in employee attitude drove a 1.3 percent improvement in customer satisfaction and resulted in a 0.5 percent improvement in revenue growth.

Of course, it isn't just the metric and measurement that made the difference for Sears. Sears had to align the organization around the model, foster a culture to reinforce the change, and then monitor and manage with the measures.

Sears also had to develop a system of ownership and accountability through every level of the company. These are all parts of a fully implemented Balanced Scorecard.

Critical Questions to Ask About Your Measures and Metrics

Following are a few critical questions to ask as you evaluate any metric you select, whether it's new or a legacy:

- What do we need to change to reach this objective?
  - Does this metric drive the change in behavior we need?
  - Does this metric measure the change in processes we need?
  - Is this metric fair and understandable by all? Can it be "gamed" by a few to circumvent the intent of the Balanced Scorecard?
- Does this metric test our hypothesis?
  - Is this metric the best measure of success or driver for this objective?
  - Will this metric enable us to prove how our business model works?
  - Will we be able to change our organization because of changes in this metric?
- Are the data available?
  - What is the source for the data?
  - Are the data clean and usable?
  - If the data are not available, are there proxies or substitutes that act the same way?
  - Can the data be captured from an existing initiative?
  - Can a cost-effective and timely program capture these data?
- What action will we take?
  - What actions will we take if this metric changes?
  - Is there a person responsible for those actions?
  - What target and alert levels would signal the need to take action?
  - If we aren't going to take action when an alert level is met, then why are we using this metric?

- How often do we measure?
  - How often are data available?
  - Is that frequency often enough for us to make an effective course correction?
  - What frequency do we need to make effective changes?

    Some metrics, such as an annual employ satisfaction survey, are done only once a year because of the expense and volume. An annual measurement is not frequent enough to drive change with any insight; however, there may be a proxy metric you capture more frequently that can give you an indication of change. For example, some proxies you can use for employee satisfaction are lost time from injuries, lost days from sickness, productivity levels, and so forth. Another alternative is to do a monthly min-survey of a small random sample of employees to monitor change from the annual survey.

- Is there a data owner?
  - Is there an individual who will be responsible for these data, their accuracy, and their entry into the Balanced Scorecard system?
  - Is there a data warehouse or portal in which to maintain these data?

Setting Targets

Executives and managers are used to setting targets, so I won't go into this in detail. But there are some nuances you might want to consider with respect to the Balanced Scorecard.

To begin with, work from the top down. Start with the financial perspective and consider what portion of change here will be attributable to each Strategic Theme. For example, if the organization wants to increase from $80M to $120M in the next three years and has three Strategic Themes, the organization will want to apportion that growth across the three themes.

Now determine how much each Strategic Theme must contribute to reach the total target. As you work down the perspectives in each Strategic Theme, you will need to ask yourself questions such as these:

- Revenue Increase Strategic Themes
  - What change will be necessary in market share, customer response, or repeat purchase?
  - What increase in infrastructure will be needed?
  - What new processes will need funding?

- Cost Reduction Strategic Themes
    - How much can we decrease production costs?
    - How much can we increase productivity?

Setting Target Values

If you use the preceding process, you will have defined the targets needed for the financial goals in each Strategic Theme. Once you break out how much each Strategic Theme contributes to the total financial goals, then you can define how each perspective in that theme needs to change to make the financial goal happen. This is usually an iterative process, working up and down the theme as well as determining whether the math produces a realistic target. Here are some ideas for sources you can use to test whether the targets you've developed are within the realm of reality:

- Historical tracking and benchmarking of organizational data
- Horizontal comparison between similar business units in your organization
- Association benchmarks
- Best practice surveys from private consulting firms
- Best estimates from a panel of experts
- Regulatory benchmarks set by legislative agencies

Setting Intermediate Targets

Your target for a three-year horizon may be a 100 percent improvement, but you'll never get your employees to believe that unless you:

- Divide the amount of change into smaller increments over time
- Tell a story that shows how each small, achievable step builds to the bigger goal
- Celebrate when you reach intermediate goals

When I work with my clients, we prioritize initiatives and projects and then schedule them over the three to five years of their strategic goal. As the next chapter explains, I help them spread initiatives across near-term and long-term schedules:

- First-year goals by quarter: Q1, Q2, Q3, and Q4
- Second-year goals
- Third-year goals
- And so forth

Moving Toward a Target Will Not Be at a Constant Rate

It's rare to approach an objective at the same rate over three or more years. You need to adjust your intermediary targets for different growth rates depending upon the type of initiative you are measuring.

Productivity programs such as Six Sigma and Lean usually get very rapid returns in the near term, with diminishing returns thereafter. Some marketing programs will have this same diminishing returns curve. During the first year there may be rapid growth, which then diminishes in rate over the next few years as the market saturates and competitors enter the same market. For example, the growth rates in the following table build to an overall change of more than 200 percent in two years:

Year 1	Year 2	Year 3
50%	25%	10%

Entering a completely new and open market with high demand, a so-called Blue Ocean, can produce a sigmoid or s curve growth. The sigmoid curve has what looks like rapid exponential growth in the beginning, linear growth during market adoption, and then asymptotic or diminishing returns as the market saturates. The first part of this curve is the infamous "hockey stick" that so many dot-com businesses bet on and failed.

The sigmoid formula is too complex for many Excel users — you can find it on Wikipedia — but Juan Carlos Méndez-García has produced a simplified formula with easy-to-understand parameters at his web site. To find his blog and web site through Google, search for "modeling market adoption in Excel with a simplified s-curve."

Summary

The measures you choose will make all the difference to the results of your Balanced Scorecard. People will work hard to give you what you measure, so choose measures that reflect the causal links on your Strategy Map.

There are many lists of measures on the Internet, through consultants, through associations, and through your own experience. Choose a combination of lead or driver metrics and lag or results metrics. Balanced Scorecards have almost all lead metrics in learning and growth, a mixture of lead and lag in internal operations and customer, and all lag measures in finance.

Make sure you document the metrics you select. People will forget, and there needs to be accountability. Part of this documentation process is selecting an owner for the data and the formula.

There is more information about operational metrics in Chapter 11, "Identifying Critical Metrics and Key Performance Indicators."

Notes

1. R. Beatty, B. Becker, and M. Huselid, *The Workforce Scorecard: Managing Human Capital to Execute Strategy* (Boston, Massachusetts: Harvard Business School Press, 2005)

2. B. Becker, M. Huselid, and D. Ulrich, *The HR Scorecard: Linking People, Strategy, and Performance* (Boston, Massachusetts: Harvard Business School Press, 2001)

3. J. Fitz-enz, *How to Measure Human Resource Management*, 3rd ed. (New York, New York: McGraw-Hill, 2001)

4. J. Fitz-enz, *The ROI of Human Capital: Measuring the Economic Value of Employee Performance* (New York, New York: AMACOM, 2000)

5. J. Kersnar, "Swamped," *CFO Europe* (November 16, 2004)

CHAPTER 7

Step-by-Step to Developing Your Implementation Plan

No decision has been made unless carrying it out in specific steps has become someone's work assignment and responsibility.

Peter Drucker
Management Consultant, 1909–2005

This is where strategy is translated into action. This is the point of translating objectives and initiatives into projects that go to budgeting, project management, and implementation.

To effectively implement your strategy, you must have the buy-in, understanding, and creative problem solving of the managers and people who will make it work. The people on the front lines usually understand best how to improve their work. Without their motivation, understanding, and agreement, it is impossible to make strategic change permanent.

This chapter covers some methods of involving and motivating middle managers and subject matter experts (SMEs). They not only translate the strategic plan into action and carry it forward, but they also augment it with their own creative ideas.

Step-by-Step to Translating Initiatives into Projects

The following process works well to capture innovative ideas while building buy-in and personal commitment from mid-level managers and SMEs.

For the teams that work on translating initiatives into projects, you will want a cross-functional selection of people who are highly experienced with planning and project management. This method quickly captures input and builds buy-in from the managers and supervisors who will be implementing projects identified within your Strategic Initiatives.

Your teams should have diverse people who are knowledgeable about existing projects and project management. Although these meetings usually involve eight to 16 people, they can sometimes involve as many as 40 people.

To follow the process outlined below, you will want the teams to meet by Strategic Theme. If there are a lot of initiatives in a Strategic Theme, you may want to limit each meeting to a few high-order initiatives. These large-group meetings can last from 3 hours to all day.

1. The Theme Team leaders guide the group through building its own case for change. This interactive process enables the group to build its own case for change that parallels the ideas and process used with the executive team. It's a good way for everyone to come to their own realization that "the iceberg is melting."

2. The Theme Team leader, or in small- to mid-sized companies, the CEO or executive vice president, then explains how the executive team feels about the needed change and the time they've put into developing a Strategic Destination Statement, Strategy Map, and initiatives.

   In this case, the CEO or vice president then says, "What we need from you today is your knowledge and expertise in how we can convert these initiatives into projects that execute our strategy." At that point, the CEO or vice president can leave.

3. Members of the Theme Team then explain the Strategic Initiatives and show how each contributes to success within the Strategic Theme. They explain the interdependence of initiatives and why projects are time-phased by dependence and by strategic priority. This usually results in some good discussion about the initiatives, and sometimes produces additional initiatives or barriers that haven't been discussed previously.

4. By that point, individuals usually have some emotional or professional tie to an initiative, so break the team into groups of four to 12 people. Each group will work on a group of related initiatives.

5. Explain the brainstorming process you want to use, how to create a unified name for each project, and how to post the projects into a schedule. What you are doing is creating an environment for an interactive work-breakdown schedule.

   Each break-out group should then:

   ▪ Identify major projects needed to accomplish each Strategic Initiative

   ▪ Determine whether each project is already funded and scheduled

   ▪ Define project dependence and sequence

- Identify major resource requirements that might impact other initiatives
- Identify dependence upon other initiatives

6. In the main room, create the framework on the wall for a large Gantt chart. Initiative names should be on the left. Timeframes, such as Q1, Q2, Q3, Q4, Y2, Y3, should be across the top.

7. Reconvene the groups.

8. The "natural leader" from each break-out group should explain their results as they post project names to the right of the initiative, under the approximate timeframe.

9. Once each group has posted its results, all the groups can see all strategic projects for this theme over the strategic timeframe. Engage everyone to look at the big picture and consider these issues:

   - Conflicts with current projects
   - Dependencies within the posted projects
   - Resource conflicts of key personnel, budget, and so forth

10. Finally, involve everyone in moving sticky notes on the wall to schedule highest-priority projects into achievable timeframes.

Everyone should be aware this is an interactive process that quickly creates a draft for Strategic Initiatives over the multiyear strategic timeframe. When you are done with this workshop, there is still considerable detail work that needs to be done to refine each project definition, build budget cases, and more.

One result of this process is buy-in and development of innovative ideas for implementing your Strategic Initiatives. It also helps you identify the people who may be your best change agents. The people who exhibit the most enthusiasm will stand out. If they also have the knowledge, authority, and resources, they may be your best change agents. If they lack one of these attributes, team them with someone who complements them.

Note: Meeting Logistics

Meetings like the implementation planning meeting can get bogged down because of poor logistics. Here's a list of items to consider:

- Ask everyone to bring current project schedules for the next year.
- Ensure the meeting room is large enough with adequate air conditioning.
- Have sufficient 3M Post-it® Super Sticky Notes (large size) and markers for all break-out groups.
- Always bribe attitudes and brains with food, snacks, and drinks. Intense thinking takes as many calories as walking. Keep them fed and happy.

- Have sufficient supplies: easels, 3M Blue Tape to tape up findings on walls, marker pens, and 3M Post-it® Super Sticky Notes.

- Set aside break-out rooms for large groups to break into smaller groups of 4–12 people dedicated to a specific project.

Monitoring Initiatives in Progress

It is rare to begin a Balanced Scorecard having all the data you need for your metrics. Sometimes one-third to one-half of the data are missing. Another reason for missing metrics is that some Strategic Initiatives won't start for 6 months to a year. So what do you display on your Balanced Scorecard?

Some Balanced Scorecard developers just put a grayed chart or metric where there are missing data or have an incomplete initiative. If possible you can give feedback on the progress of initiatives or data development.

Executives shouldn't be doing project management, but they should be aware of whether major strategic projects are ahead or behind schedule. Figure 7.1 shows a simple chart created in Excel. It's like a Gantt chart, but it displays only the difference between target and actual delivery for initiatives and projects. Creating this chart is explained in Chapter 24, "Building Powerful Charts for Decision-Making." You can use the techniques you learn in Chapter 23, "Displaying Targets and Alerts," to color each horizontal bar depending upon the size of its variance.

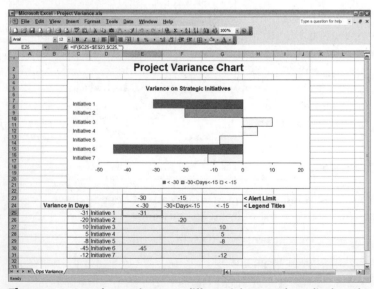

Figure 7.1: A project variance or differential Gantt chart displays the difference between target and actual delivery data for initiatives and major projects

MICROSOFT EXCEL AS A PROJECT MANAGEMENT TOOL

I really put some effort into using Microsoft Project to manage projects I was managing, but I found MS Project too burdensome for many projects.

Finally, I developed a fairly robust project management system in Excel and used it successfully for years. I've since found that many of my small- to mid-size clients have the same problem with their project management. There are a couple of nice project management systems built in Excel that work well for small projects. To see a list of Excel-based project management systems, look in the resource section of the Tor Consulting Inc. web site, www.torconsulting.com.

Summary

All the best plans are worthless if you can't implement them. And getting your people motivated and dedicated to making strategy happen is critical. The process described here has been used many times to quickly develop an implementation plan, draft schedules, develop new project ideas, and build agreement and motivation for the new direction. It works.

CHAPTER 8

Step-by-Step to Roll-Out and Strategic Reviews

*I sure wish I'd done a better job of communicating with GM people.
I'd do that differently a second time around and make sure they understood and
shared my vision for the company. Then they would know why I was tearing the
place up, taking out whole divisions, changing our whole production structure …
I never got this across.*

Roger Smith,
CEO of General Motors
–Strategic Choices
by Kenneth Primozic, Edward Primozic, and Joe Leben

The Balanced Scorecard is a tool for change. It is not just for reporting metrics. It is not just for managing performance. It is definitely not just a one-time performance project. The Balanced Scorecard is a tool for creating a strategy-focused organization. To become a strategy-focused organization, you must communicate your strategy so everyone knows how they can and will contribute.

This chapter examines a few of the processes involved in communicating and rolling out the Balanced Scorecard. It's the beginning of your journey in building a strategy-focused organization.

Creating a Culture Focused on Strategy

I have small laser pointers that I occasionally use during presentations. Each is powered by a single, small AAA battery. On a couple of occasions my kids have used two laser pointers to play "light tag" at night by shining them across the fairway of the golf course beyond our backyard. That single AAA battery gives this small, 2-inch laser enough power to light a spot on a tree 100 yards away.

Conversely, I have a small flashlight I keep in my travel kit that is also powered by a single AAA battery. However, its light barely shines across a hotel room.

The input power to both lights is the same, but the difference in output is immense. The difference is focus and alignment. The laser light comes out as coherent light. All the frequencies are the same, and they are all traveling in the same direction, so there is no need for extra effort to focus the light. On the other hand, the flashlight wastes most of its energy in heat, shines a broad spectrum, and scatters the light in all directions. A small mirror and lens attempt to focus the beam, but most of the power is wasted, and the output is dispersed. Does this sound like organizations you've worked in?

There's a profile I've noticed of the organizations I've worked with. They usually have one or more of these characteristics:

- New CEO
- New CFO
- High growth rate and the need to build the infrastructure before it gets away from them
- Merger or acquisition and a need to merge cultures and processes
- Changing workforce demographics
- Changing customer buying patterns
- Significant increase in direct or functional competition
- Current or expected changes in government regulation

All of these involve change or the preparation for significant change. The Balanced Scorecard enables organizations to manage the change, as well as to align and focus on strategy while simultaneously increasing performance. For long-lasting cultural change, you need a process to make change part of your culture. See the sidebar on "Creating Lasting Change in Your Organization" to learn how to do this.

CREATING LASTING CHANGE IN YOUR ORGANIZATION

In the last few decades there have been many tools for organizational change and performance improvement: TQM (total quality management), reengineering, learning organization (Senge), Six Sigma, Lean, and more. All of these attempt to change the culture and improve performance. For all of these methods the Balanced Scorecard acts as a management envelope to track the change and evaluate what works. But you also need a proven process of organizational change to make the change a lasting part of the culture.

One of the best processes I have seen for guiding an organization through change and making it stick comes from John Kotter, professor at Harvard Business School. In 2001 *Business Week* surveyed 504 enterprises and concluded that John Kotter was the number one "leadership guru" in the United States. His books remain in the top 1 percent of books sold on Amazon.com. I believe in Kotter's eight-step action plan for creating lasting change in organizations.

1. **Case for Change:** point to a "burning platform" that will drive an urgent need for change

2. **Leadership:** create a "guiding collaboration," a powerful, high-level team that can make change happen

3. **Vision:** create a clear picture of the objectives and the steps each person can take to reach the objectives

4. **Communicate:** create stories and images that capture every audience, through every media, all the time

5. **Empower:** give people the power to make change happen at their jobs

6. **Celebrate:** plan for and create short-term wins, because lasting change takes time and wears down motivation

7. **Adapt:** learn what works and continue to change and grow; don't let naysayers slow down the change by claiming short-term wins as the finish line

8. **Institutionalize:** cement changes into the fabric of the culture, people, and processes

When you look through Kotter's eight-step action plan, it becomes pretty clear how it works as a perfect companion for the Balanced Scorecard.

When the executive sponsor, your change agents, and your Balanced Scorecard facilitator develop your plan to roll out the Balanced Scorecard you need to be familiar with and incorporate these eight steps.

Strategy Review Meeting

In the Strategy Review Meeting the executive leadership team uses the Balanced Scorecard as a pivot point for strategic conversations that should dig deeply into the effectiveness of the strategy, the forward-looking performance of the organization, and the "learnings" and best practices that can be shared throughout the organization.

It is very important that you get the format and attitude correct for the first strategy review meeting. In the first few meetings you need to set a model for the meeting's focus, attitudes, and outcomes.

It is important to keep the momentum rolling when implementing the Balanced Scorecard. You should have your first strategy review meeting that incorporates the Balanced Scorecard within a month or two of the scorecard's completion.

Attendees for the strategy review meeting should include those leaders who have a broad vision of the organization's objectives as well as responsibility for the strategic themes. I recommend your meetings include the following:

- CEO
- Executive leadership team
- Senior strategic business unit leaders responsible for implementing strategy
- Strategic Theme sponsors
- Subject matter experts (SMEs) appropriate to the topics being discussed in that meeting. SMEs may be on standby and called when needed
- Balanced Scorecard facilitator to guide the meeting
- Data managers and the Balanced Scorecard editor, who should be "on standby" if there are questions about data freshness or validity

Because many of these functions are duplicated in the same person, a meeting can have from 8–12 people, not including the facilitator and people who are "on standby" for questions.

The two meeting agendas most frequently used are:

- Monthly meetings focused on the Strategic Theme the CEO feels is most important to discuss. The theme sponsor for that Strategic Theme should facilitate that meeting.
- Quarterly meetings that cover the entire Balanced Scorecard. Begin with a brief status report on each theme and its objectives, and then spend the majority of time on the issues of concern.

CAUTION Very few organizations are able to hold operational and strategic review meetings on the same day. Because everyone's mind is on the "alligators in the swamp," it is difficult to get into and maintain the long-term view needed for a strategy review meeting. It is far better to have the strategy review meeting on a separate day. If an operational issue comes up during the strategy meeting, put it in a "parking lot" for discussion after the strategy review meeting.

Most organizations hold their strategic review meetings monthly or quarterly. Meetings held monthly usually spend the majority of the meeting time on one

Strategic Theme. At a quarterly meeting all Strategic Themes, the Strategy Map, and its objectives can be reviewed. A strategy review meeting with good, intense discussion can take from 3 hours to all day.

If you use a meeting format that focuses each meeting on one specific Strategic Theme, then the facilitator for that meeting should be the strategic sponsor for the theme being discussed.

For the first few strategy review meetings, you should have a facilitator who is experienced with strategy review meetings. A facilitator who is used to guiding a meeting will present a good model for leading the strategy review meeting. Keeping the meeting on track and focused on strategic issues can be an issue for organizations that are used to holding only operational meetings.

Some of the first meetings may devolve into discussions on:

- Data analysis
- Balanced Scorecard charts
- Operational issues

This can be because the organization doesn't have a habit of sharing internal issues across silos or because participants are used to operational rather than strategic meetings. Your facilitator needs to bring the meeting back to its purpose: improving the organization's strategic performance and validating the model represented by the Balanced Scorecard.

Preparing for the Strategy Review Meeting

Get your data, analysis, and Balanced Scorecard ready a few days prior to the meeting. If you are focusing on one Strategic Theme, you will want that theme's sponsor to write up an analysis and comments so these can be distributed prior to the meeting. Attendees must have a chance to review data, the Balanced Scorecard, and the analysis prior to the meeting. If they can't review and analyze these before the meeting, the meeting may turn into a data presentation rather than remaining a discussion of strategy.

Prepare the attendees for the fact that the meeting will focus on issues and actions and not on presentations and data, so little time will be taken to present the data that are already available. This gives you the opportunity to jump right into discussion of strategic issues.

I meet separately with the CEO and the theme sponsor prior to each of the first meetings to reiterate the purposes:

- The meeting should discuss strategic issues.
- Operational issues need to be set aside to maintain a strategic mindset.

- The purpose is intense, strategic discussion that usually doesn't occur during the overload of operational issues. (Have I said this before?)

- It is good to have a mix of red, yellow, and green alerts. If there were no red lights it would mean you had achieved your objectives. (Another way of saying this is, "Don't shoot the messenger for a red light.")

- Fear suppresses the information about aspects you need to improve. If there is fear of reporting all information, you only get the good news.

- The meeting needs to include the sharing of best practices.

- The focus of the meeting needs to be looking forward.

- Expected results include the identification of what actions are needed, the timeframe, and the person accountable.

- Expected results also include identifying what should be communicated from the meeting to the organization.

Facilitating the First Meeting

At the beginning of the first few meetings the facilitator needs to set the behavior for the meeting by reviewing the purpose for the meeting, the same points that were reviewed in private with the CEO.

Remind everyone that it can take up to a year to get all the data for metrics on the Balanced Scorecard. You can gray out the missing data and charts, or show a miniature Gantt chart showing the progress of key initiatives in that objective.

Communication, Training, and Roll-Out

Viewing the Balanced Scorecard as a tool for creating a strategy-focused organization makes it obvious you will need programs to help your organization adapt, change, and learn new behaviors. This takes an ongoing commitment to communication, training, and motivation.

Communication

Research published in the *Journal of Strategic Communication* shows how critical the communication of strategy is to everyone in your organization. In high-performing organizations 67 percent of employees had a "good understanding of the overall organizational goals." In poorly performing organizations that level was 38 percent.

The communication program you set up should be run like any other program. It must have a project manager who is experienced with communication. Before developing your communication calendar, you need to define the basics needed in any communication program:

- **Audience.** Your communication plan must stretch from the board of directors to the individual contributor and all levels in between. Each level will have its own WIIFM — What's In It for Me — as well as thoughts like, how painful will it be for me?

- **Media.** What media works best for your culture, industry, resources, and geographic distribution? Some large corporations have created multimedia and video productions embracing the Balanced Scorecard. Smaller organizations have used recurring articles from the president in their newsletter as well as "town hall" meetings.

- **Message.** Define how this will affect your organization. Does everyone need to know the case for change? How many will need direct training on the Balanced Scorecard? Will you cascade the scorecard to business units and personal levels?

One thing is absolutely necessary: the CEO or senior executive continuously needs to give endorsement to developing a strategy-focused organization through the Balanced Scorecard.

When I interview executives and mid-managers I frequently get asked the question, "How interested is the CEO in this?" Or "How do I know this isn't just another management fad?" The only ways to dispel this attitude is with a consistent message and actions from senior executives that continuously reinforce the commitment to the Balanced Scorecard.

Communication Media

Your organization is unique. You have your own culture, communication channels, resources, and distribution. You will need to create and manage your own ongoing communications program.

Some of the different media that I've seen used for communicating the Balanced Scorecard are these:

- Recurring letters from the CEO in the organization's newsletter
- CEO personally presenting the new vision and Balanced Scorecard with Strategy Map to all employees in a presentation and webinar
- Recognition programs
- Sharing of best practices discovered through the Balanced Scorecard

- Training for all managers in aligning with objectives
- Using the Balanced Scorecard as the agenda for meetings: Are we on track? What needs to change?
- Town hall meetings
- Videos with the CEO speaking on the importance of the Balanced Scorecard
- Visual metaphors of the Strategy Map and new culture (see the following section) posted in communal gathering locations
- Web-based presentations and webinars
- Company portal front page
- Balanced Scorecard, Strategy Map, and operational metrics posted in high-traffic hallways or gathering areas
- Email postings and reminders about the Balanced Scorecard and when it has been updated (everyone likes to see how we're doing)
- Inclusion of Balanced Scorecard objectives and initiatives as a core for operational change presentations
- Focus on the Balanced Scorecard in the annual report
- Focus on the Balanced Scorecard in the message to shareholders

The importance in all of these is that you use multiple media with multiple messages to multiple audiences. It is imperative that senior leaders continually be seen endorsing the move to a strategy-focused organization.

Translating Strategy Maps into Visual Metaphors

The Strategy Map creates a visual representation of your organization's business model, but people at different levels and functions in your organization may find it difficult if not impossible to interpret. Many organizations are using another type of visual map to help them communicate to all levels of their organization.

Storytelling is probably one of our earliest forms of communicating culture, vision, and values. Combining stories with pictures that guide the storyteller and listener enables everyone to tell the story, remember it, and retell it. Many organizations are using these visual metaphors as storytelling maps that help communication.

Figures 8.1, 8.2, and 8.3 show visual maps that represent how organizations see themselves and what they want to communicate to their employees. Figure 8.4 shows a visual "scorecard" for an individual worker that demonstrates how an individual can help corporate objectives.

These visuals were produced by ALLIGN to help managers discuss with employees the organization's brand, customer perception, employee behavior, vision for the future, and more. For more information on ALLIGN go to www.allignteam.com.

With these visuals, managers can open discussion with employees and use the visuals as guides for discussing topics such as values, vision, market, customer experience, teamwork, selling, and more. Using a visual guide coupled with experiential exercises makes it much easier for managers to deliver a consistent message. Some visuals, such as that shown in Figure 8.2, even include questions and simulations to prompt discussion. Hanging visuals as posters in common areas reinforces memory and encourages discussion.

> *We have seen that individual and organizational performance dramatically improves when you give all employees a line-of-sight to the numbers that count through a visual, interactive scoreboard.*
>
> —*Scott Hamilton, Senior Partner, ALLIGN*

Figure 8.4 shows how visuals can be used to translate strategic objectives into personal goals that individuals or teams can track. Shakey's has seen a nine percent increase in measured sales that directly relates to orienting their workers to customer-facing measures.

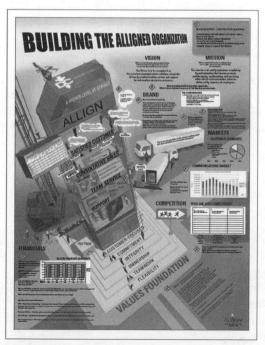

Figure 8.1: This ALLIGN map works as a visual guide for discussing how employees add value and maximize their contributions to the organization.

Figure 8.2: This ALLIGN map helps Shakey's employees understand guest expectations, teamwork, and guest demographics, as well as helps them develop signature service behaviors that distinguish the brand.

Figure 8.3: WorleyParsons, consultant to energy and complex process industries, uses an ALLIGN map to communicate its values and culture. WorleyParsons sees its internal culture as a competitive differentiator, and this "experience" engages their employees and measures how effective employee programs are in supporting performance.

Figure 8.4: Visuals can be taken to the individual level of effort so that all employees can translate their actions into strategic contributions.

Training

Using the Balanced Scorecard as a way of managing and developing a culture of high performance requires new skills and understanding. You will need to plan for motivation and training at all levels. Training doesn't need to happen all at once. Training may roll out over 6 months or more as different levels of the organization are touched by the Balanced Scorecard.

The training that I have delivered to clients to help in the transition to using a Balanced Scorecard includes these workshops clients have asked me to deliver:

- Executive level
  - Building the case for change
  - Successes in similar industries and the reasons for failure
  - Understanding the Strategy Map and Balanced Scorecard
  - Conducting the strategy review meeting with the Balanced Scorecard
- Strategic Theme teams
  - Building the case for change
  - Understanding the Strategy Map and Balanced Scorecard
  - Developing initiatives and projects

- Facilitators (you will need to train multiple facilitators if you are cascading the Balanced Scorecard down to multiple department or division levels)
    - Facilitating Strategy Map development
    - Facilitating metrics development meetings
    - Facilitating initiative and project implementation development
- Mid-managers
    - Building the case for change and motivating the workforce
    - How to present the Balanced Scorecard and capture feedback
- Human resources, change agents, and managers
    - Developing a communication plan
- Scorecard and Dashboard programmers and developers
    - Developing operational dashboards and Balanced Scorecard with Excel
    - Best practices in Excel development
    - Integrating and automating your dashboards and Balanced Scorecard

Once the Balanced Scorecard is in use, what I often see happen is that operational managers want to incorporate data-driven decision-making and operational dashboards in their operations. This drives an increased demand for operational dashboards (discussed in Part II). This in turn pushes a need for facilitators to help with process mapping and metrics definition for operations. And you will need to train people on how to efficiently create dashboards in Excel.

Summary

For the Balanced Scorecard to be effective, senior management must have strategy review meetings that use the Balanced Scorecard as the agenda. These strategy review meetings must be focused on strategic, not operational, issues.

The Balanced Scorecard is a major force in creating a culture of high performance aligned with strategy. But organizations don't change easily. You will have to continually restate the case for change, develop teams that support the change, and communicate, communicate, communicate.

Part

II

Operational Performance with Dashboards

In This Part

Developing Executive and Operational Dashboards

Strategy without tactics is the slowest route to victory.
Tactics without strategy is the noise before defeat.

Sun Tzu

Dashboards are not "the next new thing." I remember developing the first Executive Information Systems (EIS) using Microsoft Excel in the late 1980s for an international division of a major pharmaceutical company. It saved their analysts weeks of Lotus 1-2-3 and manual work. And then there were the myriad Decision Support Systems (DSS) that everyone hoped would help business decision-makers. But EIS and DSS never reached the level of impact that their proponents hoped for.

So what has changed between now and then? Many of the original EIS and DSS systems were built as a way of putting the same information online that was previously collected in printed reports or documents.

> *Scorecards and dashboards should be the lever*
> *that changes culture in an organization.*

If dashboards are to succeed in improving performance, they must:

- Be based on the causal links that drive success for organizational objectives
- Derive their metrics using a scientific process

- Increase the speed, ease, and accuracy of decision-making
- Alert decision-makers to take action
- Use "right time" data that enables timely decisions to keep objectives on track
- Communicate desired behavior in the culture

Why Are Dashboards Used with Increasing Frequency?

Dashboards are becoming ubiquitous. Forrester research estimates that 40 percent of the top 2,000 corporations use dashboards with their Business Intelligence initiatives. Managers are using dashboards to keep strategy and operations on track and to detect hot spots in the organization.

An article entitled "Giving the Boss the Big Picture: A 'dashboard' pulls up everything the CEO needs to run the show" in the February 13, 2006, issue of *BusinessWeek*, quoted Ivan Seidenberg, CEO of Verizon Communications, as saying:

The dashboard puts me and more and more of our executives in real-time touch with the business. The more eyes that see the results we're obtaining every day, the higher the quality of the decisions we can make.

Later in the same article, Jeff Raikes, president of Microsoft's Office division, explains that CEO Mike Ballmer uses dashboards to set the agenda for meetings with the seven heads of Microsoft divisions:

Every time I go to see Ballmer, it's an expectation that I bring my dashboard with me.

Executives, managers, and supervisors are using dashboards to track strategy, operations, and tactics. Smart organizations such as Verizon and Microsoft are using dashboards to set the agenda for meetings because the metrics in the dashboard are measuring the drivers for their business objectives.

Well-designed dashboards enable better and faster decision-making. In fact, surveys have shown two of the key benefits of implementing dashboards are faster decision-making and reduced administrative work in research and analysis.

Dashboards are least effective when they are developed as "the next new thing," or when management misuses them. Jeffrey Immelt, CEO of General

Electric, has stated that even though he uses dashboards, executives should be focusing on broad strategy and deal-making. These are areas that can't be captured in an operational dashboard, but they can be monitored with a Balanced Scorecard.

Another area that causes concern is the use of dashboards by managers and supervisors as a way to micromanage subordinates. The rollout and cascading of scorecards and dashboards through an organization must be done in a culture where everyone at all levels understands that the organization is looking for best practices and the fine-tuning of business models, not the daily grading of individual performance.

Balanced Scorecards and operational dashboards are highly effective tools of culture change. Bad managers who use them incorrectly to micromanage employees end up hurting the organization. But when Balanced Scorecards and operational dashboards are used as tools to build a high-performance learning organization, they monitor performance, culture, and the business model.

What Are the Differences Between Dashboards and Scorecards?

If you have listened to many discussions or web seminars on the topics of performance management, Business Intelligence, or Balanced Scorecards, you've probably heard some speakers using the terms "dashboard" and "scorecard" interchangeably — but there is a difference between the two.

Executives use scorecards to monitor strategic alignment and success with strategic objectives, and the Balanced Scorecard is undoubtedly the best known corporate strategy scorecard, used to help organizations align with strategy. Other forms of executive scorecards can show multiple dashboards that give an executive-level view into operational or functional performance.

Dashboards are used at the tactical and operational level. Managers use dashboards to monitor the success of tactical initiatives, such as marketing campaigns or sales performance during a specific new product introduction. Managers and supervisors use dashboards to monitor operational performance on a weekly, daily, and even hourly frequency. Operational uses include areas such as monitoring manufacturing quality or budget variance on projects.

Table 9.1 shows comparisons between operational and tactical dashboards and strategic scorecards.

Table 9.1: A Comparison of Operational and Tactical Dashboards and Strategic Scorecards

	OPERATIONAL	TACTICAL	STRATEGIC
Type	Dashboard	Dashboard	Balanced Scorecard
Users	Managers, Supervisors, and Operators	Managers	Executives
Information	Detailed	Detailed/Summary	Summary
Usage	Monitor daily production and operation	Monitor progress on an initiative	Monitor alignment and success of strategic objectives
Organizational level	Work unit	Department	Enterprise or strategic business unit
Updated	Intra-day	Daily or Weekly	Monthly

The Challenges in Developing Dashboards

Early predecessors to current dashboards and scorecards were in the area of Decision Support Systems (DSS) and Executive Information Systems (EIS). Overall, these systems failed to produce their hoped-for results — in large part because they were usually implemented as IT exercises, ways to move information from paper onto computer screens. They were not part of a culture change designed to align the organization around strategic objectives and focus on high performance. Often, there was little science in the selection of metrics or performance indicators; thus, these methods didn't aid managers in their daily decisions.

Operational dashboards that succeed are often part of a larger culture change. They are just one tool in an organization's shift to high-performance levels. To succeed with dashboards you need to:

- Develop a model of your business process.
- Define the causal links in that process.
- Define key performance indicators using management science methods, such as those of Lean Six Sigma.
- Be willing to change your business model and causal links if changes to a driver do not create change in the objective.
- Collect the data for "right-time" decisions — surveys have shown that the average enterprise-level dashboard system uses six to seven data sources.

- Tailor dashboards to the needs, data sources, and decision factors facing individuals.

- Build a scalable system able to expand to meet the needs of the organization.

- Absorb fact-based management and the use of dashboards into daily operations.

Developing Your Dashboard

There is a winning approach to developing operational dashboards in Microsoft Excel. This approach can be used by strategic business units of large corporations or by small to mid-sized businesses.

1. Start small, with winnable systems:

   Introduce operational dashboards to your organization by selecting a manageable, winnable problem that has high probability of success and that will have a visible effect. This will reduce your risk, prove the concept, and increase general interest in doing other dashboard projects.

   Start with a small problem and a solution you can grasp. The Business Intelligence industry is rife with stories of organizations that have purchased $250,000 systems before proving the concept or defining their needs.

2. The business manager, not IT, should own the dashboard.

   Business needs to lead the project, with IT as an enabler. Start small, with existing reporting and query systems that can feed Microsoft Excel dashboards and test business needs. Once you have winning solutions and understand your needs, look for buy-in from other groups and work with IT to create an integrated strategy.

3. Select metrics using a scientific management method.

   The metrics your dashboard measures should align with corporate strategy and operational objectives for the greatest impact and visibility. To select these metrics, you must build a model of your operational processes and understand the drivers. The next chapter touches on this with a discussion of operational mapping. Lean Six Sigma processes are a good way to pinpoint where you can get the greatest impact.

4. Limit dashboards to the "critical few" Key Performance Indicators.

   Use only the "critical few" metrics or Key Performance Indicators (KPIs) on your dashboard. More than seven per operational process or dashboard is too many. Having too many metrics can be as bad as having the wrong metrics, making it difficult or even impossible for you to understand what drives success.

5. Get results quickly.

Get a working system out in 60 to 90 days, before momentum and interest are lost. Work as quickly as possible while still following good processes. Know how you are going to roll out the dashboard and apply its use in daily work. You will need to explain to users of the dashboard the business model that was used, and how Key Performance Indicators were identified if they are to believe in its capabilities.

6. Dashboards are just part of the culture.

Remember that dashboards are just indicators of performance. Some people will view them as a threat to their personal performance or as signs that management is becoming overbearing. You must develop a culture of high performance that understands that dashboards are just tools to help the organization learn and grow.

Good executives and managers are like good pilots. They spend the majority of their time looking around, using their senses and experience. Only 20 percent or less of their time is spent looking inside, scanning the dashboard instruments. In my eight years as a military pilot, I had two near-misses while flying low-altitude missions. I would not have been able to avoid those small civilian planes flying in restricted areas if I'd had my "head in the cockpit." Running a business is much the same. Managers must constantly scan back and forth, comparing what they sense as they walk around with what they see on their dashboards. It is the comparison and balance between the two that will give you good performance.

Summary

Dashboards, whether they are operational or tactical, are essential if good managers are to stay on top of their business. Well-designed dashboards must use the business or operations model to select the "critical few" metrics or Key Performance Indicators that drive operational performance. Even if you are designing a quick operational dashboard, follow the development process described in this chapter. Use a scientific process such as Lean Six Sigma to identify the "critical few" metrics that should be on your dashboard. The next chapter describes some of the tools you can use to identify the metrics that drive your operations.

CHAPTER 10

Mapping Your Operational Processes

If you cry "Forward" you must be sure to make clear the direction in which to go. Don't you see that if you fail to do that and simply call out the word to a monk and a revolutionary, they will go in precisely opposite directions?

Anton Chekov
Short-story writer, playwright
1860–1904

Mapping operational processes creates a foundation for your improvement efforts. It creates a common language and understanding for team members and workers, and it helps identify the tasks needing improvement as well as the critical few metrics.

A process map is a visual representation of how a product is built or a service delivered. The map shows the workflow involved as a series of activities. Some process maps show additional information at each action, such as the time and resources required or the customer values added. Process maps may have multiple levels of details. A "30,000-foot-map" can show a process at such a high level that people unfamiliar with the process details can understand it. Detailed process maps show minute specifics in order to allow identification and analysis of ways to improve the process.

With Excel you can combine the clarity that comes with a process map and the monitoring and control that come with metrics and dashboards. By building your process map in Excel, your map can include formulas that recalculate time and resources as they cascade through the map. Adding sliders and spinners easily enables you to test different scenarios by changing inputs and then seeing the resulting changes in outputs.

There are many types of process maps used in operations, but they all help create a common language, bring clarity to diverse ideas, create a shared vision, and identify where the organization can best focus its resources. Using a diverse group to create process maps can increase agreement and consensus, align resources, create a unifying purpose, and communicate why specific metrics are monitored.

Before You Map, Know Why

Before you begin work on any operational or process improvement project, you must know how and why these changes will benefit your organization. Stories abound of Six Sigma and Lean proponents searching for any project and any sponsor. Failure to identify targets of greatest impact, or failure to prove the impact, can result in performance improvement projects low on the organization's priority scale. The consequence is low return on investment and lack of sustainability.

If your organization uses a Balanced Scorecard, then the areas of highest priority for long-term improvement identified through process maps should align with the Strategic Initiatives defined by the Balanced Scorecard. Aligning process improvement programs with Strategic Initiatives makes it easier to build the case and receive funding. Your long-term process improvement initiatives and process maps should align with the Balanced Scorecard themes, objectives, and initiatives.

Operational and process improvement projects face the same organizational change barriers as the Balanced Scorecard. They have the same failure points and must have an effective implementation team. You must build a case for change, get commitment from senior management, get buy-in from managers, and develop a process for communicating and sustaining the change.

Dashboards and Six Sigma

Six Sigma is the science of identifying and removing defects and variation from products and services so the quality to the customer improves while costs of production decrease. One of the key principles of Six Sigma is DMAIC. This acronym stands for:

Define

Measure

Analyze

Improve

Control

Dashboards are critical to many of the DMAIC stages. The measure and analyze stage can use dashboards to monitor data that are tracking a process. With Excel's statistical functions, it's straightforward to plot control charts and have Excel automate the statistical analysis. Examples of this are in Chapter 24, "Building Powerful Charts for Decision Making."

The completion of many Six Sigma projects should include a dashboard for the control phase. By using some of the mapping methods described in this chapter as well as normal Six Sigma statistical process control methods, you can create dashboards that well help you "control" the process you have improved so it doesn't revert back to its previous errors. Your dashboard can act as an alert for process variation, a diagnostic tool to analyze relationships in the system, and a modeling tool for performance improvement.

Types of Process Mapping

There are many process maps used in business. The concept of using process maps to identify inputs, outputs, leverage points, chokepoints, and risk points are the same for all process maps. These are leverage points where you can identify metrics and then use a dashboard to monitor performance and change. If you create your map directly in Excel, you can create an interactive simulation that enables you to monitor current status and see how changes will affect output.

A few of the many type of process maps that can be drawn and modeled in Excel are described in Table 10.1. Two of the types of maps used in performance improvement, SIPOC, and Value Stream Mapping have longer descriptions in the following text.

Table 10.1: A Sampling of the Many Process Maps You Can Draw in Excel

Supplier, Input, Output, Process, Customer (SIPOC)	SIPOC is one of the first steps taken in a Six Sigma improvement project. SIPOC takes a 30,000-foot view of the work flow from a triggering event, such as a request, to the customer receiving the finished product or service. SIPOC is described in more depth later in this section.
Value Stream Map (VSM)	Value Stream Maps are used in Lean projects to map the chain of activities in producing a product or service. Through the use of the map, Lean practitioners look for ways to reduce the seven causes of waste. VSM is described in more depth later in this section.
Supply Chain Operations Reference Model (SCOR®)	SCOR® is a model developed by the Supply-Chain Council to visualize, evaluate, analyze, and improve supply chain performance both inside and outside the organization. SCOR incorporates five hierarchical levels and five major process workflows. To learn more about SCOR go to www.supply-chain.org.

Continued

Table 10.1 *(continued)*

Program/Project Evaluation and Review Technique (PERT)	PERT is a visual model used to represent and analyze the relationships and timing between tasks in a project. One use for PERT is to identify which paths in a project can be changed to reduce the total time for project completion.
	Dashboards are useful to quickly monitor the risks, resources, and variance from schedule at critical points in a PERT chart.
Program Logic Model (PLM)	Program Logic Models are more frequently used in nonprofit, social, and organizational change situations. Program Logic Models produce a graphical map showing the relationship between input, outputs, and outcomes or impact. Outputs are segmented into activities, products, and participation. Outcomes are the changes in knowledge, awareness, and behavior, among others. Outcomes are segmented into short term, medium term, and long term.
	Dashboards are useful with PLM to monitor the variance from estimates of the input (people and money) and output (activities, products, and participation) against the hoped-for outcome, or change in behaviors.
	Search the Web for "Program Logic Model Wisconsin" for more information.

Six Sigma SIPOC Mapping

SIPOC is an acronym for Supplier, Input, Process, Output, and Customer. The SIPOC map shows high-level activities in a process from the initial request by the customer all the way to the product or service delivery.

The acronym SIPOC means:

- **Suppliers:** Major internal or external supplier to the process
- **Input:** Major materials and resources used in the process
- **Process:** Map showing the high-level activities
- **Output:** Major outputs of product or service to the internal or external customer
- **Customer:** Major recipient of the product or service

For example, the SIPOC for a biorefinery producing ethanol through the use of genetically modified enzymes acting on biomass that is the byproduct of agriculture (non-corn) or yard waste might look like this:

Suppliers	Agricultural suppliers
Input	Plant stock, genzymes
Process	Refining
Output	Fuel grade ethanol
Customer	Distributors

A SIPOC map, like the one shown in Figure 10.1, is used at the beginning of Six Sigma quality and performance improvement projects to understand the process. Building a SIPOC map is a quick way to identify your customer's needs, map the process at a high level, identify metrics, build a cohesive team with common language and understanding, identify potential areas of improvement, and build rapport with people in the process.

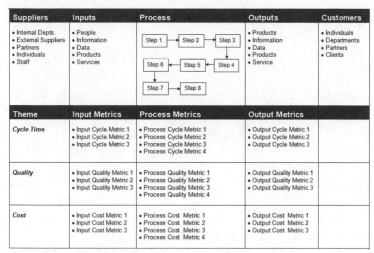

Figure 10.1: The SIPOC map shows high-level activities in a process from the initial request by the customer all the way through the product or service delivery.

Questions that will help you identify the parts of a SIPOC map are these:

- **Suppliers:** Who or what supplies the inputs?
- **Input:** What information, data, resources, and people are needed for this process?
- **Output:** What is the end result of this process that will be used by the customer? It could be products, services, data, or others.
- **Customer:** Who or what is the recipient and user of the output?

Value Stream Mapping

Value stream mapping is used by Lean practitioners to create a drawing with a set of standard symbols representing all the activities and information used to produce a product or service. Maps are then used to find areas of waste or "non-value" to the customer, which then can be reduced or removed. The "Seven Wastes" that Lean works to reduce are:

- Defects
- Inventory
- Processing
- Waiting
- Motion
- Transportation
- Overproduction

Value stream maps are produced by "walking the floor." This involves watching people do their work; following the flow of paper, products, or information; interviewing workers; and watching the work as it is performed. In many cases, an independent observer and interviewer will identify activities and inputs that individuals in the process are not aware of.

A standard set of symbols is used to draw value stream maps. (You can even do value stream maps in Excel as described in Chapter 13, "Drawing Process and Strategy Maps.") Start your value stream map at the customer, or the request for product or service, and then define the processes with data boxes. Next, draw the material flow, the push and pull of material, and follow that with the flow of information, the triggers.

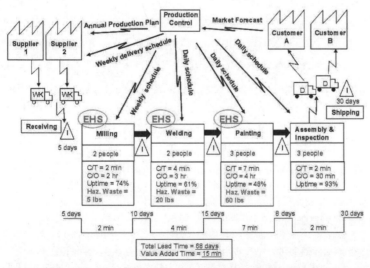

Figure 10.2: This value stream map from the EPA shows time as well as environmental data throughout the value stream.

Figure 10.2 shows a sample value stream map created by the Environmental Protection Agency. Notice the metrics in the tags below the map. These tags can include metrics such as:

- Number of operators
- Cycle time
- Changeover time
- Batch size
- Performance
- Uptime (%)
- Yield (%)

Value stream maps are created for two states: the current state and the future state. The current state map shows the activities, information, times, and resources currently used. The future state map shows the activities, information, times, and resources for the ideal state after Lean principles have been applied.

Where dashboards are valuable is in monitoring key metrics that measure the gap between current and future states. Dashboards can help you monitor the change between current and future states, and help make sure the improved future state is sustained.

Some of the tools used for value stream mapping are Microsoft Visio, iGrafx, and SmartDraw. You also can use Microsoft Excel to draw high-level value stream maps with the Drawing toolbar. Although Excel doesn't come with value stream symbols, you can create your own, and Excel gives you the added capability of developing a value stream simulation so you can see the impact of changes.

Note: Processing Mapping in Excel

Processing mapping in Excel requires some extra work, such as creating custom symbols, but it also gives you significant advantages in that you can create simulations of your process using Excel functions and formulas. For example, clicking a slider like those described in Chapter 20, "Controlling Dashboards with Menus, Combo Boxes, and Buttons," adjusts process times that cascade throughout the process model. Of course, you can also use all the Excel capabilities described throughout this book to add dashboards with trends, alerts, and statistical control charts to show the status of your process.

To see examples of process maps in Excel and for referrals for process mapping software that works with Excel, go to www.torconsulting.com.

Step-by-Step to Building a Map

Once you have aligned the goal for your process improvement with your organization's goals, the next step is to do a first pass map. The purpose of a first pass map, no matter which type of map you are creating, is to capture the big picture of the process by documenting the large processes and the metrics, and their relationships.

One of the best ways to do this is to start at the customer/recipient's end of the process and walk through the process to the trigger, or where the customer initiated the first request. (In many cases this literally means walking through the process to each person involved and each work area.) For example, to track customer shipments, you would start at the shipping dock and walk back until you reached the phone or e-commerce system where the customer first placed the order.

A high-level first pass may take a day for one person to complete. A knowledgeable person can walk through the process, interviewing participants and recording process steps, metrics, chokepoints, and waste. It is easiest to simply draw by hand the process and record important metrics at each stage. Good interviewing skills come in handy: the individuals doing the work usually know best how it can be improved.

This first pass map should give you a high-level picture of the processes, times, metrics, chokepoints, and areas of waste. At this point, you can clean up your hand-drawn map, and you may want to create a map using Excel or a drawing program such as SmartDraw.

Once you have cleaned up your first pass map, review it with people familiar with the process. They can identify and normalize any areas or metrics you may have missed. The first pass map gives you a framework on which to add more detail about where you can make performance improvement.

Creating a second-level map will give you the additional detail for subprocesses, detailed metrics, target values and ranges, additional areas of waste, and the workforce's ideas where improvements can have the greatest impact. You will want to involve a large group of knowledgeable and influential people in creating these maps. Having their contribution can help influence their buy-in and your subsequent success.

To create your second-level :

1. Use 3M Post-it® Super Sticky Notes to create a large version of your first pass map on one wall. These high-level notes should be at the highest level on the wall and each major process should have a unique color. (There will be some color duplication as 3M Post-it Super Sticky Notes have a limited color range.)

2. Gather a cross-functional group of subject matter experts (SMEs) for the process you are mapping. The room needs to be large with enough space in front of the wall to allow for people to crowd around.

3. Distribute stacks of the notes with large-tip markers. Recommend people use the note color that matches the heading for the process they work in.

4. Ask people to write on their notes a five-to-seven-word description for the most important tasks under each heading. To focus their notes to the most important tasks and because of limited wall space, I usually limit notes to no more than 40 for a map.

5. Once everyone is ready, have people post the notes themselves under the appropriate headings.

6. Rewrite any notes that are difficult to read. If any note is not understood by the group, have the SME who wrote the note briefly explain it.

7. Now, hand out small, 1.5 inch x 2-inch Post-it notes. Ask the SMEs to write on the Post-it notes the time or other resource needed for each task, and then post these on the task note.

8. Have the SMEs do a verbal walk-through for the group so everyone understands the entire map.

9. Now use "dot voting" to discover which tasks the group thinks can have the greatest impact on improvement. Hand out sheets of colored sticky dots. Green dots indicate that the product or service was transformed by adding value for the customer. Red dots indicate that the product or service was not transformed. White dots indicate the task had to be completed whether it added value or not (for example, to comply with safety or governmental regulations). Ask all members of the group to vote once for any task they feel strongly about by sticking the appropriate color dot next to the task.

10. Once everyone is seated again, it is usually obvious where the greatest impact can be gained. At this point, there is often good discussion about what changes can be made. You need to have pads and easels ready to capture this information so it isn't lost.

11. Now that you have an idea which tasks have the highest priorities for improvement, take a look at Chapter 11, "Identifying Critical Metrics and Key Performance Indicators."

**Note: Any Process Improvement Program Is Also an
Organizational Change Program**

If you want your process improvement effort to be a success, you should also
view it as an organizational change process. Process improvement changes
have all the people and cultural issues that any organizational change has. A
consultant or experienced change agent can help you manage and sustain the
culture change needed to support your performance improvement efforts.

Summary

Mapping processes is important to improving and maintaining those processes.
To improve or maintain them, you must identify which tasks are most critical,
where the greatest return will be, where chokepoints are, and where risks are
greatest. These can be identified by using a number of different mapping methods, some of which have been covered lightly here. Once you have mapped your
processes, you can use the methods described in Chapter 11 to identify which
metrics are critical and should appear in your dashboards.

Identifying Critical Metrics and Key Performance Indicators

The dashboard is the CEO's killer app, making the gritty details of a business that are often buried deep within a large organization accessible at a glance to senior executives.
"Giving the Boss the Big Picture," *BusinessWeek*, Feb. 13, 2006

Mapping processes is a big aid in identifying critical business activities and the causes and effects you need to monitor. In this chapter you will learn methods that can help you identify and select metrics for use on an executive or operational dashboard.

I have seen departments where the only public statistic was one chart hung in the hallway. I've also seen the overload caused by an overdeveloped Business Intelligence system that produced so many metrics that no one knew which metrics were the "critical few." This chapter will describe a couple of methods that can help you select those "critical few" out of the hundreds of metrics that may exist in a process.

General Rules for Metrics in Operational Dashboards

There are a few general rules for the use of metrics in operational dashboards.

- **Identify and select metrics using a scientific approach.** Heed the maxim that some attribute to Einstein: "The definition of insanity is doing the same thing over and over and expecting different results." Don't just take the metrics you've always used and slam them into a dashboard. No matter how pretty your dashboard is, and how many dials and gauges it has, you won't have any better results. Select your metrics by using a scientific method, first creating a model of the process you want to control, then developing a hypothesis of what will control that process, and finally testing the hypothesis.

■ **Test your metrics for validity.** If the metrics you are using to control a process don't help you make the change you expect, then your hypothesis is wrong. Try different metrics.

■ **Limit your dashboard to three to eight metrics per process.** Your dashboard should show only the first-order metrics, those that have the greatest impact. In almost any process there are only a few first-order metrics. Another consideration is the human mind's inability to manage more than a limited number of relationships. Experiments have shown that professional jugglers can juggle three or four balls perpetually. However, once the number of balls reaches seven, accidents start to occur, and control begins going down. With just a few more balls in the air, even the best jugglers lose control quickly. The same is true for juggling metrics and business models in your head. Keep it simple.

■ **You've got most of what you need already, but new data may be necessary.** As a general rule, 50 percent of the data for strategic and operational dashboards is already accessible form accounting systems, ERP, CRM, and HRIS systems. But there will always be some data — usually customer and employee data — requiring new data collection methods.

■ **Capturing data is often more work than defining and creating a dashboard.** Most of the small and mid-sized businesses I've worked with have good financial and operational data. They are building their customer relationship data, but they often lack data on employees and customers. This data requires setting up new data collection and validation channels.

■ **Build what you can of your dashboard, and let the missing data follow later.** It's rare that all the data is available to start with. If a metric that has been identified as critical is not available, then show it as a grey chart on the dashboard or show a "differential Gantt" chart that shows the progress of the initiative to collect the missing data. The project variance or differential Gantt chart is described in Chapter 24, "Building Powerful Charts for Decision Making."

■ **Create a Metric Definition.** Over time, people forget the how and why of metrics. Create a table for each metric with definitions that explain why it was selected, what affect it will have, what formula was used and why, and where the data comes from, and who owns it.

■ **Create a Data Map.** Surveys have shown that most Business Intelligence systems use 6 to 11 data sources. Balanced Scorecards in mid-sized companies where data is in Excel or Access files can have even more data sources. To keep your data sources straight, create a data map showing the data use, data source, file type, and so forth.

■ **Display all information necessary for decision making on one screen.** By interviewing the people who use the dashboard, you can learn what decisions they need to make and what information they need to make those decisions. Often it is a relationship between two or more pieces of data that is important. Make sure you get all the related information for a decision on one screen. If you can't do that, at least make the secondary data single-click accessible.

CAUTION You won't find long lists of metrics in this book. It would be fairly easy to fill over half this book with metrics and their descriptions, related objectives, and formulas. However, what is most important is having the "critical few" metrics, not having lots of metrics.

If what you measure is what you get and you are measuring the wrong things, then . . . you get the picture. Conversely, if you measure too many things and no one knows what is important, then … you get confusion.

If you need examples of metrics, check with your trade association or with industry consultants, or search online using the keyword "metric" and the topic that you are measuring. There are many lists of metrics; what is important is choosing the right metric.

For a list of metrics and related objectives, check the author's web site at www.torconsulting.com.

Interview the Decision Makers

Long before setting your hand on the keyboard and gathering a team to map a process, you should interview the people who will be using the dashboard for decision making. Interviewing them will give you an understanding of the purpose of the dashboard/improvement project, the alignment with corporate strategy, and the mental model they currently use to understand the system.

Some of the questions you will want to ask in the interview are

■ Who is responsible for the outcomes of this process?

■ Who controls or monitors the process?

■ Is the person who controls or monitors the process the same person who will monitor a dashboard?

■ What business decisions do you need to make routinely?

■ What business decisions are most critical?

■ What data or information do you use to make each decision?

- Do you monitor families or categories of data or information?
- What triggers your decisions —
  - Control limits or boundary limits?
  - Trends?
  - Alert levels?
  - Indexes?
- What behavior or actions do you want to effect?
- Which measure or metric will have the greatest affect on those behaviors and actions?
- How do you know whether your business decision was correct?
- Do you have reports containing these data?
- How may I speak with whoever owns the data?

Identify Metrics Using Your Map

Process maps, whether high-level or detail-level, help select the "critical few" metrics most important to monitoring status and control. Maps will help you visually identify and prioritize

- Chokepoints
- High-risk activities
- Leverage points of greatest impact
- Activities that add or do not add customer value
- Change between the current state and future state
- Degradation of processes back to old, low-performance states
- Diagnostic and troubleshooting solutions

If you have tens of years of experience with a process, you probably know the metrics that drive its results. However, you are going to need a scientific process for selecting metrics if you want to gain new insights, test causes and effects, or communicate your experience with others.

The maps discussed in Chapter 10, "Mapping Processes," are a basis for making sound decisions when selecting metrics. By mapping a process you identify major inputs and outputs, risk points, chokepoints, high waste areas, key stage gates, and much more — all of them areas that are up for nomination for membership in the "critical few" metrics that need to be on a dashboard.

> **A MEASURE IS NOT A METRIC**
>
> For the purposes of this chapter, a "measure" is what you want to evaluate. A "metric" is a quantitative value or statistical unit of that measure. Sounds confusing? Some examples might help. Measures common to all organizations are customer satisfaction, employee engagement, employee retention, and so forth. These aren't the rock-hard numbers that, for example, financials are. Usually there are many metrics for one measure. However, for each organizational process, there are only a few of these metrics that best describe the measure. Metrics that can be used to imply future employee retention are
>
> ▪ Total number of employees approaching full retirement benefits
>
> ▪ Employee engagement index
>
> ▪ Number of sick days taken
>
> ▪ Number of accidents on the line

Step-by-Step to Identifying Critical Metrics

Based on the interview questions above or on the dot voting techniques described later in this chapter in the section "Selecting a Metric," you should be able to identify the areas on your map most critically in need of measurement.

A step-by-step method useful for identifying measures and metrics involves

1. Identifying the critical areas on the map. (Chapter 10 describes dot voting as one method of identifying critical areas.)

2. Brainstorm the measures you need in order to control each critical area. Measures can be lead (drivers of the process) or lag (success measures).

3. Research metrics for each measure. If the process you are measuring is common in your industry, first try using an industry-standard measure.

4. Reduce the possible metrics to a short list by using either a dot voting technique or a weighted table.

The following sections of this chapter describe these steps in more detail.

Brainstorming and Identifying Metrics Using an Ishikawa or Fishbone Diagram

The fishbone diagram, named because it resembles the skeleton of a fish, was the brainchild of Kaoru Ishikawa, a pioneer in quality management. The fishbone diagram, also known as an Ishikawa or "cause and effect" diagram, is used as a structure for brainstorming the causes and effects in a process. It works just as well when brainstorming metrics.

Figure 11.1 shows a fishbone diagram for a chemical process. The major branches in the diagram can be labeled with the names of critical areas in your process. Chapter 10 describes how to identify the areas you want to measure.

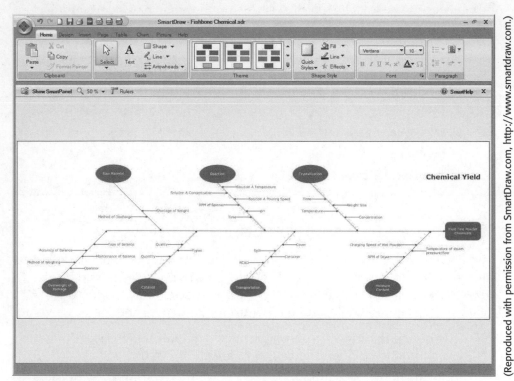

Figure 11.1: The fishbone shows critical activities from the process as branches and metrics as minor branches.

(Reproduced with permission from SmartDraw.com, http://www.smartdraw.com.)

Note: Using the Six Ms (and Two Ps) with Metrics Brainstorming

For small processes, or if time is limited, you may want to skip mapping. Instead, gather a team experienced in the process. Post a fishbone diagram on the wall, but instead of labeling branches with the names of critical process areas, label branches with the six Ms: Man, Machine, Mother Nature, Materials, Method, and Measurement. Figure 11.2 shows a fishbone diagram with the six Ms. If the process is affected by regulatory or social structures, include the two Ps, Policies and Procedures. Using the fishbone with the six Ms and the two Ps, go through a brainstorm of what the most important metrics are for each branch. Use dot voting to decide which metrics the team wants to include in the "critical few."

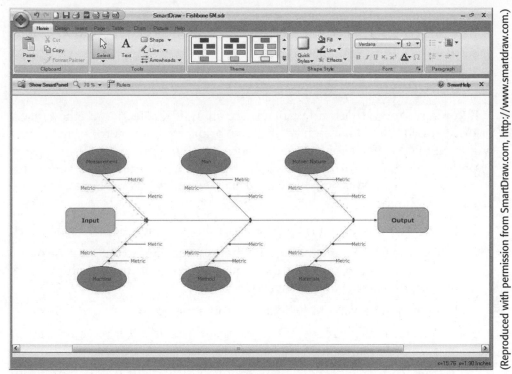

Figure 11.2: A fishbone with the Six Ms can be used to quickly brainstorm metrics for a process.

Selecting a Metric

Once you have identified possible metrics, you need to select the "critical few" that you want to track, or that feed your dashboard. Limit your "critical few" to three to eight metrics.

Two methods are frequently used to select the "critical few" from all the brainstormed metrics. One method is dot voting, a quick, subjective method. The other uses a prioritization table.

To conduct dot voting

1. Discuss the metrics you've brainstormed until everyone understands the advantages and disadvantages of each metric.

2. Distribute sticky dots to the group. Divide the number of metrics on the fishbone diagram by three. Each member gets that many dots. For example, if there are fifteen metrics on the fishbone diagram, each team member will get five sticky dots.

3. Team members then place their dots on the metrics they think need to be in the critical few. Team members can put as many or as few dots as they desire on metrics.

4. The metrics that end up marked with the highest number of dots become the critical few.

If you have more time and want a more analytical selection method, use a prioritization table with weighted values to prioritize your metrics. Again, you will need to do this with a team experienced with the process.

When I build a prioritization table with a group, we project an Excel worksheet onto the wall. We complete the Excel matrix as we work so that when we are done we have complete documentation.

1. List the metrics that you are considering down the left side of a worksheet.

2. Across the top, enter headings of what is important to the purpose of the dashboard. For example, is the change in value of the process twice as important as the change in speed?

   Here are a few weighting factors — yours may differ.

   ▪ **Value:** If this process changes, what affect will it have on output value?

   ▪ **Speed:** If this process changes, what affect will it have on output speed?

   ▪ **Quality:** If this process changes, what affect will it have on quality?

   ▪ **Cost of measurement:** Will this metric's data have a high cost to capture?

3. Under the headings, enter a value from 1 to 10 for each weighting factor. The numbers aren't as important as are their relative weights. In Figure 11.3, for example, the "value" of change is twice as important as that of "speed" to the purpose of the dashboard.

4. How does each metric affect its heading? Poll team members for a value of 1, 3, or 9 in each table cell. Using 1, 3, or 9 rather than 1 to 10 gives greater differentiation between top and bottom choices. For example, Metric 1 has a great effect (9) on value but less effect (3) on speed.

5. Sort the table in descending order by the total weight column using Excel's Data Sort command.

	Value	Speed	
Weight	6	3	Total
Metric 4	9	9	81
Metric 8	9	9	81
Metric 1	9	3	63
Metric 2	3	9	45
Metric 7	3	9	45
Metric 6	1	9	33
Metric 5	3	3	27
Metric 9	3	3	27
Metric 3	1	3	15

Weights of 1, 3, 9 in the cells are estimates of how that metric effects the column heading.

The column heading is the measure of what is important to the purpose of the dashboard.

Figure 11.3: Use a weighted table for a more rigorous selection process.

Cross-Check Your Metric

Test the critical few metrics you have by asking the following questions about them:

■ What action will I take if I see significant change in this metric?

If you aren't clear about what action you would take, either you don't need the metric, your model of what you are trying to control is not accurate, or you haven't selected the correct metric.

■ Will the action I take control the process in the way needed?

Metrics exist to drive changes to behavior and actions. There may be unintended consequences to a metric. For example, using machine use time as a measure of success could have the unintended consequence of building unneeded inventory. In that case, you may need a counterbalancing measure to watch for that unintended consequence.

■ Will measuring this metric change the behavior and action as I want?

Your purpose for measurement shouldn't be academic if you're in business. Your purpose should be to change a behavior or action. If you don't see behaviors or actions changing to create the output you need, then change the metric. It might take months or even a whole year to determine whether you have a metric that affects behavior and actions the way you want. But, if it doesn't work, change the metric. Don't be tied to it.

- Will people try to "game" or manipulate this metric?

Will your metrics work in the real world with real people? We all know of people who "game the system," explicitly lying or manipulating numbers rather than stepping up to a culture of performance. I've seen a division of an F1000 company go bankrupt and end up sold because upper management and the sales management team allowed gaming in the posting of sales numbers. I've seen contractors manipulate their project management numbers to make bonuses even though they must have known they would be caught in the end. Gaming happens when the organization's culture, executives, and management allow it to happen. As long as gaming is allowed, no performance management system will work effectively.

What's Simple Can Be Difficult, and What's Difficult Can Be Simple

Large lists of metrics are available through associations and through Web searches. But having large lists of metrics can be overwhelming. What is important is selecting one of the "critical few" that will leverage your business and understanding the ramifications behind the metric.

Some measures, such as employee contribution to a company, might seem simple, but they can actually be very complex. Others that seem difficult, such as customer satisfaction or employee engagement, can be easy. Here are two examples.

First, let's examine a measure that looks easy but is actually complex. If you want to measure how employees contribute to stakeholders, you might use the often published *Revenue per Full Time Employee Equivalent* (FTE).

When you begin to examine this metric, you realize it presents some problems. The revenue depends upon sales effectiveness, competitiveness in the marketplace, and the economy. And how can margin and the cost of capital be factored in?

Using FTEs in the divisor doesn't really make sense because different business models derive different value from employees at different levels. Perhaps a better metric would be *Economic Value Added per Strategic Employee*, where Economic Value Added could be defined as

$$\text{Net Operating Profit} - (\text{Capital} \times \text{Cost of Capital})$$

This metric uses the Economic Value Added divided by the number of Strategic Employees. Strategic Employees are those employees that have been defined through the Balanced Scorecard to have a direct impact on strategic themes and objectives.

One final adjustment might be needed for this formula. Some industries go through cyclical variations; or perhaps the organization is in a growth industry. In such cases, evaluating contribution per strategic employee requires adjustment for cyclicality or for the industry growth rate. Luckily, Excel can easily handle these calculations.

Some measures can seem impossible to quantify, but study can make them easy. For example, user satisfaction and employee engagement seem pretty inscrutable, but recent research has found that one question, "Would you refer us to a friend?" has a higher correlation with user satisfaction than do long expensive surveys that are difficult to administer.

Another important measure, employee engagement, also seems difficult to measure, but Gallup, after studying the issue, has come up with twelve short questions that do an excellent job of determining how engaged employees are with their work. Instead of trying to evaluate employee attitudes once per year with a large, expensive survey, a quick, email-based "flash" survey can be administered monthly to a statistically valid sample using a variation of these questions. Quickly and easily, you have a metric to measure your workforce's engagement.

Again, what is of value to your business is not having a lot of data and metrics, but knowing how to select the "critical few" metrics that drive significant impact.

Summary

Use a scientific method to select your metrics. Don't just use the same metrics on a new dashboard. Know why you are selecting your "critical few."

You should have a clear understanding of what behavior or action will change when you begin capturing and displaying your metrics. Metrics drive change. If you've done your job correctly, they will drive the change you want.

Part

III

Building Maps, Scorecards and Dashboards

In This Part

Creating Dashboards for Decision Making

Entia non sunt multiplicanda praeter necessitatem.
(Entities should not be multiplied more than necessary.)

"Occam's Razor," William of Ockham, 1285–1349

A dashboard's purpose is to aid decision making. It should not be a display of data, but rather a display of information that has had a template of knowledge applied to it. If your dashboard does not accelerate and improve decision making, you might as well be displaying streams of raw data onscreen.

Step-by-Step to Creating Dashboards That Aid Decision Making

You can certainly create a dashboard by just giving a client exactly what they ask for. Often this results in a dashboard that is either used for a point solution or used a few times and never again. To create a dashboard that affects the business, you need to take the time and energy up front to interview users, investigate business needs, and learn how a dashboard can help them improve their decision making. Two or three hours of prework can save a lot of downstream time and produce a more valuable dashboard.

Here is a big-picture view of the steps required to create a dashboard that will aid decision making:

1. **Learn the dashboard's purpose.** Interview the dashboard users. Learn what decisions they want to make using the dashboard.

2. **Learn how dashboard users expect the dashboard to help them.** What can the dashboard do to help them make decisions? What relationships are they looking for? What trends? What targets and alert limits? What analytics are they not using now that could be done in a dashboard?

3. **Learn what they think the dashboard might look like.** Often the request for a dashboard comes from one executive or manager who has seen another's dashboard. Users may have charts or tables they've created themselves in Excel to work with. Learn what ideas they have for their tool.

4. **Ask for business or decision rules.** Learn what can be automated in the dashboard. What logic rules can be programmed in? What about limits, boundaries, and alerts?

5. **Walk through the decision process if it is complex.** Experts are so familiar with making decisions they may not actually know the steps they take and the rules they use. Getting them to verbally walk you through their decision-making process can reveal what has been left unsaid. If you are building a process-oriented dashboard — for example, to monitor a value stream or a supply chain — then you *must* use a process map like those described in Chapter 10, "Mapping Processes," and Chapter 11, "Identifying Critical Metrics and Key Performance Indicators."

6. **Learn the parameters.** What time frames and what granularity of data (detail level) are needed? What naming conventions are used for products, regions, and departments?

7. **Gather the Excel workbooks and printed reports used in making decisions.** Ask which of the data in the reports is actually used. What totals and calculations are necessary?

8. **Check the data sources.** Make sure the data is accessible. Will it be released by IT for use in a dashboard? Who owns the data? What files are used, and how often do they refresh?

9. **Use a sketch pad to work up ideas on your own.** In the idea phase, I find that there's nothing that beats pencil and paper. It's still faster than drawing objects on a screen.

10. **Get feedback.** Once you have some ideas, get two or three of the main users into a room and present your ideas for the dashboard, user interface, results, and data flow on a whiteboard. Although you can create a prettier proposal in PowerPoint, it doesn't allow user participation. Using a whiteboard lets people step up to the board and draw their ideas.

11. **Create a limited-functionality dummy dashboard.** Present a dummy dashboard with limited functionality and dummy data. Talk through how

it works. Fill the drop-down lists or interactive portions with the actual lists used in the final. Walk through use of the dummy dashboard.

12. **Build the dashboard.** Use an Excel architecture to separate the chart and user controls from analytics from data. This is described further in Chapter 29, "Publishing Balanced Scorecards and Operational Dashboards."

13. **Release a Beta version to a few users.** Clearly label it as a Beta version, and get their feedback.

14. **Make corrections to the dashboard, and release it.**

Make Your Dashboards Actionable

Don't just report data. Great dashboards are designed to aid decision making, and your dashboards will do just that if you follow a few guidelines:

- **Group information visually by decision criteria.** Group information needed for a one type of decision into a visually identifiable "chunk."

- **Display analyzed information, not raw data.** Dashboards for decision making should display information that has already been filtered and analyzed using human knowledge, business rules, or Excel functions such as Top n, Bottom n, Pareto, or others described in this book. Automate alerts and routine business rules.

- **Automate Business Rules.** Automate business rules to identify problems and make decisions. For example, the alert charts in Chapter 23, "Displaying Targets and Alerts," automatically show the viewer where there is an issue. The Pareto chart in Chapter 24, "Building Powerful Charts for Decision Making," automatically identifies the 20 percent of issues that cause 80 percent of the problems. For example, one client needed to reduce client dissatisfaction with its software service. While continuing its program to build in quality, it wanted a dashboard that would take the data logs from its telephone support calls and provide some actionable items. The end result was an Excel worksheet that used support call logs to create a Pareto chart that identified the most frequent and highest-level support issues each week. From a parent dashboard that showed summary issues, it could drill down to identify critical areas by product line or by issue.

- **Show context, judgments, and comments.** Routine decisions that fit well-defined business rules, such as alerts, trends, and limits, can be programmed into your Excel dashboards, but the context of issues, opinions of analysts, unforeseen consequences, and so forth aren't displayed on a chart or in a table. Create a linked text box or a scrolling text box that helps analysts post comments on your dashboard.

- **Give access to source data.** Although automated alerts and business rules help identify issues, a manager with many years of experience may want to see the actual data so that he can look for nuances. To allow for this while maintaining an uncluttered appearance, include a button on the dashboard that links to a scrolling table of source data or replication of a printed report. Scrolling tables are described in Chapter 18, "Working with Lists and Tables of Data."

- **Suggest "next steps."** Include the information that makes it easy to take the next step, such as knowing what action has already been taken and contacting the issue owner. A briefing book page includes this information and can be updated by the data owner. Include a pop-up email button as described in Chapter 25, "Drilling to Details and Navigating to Locations," and Chapter 27, "Finishing Touches." Such a button pops up when a condition is met, and clicking the button opens an email message to the owner of this activity.

Rules of Design

Entire books have been written on the science and art of visually crafting a dashboard. Among the cognoscenti, it's known as "data visualization," a term you might want to search using a Web search engine. Certain psychological and mathematical rules also dictate what type of chart should be used to represent each type of data. But rather than try to compress all that into a few pages, I've tried to distill a few overarching principles.

Note: Buy the Bible of Dashboard Visualization

The "bible" of dashboard visualization is Stephen Few's *Information Dashboard Design*. Although Edward Tufte's books are beautiful and fascinating to read, Stephen Few's book focuses on how to craft dashboards that communicate with and aid decision makers. Both Stephen Few and Edward Tufte have web sites that are very informative. (URLs to their web sites are listed at the end of this chapter.)

Keep It Simple and Uncluttered

This has been said multiple times in this chapter already, and you will see it a lot in the referenced web sites at the end of this chapter — keep your dashboards and charts simple. Keep the focus on the information needed for decision-making.

Kill Cute Dashboards

Cute dashboards, like those with lots of airplane or car dashboard gauges, look cute, but when they are used frequently to make important business decisions, they become annoying. Cute doesn't last; useful does.

The space used by one cute gauge to represent one metric could display five or more bullet charts showing related information. When you need to present executives with a lot of information that they use frequently, stay away from cute.

Yes, I've made a few cute dashboards in my time, especially in Xcelsius, but I'll plead that they were either to attract attention or because the client demanded them to attract the attention of casual users.

Command the Viewer's Eye

Magicians use a technique called "forcing" to focus their subjects' minds on a limited set of responses. When the magician then guesses what someone is thinking, it looks like magic. In the same way, your dashboards should "force" a focus.

Your interviews should have made you aware of the information most important to decision making. Command the viewer's eye by putting that information together, centered at the top of the dashboard. Put the dominant colors on the critical information, and mute or eliminate other distractions.

Limit Feature Creep

I've had more than one user want to keep adding feature after feature to a dashboard (and I frequently find myself wanting to add extra features the user didn't ask for or need). The general rule of thumb I've come up with is that users are usually correct for the first two or three changes. They know what they want, and they know how they use it. But some clients have a strange glint come into their eyes, a little like Mr. Toad in *Wind in the Willows*. Suddenly, they lose control and begin asking for lots of little gadgets that are rarely used and that fog the brain.

It's up to you to know when to draw the line. Sit down with the user and discuss how much value she will get from the extra feature and how much work it will cause you now, and cause later in future maintenance.

Use a Clean, Consistent Visual Layout

Dashboard viewers in the Western world are trained to look from left to right, top to bottom. Nearly all computer programs put their menus across the top and control items, such as drop-down lists, down the left side.

Organize information into meaningful groups. For example, a chart or table with the main information should be at the top center; supporting or detail charts should be smaller and at the bottom.

Put One Decision on One Page

I lived a short while in Texas and while there came across a wonderful story that illustrates competency, force, and focus. In the late 1800s, Texas was still a wild frontier. A contingency of 80 Texas Rangers represented the only law and order for the large territory. When the first prize fights were scheduled in Dallas, the good citizens panicked with fear that riots would engulf the city. The mayor telegraphed the governor to send a company of Texas Rangers.

When a single Texas Ranger, Captain W. J. McDonald, stepped off the train, the mayor was taken aback. Albert Paine, an historical author, records the mayor as blurting out, "Where are the others?"

To this Captain McDonald responded, "Hell, ain't I enough? There's only one prize fight!" His words have been immortalized as

One riot, one ranger.

Give your dashboards competency, force, and focus. Don't cheat by including every possible piece of data and type of chart just because you aren't sure what is needed.

Using competency, force, and focus should help you build the dashboard that puts the critical information on one concise screen.

Make Dashboards Accessible to Colorblind and Aging Eyes

Design your chart elements so that they are accessible to those with less than perfect vision. Dashboards are for business decision making. I've seen dashboards created by Business Intelligence software companies that have obviously given their artists too much license. They dashboards look pretty and artistically elegant, but they contain little decision making data and are unusable.

Approximately 8 percent of males and 2 percent of females are colorblind. One of my clients, a CEO, is colorblind. Would Excel's standard conditional colors of red, yellow, and green work for his Balanced Scorecard? Yes — but only by using the following modifications.

Instead of using only conditional colors as alerts, include a conditional icon, such as an arrowhead, and adjust the color saturation. Chapter 15, "Text-Based Dashboards," describes how to combine conditional icons with conditional colors in all versions of Excel. For example, when a condition is poor, a heavily saturated red background displays behind a downward-pointing arrowhead.

When a poor but improving condition occurs, a medium-saturation yellow background displays with a left-pointing arrowhead. When the condition is good, an arrowhead points up with no background. No background is needed for good conditions, because we want to only draw attention to areas that need attention. (This is yet another area where Excel has flexibility. Numerous expensive Business Intelligence software systems have no way to compensate for color blindness.)

When you adapt colors for color blindness, in alerts and chart elements, consider how a color will translate into black, shades of gray, and white. You can still use red, yellow, and green, but change the color saturation so that each prints (or displays to a colorblind person) with a strikingly different level of grey. Color saturation is controlled in the Custom Colors dialog with the vertical bar to the right of the color box in the custom color window.

Tips on Graphical Elements

Here are just a few big-picture concepts to consider when designing the graphical layout, look, and feel of your dashboards.

Use Your Client's Branding

Your organization or client has probably paid a lot of money and spent a lot of time developing a "corporate identity." The corporate identity is the brand imaging for printed and Web materials. It includes fonts and color palettes and probably layouts.

Contact the marketing department and get the officially sanctioned corporate identity. Mid-sized and large corporations will have this in a compressed file ready to send to you.

Color Palettes and Intensities

Nearly everyone agrees: Excel has a superb chart engine, but its standard color palette for charting is garish. Create a custom color palette as described in Chapter 16, "Custom Labels, Dates, and Formatting." Use the color palette from the corporate identity, and make sure you compensate for color blindness and aging eyes.

Never put light colors on dark backgrounds, such as white or yellow on dark blue or black. This might work in PowerPoint, but never do it in a dashboard. Don't put red on black. It's a verified medical fact that 17.3 percent of viewers will find their eyes beginning to oscillate uncontrollably when viewing this color combination, causing them extreme frustration and nausea. (Just kidding — but don't do it anyway.)

Get Rid of Chart Junk

Chart junk includes all the unnecessary elements in a chart that detract from decision making. For example, why does a legend need a box around it? It doesn't, so remove it. Charts are used for trends and relationships, not for reading precise data values, so why include gridlines? Remove them.

Edward Tufte is Professor Emeritus of Statistics at Yale and has been referred to by the *New York Times* as the "da Vinci of data." As an adamant opponent of chart junk, he rails against it in his web site, www.edwardtufte.com. Tufte may have summed up his philosophy of data visualization when he said, "Good displays of data help to reveal knowledge relevant to understanding mechanism, process and dynamics, cause and effect." Get rid of everything else that detracts.

Mute the Less Important

Excel chart elements, like axis lines, are inserted at full intensity black. These aren't important to the chart. In fact, a large majority of the chart junk that Excel automatically puts in is unimportant. Remove it, or use a muted color. The only things you want to stand out with intensity are the pieces of information being used for decision making.

Use the Correct Chart Type

There are some chart types that should rarely, if ever by used. My votes for the "never" category are stacked bar charts and radar charts. In the "only in special circumstance" category are pie charts.

Use pie charts to show how three to five pieces of data relate to the total. The pie chart must include all the data elements that comprise 100% of the data set. In general, I use pie charts when the client makes a special request and it meets the previous rules; otherwise, a column chart works better.

I'd like to see some examples where a stacked column chart was the best choice of chart. I haven't seen any yet. Some people attempt to use stacked column charts to show the relative change in segments over time. But this change is nearly impossible to see. Only the bottom segment of each column has a baseline. The baseline for all other segments moves up and down, making comparison difficult. Instead of using a stacked column chart, use a normal column chart with multiple columns. If there are too many data series, give your viewer check boxes or a selection list allowing her to select and display the data series desired. The Excel techniques to do this are described in Chapter 20, "Controlling Dashboards with Menus, Combo Boxes, and Buttons."

Shadow Bands in Tables

It can be difficult for the eye to track across wide tables of numbers. If the table is so wide, it is hard to visually track a row: use alternating bands of shading behind the lines. But there is a proviso. Keep the shading as light as possible. Even the light colors that come with Excel's standard palette are too dark. Create your own custom palette, as described in Chapter 16.

Legends

Legends give references for a chart or table. They aren't a main topic of interest. Keep them small and out of the way. Reduce their clutter by reducing the size of their fonts, removing their boxes and background shading, and moving them out of the visual focus.

Text Orientation

Try not to use vertical text — it is too difficult to read. If text doesn't fit, use a smaller font; if that doesn't work, abbreviate text — and if that doesn't work, reposition the text by putting it in a floating text box and moving it out of the chart area.

Some Important Sources on the Art and Science of Visualizing Data

There is a lot of good information on data visualization that can be found in a few web sites and books. Here are a few that will help you.

Excel Charting Techniques

Ron Person
`www.torconsulting.com`
Ron is the author of this book. He helps small to mid-sized organizations become high-performance cultures. He is an expert at developing and implementing Balanced Scorecards and operational dashboards. Ron has more than a million copies of Excel books in print and was one of Microsoft's first consulting partners.

John Walkenbach
`www.j-walk.com`
I've been using Excel since 1985 — before its public release — but even so there are two invaluable books I keep nearby on my book shelf, both of them by

John Walkenbach. One is *Excel Charts*, and the other is *Excel Formulas*. When a solution doesn't immediately come to mind, I reach for one of his books, and I often find the answer.

Jon Peltier

www.peltiertech.com

Peltier's Technical Services, Inc., has many examples of Excel charting techniques at its web site. Jon's web site is a great source of all-around Excel knowledge.

The Art of Visualizing Data

Stephen Few

www.perceptualedge.com

Stephen Few has written the bible on the visual aspects of designing dashboards, *Information Dashboard Design: The Effective Communication of Data*. He contributes to blogs on data visualization as well as hosting his own web site filled with tips.

Edward Tufte

www.edwardtufte.com

Nature, one of the leading magazines of science, has described Tufte as "the world's leading analyst of graphic information." His books on representing data through visual images, not just dashboards, are beautiful and intriguing. Edward Tufte is the originator of Sparklines, the miniature minimalist charts shown in Chapter 26, "Using Excel Add-Ins for Extra Capabilities."

Dashboardspy

www.dashboardspy.com

The Dashboardspy is the place to go to see the latest in dashboards of all types. The "spy" has collected screen shots and tips from hundreds of contributors. There are over 1,000 screen shots of dashboards in many functional areas and industries.

Charles Kyd

www.exceluser.com

Charley's work in magazine quality charting with Excel is described in detail in Chapter 19, "Creating Miniature Charts and Tables." Be sure to sign up for his Excel Users newsletter — it has lots of great tips.

Junk Charts

junkcharts.typepad.com

Junk Charts has critiques on some very intriguing charts. In addition to seeing some of the bleeding edge of chartdom, you will learn about statistics, and about how *not* to present data.

TED, Inspired talks by the world's greatest thinkers and doers
`www.ted.com`
TED is one of my most favorite web sites on any topic. TED is a conference held each spring in Monterey, California, that brings together thousands of the world's most creative doers. Topics cover the gamut: design, business, religion, medicine, music, you name it. TED streams free videos of all its presentations. (Most are less than 15 minutes.) To see an impressive use of how to analyze data for insights into world problems, watch any of the TED videos by Hans Rosling. For an artistic representation on the "graphics of excess," search for Chris Jordan.

Summary

The purpose of any dashboard you create should be to aid decision-making. By interviewing users and understanding their reasons for requesting a dashboard, as well as how they make decisions, you can create a tool that will help them make better decisions faster.

Most of the rules for visualizing data can be condensed to a few:

- Eliminate chart junk.
- Keep the focus on the information required for decision-making.
- Help the user make better decisions faster.

CHAPTER 13

Drawing Process and Strategy Maps

As I grow older, I pay less attention to what people say. I just watch what they do.
Andrew Carnegie
Industrialist, 1835–1919

Strategy Maps, value stream maps, and process maps of all types provide visual clarity. They make complex processes understandable and memorable. They also make it significantly easier to identify the points in a strategy or process at which we can get leverage to create the greatest effect. Once we have identified those points, we can identify the most important metrics.

Selecting the right tools to create your Strategy Map or process map can save you a lot of work and rework. This chapter describes the leading tools in three different classes of mapping software.

Which Drawing Tool Should You Use?

Strategy Maps and process maps range from simple maps you do once, which only need to be "good enough," to maps dynamically linked to databases that update continuously and are critical to operations. But a range of software exists that can satisfy your needs across that full spectrum.

This chapter describes three different software solutions with three different levels of user knowledge and three different levels of output. Of course, there are three different levels of pricing.

If your needs are minimal and you only need to create one or two Strategy Maps or simple process maps, then the Drawing toolbar in Microsoft PowerPoint may be all you need. If you don't have a lot of time to invest in learning but want access to a wide range of maps and charts, including Strategy Maps, affinity maps, value maps, process control maps, Six Sigma maps, and hundreds of other types of maps and charts, check out SmartDraw. Those who need unlimited flexibility, manual control, and the ability to link data tables or databases to the map's display should use Microsoft Visio.

Table 13.1 breaks down the features of these three products.

Table 13.1 Feature comparison of three drawing tool software options

	MICROSOFT OFFICE DRAWING TOOLBAR	SMARTDRAW	MICROSOFT VISIO
Price	Free	$	$$$
Ease of creation	Mid-level manual work	Easy; Start with examples or template and modify with SmartPanel	Mid-level manual work
Start from	Blank page	Blank page; complete example or template	Blank page; a few templates available
Ease of editing or changing existing maps	Mid-level manual work	Easy	Mid-level manual work
Ease of applying color and graphical themes	Manual; lots of work	Easy; apply predefined color themes	Easy; apply predefined color themes
Drawing objects available	Basic mapping objects; special symbols such as those for EVA may have to be created manually	Thousands	Thousands
Connector lines and arrows (remain connected when objects move)	Yes, for some objects	Yes	Yes
Guidance or Wizards	Minimal help	SmartPanels that act like wizards; help; online tutorials	Help; online tutorials
Multipage	Yes, banner format	Yes	Yes

Continued

Table 13.1   *(continued)*

	MICROSOFT OFFICE DRAWING TOOLBAR	SMARTDRAW	MICROSOFT VISIO
Large-format printing	Yes, in PowerPoint with banner or custom page setup	Yes	Yes
High-quality output to large-format commercial printing	In PowerPoint with limitations	Online download to commercial print partners	Yes
Templates	None	Hundreds	Some online
Industry templates	None	Medical, Legal, Crime Scene, business forms	Through Microsoft Partners
Export to MS Office	Native	Yes, but objects are broken into many components	Yes
Training	Minimal	30 minutes to get started; free training available online	30 minutes to get started; free training available online
Data entry tables that link to object text and numbers	No	No	Yes
Objects link to Excel tables or databases for auto-update of text and numbers	No	No	Yes
Database analysis with PivotTable-like capability	No	No	Yes
Programmable	Complex, but possible with VBA	No	Yes, using VBA and API

Drawing with Microsoft Office Drawing Tools

The Drawing toolbar in Microsoft Word, PowerPoint, and Excel gives you access to drawing tools that are adequate for simple Strategy Maps, simple process maps, and flowcharting. The Drawing toolbar gives you basic drawing tools, lines and arrows that stay connected, and enough formatting capability to make your work look pretty good.

Microsoft PowerPoint is the most common application used when drawing Strategy Maps with the Drawing toolbar. This is because the maps will usually be displayed in PowerPoint. Also, PowerPoint can print large formats using a banner or custom page setup.

Here are some basic guidelines for drawing maps in Microsoft PowerPoint. Figure 13.1 shows a Strategy Map drawn in Microsoft PowerPoint. The Drawing toolbar has been docked at the bottom of the screen. The Basic Shapes toolbar was "torn" off the Drawing toolbar so it is constantly accessible. The Connector toolbar hangs from the sides of the AutoShapes menu on the Drawing toolbar.

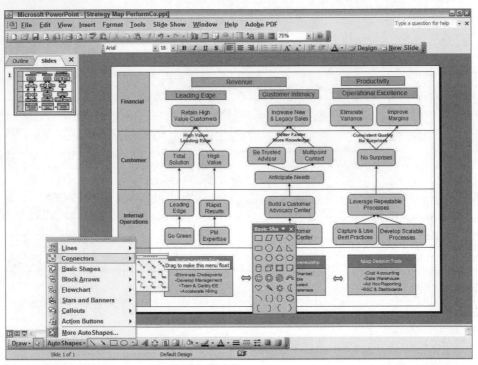

Figure 13.1: Use the Drawing toolbar in Microsoft PowerPoint to create effective Strategy Maps.

Displaying the Drawing Toolbar

To display the Drawing toolbar, if it is not already visible in Microsoft PowerPoint

1. Using your mouse, right-click on a toolbar and choose Drawing, or select View ➪ Toolbars ➪ Drawing.

2. Drag the toolbar to the location you want by dragging the title bar or dotted "handle" at an end of the toolbar.

In PowerPoint 2007, the Drawing toolbar has been removed. For information on how to draw in PowerPoint 2007, see the steps in the following procedures.

Drawing Objects and Connectors

The drawing objects you will use most frequently are the Basic Shapes, Flowchart, and Connector tools. To put a shape onto the PowerPoint slide

1. Click AutoShapes.
2. Point to Basic Shapes or Flowchart, and then click on the shape you want to draw.
3. Move the crosshair pointer to one corner of where you want the shape, drag it to the opposite corner, and release it.

In PowerPoint 2007, on the Home tab, in the Drawing group, click Shapes. Click the shape you want, and then click in the document where you want the shape; drag to size it. Holding the Shift key down as you drag will enable you to draw circles or squares. Additional tabs for applying formatting and effects to drawing objects will appear on the ruler when you have a drawing object selected.

Connector lines or arrows stay connected between objects you draw, even when you move the objects. Figure 13.2 shows a connector arrow being drawn from its starting point to its end point. As the pointer moves over an object, blue connector sites appear on the edges of the object. These connector sites are locations where you can anchor the end of the connector. Lines and arrows stay attached to an anchor, even when objects are moved.

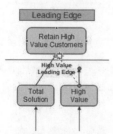

Figure 13.2: Connector sites appear on the edges of objects where connector lines or arrows can be attached.

To draw and connect a connector between two objects

1. Click AutoShapes.

2. Point to Connectors, and then click the type of connector you want. You can later modify a connector by double-clicking it to change the style of its line or arrowhead.

3. Move the pointer over the first object, and click the blue connector site where you want to anchor the tail.

4. Move the pointer over the second object, and click the blue connector site where you want to anchor the head.

In PowerPoint 2007, on the Home tab, in the Drawing group, click Shapes. Click the line or connector you want. Point to the first object you want to connect, and click on the connection site. Drag to the next object and click on the connection site you want. You can move endpoints of connectors by dragging them to a new location.

Adding Text to Objects or Connectors

Add text inside objects by clicking in the center of the object and typing. You also can right-click on an object, select Add Text, and begin typing. To format the text in an object, select the text, right-click, and choose Font. Select the text formatting you want. To adjust the positioning or layout of text in an object, right-click the object and select options you want in the Text Box tab.

Lines, arrows, and connectors do not have text associated with them, but you can click the Text Box tool in the Drawing toolbar and create a text box next to the connector. Use Grouping to keep the connector and text box together when they are moved.

Moving Objects or Connectors

Move objects by dragging them to new locations. If you have connectors attached to an object, the connector will move and realign itself with the object in its new location.

Formatting Objects or Connectors

The size, line style, and color of all objects, lines, and connectors can be formatted. Right-click the object or connector you want to format, choose Format *Shape*, and browse through the tabs to find the formatting options you need.

Grouping Objects So That They Act As One

Some objects need to stay together and act as a unit. To group objects

1. Select all the objects you want to group by clicking the first object, and then hold the Ctrl key down as you click the other objects.

2. Right-click on one of the objects and choose Grouping ➪ Group.

   To ungroup a group of objects, right-click the group and choose Grouping ➪ Ungroup.

In Excel 2007, select the objects you want to group, and then, on the Format tab, in the Arrange group, click the Group icon, and then click Group. To ungroup a group of objects, select the group; then, on the Format tab, in the Arrange group, click the Group icon, and then click Ungroup.

Using Grid and Nudge for Accurate Positioning

Move objects in large increments by selecting them and then using the arrow keys. To move objects in small increments, hold the Ctrl key as you press the arrow keys.

The Grid and Guides dialog box, shown in Figure 13.3, enables you to accurately position objects. With the appropriate selections in the dialog box, you can create a visual grid of a size you specify and make objects snap to that grid.

Figure 13.3: The Grid and Guides dialog box makes it easier to align and position objects when you are working on finishing touches.

If you are having trouble getting objects to align, use the Zoom tool or View ➪ Zoom to expand the map to 200% or 400%. This magnified view makes it easier to make minor adjustments and to see corners and alignment.

Controlling Objects That Overlap

Objects appear in layers. Layers are like virtual sheets of glass each holding one object. Visually, the objects can cover each other. Moving the order of the layers enables you to make different objects appear on top of others. It gives you the ability to overlap objects.

However, you will find that sometimes you want to change an object's layer. To change an object's layer, right-click the object and choose Order; then select one of the four commands to shift the layer.

Saving Time When You Draw

Figure 13.4 shows how to save yourself considerable time when creating a map in PowerPoint using the Drawing toolbar. As you begin your project, decide which objects you will need and what their format should be. Create and format one of each object and drag them off the slide to the side. These objects on the side will be your library.

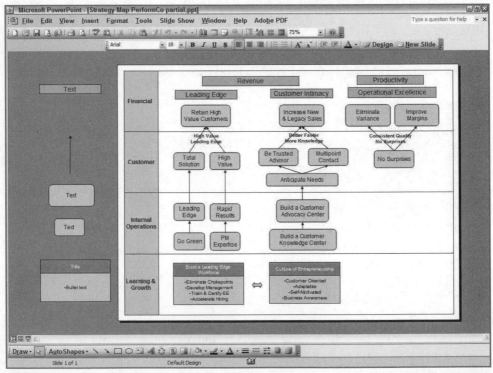

Figure 13.4: Save time by creating a library of frequently used objects outside the viewing area of your slide.

Whenever you need one of your pre-formatted objects or connectors, select it from the side area and hold the Ctrl key as you drag a duplicate onto the slide. This will ensure that all your objects have the same formatting and size.

You may find it easier to work by starting at the macro or global view and working toward the micro or detail view. Begin with a 66% view or one that enables you to see the entire slide as well as your library of objects on the side. Create and format a library of objects to the side of your slide, then drag them into their general location. Now, zoom to a closer view and begin entering text, aligning objects, and attaching connectors.

Drawing with SmartDraw

SmartDraw bills itself as the world's most popular business software. I can't vouch for that, but I will say it has saved me a lot of time with all of its templates. The results are also more attractive than what can be done with the Drawing tool.

One of SmartDraw's chief distinctions is that you start by selecting an example or illustration of what you want to accomplish. Most business drawing programs start by presenting a blank form and then expecting you to know exactly what you want and how you want to do it. SmartDraw comes with hundreds of examples whose topics range from Strategy Mapping to value stream and business process mapping to Six Sigma analysis to crime scene investigation. It is quite likely you will find what you need. In fact, while browsing the examples, I have found other tools that can help clients. Figure 13.5 shows just a few of the examples from which you can choose. To see more examples, go to SmartDraw's web site, www.smartdraw.com, and look in the Solutions tab for the Encyclopedia of Business Graphics. You can also download a trial copy.

Once you select something similar to what you want, begin to modify it. You can manually select symbols from the Library tab of the SmartPanel on the left. If the example or template doesn't have all the symbols you need associated with it, then select additional symbol libraries from the More Symbols dialog box, as shown in Figure 13.6. (SmartDraw comes with more than 20,000 symbols.)

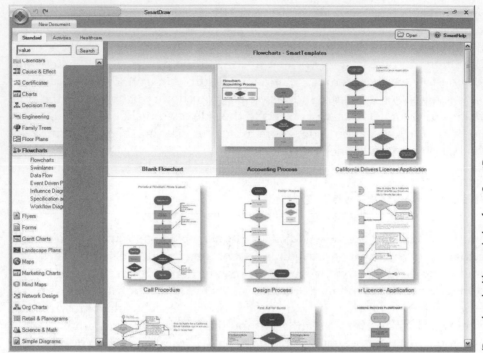

Figure 13.5: SmartDraw has hundreds and hundreds of examples and templates from which to choose.

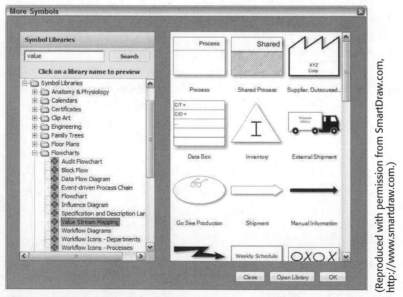

Figure 13.6: SmartDraw has symbol libraries containing hundreds and hundreds of symbols for different areas of business, science, and industry.

Once you have selected an example or a blank template and symbol libraries, you can modify your drawing. You can drop and manipulate individual symbols and connectors as you would with the Microsoft Office Drawing toolbar or Microsoft Visio. However, SmartDraw has added a wizard-like feature called SmartPanels. Figure 13.7 shows the SmartPanel on the left being used to add two sub-topics to the selected topic in the Mind Map.

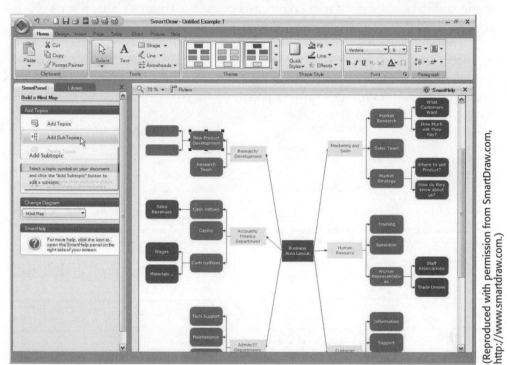

(Reproduced with permission from SmartDraw.com, http://www.smartdraw.com.)

Figure 13.7: If you don't want to manually modify an example or template, the SmartPanel options, shown on the left, will make appropriate modifications, such as adding a subtopic to the selected topic in this Mind Map.

After drafting your map, you will need to make it look good. Choosing well-coordinated palettes of colors is where I always have trouble, but SmartDraw makes this pretty easy. SmartDraw has sets of predefined color palettes and effects. Once you choose a theme, the color palette from which you make choices is all in the same color family.

Drawing with Microsoft Visio

Microsoft Visio is the drawing tool for heavyweight production. It can lift any load, but you need to be able to spend dedicated time with it. If you want to create a quick Strategy Map or process map, Visio may take more time to learn than you want to spend. But if you face large EVA models or need to link process maps to databases so that text and numbers update dynamically, then Visio is your tool.

Microsoft Visio gives you a blank sheet on startup, so you need to know what type of map you want, rather than looking through a library. There are a few templates available at the Microsoft Office download web site, but not nearly as many templates, and of such variety, as are available for SmartDraw. Figure 13.8 shows one of the templates available online.

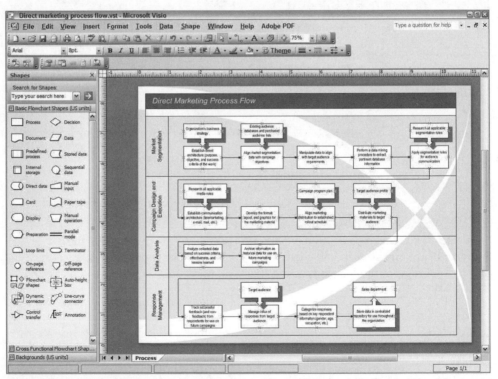

Figure 13.8: Microsoft Visio is a heavy-duty workhorse that can handle any type of business process mapping.

After selecting a symbol from one of Visio's many symbol libraries, position and connect the symbol on the map using the same methods you would use with the Drawing tool. When you need to apply formatting and color, you can use Visio's predefined color themes.

Microsoft Visio really excels in the areas of data connectivity and analysis. Maps and charts you draw can be linked to data in Excel workbooks or databases. This enables displayed data in symbols to automatically update when the data changes. You can even assign alert levels to connected data so that areas out of tolerance are flagged with a warning color.

Figure 13.9 shows a human resource recruiting map linked to an HR database. As data in the database changes, the graphs and alerts change on the map.

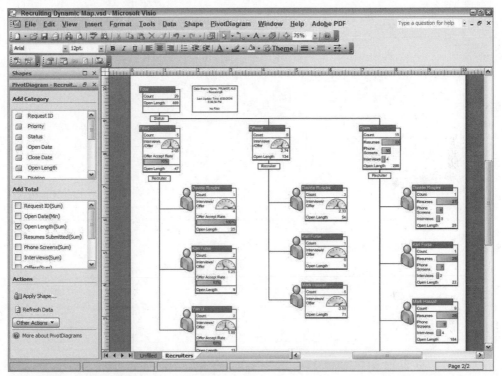

Figure 13.9: Visio's PivotDiagram enables you to link maps and charts to databases so that information updates dynamically.

Summary

At in-house workshops or when giving a presentation someone often remarks how the Strategy Map or operational map has brought clarity to a problem. Don't lose that clarity. When you need to capture the Strategy Map or to process it and communicate it to your organization, use a drawing tool that is up to the task. If you are creating a single Strategy Map, the Microsoft Drawing tool is sufficient. If you need a wide variety of visual decision-making tools but don't want to become mired in software, choose SmartDraw. And if you need maps that have no limits to their robustness and that can work dynamically with data, choose Microsoft Visio.

CHAPTER 14

Using Microsoft Excel for Balanced Scorecards and Dashboards

Once we accept our limits, we go beyond them.
Albert Einstein
Theoretical Physicist, 1879–1955

I'll come right out and say it: IT departments don't like Excel. I'll admit that they do have some justifiable issues with using Excel for complex business systems, or as a Business Intelligence engine in some environments.

But the truth is, Excel is ubiquitous. According to my highly unscientific and impromptu polls over the last few years, Excel is the most used software for Balanced Scorecards, and I would bet that there are far more operational dashboards in Excel than in enterprise-level Business Intelligence systems.

So how do we handle this disparity between business users' needs for fast, personally controlled analysis and IT needs for management, security, and control? Perhaps there is a middle way.

Excel is the Most Widely Used Balanced Scorecard Software

At a meeting of fellow Six Sigma Black Belts, I asked the 32 Black Belts present, "How many of you are using Balanced Scorecards and operational dashboards created in Excel?" Everyone raised their hands. Only one, in a very large corporation, had access to an IT-governed Business Intelligence system.

The night before I started this chapter, at a meeting of the Association of Strategic Planning, someone raised the question, "What software is everyone using for Balanced Scorecards?" Everyone in the room acknowledged using Excel. The Balanced Scorecard sponsor for one major bank told how it had attempted to build its scorecard using an enterprise software package. After six months, the bank realized that doing so had been a serious mismatch. It rebuilt its Balanced Scorecard using Excel and went on to have a successful Balanced Scorecard implementation — so successful, in fact, that the parent bank will be using Excel for subsequent Balanced Scorecard implementations in its other holdings.

The ubiquitous nature of Excel isn't just in Balanced Scorecards. I always keep an eye out for dashboards when walking through my clients' financial or manufacturing facilities. Perhaps it is selective perception, but it seems that every other corridor has a posted collection of Excel charts showing targets vs. actuals. I'm coming to the conclusion that the Western world is being measured using Excel scorecards and dashboards.

Consider the Trade-Offs Between Excel and Large BI Systems

It is pretty easy to claim that Microsoft Excel is the most widely used numeric analysis and financial software in the world. It has made business and financial analysis available to millions of business people. In the context of this book Excel is used for

- Ad hoc queries to databases
- Analysis of business data
- Business modeling
- Planning and budgeting
- Presentations of charts and tables
- Reporting
- Scenario testing

With all its use, Excel is still held in low esteem by IT. Whenever Excel is discussed with IT departments, three issues arise:

- **Excel isn't scalable.** It is difficult to distribute, manage, and control Excel applications — for example, scaling an Excel dashboard for use by 1,000 users.
- **Excel produces multiple versions of the "truth."** When users get personal copies of data, it spawns different versions that, though they have the same title, may have different source data and origination dates and may have been manipulated using user-defined formulas.

- **Excel lacks referential integrity.** There is no way to track where the data in an Excel spreadsheet came from, when changes were made (and by whom), and what business rules lie behind the formulas.

Business users, however, are less concerned with a manageable IT environment and data integrity. They are more concerned about managing the alligators in the swamp. Some of the alligators that keep users on Excel and away from Business Intelligence systems are:

- **Business changes quickly.** Analysis is needed rapidly. It can't wait for IT that is short-staffed or unresponsive.

- **Users know their own assumptions and rules.** In Excel, users can modify variables and formulas quickly as the environment changes.

- **Low-cost solutions are needed.** Some situations require simple, low-cost solutions that would never stand up to the rigor and resources required of a system sent through the entire IT process.

- **Users know Excel.** Business users don't have the time to learn a new Business Intelligence system when they already know Excel.

- **Users have existing solutions in Excel.** Implementing a Business Intelligence system would also force users to recreate all their existing tools and solutions they use to manage daily crises. Without their existing tools, they would fall even farther behind.

Disadvantages of Excel

The IT department raises valid objections to Excel. We need to understand IT's concerns before assuming that Excel can always replace a Business Intelligence system.

Many Versions of One Truth

A fairly common scene in corporate America is the business user with a special need who puts in a request to IT. IT can't build the analysis or report quickly, so the user says, "Can you just export the data for me?"

The user then sucks the static data into Excel, manipulates the data to fit his needs, uses unaudited formulas to add or forecast more data points, and then prints the report or sends the resulting data on to other users. Nowhere is there documentation or version control. Two people doing this to similar data sets the stage for a fight about whose data is correct.

Technical Scalability vs. User Scalability

A common IT refrain is that Excel is not scalable. This depends upon the type of scalability needed. In the area of multidimensional work, Excel doesn't scale well. Excel is great for building a budget and forecast for a single department, but it doesn't work well for rolling up the budget and forecast for tens of departments and divisions. If you want to build a Balanced Scorecard that rolls up through ten levels of your organization, Excel is not what you want.

Many Excel systems, like those for Balanced Scorecards and operational dashboards, work well without needing to scale to large levels.

One area of scalability where Excel wins is in cost and time. The cost of licensing Business Intelligence seats per user is growing rapidly. With Excel, that cost is already paid.

Another cost in large-scale production is in training and support. Although most Excel users can use more job-specific training, the cost is minimal. The cost for training on enterprise Business Intelligence systems can be thousands of dollars per user. And then the users must return and use the new system while facing the pressure of daily work. Such a solution usually takes a long time to work. The cost to the business is huge.

In one case, a large northern California bank implemented an enterprise-wide Business Intelligence system from one of the largest Business Intelligence vendors. After 3 days of training, business and account managers returned to their desks unable to use the new, very expensive BI system to do the simple analysis they all had existing Excel worksheets for. They understood how their Excel analyses worked, and they knew how to make corrections to them. Within the week, everyone had returned to using Excel just so they could get their work done. Within weeks, the minimal skills they had learned on the new system were forgotten.

Hidden Errors

Spreadsheets contain errors. Poorly constructed spreadsheets make it worse by mixing formulas and data so it is easy for users to type over formulas. The users are never taught how to structure their spreadsheets or how to audit the results, so spreadsheets go out to the world containing errors.

Spreadsheets Spawn Spreadsheets

Spreadsheets spawn spreadsheets, and that spawns trouble. When one department or user sees an application or data set that is useful, it asks for it. Even if the original application was well maintained, the spawned spreadsheet gets changed, spawns again, mutates, and soon spreads throughout the organization with neither version control nor documentation.

KNOW SPREADSHEET BEST PRACTICES

In one Excel system I audited for a major pharmaceutical, the spreadsheets had numeric values typed over where critical formulas should have been. The result was that decisions had been made using incorrect sales reports and forecasts.

IT would say it was the fault of Excel. However, I've also found SQL statements that were incorrect and data warehouses with incorrectly defined data. In all these cases, good training and time spent testing and auditing would have found the errors.

In Excel, you can significantly reduce errors by using a few best practices:

■ Use a spreadsheet architecture that separates data, formula, and chart and reporting areas.

■ Link Excel spreadsheets to shared data that refreshes on a recurrent basis.

■ Use range names in formulas.

■ Include a documentation sheet that lists critical formulas, assumptions, and range names. Use Insert ⇨ Name ⇨ Paste to document named ranges in the worksheet.

■ Use the Formula Audit Toolbar to check for values in formula areas, track formulas, trace circular formulas, and more.

■ Use the F9 key to evaluate nested formulas.

■ Include date and data source on all dashboards and reports.

These are all simple disciplines that are easy to learn and monitor. Make sure your developers know them. I teach them to my clients.

The Ineluctable Modality of User-Built Conundrums

Excel's very popularity with businesspeople causes problems. It puts power in the hands of users. Business users love Excel for its ability to quickly analyze data. But the majority of business users have not had even rudimentary training in spreadsheet design, security, and audit. They were shown how to enter formulas, create charts, and perhaps build a PivotTable, and then they were let loose without the discipline or structure of trained or experienced programmers.

Spreadsheet applications may work fine, but when the original developer leaves, there can be problems of maintaining and documenting a proprietary system. Again, this is really a problem of user training. What is needed is a professional system of documentation and development.

Advantages of Using Excel

In business users' minds the advantages of Excel clearly outweigh those of other analysis software. And in most cases, there are no alternatives to Excel. Furthermore, the advantages of using Excel are many. Knowledgeable users and consultants are everywhere. Excel is basically free, since it is a part of Microsoft Office. And it has the add-ons and calculating power necessary to solve most business analysis problems in the hands of the average user.

Get It Done Now!

One of the biggest advantages to the use of Excel is that the analysis can be done *now*, by the person who needs it. Excel's 300+ functions and hundreds of add-ons allow users to solve almost any business analytic and reporting problem they face, so long as they can get the data. Of course, this is also one of Excel's biggest problems. Jamming out quick solutions usually means that the spreadsheet application wasn't constructed with a good architecture and certainly wasn't documented.

Prove the Business Intelligence and Dashboard Concept

Excel is an excellent, low-cost way of proving the need and value of a Balanced Scorecard or operational dashboard. It makes good sense for management to want to see a working system to test the concepts before budgeting the year of development and hundreds of thousands of dollars that a full Business Intelligence system can cost.

Experienced Users

Excel knowledge is pervasive. And most organizations have one person they turn to as the Excel guru who knows most features, and perhaps a little Visual Basic for Applications. The Web has numerous excellent sites with databases full of tips and examples. This means that the support load is low. Users can help each other.

Total Costs for Scalability

IT departments talk about the technical limits of scalability for Excel. But there is another area that needs to be discussed. That is the true cost of scaling or expanding a Business Intelligence, Balanced Scorecard, or dashboard effort.

License fees and the definition of a user are making Business Intelligence systems from large vendors more and more expensive, whereas the cost of Excel is a sunk cost, having been included in Microsoft Office.

Another even larger cost that is rarely discussed is the total cost for retraining and redeveloping existing business systems. Converting users to a large Business Intelligence system requires a couple of days of training at a thousand dollars or more per day. Then, when users return to work, they are expected to leave behind their existing spreadsheets and use the new system for their analysis. The reality is that it doesn't happen. People return to their desks with high hopes, fail to get the results they need (the examples in class are always dumbed down), and, under the pressure of deadlines, return to their old Excel spreadsheets.

If users are forced to use a BI system, they must take time from being productive to create new solutions that replace the Excel solutions that have taken them years to create. That time away from production damages the bottom line.

Excel Is Flexible and Extendible

I've been using Excel for over 20 years, since back when it came on a stack of diskettes about six inches high and ran on a run-time version of Windows. Since that time, Excel has polished out the glitches and has developed a warehouse full of analytical add-ons you can use to extend its analytical capabilities. Also, the Excel format has become a *lingua franca* for data interchange between computer systems, almost like CSV files.

Excel's Chart Engine Is a Powerful Standard

One of the best chart engines available is in Microsoft Excel. You can customize almost any part of a chart you want. A common request I hear when doing Business Intelligence work is to make the chart look as good as it does in Excel while having the same analytic capability. I haven't found a Business Intelligence system that allows that.

When to Use Excel

Excel works well for Balanced Scorecards at a single level in the organization and for scorecards and dashboards that drill down only one or two levels. For that reason, and because of its excellent charting and math capabilities and its common use in business, Excel is the preferred choice for initial development of Balanced Scorecards.

Using Excel for the first year gives organizations the chance to evaluate their objectives and causal links, to refine their metrics, and to gather their data without spending a lot of time and resources on a large IT project. Stories abound of companies who have bypassed the "functioning prototype" Excel stage and then have failed to deliver with their too-large BI system. Only upon restarting the Balanced Scorecard process and rebuilding with Excel were they able to succeed.

Excel also works well for operational dashboards that are point solutions working with narrow sets of data and that aren't shared between large numbers of users. Excel doesn't work well for dashboard systems that give users ad hoc query capability. You can build dashboards that allow queries, but these usually are used against narrowly scoped data sets.

If you are a small to mid-sized business or a department within a large corporation, using Excel within these limits, and when linked to a good database, may be all you need. It may fit your BI needs, your budget, and your time constraints far better than a large, resource-intensive BI system.

When Not to Use Excel

You don't want to use Excel if you are considering Business Intelligence solutions that are large scale. For example, some government agencies have Balanced Scorecards that cascade and roll up through 14 layers of the organization. I wouldn't recommend using Excel by itself to cascade even 2 layers in an organization.

Excel can drill down into data when it has the appropriate relational database or OLAP cube back end. In most Balanced Scorecard systems, however, Excel is using static data imported into an Excel worksheet. This makes drill-down of more than one or two layers difficult. If you need extensive ad hoc queries and drill-down capability, you may need a Business Intelligence system.

If you plan to cascade your Balanced Scorecard and dashboards through multiple levels of the organization and through hundreds of users, then I recommend prototyping in Excel to determine users' needs before developing the Business Intelligence system.

Solutions

Although there are IT reasons for not using Excel for Business Intelligence, doing so works well for Balanced Scorecards and point solution operational dashboards.

Excel will also help small and mid-sized business units (SMB) or departments within large organizations that need agile systems that are easy to support, that cost little to develop and maintain, and that can handle flexible analysis. Balanced Scorecard and dashboards developed in Excel have the advantages of

- Less time to development
- Low or non-existent licensing fees
- Accessible developers
- An established, knowledgeable user base
- Easily accessible user training
- Quick and inexpensive testing of user requirements
- Excellent analytical capability with over 300 functions
- Extensibility that allows additional features, such as Monte Carlo techniques, for nominal cost
- Arguably one of the best charting engines around

What about the scalability and data integrity issues? The solution might be using Excel as the analysis and presentation layer and storing all data in a relational database or OLAP cube, then linking in the Excel scorecards or dashboards. This enables you to share common data, to maintain backups, to maintain standard metric definitions, to have secure access, and to scale to a large number of users. Increase the integrity and professionalism of your spreadsheets by giving your power users a one- or two-day course that specifically targets those rules described earlier for professional spreadsheets.

Summary

Excel is the world standard for financial and business modeling. Combine this with its powerful charting engine and broad user base, and it's easy to see why it continues to be the most widely used platform for Balanced Scorecards and operational dashboards. But there are caveats. You must be aware of Excel's limits, and the systems you build must subscribe to spreadsheet best practices, or you may develop systems that are difficult to maintain.

Text-Based Dashboards

This report, by its very length, defends itself against the risk of being read.

Sir Winston Churchill
Statesman, 1874–1965

Knowing that Excel has one of the best graphical engines available in business software, why would you consider creating text-based dashboards? Actually there are numerous reasons.

The text-based dashboards described in this chapter use text elements that fit within worksheet cells. They take up little room in a printed report, yet give the reader a quick comparison between relative values.

With the addition of conditional colors and conditional icons, we can create information-rich screens or printed reports that contain a great deal of data, yet also convey a great deal of information. The text-based dashboard techniques in this chapter enable you to

- Create information-rich printed reports to complement dynamic and chart-oriented dashboards

- Match the information-rich format used in some Business Intelligence software

- Create color alerts and icon alerts that draw attention to text data

- Create report elements that make alerts more readable for the color-blind

- Create text elements compatible with any version of Excel

CROSS-REFERENCE More examples of in-cell or text-dased dashboards: Chapter 19, "Creating Miniature Charts and Tables," and Chapter 26, "Using Excel Add-Ins for Extra Capabilities," describe in detail how to create miniature charts and use some cool charts that fit within a worksheet's cells. If you're looking for additional ways to create miniature charts, check out Chapter 19 and the sidebar on techniques Charley Kyd has developed for magazine-quality displays.

Alerting with Conditional Formats

Conditional formats change text and cell formatting depending on a condition you prescribe. They are an excellent way of highlighting data that exceed alert levels you have set. In some very simple Balanced Scorecards, conditional formatting is used on a single page of metrics to highlight whether values are within green, amber, or red limits.

Figure 15.1 shows how a color created with conditional formatting in combination with a text icon arrowhead draws attention to a miniature chart in a Balanced Scorecard. The conditional color and arrowhead icon are set to appear when an alert limit is exceeded. This type of alert system can be done in any version of Excel with conditional formatting.

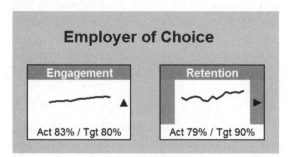

Figure 15.1: Using any version of Excel, you can combine conditional formatting with a conditional icon to create an alert system for Balanced Scorecards.

Conditional Formatting with Earlier Versions of Excel

Earlier versions of Excel have conditional formatting that allows for four formats, the original cell format and three formats that depend upon a cell's content. The condition can be tested against a simple value or with a complex formula. Figure 15.2 shows a simple list where the format of the numbers in the Sales column depend upon the numeric value in the cell.

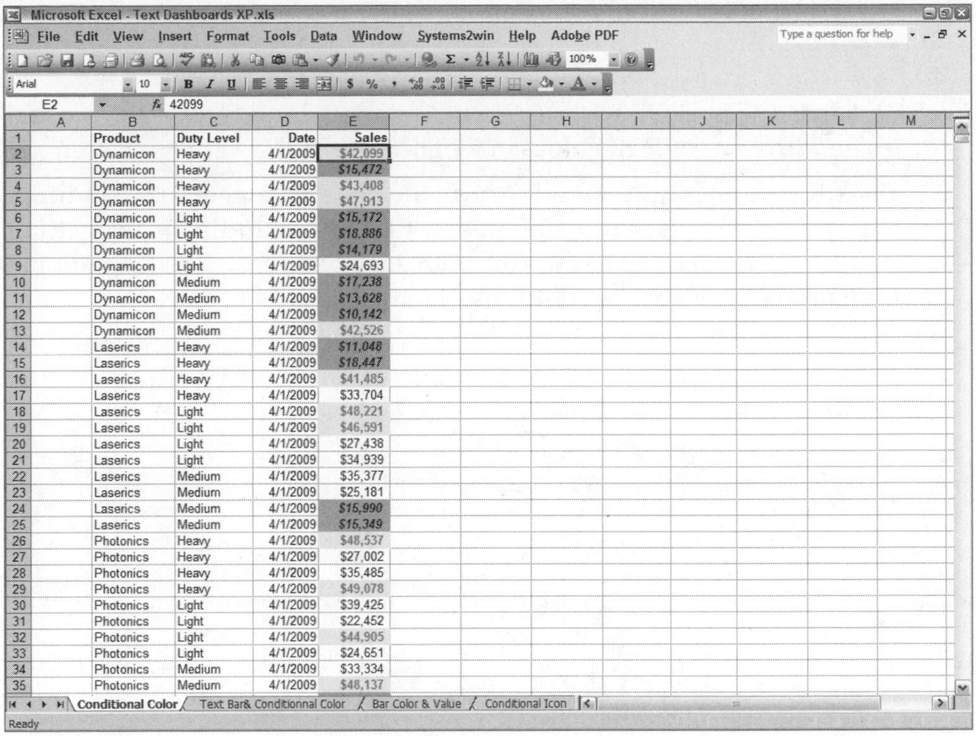

Figure 15.2: Conditional formatting helps you quickly identify numbers and dates that exceed limits.

The following steps set a conditional format that changes the appearance of sales values if they are greater than the 75th percentile or less than the 25th percentile:

1. Select all cells down the column that will have the conditional formatting.

2. Choose Format ⇨ Conditional Format to display the Conditional Formatting dialog box.

3. For Condition 1, select Formula Is and enter the formula.

   ```
   =E2>=PERCENTILE($E$2:$E$625,0.75)
   ```

   This formula is TRUE when the contents of E2 are greater than or equal to the 75th percentile of values in E2:E625.

4. Click the Format button and format the cells that meet this condition with a bold, dark green font and light green background. This formatting will enable color-blind readers to see the bold difference.

5. Click Add>> to add another condition.

6. For Condition 2, select Formula Is and enter the formula

```
=E2<=PERCENTILE($E$2:$E$625,0.25)
```

This formula is TRUE when the contents of E2 are greater than or equal to the 75th percentile of values in E2:E625.

7. Click the Format button and format the cells that meet this condition with bold, italic black font and light pink background. This formatting enables color-blind readers see the bold italic difference. The Conditional Formatting dialog box will look like Figure 15.3.

8. Choose OK.

Figure 15.3: Apply up to three conditional formats in older versions of Excel to help you identify four different alert ranges.

TIP Excel versions prior to Excel 2007 allowed three conditional formats. However, that actually means there are four conditional formats for each cell. The normal format is a separate color, so if you correctly write your conditional format, you can have four distinct conditions.

Conditional Formatting with Excel 2007

Excel 2007 takes conditional formatting even further with the ability to show data bars, color scales, and icons depending on a cell's contents. You aren't limited to three conditions as in previous Excel versions. There are many built-in rules and conditions, such as Top *n* and Bottom *n*, which identify the Top or Bottom number of cells.

Conditional formatting does more than just change cell formatting. In addition, each cell meeting a condition can display one of these conditional formats:

- Data bars: shaded horizontal bar charts
- Color scales: color backgrounds
- Icons: colored graphical icons

Excel 2007 conditional formatting has limited backward compatibility with earlier versions of Excel. Saving to earlier versions keeps the first three conditional formats for cell formatting; however, you will lose other Excel 2007 features such as data bars and icons.

To apply simple cell formatting based upon on a condition,

1. Select the cells that will have a conditional format

2. On the Home tab, in the Styles group, select Conditional Formatting to display a list

3. From the list, select Highlight Cells Rules ⇨ More Rules to display the New Formatting Rule dialog box shown in Figure 15.4

4. In the Select a Rule Type list, select Format Only Cells that Contain

5. In the Edit the Rule Description group, select Format Only Cells with Cell Value Greater Than

6. In the reference box type the function

   ```
   =PERCENTILE($E$2:$E$625,.75)
   ```

7. Choose the Format button and select a format for those cells containing values greater than 75 percent of the range

8. Choose OK, OK

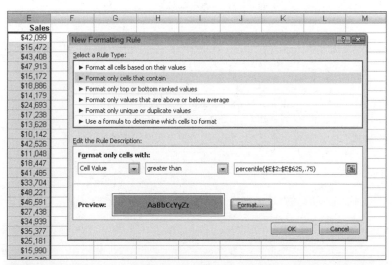

Figure 15.4: Many conditional options are predefined in Excel 2007.

TIP To edit, delete, or set priorities on Excel 2007 conditional formats, open the Home tab. Then, in the Styles group, select Conditional Formatting and then select Manage Rules.

Creating In-Cell Charts with Text

Creating charts with text characters sounds like returning to the 1970s and drawing text charts with mainframes. But, with all of Excel's great charting capabilities there is still a place for in-cell charts made with text.

> **TIP** MicroCharts, described in detail in Chapter 26, is an add-in for Excel that creates many forms of in-cell charts, ranging from the simple bar charts shown in this section to the very effective Sparklines and more.

Text charts, like the one in Figure 15.5, work well to identify relative differences in reports with long columns of data. Text charts like this can also be combined with conditional formatting so the characters change color to indicate an alert condition as well as show their relative size. The technique works in all versions of Excel.

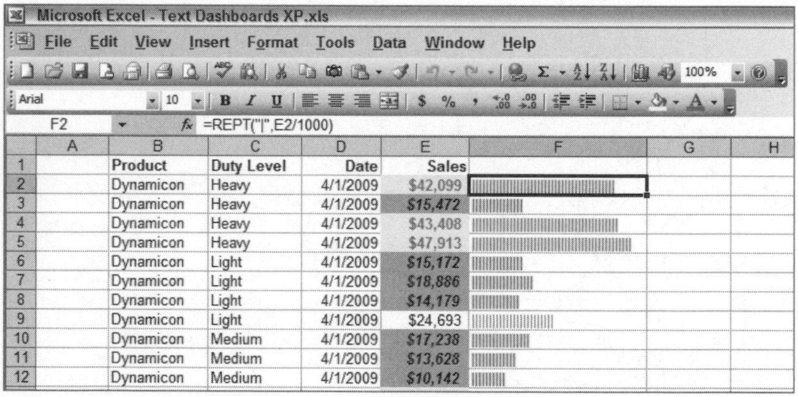

Figure 15.5: Text charts work well to identify relative differences in long columns of data. This figure shows text bars combined with conditional colors.

Creating Text Charts with Earlier Versions of Excel

The REPT function is used in Excel to create text charts. The syntax is

```
REPT(text,number_times).
```

The text is repeated as indicated by *number_times*. The *text* character must be typed in quotes, such as "|". A vertical bar, co-located on the \ key, is often used for simple bar charts.

You can use other non-keyboard characters as repeated characters. To do that, use the CHAR function to convert an ASCII number into a character. The font format of the cell must also match the font set containing the non-keyboard character. You can see the font and the ASCII numeric codes for available symbols by choosing the Insert, Symbol command. Look for the symbol you want, its numeric code, and its font.

Figure 15.6 shows text bars adjacent to the Sales values. The formula in F2 is

```
=REPT("|",E2/1000)
```

This formula is copied down column F. The cell is formatted with the Arial font so the bar character, co-located on the backslash key, appears as a vertical bar in the cell. The value in E2 is divided by 1,000 to scale the number of bars to an appropriate width.

Another technique is to apply conditional formatting on the text charts. This enables you to color the bar charts depending on the values in adjacent cells.

You may also want to show the numeric value or a scaled value next to a bar chart. To do this, concatenate the REPT function with a TEXT function that specifies the value. In this example, the value following the bar is scaled down by 1,000 and has a "K" following it for thousands. F2 contains

```
=REPT("|",E2/1000)&"  "&TEXT(E2,"$#,K")
```

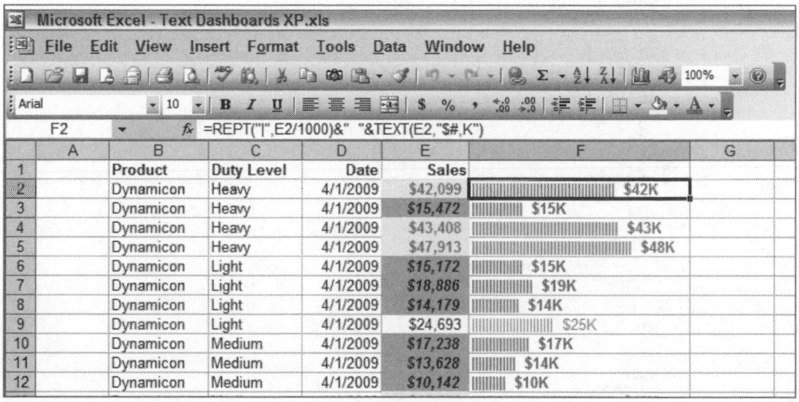

Figure 15.6: Combine the REPT function with a text bar chart, a concatenated value, and conditional formatting to create conditionally colored bar charts that show a value.

There are many "tricks" you can play to create more informative bars. For example, the formula,

```
=REPT("-",E2/1000)&"  "&"o"
```

creates a line the length of the scaled number and then ends with an o.

Another text chart that is useful for variances has two columns, the left for negative values and the right for positive values. The left column is formatted with right justification. The formula in cell F2 is

```
=IF(E2<0, REPT("|",E2/1000),"")
```

The right column is formatted with left justification, and the formula in G2 is

```
=IF(E2>0, REPT("|",E2/1000),"")
```

By formatting the left column with a red font and the right with a green font and then copying these formulas down columns F and G you can make positive and negative variances stand out.

Creating Data Bars with Excel 2007

Excel 2007 includes data bars, a conditional display that seems to replicate the function of the in-cell bar charts just described. As you can see in Figure 15.7, the new data bars are pretty with their subtle colors and gradient shading; however, they are not very effective for visualizing data. They are not distinct and precise enough to give a good representation of data.

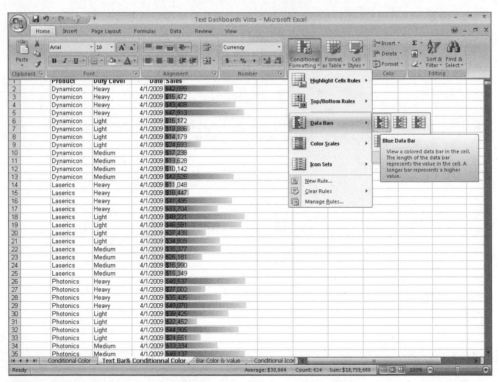

Figure 15.7: Data bars are visually attractive but are neither distinct enough nor precise enough for good data visualization.

CAUTION Excel 2007 data bars are not backward compatible. If you want a backward compatible "data bar," use the conditional text charts described in the previous section. You can combine conditional text charts with conditional formatting so the in-cell chart appears with special color formats and fonts.

To create data bars,

1. Select the cells that will have a conditional format

2. On the Home tab, in the Styles group, select Conditional Formatting to display a list

3. Roll the mouse over the Select Data Bars

4. Select the Blue Data Bars icon

Excel immediately inserts data bars with a blue gradient. Each bar's width is proportional to the value in the adjacent cell.

Alerting with Conditional Text Icons

Text icons help draw attention to specific conditions. They are very helpful in augmenting colors for color-blind readers and indicating trends within the small area of one cell.

You can create conditional text icons both in Excel 2007 and in earlier versions of Excel. To create conditional text icons in earlier versions of Excel, use text symbols. When created as shown in figure 15.8 they work with any version of Excel.

Excel 2007 has additional capabilities for conditional icons and has many unique icons. However, Excel 2007 conditional icons are not backward-compatible, so they cannot be used with older versions.

Creating Conditional Icons with Earlier Versions of Excel

With Excel versions prior to Excel 2007, you can create conditional icons that appear in a space as narrow as one character. You can combine these conditional icons with conditional formatting to create icons and color schemes that identify complex conditions and alerts. Figure 15.8 shows a magnified view of two miniature charts in the Learning and Growth section of a Balanced Scorecard created in Excel 2003. The Sparkline trend chart created with the techniques outlined in Chapter 19, "Creating Miniature Charts and Tables," shows the trend, while a conditional icon and conditional formatting enable the executive to see at a glance whether that metric is yellow or red. The arrowhead icon reinforces the color by showing whether the alert status is poor or marginal.

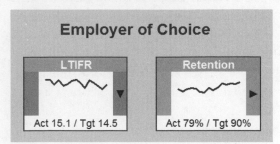

Figure 15.8: These conditional arrowheads in a magnified view of an Excel 2003 Balanced Scorecard change colors and directions depending upon alert conditions.

Conditional text icons are just text symbols that display depending upon the conditions in a conditional statement such as IF or CHOOSE. The symbols you can choose from are the symbols you see when you choose Insert, Symbol and scroll through symbols in the Symbol dialog box of Excel versions prior to 2007 shown in Figure 15.9.

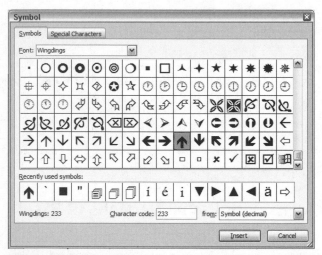

Figure 15.9: Select the symbol you want as an icon from the Symbol dialog box.

To select an icon, select a font from the Font list, then scroll through until you see the symbol you want. Click on it and note the font name, the character code, and the decimal ASCII code. The Wingding fonts have many symbols that are available on printers. For example, if the cell is formatted with the Wingding font, then CHAR(233) creates an upward-pointing arrow.

Note: Which Symbol? Which Font?

The symbol you select must be from a font set that you know your scorecard or dashboard users have. If they do not have the font set, then the symbol will show on their displays as a different symbol than what you want. You are usually safe if you use a character or symbol from Arial, Times New Roman, Wingdings, Wingdings 2, or Wingdings 3.

You must format the cell containing the CHAR function with the same font you saw in the Symbol dialog box, for example Wingding. If you don't, you will see the character with that decimal ASCII code from a different font set.

Figure 15.10 shows the example we have used previously; however, a column has been inserted at column F and the formula in cell F2,

```
=IF(E2>=PERCENTILE($E$2:$E$625,0.75),
    CHAR(236),IF(E2<=
    PERCENTILE($E$2:$E$625,0.25),CHAR(238),""))
```

has been copied down. If E2 is in the 75th percentile of the column, an arrow, CHAR(236), pointing up at a 45-degree angle displays. If E2 is in the 25th percentile of the column, an arrow, CHAR(238), pointing down at a 45-degree angle displays. If E2 is in between, nothing displays. In this example, the arrows do not point directly up or down because perfectly vertical arrows are too difficult to tell apart.

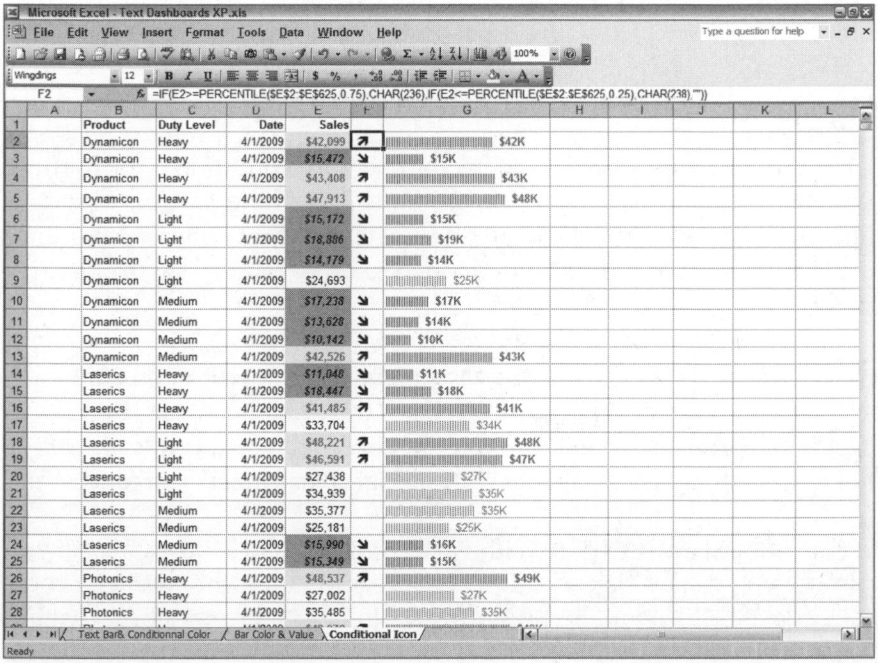

Figure 15.10: Conditional icons can be used in any version of Excel to help readers identify trends or alert limits.

The Wingdings fonts have many useful symbols. The ASCII codes from 219 to 248 in the first Wingdings font set are all arrows. Some examples are shown in Table 15.1.

Table 15.1 Sample Wingdings Symbols with Corresponding ASCII Codes

WINGDINGS	ASCII
←	231
→	232
↑	233
↓	234
↖	235
↗	236
↙	237
↘	238

TIP In printed reports or on Balanced Scorecard home pages, you can indicate trends by showing conditional arrows. Use a conditional IF or CHOOSE function with the SLOPE function to display one of five different arrows, depending on the value and sign returned by SLOPE.

Creating Conditional Icons with Excel 2007

Excel 2007 presents a wide choice of icons for use with conditional formatting. The Excel 2007 conditional icons appear in the cell with the data being examined. Figure 15.11 shows red, yellow, and green arrows that appear depending on the value in column F. Conditional icons are an excellent way to identify trends or data that have exceeded alert limits.

CAUTION If you want to ensure the conditional icons in your dashboard or report work with earlier versions of Excel, use the conditional text icons described in the previous section. You can combine conditional text icons with conditional formatting so they appear with special color formats and fonts.

To add conditional icons to data with Excel 2007,

1. Select the cells that will have a conditional format.
2. On the Home tab, in the Styles group, select Conditional Formatting, Icon Sets, More Rules.
3. In the New Formatting Rule dialog box, shown in Figure 15.12, select Format All Cells Based on Their Values.

4. Select Icons as the Format Style.

5. Select 3 Arrows Colored as the Icon Style.

6. Specify the icons as follows:

   Up arrow for >= 75%.

   Sideways arrow for >=25%.

   The down arrow will default to values less than 25 %.

7. Choose OK.

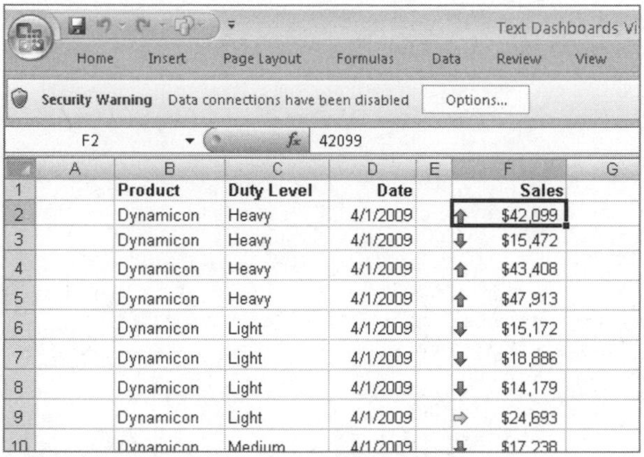

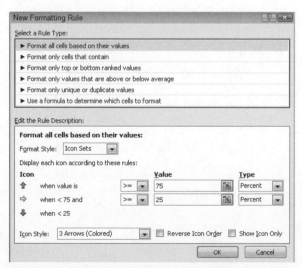

Figure 15.11: Conditional icons identify alerts or conditional levels with a set of variable icons.

Figure 15.12: Excel 2007 presents a wide choice of icons and many types of rules for their display.

Summary

Text charts and conditional formatting are powerful additions that make dense reports more informative. When well used, they can show more information in a smaller area than any other format. If you use conditional formatting to focus a user's attention, also consider using a text icon to assist color-blind users or to give additional information such as trends. Don't forget to look at Chapter 19, "Creating Miniature Charts and Tables," and Chapter 26, "Using Excel Add-Ins for Extra Capabilities," for more information about and examples of using small or in-cell graphics.

Custom Labels and Formatting

To conquer the enemy without resorting to war is the most desirable. The highest form of generalship is to conquer the enemy by strategy.

Sun Tzu, *The Art of War*

Balanced Scorecards and dashboards always seem to need custom titles, custom dates, custom formatting, and custom data labels. These needs usually can be addressed with a few special techniques.

The need for custom date formats often appears when you need a label with a specific format, or you need a database query constructed a certain way. Organizations also often need calculated dates for the beginning or end of a financial quarter or the beginning or ending day of a workweek.

Most organizations have a unique "corporate identity." The corporate identity includes the font, color palette, layout, and logo used on the organization's web site, letterhead, and forms. If you want your executives and managers to identify your scorecard as one of their own, then use your organization's color palette, layout, and logo. Using your organization's "official" colors adds credibility and a feel of professionalism to the Balanced Scorecard and dashboard you produce.

Knowing how to combine text, numbers, and dates will give you the ability to create dynamic custom titles for your scorecards, dashboards, and reports. You won't be limited by the automatic chart titles created by Excel. You will be able to combine calculated text, numbers, and dates for any title you need.

Combining Numbers, Text, and Dates to Create Custom Labels

Some labels and titles need a combination of numbers, text, and dates. These titles often need to recalculate as data change. This is easy to do with two functions, the &, or concatenation function, and the TEXT() function.

The & (ampersand) function joins text strings together. Text must be enclosed in double quotes, for example:

```
="Balanced "&"Scorecard"
```

Of course, the real power comes when you combine text with the result of a numeric or text formula. In that case, if the formula in cell C5 results in 542, then the formula:

```
="Number of Units Sold is "&$C$5
```

produces this result:

```
Number of Units Sold is 542
```

Concatenation and calculation give you the power to create dynamic titles. Fixed text in quotes can be joined with text, numbers, and dates generated by formulas. You get even more power when you use a conditional formula, such as an IF condition, or lookup data and titles from lists using VLOOKUP, HLOOKUP, or INDEX.

Joining Text and Custom-Formatted Numbers

Although a concatenation formula like those just described joins text and a date or number, it will probably not produce the formatted appearance you want. For example, consider that cell B4 contains the number 2,400. Cell B4 is formatted to show Currency formatting with no decimal values. A concatenation formula like this:

```
="The dollar value is "&$B$4&"."
```

will look like this in the display:

```
The dollar value is 2400.
```

The Currency formatting on the cell does not appear in the concatenation formula's result. To format numbers or dates when they are displayed as text, use the TEXT() function. The TEXT() function has this syntax:

```
=TEXT(value, format_text)
```

The *value* is the cell reference containing the number or date. The *format_text* is the same formatting syntax used to create custom numeric and date formats in the Format Cells dialog box. For example, if cell B4 contains 2,400 as in the previous example, we would want to use:

```
="The dollar value is "&TEXT($B$4,"$#,##0")&"."
```

to create a display that looks like this:

```
The dollar value is $2,400.
```

You can see examples of these custom formats usable in TEXT by choosing Format, Cells, selecting the Number tab, and then selecting Custom from the Category list.

In Excel 2007 on the Home tab, click the dialog box launcher, the small icon at the lower right in the Number group. In the Category box, click Custom. In the Type list, select a custom numeric format that is close to what you want and modify it.

Note: Use the TEXT Function to Fit Wide Numeric Results

When a calculated numeric result will not fit in the cell width because the column is not wide enough, the cell fills with ####. Work around this by using the TEXT function to format the result of the formula. The textual result that appears as a number will now display and flow outside the column width as long as the adjacent cell is empty.

Formatting numbers and dates for inclusion in titles or creating custom formats for use in your worksheets is easy; you just have to know a few rules. You can create a different format for the positive, negative, zero, and text-only portion of a numeric or date format. These custom formats have four parts. The syntax is as follows:

```
positive_format;negative_format;zero_format;text_format
```

To continue with the previous example, you could create a custom format for both positive and negative currency. It might look like this:

```
="The dollar value is "&TEXT($B$4,"$#,##0_);($#,##0)")
```

This produces a negative dollar value enclosed in parenthesis. The positive format ends with "_)" so that a space is left at the trailing end of positive numbers that is the same width as the trailing parenthesis behind negative numbers. This enables positive and negative numbers to align in columns.

Some of the symbols you can use for formatting numbers are shown below.

SYMBOL	RESULT
#	A placeholder. 0 is not displayed if a trailing digit is absent, so use a trailing 0 as in the example above. Fractions round up.
0	A placeholder. Displays a 0 when there is no number. Fractions round up.
,	Comma marks the place of the first thousands' separator.
.	Decimal marks the location of the decimal point.
_	Skip the width of the character following _. As the previous example shows, you can use this to allow space for the formatting difference between positive and negative numbers when the negative number is enclosed in parenthesis. Using the appropriate trailing space enables numbers to right align.

Joining Text with Custom Formatted Dates and Times

Dates and text can also be joined with concatenation. This is frequently done for titles or notations to show the date of the dashboard's data. A frequently used combination is:

```
="Data as of "&TEXT(NOW(),"mmm d, yyyy h:mm AM/PM")
```

A formula like this enables you to put a date/time stamp on a dashboard. When the dashboard is printed, you can see the date of the data. This reduces the arguments people may have when their data don't match the dashboard because they were acquired and published at different times. The result of the concatenation above produces this:

```
Data as of Mar 9, 2009 9:52 PM
```

Note: Always Show a Date/Time Stamp on Dashboards

Put a date/time stamp in a consistent location on dashboards to show the date and time of printing. This will prevent confusion when printouts of the same dashboard show different data.

You can create your own date and time formats within TEXT(). Look at the custom date formats in the Custom Category of the Cell Formats dialog box for examples. Some of the symbols you can use for formatting dates and times are shown below.

DATE/TIME	FORMAT CODE	DISPLAY EXAMPLE
Month	m mm mmm mmmm	9 09 Sep September
Day	d dd ddd dddd	8 08 Tue Tuesday
Year	y yy yyyy	9 09 2009
12-hour clock	H:mm AM/PM	7:45 PM
12-hour clock	H:mm:ss AM/PM	7:45:33 PM
24-hour clock	hh:mm	19:45
minutes:seconds	mm:ss	45:33

Time and Data Calculations

Although most Excel users are familiar with often-used time and date functions such as NOW(), TODAY(), DATE(), DAY(), HOUR(), MONTH(), and YEAR(), there are times you will want to do more. Usually, you need these additional time and date functions for an information label on a dashboard or for a limiter in an SQL query to the database feeding your worksheets with data. The following sections include a few date/time functions you may find useful.

CAUTION There are some helpful date conversion functions in the Analysis ToolPak. However, whenever possible, avoid using functions that are found only in Excel's Analysis ToolPak. Not all users of your scoreboards and dashboards will have the Analysis ToolPak installed.

The X-axis on charts and headings on tables usually requires a series of dates. For example, it might require the workdays of each week in a month, the first day of each month in a quarter, or the first days of each month in a year. By creating these date series with formulas, you can update them easily when you update data. Later in this book, you will learn how to use a calculated date series to create animated charts that show how data change over time.

Calculating the Beginning and End of Any Month

It's easy to calculate the beginning of a month since they all start with day 1. The formula for the first day of any month is:

```
=DATE(YEAR(ref),MONTH(ref),1)
```

If you assume a "seed" date for the first date in a series of months is in cell B5, then the next date for the series in the cell to the right is:

```
=DATE(YEAR(B5),MONTH(B5)+1,1)
```

Copying this formula to the right creates a series of months with the same day as the original. Excel automatically skips to the next year when appropriate.

To find the last date of any month, you need to know a little trick about Excel. The DATE function calculates the last day of a month as day 0 of the following month. For example, if the "seed" date is in cell B5, then the last day of the month prior to B5 is:

```
=DATE(YEAR(B5),MONTH(B5),0)
```

Creating a Month Series

The most common type of date series used in dashboards is a month series. Monthly financial data is most frequently viewed over a 12-month or 15-month span. Showing data over a 15-month span allows month-to-month comparisons and last-quarter comparisons against the prior year.

It is rare in dashboards to create a fixed monthly series. Instead, you want a date series that will update when the start or end date changes. To create a monthly series based on a single "seed" date in cell B5, follow these steps:

1. Enter a starting date in cell B5

2. Enter this formula in cell C5

    ```
    =DATE(YEAR(B5),MONTH(B5)+1,DAY(B5))
    ```

3. Copy this formula to the right to fill cells you want to contain sequential months

This formula works by calculating a new date from the year and day of the date in the cell to the left. The month that is used for the calculated date is one more than the month to the left. Each new copy across row 5 looks to the formula to its left and adds one month. When the calculated date gets to month 13, a new year is automatically started. By using this formula, it is easy to create a date series that updates when the "seed" date changes. If this date series is used to look up the data from a historical list of data, you can animate a data series so it scrolls through time. Chapter 18, "Working with Lists and Tables of Data," describes this.

Calculating the Beginning and End of a Quarter

Financial reports frequently report data in quarters. You may find that you have to summarize monthly data and report them in charts or tables using the appropriate quarterly headings. The upper portion of Figure 16.1 shows the formulas used to calculate and format a quarterly title given a date.

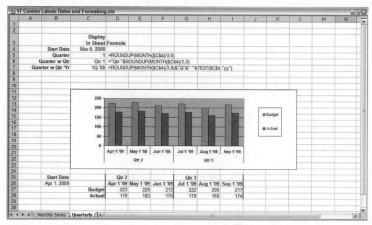

Figure 16.1: Use formulas to calculate quarterly titles as dates change.

You can calculate the financial quarter for a date entered in cell C4 using the following formula:

```
=ROUNDUP(MONTH($C$4)/3,0)
```

To display a more finished expression like "Qtr 1" as shown in cell C6, use a concatenation formula:

```
="Qtr "&ROUNDUP(MONTH($C$4)/3,0)
```

A longer concatenation formula such as the one in C7 produces "1Q '09." Note in this formula that there is an apostrophe within the set of double quotes that creates the apostrophe for the year abbreviation:

```
=ROUNDUP(MONTH($C$4)/3,0)&"Q"&" '"&TEXT($C$4,"yy")
```

Automatically Updating Quarterly Titles on the Category (X) Axis

The lower portion of Figure 16.1 shows how these calculated quarterly titles can be used effectively in a dashboard chart. Although this example is simple and uses a manually entered start date to update the quarterly titles, you may want to use a menu selection to update the dates and titles displayed. This will enable you to create charts that will automatically reformat and retitle with data retrieved from a database.

In Figure 16.1, you will see a starting date has been entered in cell B26. This date must be in the first month of any quarter. Cells D26 to I26 contain a calculated series of months that begin with the start date. The formula in cell D25 is

```
="Qtr "&ROUNDUP(MONTH($F$26)/3,0)
```

This formula examines the third date from the start in F26 and calculates the quarter. The quarterly text formula in G25 examines the last date in I26. As long as the starting date is the first month in a quarter, the text quarter labels will update automatically.

The chart uses a dual row of Category (X) axis titles. The chart was created using the Chart Wizard and selecting C25:I28. Selecting contiguous rows for the Category (X) Axis will create dual or triple-row Category (X) Axis titles.

Scaling Numbers with Formatting

Financial and production data are usually large numbers. You will probably want to adjust the appearance of these large numbers for two reasons. First, executives and managers who are monitoring Balanced Scorecards and management dashboards should be concerned with the big picture, not minute details. If financial results are in the millions, they shouldn't be looking at numbers with hundreds or thousands. Second, without scaling, the numbers might not fit in the cells or chart.

An obvious way to scale data is to divide it by a scaling factor. For example, if you are working with numbers in the hundreds of thousands, you can divide by 1,000 and use ROUND() to round to the precision you want.

A better way to handle this is to leave the original data intact and use custom formatting to scale the data. You can use custom formatting to scale numeric displays for display in cells and charts. Figure 16.2 shows the use of custom formatting in cells to change the display. A comma is used after the 0 (zero) to indicate the hundreds or thousands separator in the custom format.

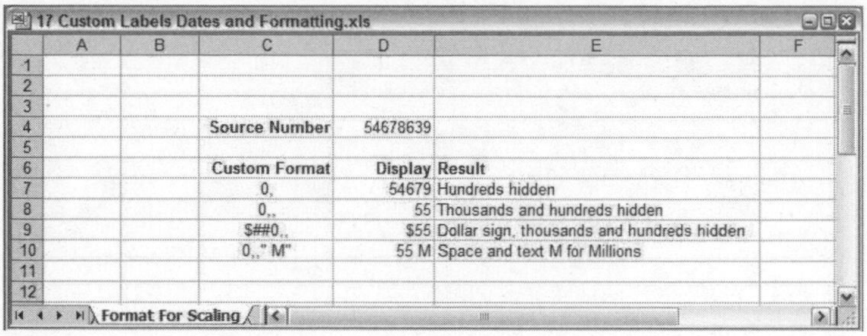

Figure 16.2: Use custom formatting on numbers to retain precision, but change the display in tables and charts.

A text character can be included in custom formats to indicate millions (M) or thousands (K). For example, in the Number tab of the Format Cells dialog box, select the Custom category and enter a format like this:

```
$##0,," M"
```

This formats the number 57897463 as

```
$58 M
```

Creating a chart from custom-formatted data produces a chart that shows the data with the custom format.

Scaling Charts and Sheets Separately

You can keep high precision in the data on your sheet while charting with scaled data. Excel 2000 and later enable you to do this by formatting the chart's Y-axis scale.

To format the Y-axis scale so it shows shortened values:

1. Double-click the Y-axis to display the Format Axis dialog box shown in Figure 16.3. Select the Scale tab.

2. Select the scaling factor you want to use from the Display Units list. For example, select Millions if you want to round displayed values to millions.

3. Select the Show display units on chart check box if you want the scaling factor, Millions, Thousands, and so on to appear at the top left of the Y-axis.

4. Choose OK.

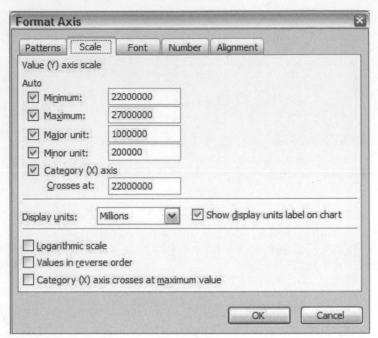

Figure 16.3: Use the Format Axis dialog box to scale Y-axis values and display a units label showing the scaling factor.

Creating Custom Titles and Floating Text

Excel has arguably the best chart generation engine available. But just because you can create very complex charts with fancy formatting, colors, textures, and patterns doesn't mean you should.

Your purpose should be to create Balanced Scorecards and dashboards that communicate information and allow clear decision-making. The addition of nonessential colors, patterns, and text may make your charts look prettier, but the extra "noise" is distracting and can lead to misinformed decisions. I hope some of the following tips will help you communicate more clearly with your charts and keep embellishments to a minimum.

Keep it clean and simple.

Creating Dynamic Chart Titles

When you first create an Excel chart, the main title, X-axis, and Y-axis titles are static. However, it is easy to link any of these titles to cell contents. If the cell contains a formula that calculates a title, like those shown earlier in this chapter, then the titles will update when the cell content recalculates. This is useful for displaying dates or product information in a title.

To create chart titles that display cell contents:

1. Create your calculated title in a cell. For example, a formula for a main title or X-axis title might look like:

```
="Sales Ending "&TEXT($D$6,"mmm d, yyyy")
```

If cell D6 contains the formula =NOW() that calculates the current date and time, then the text for the subtitle will look like this:

```
Chart data as of Mar 30, 2009
```

2. Create the chart.

3. Click the main title, Value (Y) Axis label, or Category (X) Axis label you want linked to the cell.

4. Type an equal sign (=) in the formula bar, then select the cell containing the calculated title. You can also type the cell reference if you include the worksheet tab's name within single quotes followed by an exclamation mark. For example:

```
='Joining Text, Dates and Numbers'!$D$8
```

5. Press Enter.

If the chart does not have a title for you to select, then select the chart and choose Chart ➪ Chart Options; then select the Titles tab and type a title in the Chart title entry box.

Note: Create Two-Line Titles

Create static subtitles with two lines by typing the title and subtitle as one long title in the Chart title entry box of the Chart Options dialog box. Close the Chart Options dialog box. In the chart, click the title to select it, then move the insertion point to where you want the line break and press Shift+Enter. The title and subtitle will break into two lines. Select and format each line separately with size, color, and attributes.

Creating Floating Titles in Charts

Excel charts automatically create a main title, Value (Y) axis label, and Category (X) axis labels. What you will frequently find is that you will want to add a subtitle or a comment in the chart for additional information. These "floating titles" can be dragged anywhere on the chart. You can link these floating titles to cell contents so they display a calculated title like the concatenated text described earlier in this chapter.

To create a floating title in versions prior to Excel 2007:

1. Enter a formula or text in a cell

2. Click on a clear area of the chart

3. Type = in the formula bar

4. Click on a cell or type the cell reference and press Enter

A floating text box will contain the cell's results. You can drag this text box anywhere on the chart, including over other chart elements. Format the floating text box by double-clicking it and selecting from the Format Text Box dialog box. You can format the font, alignment, colors, lines, size, protection, properties, and margins.

If you want line breaks and paragraphs of text to appear in your floating text box, use Alt+Enter to create line breaks in the cell containing the text box contents or format the cell contents with the Alignment tab to allow word wrap.

Floating text boxes that do not have borders can be difficult to select. Don't click directly on the text. Click where you think the border of the floating text box is.

Creating Dynamic Titles That Float in Worksheets

You can create floating text or titles in worksheets that reflect the results of calculations. Floating titles in a worksheet enable you to create titles that are larger than cell size allows or to show text boxes that contain comments without distorting the size and position of nearby cells.

To create floating text on a worksheet:

1. Enter the text or formula in a cell on the worksheet.

2. Display the Drawing toolbar if it is not displayed by choosing View, Toolbars, and selecting Drawing. In Excel 2007 on the Insert tab, select the Shapes group.

3. Select a shape from the toolbar or Shapes group to contain the floating text. An AutoShape, text box, rectangle, or circle will work.

4. With the shape selected, type an = in the formula bar and click on the cell containing the text or formula you want displayed.

5. Press Enter.

You may want the text in the floating shape to have a different orientation, for example, a Category (Y) axis title and subtitle. To change the orientation of the text in the shape, select the shape, right-click on its edge, and choose Format AutoShape. Select the Alignment tab in the Format AutoShape dialog box, and then select the text orientation from the Orientation box.

In most cases, you will want the text in your shape to be in the center of the shape. To format the shape so the text is where you want it, select the shape, right-click on its edge, and choose Format AutoShape. Select the Alignment tab and then select the text positioning from the Horizontal and Vertical alignment lists.

Rotating Text, Shapes, and Charts in Any Direction

The text inside shapes you draw can be formatted, aligned, and positioned, but it can't be rotated in all directions. However, as with many things in Excel, there is a trick that will get you past this.

Create the shape you want and link the text with a formula as described previously. Notice that if you select the shape and drag the green selection handle, you can rotate the shape, but the text does not rotate.

To rotate the text to any position, you will need to use Excel's Camera tool to create a picture of the shape, and then rotate that picture and text. Shapes with links to text appear at the top of Figure 16.4. In the lower half of Figure 16.4 are rotated camera pictures of these same shapes. The text inside the AutoShape rotates to any angle with the camera picture.

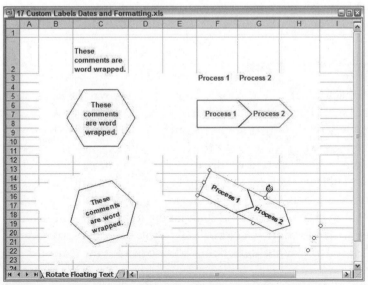

Figure 16.4: Rotate shapes and the text in them by using the Camera tool.

To create text, shapes, and charts that can be rotated in any direction, take a picture of the shape and then rotate the picture following these steps:

1. Create the text, shape, or chart.

2. Remove the cell edges by selecting all cells in the background and choosing Format ➪ Cells.

3. Select the Patterns tab and select the background you want. In most cases, this will be white. Choose OK.

4. Select the cells containing the text, shape, or chart you want to rotate.

5. Hold down Shift as you choose Edit ➪ Copy Picture. The Copy Picture and Paste Picture commands only display in the Edit menu when you hold Shift.

6. From the Copy Picture dialog box that appears, select Appearance as Shown on Screen and Format Picture, then click OK.

7. Move in the workbook to where you want the picture. This can even be in another worksheet or over a chart.

8. Hold down Shift as you choose Edit ➪ Paste Picture.

This picture is linked to the original area. The picture will also change, when the original text, shape, or chart changes. You can resize this picture of text, shape, or chart while maintaining proportions by dragging one corner.

Rotate the picture of text, shape, or chart to any angle by selecting the picture and then dragging the green handle.

Creating Custom Data Labels

Data labels are labels that appear adjacent to a data point as shown in Figure 16.5. When you create an Excel chart using the Chart Wizard, you have the choice of displaying data labels in the third step of the Chart Wizard as shown in Figure 16.5. You have the choice of showing the Series Name, Category Name, and Value for each data point. If you have already created a chart, double-click an element in the chart series, such as a column. From the Format Data Series dialog box, select the data labels tab.

In Excel 2007 select the chart area to add data labels to all charts or select a single chart element. With the chart selected, the Chart tools menu appears. In the Layout group, select data labels and choose the position you want for the data label.

Data labels may not show the content you want or they may be positioned so they cover chart elements. When there are lots of data, you may not want all data to show, or you may only want to show data labels for those points that are of special interest.

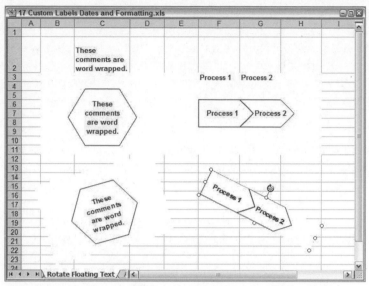

Figure 16.5: In Step 3 of the Chart Wizard, you can select the data label that will appear next to each data point.

To select an individual data label, click on any data label to select all of them. When you see the entire series of labels selected, click once more on the individual data label you want.

If an automatically created or custom data label does not appear where you want, you can select one and drag it to a new position. It will maintain this position as the data point moves on the chart.

If you want to create custom data labels, start by entering into the worksheet the text or numbers you want as labels. Select a data label. Type = in the formula bar, then click the cell containing the custom content and press Enter. If you want to create a custom label for each data point, you will need to link each data point individually.

Data points can clutter a chart. Instead of displaying data points, an alternative is to use a data table below a chart. Chapter 19, "Creating Miniature Charts and Tables," describes how to create custom data tables that are easy to position and format.

Creating Pop-Up and Alert Data Labels

A great way to use data labels is as alerts that appear only over data points of special interest. You can specify alert limits so that if a data value is outside a specific range or criteria, that individual data label appears.

Using the same techniques as above, you can create data labels that display or hide depending on whether a check box is selected. This enables executives or managers to turn the labels on or off, removing them when they aren't needed.

The Variance chart in Figure 16.6 shows data labels that only appear when the budget variance is outside 10 percent. The appearance of a data label acts as an alert to help identify a data point that exceeds limits. The formula in cell C9 of the Alert data label row is:

```
=IF(ABS(C8)>0.1,C8,"")
```

This formula displays the variance in cell C8 if the positive or negative variance is greater than 10 percent. Copying this across row 9 creates formulas that only show the variance percentages when they are outside the 10 percent alert limit.

Each data label in the chart is then linked to its corresponding cell in row 9. The data labels have all been selected and formatted with no background pattern and a red font.

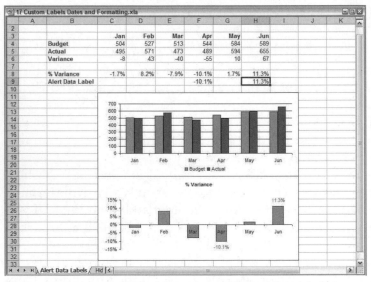

Figure 16.6: Use conditional formulas and linked data labels to create labels that appear as alerts when a limit has been exceeded.

Figure 16.7 shows how you can use a check box control to turn data labels on and off. The check box control puts TRUE or FALSE into cell B10 depending on whether it is selected or not. The formula in cell C10 then checks this TRUE/FALSE status to see whether data values should appear. The formula has been copied across row 10 to show or display all data values. The formula in cell C10 is:

```
=IF($B$10,C6,"")
```

If you now link each individual data label to its appropriate cell content in row 10, the data labels will only appear when the check box is selected. Chapter 20, "Controlling Dashboards with Menus, Combo Boxes, and Buttons," describes how to use check boxes in more detail.

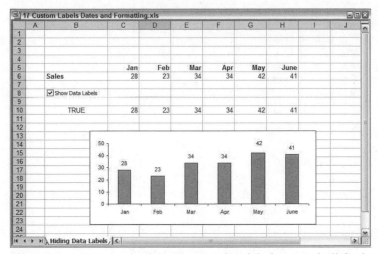

Figure 16.7: Using a check box to turn data labels on and off displays a cleaner chart until more detail is needed.

Creating New Color Palettes

Most people are used to seeing the stark colors in Excel's default palette. Excel's color palette of 56 colors contains 40 standard colors, 8 chart fill colors, and 8 chart line colors.

The ability to place any color in your palette lets you create a much more professional appearance than is normally seen in Excel worksheets. Customizing Excel's color palette to match your organization's branding will make your Balanced Scorecard or dashboard seem more professional and give it a sense of integrity. Being able to select your own palette also enables you to make the information in your dashboards more understandable. I frequently find that I need different alert colors than what are available, and that I need more muted shades of tan, cream, or yellow as backgrounds for text, titles, and notes.

Creating a Custom Color Palette in Excel

To create a custom color palette in Excel versions prior to Excel 2007:

1. Open the Excel workbook you want to contain the custom palette.

2. Choose Tools, Options to display the Options dialog box with Standard color palette as shown in Figure 16.8.

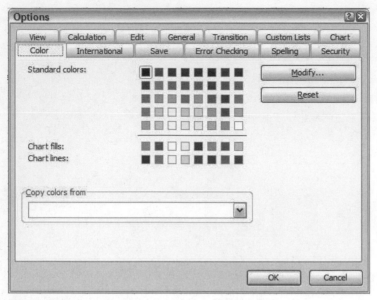

Figure 16.8: Use the Color tab in the Options dialog box to create your custom color palette.

3. Choose the Color tab.

4. Select the color you want to change; then choose the Modify button.

5. To change your selected color to a Standard color, select the Standard tab and click on a color.

   Or,

   To modify the existing color or create a new color, select the Custom tab and modify the existing color or create a new color.

6. Choose OK.

7. Modify another color or choose OK if you are finished.

To reset colors to the original palette of Standard colors, click the Reset button in the Options dialog box.

Excel 2007 uses a different system for controlling available color selections. You can select a color for a cell that is independent of other colors, or you can select colors from a color theme. You can use the color themes built into Excel 2007 or create your own color theme. When you modify a color in a color theme, that color will change throughout the workbook wherever it has been used.

To create your own color theme:

1. On the ribbon, choose Page Layout and then in the Themes group select Colors.

2. If you want to use a different color theme, you can select one of these themes displayed. If you want to create a new color theme, choose Create New Theme Colors. This opens the Create New Theme Colors dialog box.

3. Select the color in the theme you want to change. A Theme Colors dialog box will open, enabling you to select from predefined colors for that theme, or you can select More Colors and define your own color.

4. Enter a Name for your theme in the Create New Theme Colors dialog box and choose OK.

Matching Your Dashboard to the Corporate Identity

Most organizations, especially large corporations, have well-defined "corporate identities." The corporate identity consists of a corporation's colors, fonts, logo, signature, signage, and all those elements that visually represent the corporation's brand. As you begin developing your Balanced Scorecard or dashboard, check with the marketing department and get a copy of their corporate identity package. It should contain the colors as RGB values, fonts, allowed spelling of business entities and products, usage of the copyright (©), trademark (™) and registered trademark (®) symbols, as well as files of logo images.

Transferring Color Palettes between Workbooks

If you have a color palette you want to use in a different workbook, you can transfer the palette between workbooks. To transfer palettes between Excel workbooks in Excel XP or Excel 2003:

1. Open both workbooks

2. Activate the workbook in which you want the new palette

3. Choose Tools ⇨ Options and select the Color tab

4. From the Copy colors from list, select the workbook containing the palette you want to transfer

5. Choose OK

Note: Create a Template for Frequently Used Color Palettes

If you will frequently use the same color palette, create a workbook with the palette you want, and then save it as a template. When you open that template, the new workbook will include your custom palette.

Creating Aesthetically Pleasing Color Palettes

For those of us who are color impaired and couldn't create an aesthetically pleasing color palette if our jobs depended on it—which they might—there are excellent ways to "grab" well-coordinated color palettes. There are also tools that will help you to select colors from web sites or images.

Selecting Predesigned Color Palettes

Thank heavens artists are willing to share their color aesthetics. There are numerous web sites where artists have posted, for free, thousands of color palette combinations of every imaginable type and energy level. Three of these web sites are listed here.

The web site Kuler, at `kuler.adobe.com`, has beautiful color palettes to select from, tools to create new palettes that are automatically color coordinated, and a tool that enables you to capture the color palette from an image that you upload.

Figure 16.9 shows Kuler's Create tool being used with a Custom rule. Dragging the spokes of the color wheel at the top of the screen creates color combinations in the color swatches below. Color RGB codes are listed below each swatch.

On the Kuler web site, you can use rules that recommend a palette when given a main color. The rules are summarized below.

Analogous	Matches colors with adjacent hues
Monochromatic	Has one color with varied intensity
Triad	Shows colors spaced around the wheel for a contrasting palette
Complementary	Uses two opposite colors and their hues
Compound	Uses interesting color combinations
Shade	Shows variations on the base color
Custom	Lets you drag the color spokes to any position

In addition to creating your own palettes in Kuler, you can select Create ⇨ From an Image, then upload an image and create a palette from the colors in the image. To see collections of palettes that have been shared by a community of color-adepts, select Themes. Figure 16.10 shows a few of the most popular themes. You can also view different color themes, or palettes, by selecting Themes, then Newest, Most Popular, Highest Rated, or Random; you can also use the Search box to search for key words.

Two other web sites can help you with your color palettes. Colorcombos.com is, of course, located at `www.colorcombos.com`. The ComboLibrary tab will display hundreds of color palettes. The color codes for these colors are in hexadecimal HTML codes, but you can use ColorPic described later in this chapter to pickup the RGB colors for use in Excel.

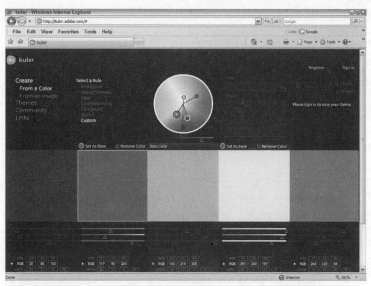

Figure 16.9: Kuler enables you to create color palettes that are coordinated by different rules such as Complementary or Monochromatic.

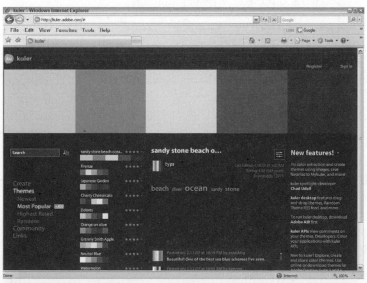

Figure 16.10: You can search for or select from lists of predesigned palettes in Kuler.

Colorcombos.com has another useful feature. As Figure 16.11 shows, it will capture the color palette used on a web site's home page and even generate its complementary colors. To do this, select the ComboLibrary tab, type the web site's home page URL in the Grab Website Colors box at the top right, and click

GET. The ComboTester tab enables you to see different variants of the home page palette. Figure 16.11 shows the results of capturing the palette on my home page, www.torconsulting.com.

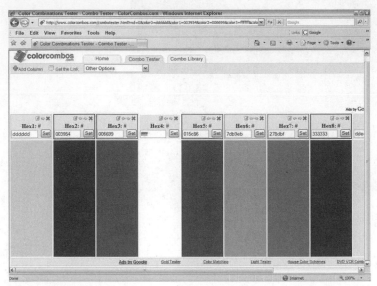

Figure 16.11: Colorcombos.com has captured the palette from my home page at www.torconsulting.com.

The web site COLOURlovers has thousands of color palettes available for free. COLOURLovers is located at www.colourlovers.com. Use ColorPic, described later in this chapter, to select RGB colors from the screen.

Capturing Colors from Onscreen

ColorPic is a time-saving, free tool from Iconico, located at www.iconico.com. With it, you can read the color code from any portion of the screen. Figure 16.12 shows ColorPic displaying the color code of the dark blue next to the word "Action" on the Tor Consulting web site. Use the RGB (Red, Green, Blue) code or the Hue, Saturation, Value code to enter the color on the Custom tab of Excel's Colors dialog box. ColorPic enables you to store the color codes you capture and group them as palettes.

Figure 16.12: ColorPic gives you the ability to select colors from anywhere onscreen and see their RGB codes.

Summary

Although the topic of this chapter isn't about the decision-making part of a dashboard, the custom labels, dates, and color formatting make a significant difference in how pleasing your dashboard is and whether it ties in with the corporate portal and culture. Custom labels can make your dashboard titles update automatically to reflect the data. Custom dates and numbers can help you format dates and numbers to match the format expected by your organization. They can also help you fit data in when there isn't enough space for a long format. Of course, custom colors or themes are important for creating a look and feel that matches your organization's identity.

CHAPTER 17

Working with Data That Changes Size

*What business strategy is all about; what distinguishes it from
all other kinds of business planning—is, in a word, competitive advantage.
Without competitors there would be no need for strategy, for the
sole purpose of strategic planning is to enable the company to gain,
as effectively as possible, a sustainable edge over its competitors.*

Kenichi Ohnae
"One of the top five management gurus in the word"—*The Economist*

A useful skill when creating Balanced Scorecards and dashboards is being able to handle data that changes size or location. This is useful if you want to import new data and the size of the data source changes, and it is also useful with charts. For example, you might have one chart, but you might want to allow the user to choose between four different data sources. In another situation, you may have one chart and want it to use different starting dates or different periods of time.

The ability to work with data that changes size or shape also comes in handy with source data that changes size or shape. You will find this useful whether your dashboards work from manually entered data or from data retrieved through a dynamic link to a database.

This chapter begins by describing how to use range names. Range names are a very useful Excel feature that every intermediate to advanced user should be familiar with. They are a foundation for solving the problems of varying data size and shape.

Naming Ranges for Ease of Use and Functionality

Range names are English-language names used in place of range references such as B5:G26. Range names can be used in formulas and in a chart's data series just as cell references but are much more readable than cell references. For example, using the word Revenue as a reference in a formula is easier to understand than using $B$5:$I$20.

Range names also make it easier to navigate in a worksheet. You can go to a name by choosing Edit, Go To or by pressing Ctrl+G or F5 and then choosing a name from the Go To dialog box. Excel will move to that named range and select it. When you insert or delete rows or columns through a range name's reference, the range name expands or contracts like a normal cell reference.

Range names should explain what they are referencing, as Revenue does. This helps you when you return to a worksheet you haven't seen in a long time, makes it easy for others to understand your worksheet, makes diagnostics easier, and, as you will soon discover, can be used to name powerful formulas.

Creating Named Ranges

To manually create a named range:

1. Select the cell or range of cells you want to name. You even can select non-adjacent cells or ranges by holding Ctrl as you make your selection.

2. Type the range name inside the Name box. The Name box is to the left of the formula bar and normally shows the currently active cell.

3. Press Enter.

Instead of typing a range name in the Name box, you also can select the cell or range and then choose Insert ⇨ Name ⇨ Define and type a name in the Names in Workbook box. Click Add to add the name. The Define Name dialog box can also be used to view and edit names and their references.

TIP In Excel 2007, right-click a cell and choose Name a Range. In the Name box, type the range name. Select the Scope. In the Refers To box, enter the formula. Click OK.

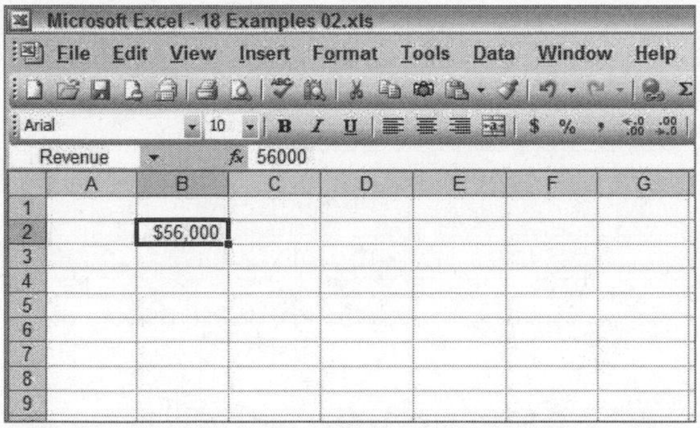

Figure 17.1: Type a name for a new named range in the Name box to the left of the formula bar.

Some conventions for naming your named ranges are:

- Type names without spaces.

- Never use a hyphen (-) to separate words in a name. You or Excel may misinterpret this as a minus sign in a formula. If you want to separate words, use an underscore (_).

- Use a leading capital letter at the beginning of each word in a name, for example, RevenueNewProduct. This will help you prevent errors. Get in the habit of always typing range names in lowercase in formulas. When you press Enter, they will convert to leading caps if Excel recognizes them as a valid range name. If they do not automatically convert, you have mistyped or the name has not been created.

- If there are a lot of names in a workbook, they will be easier to find if you use the military naming convention of putting the category first, such as RevenueNewProduct instead of NewProductRevenue.

- Names for special types of ranges are easier to understand if you use a prefix convention. You can make up your own prefixes—just be consistent. Table 17.1 shows a few examples of prefixes you could use.

- Never use names that look like cell references, such as D250.

- If you use a name that has not been defined, Excel returns the value #NAME?

Table 17.1 Sample Prefixes for Range Names

TYPE OF RANGE	PREFIX	EXAMPLE
Forms lists (drop-down boxes, etc.)	fl	flStates
Database	db	dbMfgrProduction
Report	rpt	rptDailyQuality
Chart Range	ch	chBudgetVariance

TIP In large systems, you may have many range names, and the spelling can be hard to remember. Rather than typing range names, you can paste range names into formulas by moving the insertion point in the formula to where you need the range name, then pressing F5 to display the Go To dialog box with the list of names. Double-click the name you want to paste it in. This saves you from possible typing errors and is definitely superior to trying to remember what may be hundreds of names in one workbook.

If you know in advance that you will be using names for cells adjacent to lists of labels, you can create multiple range names at one time. To create range names from labels on the worksheet:

1. Select the cells containing the labels and adjacent cell or range to be named with the label. Figure 17.2 shows multiple cells selected and about to be named.

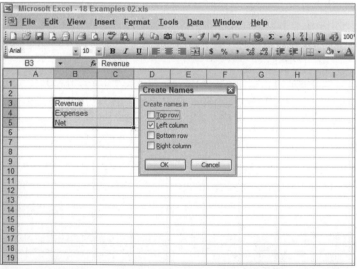

Figure 17.2: Name multiple cells from adjacent labels using the Create Names dialog box.

2. Select Insert ⇨ Name ⇨ Create.

3. Select the check box or boxes that describes where the labels are that can be used as names. Name rows and columns at the same time by simultaneously selecting row and column check boxes.

4. Choose OK.

WORKING WITH GLOBAL AND LOCAL NAMES

There are two different types of range names: global and local. To learn more about creating and managing range names and working with local and global names, names that apply across multiple sheets, and names that apply to a specific sheet, please refer to a book on the fundamentals of Excel such as the *Excel 2003 Bible*, by John Walkenbach (Wiley, 2003). If you are using Excel 2007, you can look at *Excel 2007 Bible*, also by John Walkenbach (Wiley, 2007).

TIP Even with the use of range names, the logic behind some formulas can be very obscure. It is a good idea to document complex formulas. In addition to using the Insert ⇨ Comment command to add documentation on a cell, you can add a comment directly to the formula in a cell. To do this, use the N function:

```
=CHOOSE($F$3,rptQuality,rptProduction)+N("Option button value, F3,
selects the report range")
```

   The N function returns 0 for text, so you must enclose your comment in quotes.

Creating Dynamic Range Names That Automatically Adjust When the Size of Data Changes

Although range names are great for reducing errors and making formulas easier to decipher, their real power comes when they are used to name formulas. Named formulas recalculate just like formulas in cells do. You can use them within other formulas or within chart series as you would use a reference or result.

   The Figure 17.3 shows cell B5, containing the simple SUM formula

```
=SUM(RevenueData)
```

where RevenueData is the range name for C5:H5. Although the range name makes this formula more readable, it doesn't help you if you want to add up the data in cell I5 and automatically add the total into the SUM.

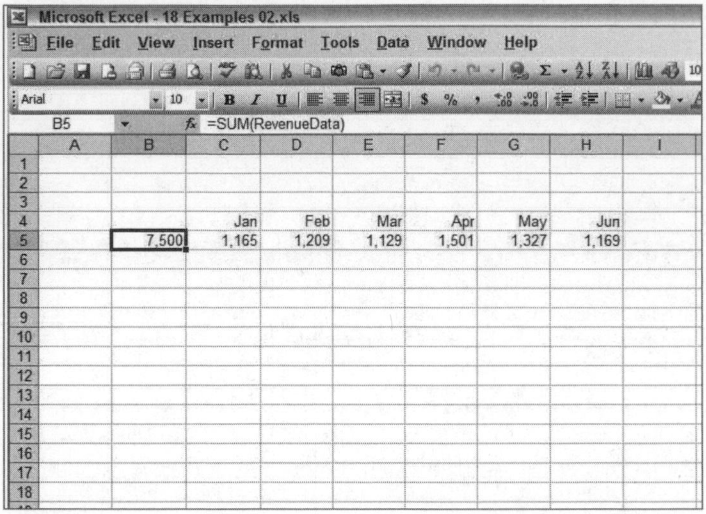

Figure 17.3: A simple SUM formula totaling the range named Revenue.

The following section will show you how to make a dynamic range name that expands or contracts so that it continues to function as data is added or deleted. The principle used in this simple example will be used next to create a dynamic range for chart data.

The OFFSET function can be used to calculate a range that changes shape. The OFFSET function returns a reference, cell, or range based on a single reference cell. Its syntax is:

```
OFFSET(reference,rows,cols,height,width)
```

where

- Reference: The base point or upper-left corner of the calculated range

- Row: The number of rows the calculated range is offset from *reference*

- Cols: The number of columns the calculated range is offset from *reference*

- Height: The height of the calculated range

- Width: The width of the calculated range

There is one other function you need to create a range that automatically updates itself. As you add data to the right of existing data, you will need to know the new width to encompass the new data. To do this, use COUNTA to count the number of filled cells in the range C5:M5. This enables you to add data from left to right in the range C5:M5, and the SUM function will automatically include it, because the range name RevenueData dynamically expands.

The OFFSET formula you need is:

```
=OFFSET(DynamicRangeSum!$C$5,0,0,1,COUNTA(DynamicRangeSum!$C$5:$M$5))
```

OFFSET begins the calculated range at C5 in sheet DynamicRangeSum. There is no offset from C5, because the offset row and column are 0 and 0. The height of the calculated range is 1 row. The width of the calculated range is the number of filled cells in $C$5:$M$5. The name of the worksheet, the tab name, is included with the cell references so that this range name applies only on this worksheet. If the worksheet/tab name had spaces in it, then you must enclose the worksheet/tab name in single quotes (').

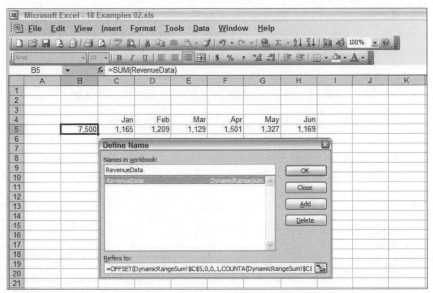

Figure 17.4: The Define Name dialog box is where you create a dynamic range name formula.

To make this work, you must create the formula in the Define Name dialog box. Choose Insert ➪ Name ➪ Define to display the dialog box. Type the name **RevenueData** in the Names in workbook box. Type or select the formula in the Refers To box. Click Add and OK.

Now enter the formula

```
=SUM(RevenueData)
```

in any cell.

As you type data in the range C5:M5, it will be included in the SUM. There is one caveat with using COUNTA to calculate a new width or height. Data you enter must be from left to right or top to bottom, without blank cells.

You can see how the range RevenueData expands as you add more data by selecting the RevenueData range. Named formulas do not appear in the Go To dialog box. To select a dynamic range name:

1. Press F5 to display the Go To dialog box. Notice that RevenueData does not appear in the Go To dialog box. Named formulas are not visible.

2. Type the name `RevenueData` in the Reference box and click OK.

Excel will select the new range associated with RevenueData.

Note: Viewing or Editing Named Formulas

Named formulas do not show in the Go To dialog box, but you can always see them and edit them by choosing Insert ⇨ Name ⇨ Define and selecting the named formula.

Creating Charts That Expand to Include New Data

Adding data to the right edge of existing chart data does not expand the chart. Without the following technique, you would need to recreate charts as data expands. However, you can use a named formula in a chart's series to automatically expand the chart's data range. This could save you a lot of work and make for cleaner charts.

To create charts that automatically adjust as new data is added, you must first create a dynamic range name, as described above, and then enter that range name as the reference for the chart's data series.

Enter the range name in a chart's series formula by clicking on the chart; then, choose Chart ⇨ Source Data. In the Source Data dialog box, shown in Figure 17.5, select the Series tab. The figure shows the dynamic range names, NPSales and NPMonths used in the chart's data series.

The dynamic formula for NPMonths, the chart's date range, is

```
=OFFSET(DynamicChart!$C$6,0,0,1,COUNTA(DynamicChart!$C$6:$N$6))
```

The chart's date range can include a changeable range of dates from C6 to N6.

The dynamic formula for NPSales, the chart's data range, is:

```
=OFFSET(DynamicChart!$C$7,0,0,1,COUNTA(DynamicChart!$C$7:$N$7))
```

The chart's data range can include a changeable data title and data range from C7 to N7.

If you have multiple series of data in the chart, select the series to receive the name from the Series list. Enter the dynamic range name for the data in the Values box. Enter the dynamic range name for the Category (X) axis labels in its box.

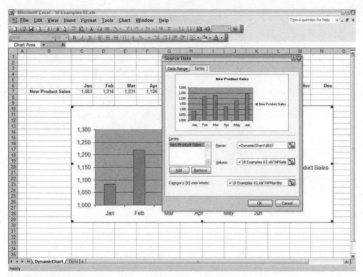

Figure 17.5: Typing dynamic range name formulas into a chart's data series creates charts that automatically adapt as the size of their data changes.

Dynamically Changing the Start Date of a Chart

When the dashboard user needs to record and review large amounts of historical data, you can give the user the ability to change the start date of the chart. This enables him to select any starting date. By combining what you learn here with what you learn in Chapter 20, "Controlling Dashboards with Menus, Combo Boxes, and Buttons," you can allow your dashboard users to select start dates from a menu or scroll through historical data by moving a slider bar.

DOWNLOAD ALL THE EXAMPLES FOR THIS BOOK

Refer to the Introduction for information about how to download the examples in this book.

Figure 17.6 shows a chart displaying 6 months of the data in range C7:N7. Changing the start month in C3 changes the starting and subsequent months in the chart. By linking a slider bar to cell C3, your dashboard's users can scroll through the data a month at a time.

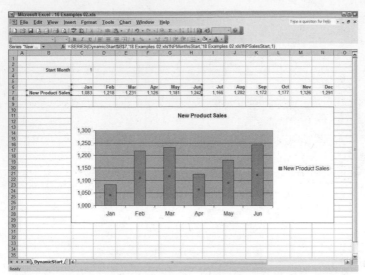

Figure 17.6: The Category (X) axis and data range for the New Product Sales chart use dynamic ranges so that the chart can animate across time periods.

Two dynamic range names are needed to create this dynamic chart. Create these names using the Insert ⇨ Name ⇨ Define command as described previously. The dynamic range formula to calculate the Category (x) axis series is:

```
NPMonthsStart=OFFSET(DynamicStart!$C$6,0,DynamicStart!$C$3-1,1,6)
```

NPMonthsStart uses C6 as the starting reference point. The row offset for the start is 0, because the months are always in this row. The height and width for the range is 1 and 6, so the chart always shows 6 months. The animation occurs in the formula:

```
DynamicStart!$C$3-1
```

This is the column offset for the starting point of the range. When the value in C3 is 1, the first month, then the offset is 0. Increasing the value in C3 moves the starting point for the range farther to the right.

The data series is almost the same formula as the axis, but the data series references the row containing formula data.

```
NPSalesStart
```

```
=OFFSET(DynamicStart!$C$7,0,DynamicStart!$C$3-1,1,6)
```

Enter the NPSalesMonth and NPSalesStart names by selecting the chart, then choosing Chart ⇨ Source Data, and selecting the Series tab. Do not forget to enter the worksheet/tab name when you enter the formula. For example, in the Values box you will enter:

```
='DynamicStartData'!NPSalesStart
```

because the name of the tab containing the dynamic range name is DynamicStartData.

Dynamically Changing the Start Date and Width of a Chart

With a small modification you can make the dynamic chart adjust so it displays variable amounts of data. This makes charts extremely flexible for tasks like switching views from one year of financial data to multiple years or switching from a week of manufacturing data to months of data. Figure 17.7 shows the chart and data entry fields for a chart that allows users to adjust its start date and the number of months it displays.

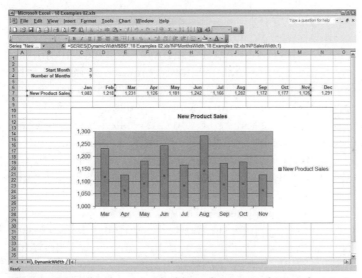

Figure 17.7: Allowing your dashboard users to change the start date and amount of data plotted gives them the power to display what they want.

In this example, the DynamicStart worksheet from the previous example has been copied and the tab renamed as DynamicWidth. This preserves the two dynamic range names, so you only need to make two small modifications. First, type a number from 1 to 12 in cell C4. C4 will contain the width of data plotted.

Second, you'll need to modify the width of the OFFSET in each dynamic range formula so it references cell C4. When the contents of C4 change, the amount of data in the chart changes.

The dynamic range names have changed from referencing the DynamicStart to the DynamicWidth sheet, and the width has changed, so they now look like:

```
NPMonthsWidth=OFFSET(DynamicWidth!$C$6,0,
DynamicWidth!$C$3-1,1,DynamicWidth!$C$4)

NPSalesWidth=OFFSET(DynamicWidth!$C$7,0,
DynamicWidth!$C$3-1,1,DynamicWidth!$C$4)
```

Dynamically Charting the Last 13 Months of Data

Executives and managers usually want to see the most current data series. For financial data, this is usually the last 12, 13, or 15 months of data. Displaying 13 months of data allows comparison between the current month and the same month in the year before. Displaying 15 months of data allows comparison between the months in the current quarter against the same months in the prior year.

When static charts display this type of information they usually resort to one of three solutions, none of which are good. First, you can waste time by recreating the charts over the range of the new data. Second, you can waste time by reentering data on top of the previous data, or third, you can create aesthetically offensive charts by making the chart so wide it leaves blank spaces on the right in anticipation of forthcoming data.

Using a range name formula to calculate the range to be plotted produces a much better solution. It creates a clean-looking chart with no gaps, and data can be added at the end of existing data. The chart will automatically determine the most current data needed. In Figure 17.8, for example, the dynamic range names have calculated the most current 13 months of data in E6:Q7.

```
NPMonths13Mo=OFFSET(ChartLast13Mo!$C$6,0,
COUNTA(ChartLast13Mo!$C$7:$Z$7)-13,1,13)

NPSales13Mo=OFFSET(ChartLast13Mo!$C$7,0,
COUNTA(ChartLast13Mo!$C$7:$Z$7)-13,1,13)
```

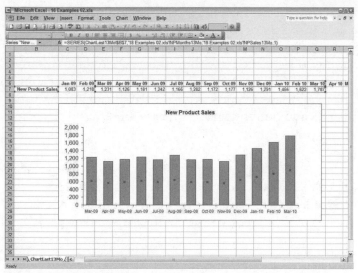

Figure 17.8: Use dynamic range names to automatically chart the most current data from a larger range.

Creating Dynamic Range Names for Lists

Dashboards and scorecards in Excel use a lot of lists. Lists are used to hold data for analysis, data for charting, menu contents, lookup tables ranges, and so forth. Over time, and with changing requirements, these lists change in height and width. More data may be added manually, data retrieved from a database may be larger or smaller than expected, or user requirements may change.

Changes of this sort would normally require that formulas be rewritten. But changing formulas not only wastes time, but can introduce errors. And those errors can affect critical business decisions.

What you will be learning in this section will be used multiple times in Chapter 24, "Building Powerful Charts for Decision Making."

CAUTION Before I develop a Balanced Scorecard or operational dashboard, I usually audit the worksheets the organization has been using to accomplish the same task. One of my client's worksheets contained formulas that had been replaced by fixed values and formula references that didn't refer to all the data. For almost two years, the pharmaceutical company that had been using the worksheets had been making tactical decisions based on international sales margins that were drastically incorrect.

Excel 2003 and Excel 2007 contain commands that automatically expand lists as data is manually added directly below or adjacent, on the right. This functionality works well for manual data entry into simple lists you may keep in Excel.

The ranges and lists we will be working with in this section have different needs and require more capability. The lists we are working with here will be used in scorecards and dashboards as references by LOOKUP and INDEX functions, as references for menus and buttons, and as sources for dynamic charting and scrolling tables, among other things.

TIP Excel recognizes a list as a rectangular block of filled cells. The block may contain unfilled cells, but all filled cells must touch each other at one edge. The list must be surrounded by unfilled cells and may or may not have a row of headers. To quickly select a list, click on one cell in the list and then press Shift+Ctrl+*.

Creating range names that update dynamically for lists is much the same as creating dynamic range names for charts. You will assign a formula to a range name, and that formula will calculate the height and width of the list. The difference about charts is that lists may expand downward, as well as to the right.

In the following example, a dynamic range will be created for the list

```
MedianHouseHoldIncome1996_2006_US_State_CAcounty.xls
```

This file is available for download. Instructions for downloading it are in the Introduction. The list contains the Median Household Income for the U.S., fifty states, and the counties in California. It covers the years 1996 to 2006.

You expect that additional U.S. Census data will extend the list each year, and you want the list's range to expand to account for years up to 2012, or column S. Also, additional counties from a few other states may be added, so the last row may go from its current 111 entries to as many as 300. Figure 17.9 shows the list.

To reference this range, even if it grows to row 300 and column S, you will need to use a dynamic range name that expands vertically and horizontally. You can do this with two COUNTA functions inside an OFFSET function.

To create a dynamic named range for this list

1. Choose Insert ➪ Name ➪ Define.

2. Type the range name **dbMdnHseInc** in the Names field in the Workbook box.

3. Type or enter the formula that calculates the range in the Refers To box.

```
=OFFSET(Data!$B$2,0,0,COUNTA(Data!$B$2:$B$302),COUNTA(Data!$B$2:$S$2))
```

Notice that Data is the name of the tab.

4. Click OK.

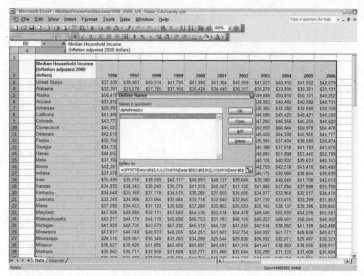

Figure 17.9: Dynamic range names can automatically adjust as the height and width of the list change.

`Data!$B$2` is the base reference at the top left corner of the list. The 0,0 indicates that the base reference is not moved from B2. `COUNTA(Data!$B$2:$B$302)` calculates the height of the range by counting the number of filled cells between the base reference and row 302. `COUNTA(Data!$B$2:$S$2)` calculates the width of the range by counting the number of column headers between the base reference and column S.

TIP The Define Name dialog box can be frustrating to edit or type in until you realize it works like the formula bar. Press F2 to go into edit mode before attempting to use arrow keys to move the insertion point or select portions of the formula with the mouse. Once in edit mode you can move the insertion point in the formula and then click or drag in the worksheet to enter a reference.

Now, test to see whether you created the dynamic range name dbMdnHseInc correctly. Choose Edit ⇨ Go To or press F5 to display the Go To dialog box. You cannot see named formulas, so type the name **dbMdnHseInc** into the Reference box and click OK. The range of cells should be selected.

TIP When you use the Go To dialog box to select a dynamic range name, the range may be so large you may only see the upper-left corner of the range. While the range is still selected from using Go To, press Ctrl+. (period). Each press of Ctrl+. (period) moves the active cell to the next corner. Four presses, and you've gone round-robin and seen all four corners of the selection.

The reason you went through all this work is to create a named range that automatically expands. Check to make sure your dynamic range expands downward and to the right. Type **2007** to the right of 2006 in the headers. Type the name of your county in the last cell of column B, below the California counties. Press F5, type in **dbMdnHseInc**, and see whether the range expands to include the new column and row. If it does, you'll be ready to start creating dashboards that automatically update themselves.

Summary

With the minor amount of work required to create a dynamic range name, you will save yourself from the repetitive work of updating your scorecard or dashboard. As you become more comfortable creating dynamic range names, you will find that they have uses beyond databases and charts. You also can use them to create scrolling lists that automatically expand, combo boxes that expand, or combo boxes that change contents.

CHAPTER 18

Working with Lists and Tables of Data

Information is a source of learning. But unless it is organized, processed, and available to the right people in a format for decision-making, it is a burden, not a benefit.
William Pollard, Historian

Although charts are what people usually look at first in Balanced Scorecards and dashboards, it is tables and lists that are the source of the information. They contain the data from which Excel builds charts, displays tables, fills menus, and builds printed reports. They are also what managers and executives refer to when they want more detail. Being able to manage your lists and tables dynamically will save you a significant amount of time, give your dashboard users more capabilities, and reduce chances for error.

Other techniques you will learn in this chapter include sorting lists using a function rather than a command. This enables you to retrieve or import data from any data source, sorting it multiple ways according to your user needs.

Banish VLOOKUP—Use INDEX and MATCH

One of the first powerful Excel features people learn as they move from novice to intermediate level is the use of the vertical and horizontal lookup functions, VLOOKUP and HLOOKUP. The VLOOKUP function searches the first column in a list for a term, and then returns the value in the row of the item found, but in a column you specify. HLOOKUP accomplishes the same function on horizontal lists. These functions are usually used to retrieve items, such as purchase amounts, when given a search item, such as a transaction code.

Although the VLOOKUP and HLOOKUP functions are powerful, they can get you in trouble. They are easy to use incorrectly and, if used incorrectly, return the wrong values.

VLOOKUP and HLOOKUP use the syntax

```
VLOOKUP(lookup_value,table_array,col_index_num,[range_lookup])
HLOOKUP(lookup_value,table_array,row_index_num,[range_lookup])
```

Errors most frequently occur with VLOOKUP and HLOOKUP when someone is looking for exact matches and fails to use FALSE for range_lookup. If range_lookup is TRUE or omitted, VLOOKUP and HLOOKUP expect the list to be in sorted order. When they cannot find an exact match, they return an approximate match, which is usually worse than returning an error.

Another failing of VLOOKUP is that the column being searched must be the left column. The row being searched with HLOOKUP must be the top row. When you create dashboards that use multiple drop-down lists to search on different search fields, you will want to be able to search on the columns or rows of your choice.

A more flexible and more powerful approach to finding data in a list is with the combination of INDEX and MATCH. INDEX has the syntax

```
INDEX(array,row_num,[column_num])
```

In an array or table of data, INDEX returns the value at the intersection of the row and column number specified. You can determine the row or column containing the value you use as a lookup_value with MATCH. MATCH finds the row or column where data is stored and INDEX retrieves it.

The syntax for MATCH is

```
MATCH(lookup_value,lookup_array,[match_type])
```

The lookup_value is the value being searched for—the value used to identify the information, such as a transaction code or invoice number. The lookup_array is the column or row being searched. The match_type specifies how close we want the match. The values for match_type are shown in Table 18.1.

Table 18.1: Values for match_type

IF MATCH_TYPE IS	THE RETURNED VALUE IS
-1	The smallest value that is greater than or equal to lookup_value. Lookup_array must be in descending order.
0	The first value that is exactly equal to lookup_value. Lookup_array can be in any order.
1	The largest value that is less than or equal to lookup_value. Lookup_array must be in ascending order.

The MATCH syntax you will almost always use for Balanced Scorecard and dashboards uses a match_type of 0 to find exact matches in unsorted lists. If MATCH does not find an exact match, then it returns the #N/A error value. We can trap for this error with the ISNA function.

The ISNA function returns TRUE if the calculation inside ISNA returns an error and returns FALSE if the calculation does not return an error. By combining ISNA with an IF function, you can trap errors so that the user does not see them. (In this explanation of ISNA, the INDEX and MATCH functions are used to illustrate how to trap for errors. INDEX and MATCH are described in the following section.) For example, in the following formula, INDEX returns the value in the second column (2), of the array C4:D17. The row is determined by the MATCH function. The MATCH function finds the row in C4:C17 that matches the search term in F2.

```
=INDEX($C$4:$D$17,MATCH($F$2,$C$4:$C$17,0),2)
```

But what happens if someone enters a term in F2 that is not in the array C4:C17? Then MATCH returns an error and causes the entire INDEX function to return #N/A. You don't want your dashboard returning incorrect data, and you don't want your users getting errors. Here's how to handle it.

Use an ISNA function to determine whether MATCH is going to cause an error and then handle that error by returning a message to the user that the item was not found in the list. This formula either finds and returns a valid item or returns the message "Value not found in list."

```
=IF(ISNA(MATCH($F$2,$C$4:$C$17,0)),"Value not found in
list.",INDEX($C$4:$D$17,MATCH($F$2,$C$4:$C$17,0),2))
```

The condition in the IF function is `ISNA(MATCH())`. If the MATCH is not found, then ISNA returns TRUE, so the text appears in the cell. If MATCH does find a value, then the INDEX function calculates and returns the value found in the array.

Once you understand how to combine IF and ISNA, there are many ways of using the pair to trap errors so that your scorecard and dashboard users aren't left perplexed.

Another way of preventing lookup or `INDEX(MATCH())` errors is by using Combo Box or Lists from which users select the item they are searching for. By only giving users valid choices from a Combo Box or List you eliminate the chance for data entry errors. Chapter 20, "Controlling Dashboards with Menus, Combo Boxes, and Buttons," describes how to add these interactive controls to your dashboards.

The Key to Creating Most Interactive Dashboards

In this section, you will see how to use INDEX and MATCH together to find and retrieve a value from a list. You can search for and retrieve data from any row or column, whether it is sorted or not.

This first example shows you how to select median family income for a state from a list and then chart the retrieved data. This process is fundamental to creating most interactive dashboards. In the next section, you will learn how to add a drop-down list so that you won't have to type the state's name. After that, you will see how to retrieve and chart data using multiple keywords.

Using a Keyword to Retrieve and Chart Data

Figure 18.1 shows a chart plotting a state's median family income. The charted data in row 18 was retrieved from the named range dbMedianIncome, B25:M75.

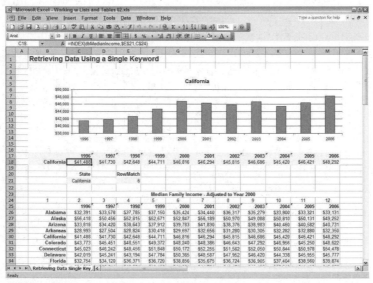

Figure 18.1: Use INDEX and MATCH to find data in a list and retrieve it for charting.

DOWNLOAD SAMPLE DATA FILES

See the Introduction for information on downloading the sample files and data used in this book, as well as for additional valuable information.

The INDEX and MATCH functions are used to retrieve data to chart from the list. When you type a valid state's name in C21, the MATCH formula finds the row in the list containing that name and returns the row number within the list. That row number is then used by the INDEX formulas in row 18 to retrieve the appropriate data for charting.

Cell E21 contains the formula

```
=MATCH($C$21,$B$25:$B$75,0)
```

The MATCH function finds which row in B25:B75 contains an exact match for the state in cell C21. The MATCH function looks through the range B25:B75 to find the state's name the user entered in C21. The 0 in the MATCH function forces MATCH to look for only exact matches. MATCH returns the row number within the range B25:B75. This row number is the same as the row containing California's data in the list range dbMedianIncome.

Cells B17:M18 feed data to the chart. The data in B18:M18 changes depending upon the state entered in C21. Each cell in B18:M18 uses INDEX to retrieve from the list the row calculated by MATCH.

Cell C18, for example, contains the formula

```
=INDEX(dbMedianIncome,$E$21,C$24)
```

This INDEX function looks at the list with the range name dbMedianIncome, B25:M75, and retrieves the row specified by $E$21. The column number for the data to be retrieved is in C$24.

Column numbers for each column of data were entered in row 24 to make this example easy to understand. Later in this chapter, you will see how rows and columns can be selected by function, no matter what their order is.

Using the relative reference C$24 enables you to copy the first INDEX formula across from B18 to M18, and the formula will continue to reference the correct column number in row 24. For example, the formula in cell B18 to retrieve the state's name is

```
=INDEX(dbMedianIncome,$E$21,B$24)
```

LEARN HOW TO USE DYNAMIC RANGE NAMES FOR TABLES

To work effectively with lists and tables, you will need to understand dynamic range names. These are range names that automatically update themselves as the list or table changes. Chapter 17, "Working with Data That Changes Size," describes how to create dynamic range names.

Adding a Drop-Down Selection List to Make Retrieval Easier

When your keywords are long or complex, you will want to give users a drop-down list instead of forcing them to type an entry. Typing requires memorization of often-complex names or numbers and is error-prone. It is very easy to create a simple drop-down list from which you can select, rather than type, what you are looking for. Chapter 20 shows many more examples of how to use drop-down lists, buttons, and menus.

Figure 18.2 shows a drop-down list that has been added to the previous example. This is done with the Data ⇨ Validation command.

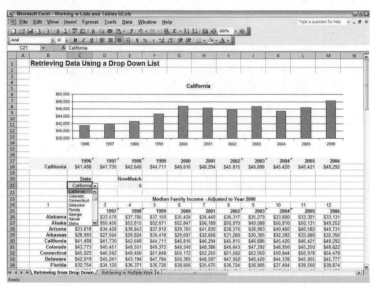

Figure 18.2: Using a drop-down list to select data is easier and less error prone.

To add this drop-down list:

1. Select the cell where you want the list to display. In this case, the cell is C21.

2. Choose the Data ⇨ Validation command to display the Data Validation dialog box shown in Figure 18.3. Select the Settings tab.

3. In the Allow box, select List.

4. Select the Ignore Blank and In-cell Dropdown check boxes.

5. In the Source box, select the range containing the list of entries. In this case, it is B26:B75.

6. Choose OK.

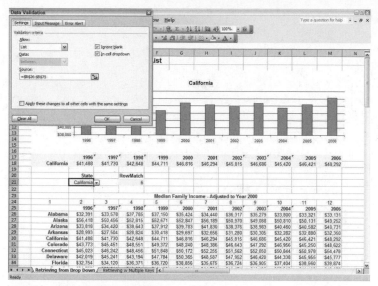

Figure 18.3: The Data Validation dialog box makes it easy to create drop-down lists for data entry.

Retrieving Data Given Multiple Keywords

When you need to access large amounts of data on your dashboard, you will probably have to use multiple keywords as a way of selecting the data to chart. For example, you might select a product line and then select a product within the product line, or you might select a division and then a department within the division.

Retrieving data using multiple keywords is very similar to using a single keyword. The difference is that you will use the concatenation function, &, to join multiple keywords together to form a single key on which you can search. In Figure 18.4, for example, the Product Line and Region columns in columns C and D of the list have been concatenated to create a new key found in column B—labeled, surprisingly, Key. This key is unique for each row, so when you search with MATCH, only one possible row will match the selected Product Line and Region.

The Key column is created by entering in cell B26 the formula

```
=C26&D26
```

and copying it down the column. The concatentated values from B26 down will be used as the search array for MATCH.

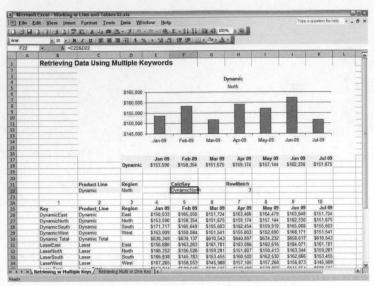

Figure 18.4: Retrieve data using multiple keys by creating a new key using concatenation.

Now, when you enter a Product Line name in cell C22 and a Region in cell D22, the formula in cell F22

```
=C22&D22
```

creates the term used for search down the Key column. If you enter Dynamic and North, then cell F22 will contain DynamicNorth.

The MATCH function in cell H22

```
=MATCH($F$22,$B$25:$B$46)
```

calculates the row number that matches DynamicNorth. That row number is then used by the INDEX functions in row 18 to retrieve the row of data that matches Dynamic and North. Cell E18, the first data cell, contains the formula

```
=INDEX($B$25:$K$46,$H$22,E$24)
```

TIP Your list of data may contain more content than you need for searching. For example, a column may contain the combined text LastName, FirstName in a cell, but you want to only search by LastName. Use the text functions LEFT, RIGHT, FIND, LEN, MID, &, and TEXT to extract the piece of a larger cell content that you need and search on that extracted content. Many examples of how to do this are available on the Internet.

Retrieving Multiple Rows Using a Single Keyword

A common need is to retrieve multiple rows of data when given a single keyword; for example, for a hospital you might select a clinical value, such as whether aspirin was administered for heart attack on arrival, and then retrieve and chart three associated rows of data: the actual data, a benchmark derived from similar hospitals, and the level of aspirin on arrival recommended by an association. As in the previous example, this is done by concatenating multiple words, but the additional search terms, such as Actual, Benchmark, and Recommended, are hidden from the user.

Figure 18.5 shows a list of hospital clinical quality data. The list is in the range dbClinical and contains "actual," "benchmark," and "recommended" data for each of 17 clinical measures. What is needed is a dashboard where the user can enter the desired measure so that the chart will show the associated data for Actual, Benchmark, and Recommended for the measure entered.

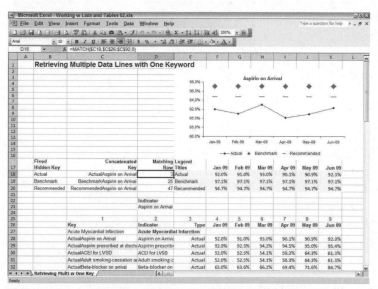

Figure 18.5: Retrieve multiple rows of data associated with an entered key by using fixed keys hidden from the user.

Each measure in dbClinical has three entries, one each for Actual, Benchmark, and Recommended data. The measure's name is in column D or column 2 of dbClinical. Whether the data is Actual, Benchmark, or Recommended is entered in column E or column 3 of dbClinical.

The key used to identify each unique row of data is in column C and is created by concatenating D and E. For example, C28 contains

```
=E29&D28
```

and produces

```
ActualAspirin on Arrival
```

a unique key in the list.

To examine how this works, consider row 18. Table 18.2 shows what specific cells should contain if you enter Aspirin on Arrival in D23.

Table 18.2: Formulas Used to Retrieve Data and the Returned Value

CELL ADDRESS	CELL TITLE	FORMULA	RESULT
B18	Fixed Hidden Key	Actual	Actual
C18	Concatenated Key	=B18&$D$23	ActualAspirin on Arrival
D18	Matching Row	=MATCH($C18,$C$26:$C$92,0)	3
E18	Legend Titles	Actual	Actual
F18	Jan 09	=INDEX(dbClinical,$D18,F$25)	92.0%

Cell C18 creates the lookup term for actual data by concatenating the fixed text Actual with the entered term Aspirin on Arrival to create the term ActualAspirin on Arrival, which can be found in column C. This will be used to retrieve Actual data.

The MATCH function in D18 then uses ActualAspirin on Arrival to find the row that contains that term, row 3.

Cell E18 contains a text title, Actual, that is used by the chart to create the legend.

Cell F18 retrieves the data from dbClinical for row 3 and column 4, Jan 09, in dbClinical. This formula is written with relative references so that it can be copied across to the right.

Rows 19 and 20 use the same process to create a unique lookup term for Benchmark and Recommended data that match Aspirin on Arrival.

The data series in the line chart were formatted so that only the Actual data shows a line. The other two series hide the line and show only the data markers. To do this, right-click a line and choose Format Data Series, which will display the Format Data Series dialog box, shown in Figure 18.6. Set Line as None. Choose Custom for Marker and select a marker size of approximately 10.

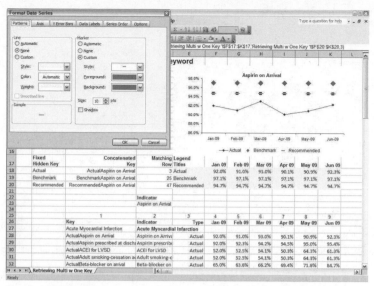

Figure 18.6: Create benchmark or target points by hiding the line and increasing the size of the data marker.

Retrieving Data with a Two-Way Lookup

Data may not always import in the layout you expect it to, and you want a product that isn't going to require manual data entry or corrections whenever it updates. You want a dashboard that can adjust for data where rows or columns are in the wrong order or where there are additional unexpected rows or columns.

The previous examples have shown how to calculate the row containing the data you want. In the following example, you will see how to calculate which column contains the correct data. Usually this technique is used to find the column containing a specific date header.

The example in Figure 18.7 uses MATCH to look across the list's column headings to find the appropriate column, just as MATCH was used to look down to find the appropriate row.

Consider the INDEX function in C18.

```
=INDEX(dbMedianIncome,$E$21,MATCH(C$17,$B$25:$M$25))
```

It looks in the array dbMedianIncome across row 3, which is found in E21, as shown earlier.

The column for the data in C18 should match the heading 1996 in C17. So MATCH looks for a match to C17 in the row of date headings in B25:M25. The match is column 2 of dbMedianIncome, with the heading 1996.

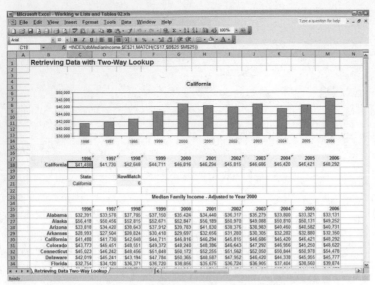

Figure 18.7: A well-done dashboard will use MATCH to find the data row and column.

CAUTION F9 is a wonderful key to know for an Excel user of any proficiency level. The F9 key enables you to see the result of a portion of a formula. For example, if the formula

```
=INDEX(dbMedianIncome,$E$21,MATCH(C$17,$B$25:$M$25))
```

is not returning the results you expect, you may want to see the results for the MATCH function to see whether it is correct. To do that, select in the formula bar the portion of the function that can calculate on its own, for example,

```
MATCH(C$17,$B$25:$M$25)
```

then press F9. You will see the result of the MATCH. Do not press Enter, or you will replace MATCH with its results. Press Esc to return to the original formula. If you make a mistake, press Ctrl+Z to undo.

Sorting Lists by Formula

When we manually create worksheets and analyze data, we are used to sorting lists by manually selecting a command from the menu. However, you rarely want users of Balanced Scorecards or dashboards to manually manipulate data; I usually try to limit the use of macros as well.

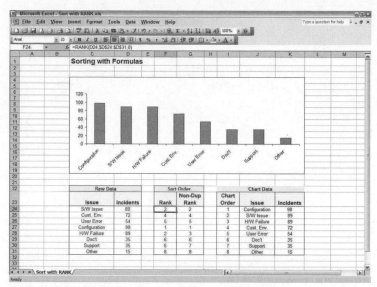

Figure 18.8: Sorting by formula enables the dashboard to order and reorder data without the use of macros or manual intervention.

So what is the solution? Use formulas to sort your data. Formulas can sort data that is stored in unsorted order or re-sort data as the user needs. Doing this also enables you to prepare data for Pareto charts, as illustrated in Chapter 24, "Building Powerful Charts for Decision Making."

Figure 18.8 shows a typical example of high-level data from a report on customer trouble incidents. Management will want to know which issues are most frequent and what their frequencies of occurence are.

The raw data is in C24:D31. Notice that it is not sorted by incident. If C24:D31 were charted, the chart would be difficult to interpret.

The RANK function is used in F24:F31 to calculate the RANK order for each incident. The RANK function in F24 is

```
=RANK(D24,$D$24:$D$31,0)
```

This function compares the value in D24 against the values in D24:D31 and determines its rank in the list. If you sorted the list, the rank would be its position in the sorted list. The 0 indicates that the rank is for a descending list. The formula in F24 has been copied to F31.

If this were all there was to it, it would be easy. This example shows that problems occur if there are matching RANK values. In this case there are two issues with 89 incidents, and therefore both rank at 2. Notice that because they both rank as 2, there is no incident ranked 3. There are also two issues with 35 incidents; both rank as 6. Again, notice that because these both rank at 6, there is no 7.

The tough part comes when you attempt to put this list in ascending or descending order using the RANK values in F24:F31. How do you create a new list ranked most to least severe if there are two values ranked 2 and two values ranked 6? VLOOKUP or INDEX(MATCH()) won't work; because there are duplicate numbers; only one will be found.

The formula in G24

```
=F24+COUNTIF($F$23:F23,F24)
```

works out the difficulty. Because F24 equals 2, G24 will be at least 2. However, the portion

```
COUNTIF($F$23:F23,F24)
```

counts matches to the 2 in the range above. Because there are none, G24 remains 2.

The formula in G24 is copied down the column. The dollar signs that create the fixed reference must be exactly as shown in the formula for this to work. Note that in the COUNTIF function, $F$23 anchors the top of the COUNTIF range, and the F23 allows the bottom of the range to move down with the copied formula.

Let's see what happens when a second rank of 2 is met. Cell G28 evaluates a second 2. In G28, the formula

```
=F28+COUNTIF($F$23:F27,F28)
```

finds that F28 is 2, and the COUNTIF counts one other 2 in the range above. The result is that G28 is 3. Because both of these issues have the same number of incidents, it is not important which is second or third so long as they are charted together.

Now that there is a unique ranking order with no duplicates, INDEX and MATCH can be used to create a list for charting. (In this case, a VLOOKUP could also be used to create the ordered list for display.) The range I24:I32 contains the numeric values 1 through 8. Cell J24 contains the formula

```
=INDEX($C$24:$G$31,MATCH($I24,$G$24:$G$31,0),1)
```

which retrieves the first issue name. Cell K24

```
=INDEX($C$24:$G$31,MATCH($I24,$G$24:$G$31,0),2)
```

retrieves the number of incidents for the first issue. These formulas are copied down their columns.

Summary

A critical part of developing interactive dashboards is being able to retrieve only the data you want for analysis. Using the methods described in this chapter, you can have a workbook that contains hundreds or thousands of rows of data imported from or linked to a database. If you use the INDEX and MATCH functions, you can give your dashboard users the power to extract just the data they want or sort on just the column they want.

Initially the INDEX and MATCH functions seem as if they are more work than a simple VLOOKUP, but they actually are more flexible, allow greater functionality, and are less prone to errors. Once you've used them a few times, you will find them as easy to understand as VLOOKUP, and well worth learning.

CHAPTER 19

Creating Miniature Charts and Tables

Good business leaders create a vision, articulate the vision, passionately own the vision, and relentlessly drive it to completion.

Jack Welch, 1935–
Chairman and CEO, GE

When possible, business dashboards should have the information necessary for a business decision on a single information-rich dashboard. To create information-rich dashboards, you can't use glitzy gauges or large charts; what you need are sets of miniature charts that fit in a single display.

Balanced Scorecards show a collection of information all related to the drivers and success of an organization's strategy. If you want to see all of these metrics at one time, and any related trends and alerts as well, you need to use miniature charts arrayed on a larger scorecard. As illustrated in Chapter 29, "Publishing Balanced Scorecards and Dashboards," clicking on the titles of these miniature charts drills down to detailed charts and data.

Miniature charts are not used for a detailed examination of data values. Rather, by putting numerous miniature charts in one display, it is possible to see many trends, relationships between many metrics, and proximities to target values.

Using Miniature Charts, Tables, and Sparklines for Greater Information Density and Improved Layout

When you try to put multiple Excel charts on a dashboard, you find that you can put about four charts to a dashboard by just reducing the size of a normal chart. However, when you need more than four charts on a screen, the chart's content becomes so crowded that it is difficult to read. Figure 19.1 shows 17 miniature charts used to give a summary overview for a Balanced Scorecard or executive dashboard. As other chapters explain, each of these miniature charts is live and contains a hyperlink to drill down to more detailed charts. Additional examples of miniature charts being used in a Balanced Scorecard are in Chapter 29.

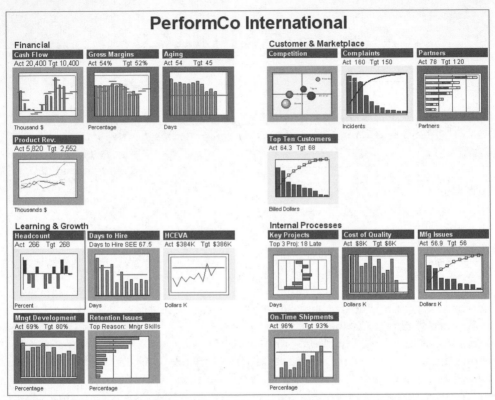

Figure 19.1: One use for miniature charts is to show a summary overview in Balanced Scorecards or executive dashboards.

Another situation where you need miniature charts is when you have tables of data and want a chart adjacent to them to show relationships and trends. Miniature charts can fit perfectly next to tables. Figures 19.2 and 19.3 show pages from printed reports using miniature charts next to supporting data.

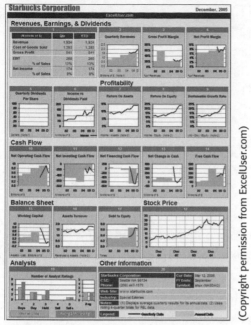

Figure 19.2: Seeing relationships and trends across related metrics enables you to form a mental model for different aspects of your business.

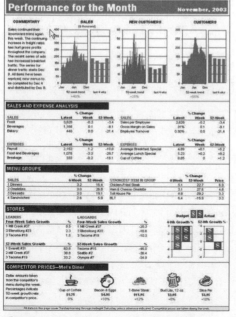

Figure 19.3: Miniature charts enable you to create dashboards and reports with near–magazine layout quality.

LEARN MORE ABOUT MINIATURE CHARTS AND MAGAZINE-QUALITY REPORTS

Charles Kyd is a master at using Excel to convey a maximum amount of information in a minimum amount of printed space. He has perfected the art of creating, in his words, "magazine-quality" reports. Figures 19.2 and 19.3 are examples of his work.

Charley's web site, www.exceluser.com, contains lots of tips on using Excel to create concise, high-quality reports. It also includes numerous articles about how to display unique financial problems with Excel charts. Sign up for the free ExcelUser's newsletter at www.exceluser.com.

ExcelUser has two versions of the downloadable e-book, Dashboard Reporting for Excel, for sale; one covers the older versions of Excel, and the other covers Excel 2007. These e-books describe additional tips on miniature charts and creating dashboards. In Charley's e-book you'll find topics such as:

■ How to Set Up Common Y-Axis Scaling for Multiple Charts

■ How to Use the Camera Tool to Create Stoplights

■ Multiple Methods of Integrating Data into Excel

■ How to Lay Out Magazine-Quality Reports

If you do a lot of financial reporting, you might also be interested in his Plug-N-Play Dashboard Kit. This kit has preformatted tables, miniature charts, and multiple color schemes; all you add is data.

MICROCHARTS CREATES FONT-BASED MINI-CHARTS

Chapter 26, "Using Excel Add-Ins for Extra Capabilities," shows examples of the miniature charts and Sparklines possible with MicroCharts. MicroCharts uses a custom font set to create many types of miniature charts that fit within a cell.

Creating Miniature Charts from Standard Excel Charts

Creating miniature charts from standard Excel charts is pretty straightforward — just get rid of all the "chart junk" that doesn't add any communication value and then reduce the size. Although doing this is straightforward, a few tricks are helpful. Figure 19.4 shows a typical chart created — in Excel prior to Excel 2007 — by selecting the data to be charted and pressing F11, the create chart key. Figure 19.5 shows a chart with the "chart junk" removed, prior to being reduced in size.

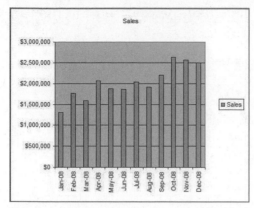

Figure 19.4: When charts are created with the default settings, they contain a lot of unnecessary "chart junk."

Figure 19.5: Miniature charts should show just the information they want to communicate. Remove all the clutter.

Removing Titles, Gridlines, and Legends

Prior to its 2007 release, Excel created its default charts (like that in Figure 19.4) with an unnecessary grey background that made them difficult to read. To remove the grey background, click the background and press Delete.

Now make the chart even more readable by removing the titles, grid lines, and legend. Miniature charts are usually used adjacent to the data they represent; data represents only one or two data series, so the chart title and legend may be unnecessary. Deleting the title and legend helps reduce the size, as fonts and legend do not adjust well when reduced and may require a lot of manipulation.

Gridlines also can be removed, because they do not convey information necessary for decision-making. If actual numeric values are needed, then the chart should be accompanied by a table with numbers. To delete gridlines, click on the gridlines and press Delete.

Legends also are unnecessary in miniature charts or Sparklines. Remove the legend by clicking on it and pressing Delete.

At this point, your chart should look like the chart on the right in Figure 19.6.

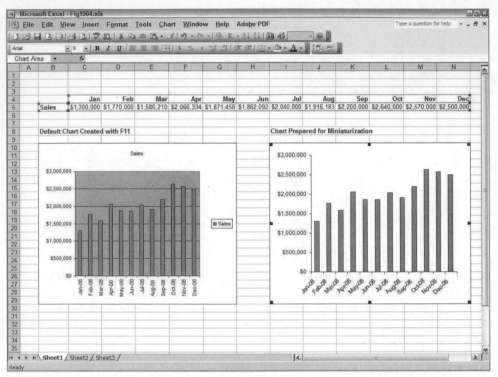

Figure 19.6: Removing "chart junk" from a chart makes it more readable and is essential before reducing its size.

Formatting the Y-Axis to Remove Unnecessary Scales and Width

At this point, you need to decide what you want to retain on the Y-axis. Values along the edge of the Y-axis on a full-sized chart are helpful when reading approximate values for data points. In miniature charts, values are usually not needed; miniature charts are primarily used to see general trends, relationships with other trends, and proximity to target values.

Tick marks on the Y-axis are the small dashes that appear on the axis. Just as with gridlines, there is no need for tick marks, because users are looking at miniature charts for trends and relations, not to read data values.

To remove the values and tick marks, right-click the vertical or Y-axis and choose Format Axis to display the Format Axis dialog box. In Excel, prior to 2007, select the Patterns tab and select None for Major and Minor Tick Mark Type.

If you do not want values to show, select None for Tick Mark Labels. Choose OK. In Excel 2007, select Axis Options and remove tick marks on the Major and Minor Tick Mark Type. Figure 19.7 shows how the default chart appears at this point, with Y-axis values still displayed.

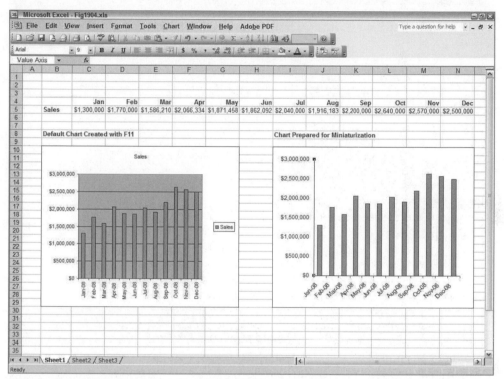

Figure 19.7: Removing tick marks removes additional "chart junk," but you still need to manage the Y-axis values.

Reducing the Size and Width of Y-Axis Numeric Values

You may want to keep Y-axis values, but if you do you will need to reduce their size and width so they don't take up unnecessary width and push the Y-axis out of position. Here is how to reformat numbers on the Y-axis so they are narrower.

To make Y-axis values like $1,500,000 appear shorter, like $1,500, use a custom numeric format command in the Y-axis format dialog box. Right-click the Y-axis to display the Format Axis dialog box. Select the Number tab and then select Custom from the Category list as shown in figure 19.8. In the Type box you can type in the custom numeric format you want to appear on the Y-axis. Choose OK. Examples of custom formats are in the following table. Notice that you can even create a custom format that automatically adds text to show your scaling value, such as K for thousands or M for millions.

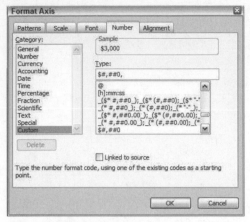

Figure 19.8: Use the same custom formats you use in the worksheet to modify displays on the X- and Y-axis.

Table 19.1: Use Custom Numeric Formats to Scale Y-Axis Values

	ORIGINAL FORMAT AND Y-AXIS APPEARANCE	CUSTOM FORMAT AND Y-AXIS APPEARANCE
Currency Shortened by Thousands	$#,##0 $2,000,000	$#,##0, $2,000
Currency Shortened by Millions	$#,##0 $2,000,000	$#,, $2
Currency Shortened and Text Added	$#,##0 $2,000,000	$#,," M" $2 M

In Table 19.1 notice that custom formats have one or more trailing commas (,). The trailing comma tells Excel to drop a trailing three zeros — one trailing comma drops three zeros, two trailing commas drops six zeros. You can add quoted text at the end of a custom format for text to appear after the number. In this example the M indicates millions. You can further reduce Y-axis width by not adding a text label of K or M to every number as shown in the last custom format, but instead creating a floating label with $M that appears at the top of the Y-axis.

At this point the chart is using a $#,, custom format that appears as shown in Figure 19.9.

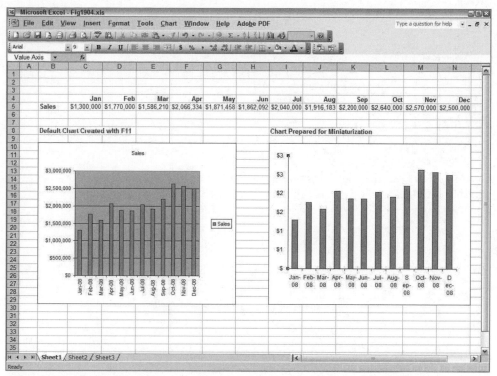

Figure 19.9: Reduce the width of values on the Y-axis by using custom labels.

The right-hand chart in Figure 19.9 contains repeated Y-axis values. You need to eliminate ones that are showing for the ½-scale values. Also, a small chart won't need all the values along the Y-axis. Often just a top and bottom value are needed to give a sense of proportion. You can take care of either of these by adjusting the Scale tab in the Format Axis dialog box.

To adjust which numbers display on the Y-axis, display the Format Axis dialog box again by right-clicking the Y-axis. In Excel, prior to 2007, select the Scale tab. In Excel 2007 select Axis Options. Clear the Maximum, Major, and Minor Unit check boxes. These check boxes tell Excel to automatically format the scales. For the example shown, we want a maximum value at the top of the Y-axis of 3,000,000, so enter 3000000 in the Maximum box. To use a minimum number of extra numbers on the scale, show the value at every 1,000,000 point. Enter 1000000 in the Major Unit box as shown in Figure 19.10. Choose OK to see a chart that appears like the one in Figure 19.11.

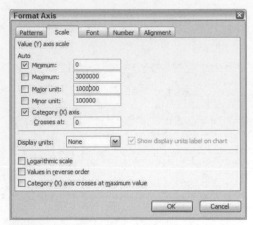

Figure 19.10: Clear the check boxes and use large Major Unit values on the Scale tab to remove unnecessary numbers along the Y-axis.

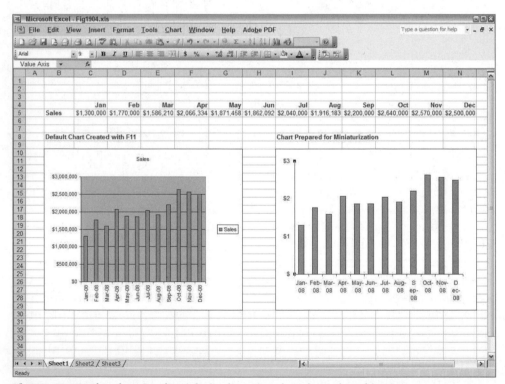

Figure 19.11: The chart on the right is almost ready to be reduced in size.

Formatting the X-Axis

As you can see in Figure 19.11, the X-axis is crowded. Reducing the chart in size would make the X-axis look even worse. Luckily, there are a couple of ways to handle this. One of the easiest methods is to reformat the numeric values on the X-axis to a display format with a smaller size.

To reformat the X-axis so it will display every other month on the X-axis, right-click the X-axis to display the Format Axis dialog box. In Excel, prior to 2007, select the Scale tab. Clear the Major and Minor Unit check boxes. Enter 2 in the Major Unit check box. Choose OK.

In Excel 2007, select Axis Options. Then, in the Interval Between Labels group, select Specify Interval Unit and enter 2. Choose OK.

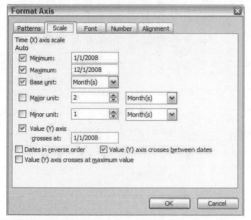

Figure 19.12: Reformat the axis so that you get the display you want.

Only displaying every other month gives more space on the X-axis, but you can improve it more. Return to the Format Axis dialog box for the X-axis and select the Number tab. By entering a custom format, as you did for the Y-axis, you can make the date displays appear in almost any format you want.

Select Custom from the Category list. In the Type box, enter mmm as the custom format. This will display a three-letter abbreviation for each month. For example, Mar-08 will now appear as Mar. Choose OK. The X-axis should now look like the simplified version shown in Figure 19.13.

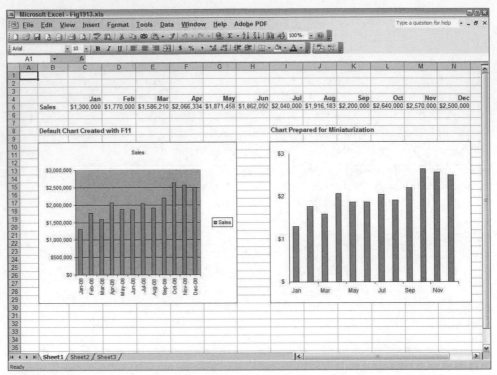

Figure 19.13: Using a custom date format and displaying alternating months makes the X-axis easier to read.

Make sure the plot area of your chart is filling the chart area completely. Click inside the plot area and drag the corner handles as far to the corners as possible. This reduces the white space around the edges of the chart.

Finally adjust the font sizes of the X- and Y-axis so they are legible. Usually an 8- or 9-point font will work.

You can now reduce the chart to miniature by dragging a corner of the chart. Hold the Alt key as you drag to make the chart's corners align with cell corners. Figure 19.14 shows this example reduced in size. If you want to make the chart even smaller, eliminate the X- and Y-axis fonts or follow the steps later in this chapter on creating a Sparkline.

TIP Some items in a chart are hard to select by clicking. They may be small or hidden. You can still select them. Click on anything in the chart so that the selection handles (small black squares) show. Now slowly press any direction arrow key to move through all the selectable items in the chart until the one you want is selected.

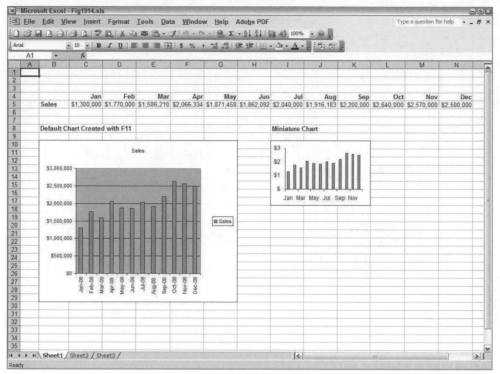

Figure 19.14: You can place many miniature charts on a single display.

Formatting Multiple Miniature Charts

It takes a lot of work to remove chart junk so that you can reduce a chart in size. Thank heavens, there is an easy way to duplicate this process for other charts.

Format multiple charts with your miniature formatting by first formatting one chart the way you want it. Select that chart and choose Edit ⇨ Copy. Now select the other charts and choose Edit ⇨ Paste Special. From the Paste Special dialog box select Formats, and choose OK. The charts you have selected will change to match your master copy.

Creating Sparklines

Edward Tufte is an acknowledged thought leader in the visual display of information. One of his many innovations is the Sparkline. His premise is that many charts are used to show trends or relative changes. Sparklines are line charts reduced to show just that trend or relationship. Sparklines are usually presented in the context of textual discussion or tables so that specifics are available if needed. Figure 19.15 shows the previous example further reduced to a Sparkline chart.

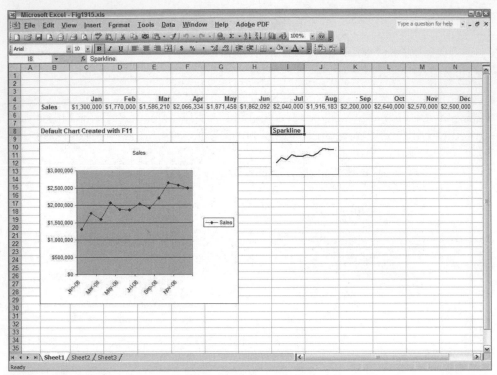

Figure 19.15: When you consider that these two charts are designed to convey a trend, it becomes obvious that the default Excel chart has far too much clutter when compared to the Sparkline on the right.

LEARN MORE ABOUT EDWARD TUFTE

You can learn more about Edward Tufte, Sparklines, and the visual display of information at www.edwardtufte.com. It is an intriguing site with lots of content about the visual display of information. For information specific to Sparklines, look for the article titled "Sparklines: theory and practice." Chapter 26 has examples of Sparklines produced with the Excel add-in MicroCharts.

With a few additional steps, you can convert your Excel charts into Sparklines. To convert the default Excel line chart to a Sparkline, follow the preceding steps to remove unnecessary clutter.

Remove the X- and Y-axis by clicking on an axis to select it and then pressing Delete.

Reformat the line and markers by right-clicking on the data series line and using the Format Data Series dialog box to change the line width and marker to your liking.

A Sparkline illustrates a single data series, so remove data series that are not the focus of the chart. I violate some of Tufte's tenants by including a trend line or control limits in some of my miniature charts, but a Sparkline should just show a single data line. When you make modifications, remember the three C's — make your charts concise, crisp, and clear.

Finally, take pity on those of us over 40 or those who wear glasses. Colored lines may be visible in large charts, but colored lines, especially red hues, are difficult to differentiate in miniature charts. Color your lines with darker hues such as black and blue.

Excel's Amazing Camera Tool

Hidden deep within the caverns of Excel's inner recesses is the Camera tool. Once you learn the pathway to the Camera tool, you will be able to access its powers. The Camera tool enables you to escape the limits of Excel's dashboard and report layouts. With the Camera tool, you will be able to:

- Create pictures that are live windows to another worksheet
- Arrange live pictures of charts and tables unhampered by row height or column width
- Shrink or magnify charts and tables
- Rotate sections of a worksheet or chart

The Dark Side of Excel's Camera Tool

While the Camera tool is an instrument of power it has its dark side. The Camera tool has two nasty personality problems you should be aware of before using it.

In every Excel version since Excel 2000, linked pictures created with the Camera tool have acted quirky for some computer and printer combinations. If you have a certain combination of computer and printer and print a page containing a picture linked to a worksheet area or chart, then the linked picture may resize or disappear. This doesn't happen for all computer and printer combinations. On some of my computers it works fine, and on others it doesn't.

Microsoft doesn't seem to know how to fix this problem, since it has had a warning about the problem in its knowledge base since Excel 2000. This problem only occurs with linked camera objects, which are the most useful type. To learn more about this problem, go to the Microsoft Support Developers Network at `msdn.microsoft.com` and search for the knowledge-base article ID: 211633 or the title "XL 2000: Linked Picture of Cells Changes Size with Print Quality."

The other issue with the Camera tool is that putting a large number of camera pictures on a page will slow recalculation. This is a hindrance, but you can turn off worksheet calculation by choosing Tools ➪ Options and selecting Manual on the Calculation tab. Pressing F9 will force a recalculation.

TIP Dashboards and reports look more professional when all the elements are aligned horizontally and vertically. To make sure you align chart or picture corners, and therefore the edges, hold down the Alt key while dragging the corner handle of a chart or picture. Holding the Alt key forces an object's corners to align with the nearest cell corner.

If you want to manually align objects and the edge is not at a cell corner, then use the Zoom button or View Zoom to magnify the worksheet to 200% or 300% and then position the elements you want to align. Select the object and then use the arrow keys to move it, rather than the mouse. The magnified view enables you to see smaller imperfections in alignment.

Taking Pictures with the Camera Tool

The Camera tool is very easy to use; you select a portion of a worksheet, take a picture with the camera tool, and then paste the Camera's live picture in another location.

It is like having a video camera trained on the area you took a picture of. Anything that changes in the original area is shown in the picture. Everything in the range you select will appear in the picture, and when any change occurs it will be reflected in the camera's picture.

You can move the camera's picture after you have pasted it by dragging it as you would any drawn object.

To capture a picture using keystrokes:

1. Select the range you want pictured.
2. Choose Edit, Copy or press Ctrl+C.
3. Select a cell where you want the camera picture.
4. Hold the Shift key as you choose Edit, Paste Picture Link. In Excel 2007, on the Home tab, in the Clipboard group, click the down arrow on the Paste button. Select As Picture, Paste Picture Link.

You can also add a Camera tool to your toolbars. The Camera tool is accessible two ways: either through the menu, while holding down the Shift key, or via a button you can add to your toolbar.

To add the Camera button to a toolbar in Excel prior to Excel 2007:

1. Choose Tools ➪ Customize.
2. Select the Commands tab, and then select Tools from the Categories list.
3. Scroll through the Commands list until you see the Camera.

4. Click and drag the Camera onto a toolbar and drop it between two existing buttons.

5. Choose Close.

To capture a picture:

1. Select the range you want pictured.

2. Click the Camera tool.

3. Click in the same workbook where you want the upper-left corner of the picture.

4. Once the picture appears, you can drag it to a new location like any drawing object or resize it by dragging a handle on the edge of the object or rotate it by dragging the rotate handle.

USING THE CAMERA TOOL IN EXCEL 2007

The Camera tool is also available in Excel 2007 to move onto a ribbon. Select the Office button ⇨ Excel Options ⇨ Customize ⇨ Choose commands from ⇨ Commands Not in the Ribbon. Scroll through the alphabetical list to the Camera and add it to a toolbar.

TIP If you captured too large or too small a range with the Camera tool, you can increase the "view" of the picture you have already taken without reshooting the picture. Display the Picture toolbar, click on the crop tool, and then use the Crop tool to drag an edge or corner of a picture. The view of the source worksheet shown in the picture will expand correspondingly.

Using Camera Pictures of Charts, Tables, and Miniature Charts

With the Camera tool, you can take a picture of anything in or over a range of cells. Your picture can include cell contents, a chart, multiple charts, or charts and tables.

TIP The Camera tool does an excellent job of maintaining fonts and proportions when shrinking charts, but don't expect it to make a readable miniature chart from a large chart containing titles, legends, backgrounds or more. When you make a miniature chart it is best if the large chart being captured has its elements reduced to a minimum using the methods the beginning of this chapter describes.

The Camera tool takes a picture of everything over a range of cells. For example, to take a picture of a chart, do not select the chart itself. Select the cells behind the chart. Take the picture using one of the methods previously described and then paste the picture on a worksheet where you can move it as needed.

Figure 19.16 shows an example of a Camera picture containing both a chart and a table. This is done by selecting the cells under the chart and the table before clicking the Camera tool. Notice that the camera picture at the top left does not have to be aligned with rows and columns. The X-axis labels are actually the titles across the top of the data in row 31. By eliminating row and column alignment and being able to group charts, tables, and objects into a single entity, you can create impressive layouts. Dragging the corner of a camera picture so that the picture is smaller creates reduced charts and tables that are very readable.

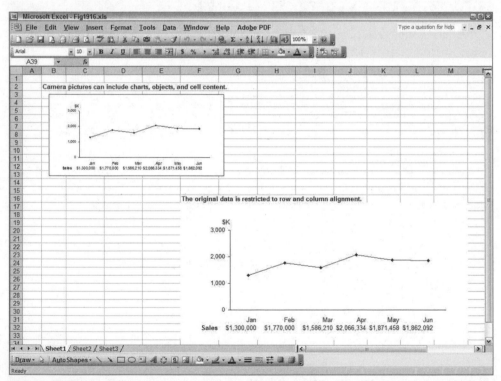

Figure 19.16: Camera pictures can contain charts and cell contents and can be positioned anywhere on the worksheet.

You can position a Camera picture without regard to rows or columns. Change the size of the Camera pictures by dragging the corners. This enables you to create miniature "detail" boxes alongside data in a report, as you might see in a magazine layout.

Simultaneously Formatting the Size of Multiple Charts or Camera Pictures

In most arrangements of charts and miniature charts, you will want all of them the same size. There are two ways to do this quickly. The first way is useful if you have a few charts and you want to arrange them in free form with no alignment to rows and columns. To do this, select all the charts using Ctrl+click. Right-click one of the selected charts and choose Format Object. Select the Size tab and then set the Height and Width in either the Size and Rotate or the Scale groups. All selected charts will change size. To make further changes, you will have to repeat the process.

The second method works well when you have many mini-charts you want to arrange and keep aligned with rows and columns. This method also enables you to easily experiment with different heights and widths by changing all the charts' heights and widths at the same time.

In this method, you "embed" mini-charts in the cells of a row or column and then adjust their sizes by changing row height or column width. For example, if you have multiple mini-charts you want aligned vertically, put them in the same column. Drag the mini-charts over each cell in the column where you want a mini-chart. Align the corners of each chart with the cell under it by holding the Alt key and dragging the chart corner to snap to the cell corner. Each mini-chart should now exactly cover the cell. Don't worry about chart height — that will be adjusted later.

Now change the mini-chart's properties so they will keep the same size as the cells they cover. To do this select all the mini-charts using Ctrl+click. Right-click on a selected mini-chart and choose Format Object. Select the Properties tab, then select Move and Size with Cells, and click OK. All mini-charts will now keep the size of the cells they cover.

Now format the heights of all the mini-charts by selecting all the rows containing mini-charts and dragging the row header to a new height. All mini-charts in a row will keep the same height as you change the row height, and all mini-charts in a column will keep the same width as you change the column width.

Summary

Miniature charts are essential to creating an information-rich display. You want a display where all the important information for decisions can be grasped quickly.

An important lesson to take from this chapter is that you should eliminate unessential information from your charts. Doing so will enable you to reduce the chart size and present additional information that is important to decision-making. (You don't want to present superfluous data.)

Chapter 26 describes how to use the MicroCharts add-in to add a suite of miniature charts to Excel. Chapter 29 shows examples of miniature charts used in a Balanced Scorecard.

20

Controlling Charts with Menus, Combo Boxes, and Buttons

The vision is really about empowering workers, giving them all the information about what's going on so they can do a lot more than they've done in the past.

Bill Gates
Founder, Microsoft

Microsoft Excel gives you the ability to create a user interface for your scorecards and dashboards that looks and operates like any Windows application. Just a few of the controls you can add to your scorecards and dashboards include lists, combo boxes (also called drop-down lists), scroll bars, and option buttons. As Figure 20.1 illustrates, with the addition of combo boxes, check boxes, and option buttons, you can make your dashboards more interactive, easier to use, and prevent many errors.

Chapter 18, "Working with Lists and Tables of Data," describes how to select data from a database and manipulate it through the use of INDEX and MATCH. Now, by combining INDEX and MATCH with controls, you can create interactive charts, data selectors, scrolling charts, and more.

Adding Combo Boxes, Lists, Check Boxes, and More to Your Dashboards

As Figure 20.2 shows, there are many controls you can add to your dashboards: menu buttons, check boxes, option buttons, list boxes, combo boxes, scroll bars, and spinners. There are many form controls, but they all work in a similar way. In order to use a form control, you must display the Forms toolbar shown in

Figure 20.2. To display the Forms toolbar, choose View ⇨ Toolbars ⇨ Forms. Table 20.1 describes each of the form controls displayed on the toolbar.

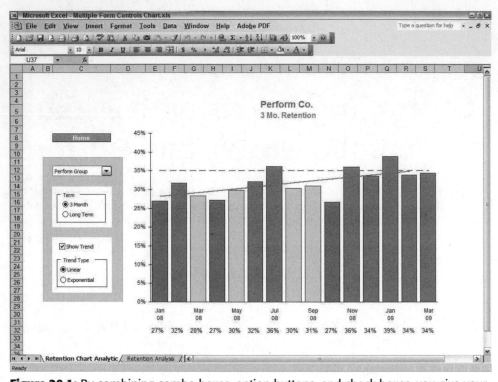

Figure 20.1: By combining combo boxes, option buttons, and check boxes, you give your users the ability to easily interact with the scorecards and dashboards you create.

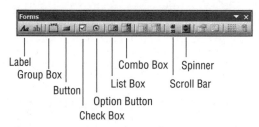

Figure 20.2: The Forms toolbar enables you to drag and drop controls onto your worksheets.

TIP Form controls are not automatically available in Excel 2007. To enable their use, you must enable the Developer tab. To do this, click the Microsoft Office Button, then click the Excel Options buttons. On the Popular tab, select Show Developer Tab in the Ribbon check box. Click OK.

To insert a form control when using Excel 2007, on the Developer tab, in the Controls group, click the Insert button, and then select the Form Control you want. Click and drag in the worksheet where you want the control.

To format a control in Excel 2007, right-click on the control and then select Format Control to display the Format Control dialog box. This chapter's instructions on formatting controls apply to Excel 2007 and earlier versions of Excel.

Table 20.1 The controls available on the Forms toolbar

FORM	FUNCTION
Label	Add a floating text box.
Group Box	Draw a box with an editable title. Use this tool to enclose multiple option buttons so that only one option button in the box at a time is selectable.
Button	Draw a button that will run a macro.
Check Box	Draw a single check box with an editable title. When selected, it enters TRUE in the linked cell; when unselected it enters FALSE. Check boxes are independent of each other.
Option Button	Draw a single option button (radio button). Place multiple option buttons within a group box so that only one option button is selectable from within the group. The selected button inserts its rank order into the linked cell. (Selecting the third button puts 3 in the linked cell.) Option buttons are normally used in the place of a combo box or lists when there are three or fewer items.
List Box	List boxes contain a list within a cell range on the worksheet. Selecting an item from the list inserts that item's numeric position in the list into the linked cell.
Combo Box	Combo boxes are drop-down lists that have the functionality of a list box but require little screen space when they are not in use.

Continued

Table 20.1 *(continued)*

FORM	FUNCTION
Scroll Bar	Scroll bars are like the scroll bars on the side or bottom of the Excel worksheet. Use a scroll bar to quickly "drag" from one end of a numeric range to another. Scroll bars are good when someone wants to test numerous approximate numeric entries. Once the range is found from dragging the slider, the exact number can be manually entered if needed. The "thumb" is the small movable box within a scroll bar. Dragging the thumb within the scroll bar inserts a number into a cell. You can control the range of the number. When you create a scroll bar the direction you initially drag to create the shape determines whether it is vertical or horizontal.
Spinner	Spinners are vertical up and down arrows that enable you to quickly "spin" through numbers. Unlike the scroll bar, which allows large jumps between numbers, the spinner increments through every number in its range. The numeric result from the spinner is inserted in a linked cell.

To draw a form control, display the Forms toolbar, click on the toolbar icon you need, and then click on the worksheet where you want your form control.

To move, resize, or format a form control, you must first select it. At first, this may cause you some confusion, because left-clicking on some controls checks or unchecks the check box, selects an option button, or selects an item from a list. To select a form control so that you can move or format it, hold Ctrl and click on the form control.

Drag a form control once it is selected by dragging the hatched outside border. To format a form control, right-click the control and select Format Control. To delete a control, select it then press Delete.

TIP You can align form controls with cell corners so multiple controls are in vertical and horizontal alignment. To align controls, select them, and then, as you drag a selection handle, hold down the Alt key. This forces that selection handle to align with cell boundaries.

To modify a form control, right-click the form control and choose Format Control from the context menu. In the Format Control dialog box, all form controls contain the same four tabs: Size, Protection, Properties, and Web. These are fairly self-explanatory. Most of the form controls also contain a tab named Control. The Control tab is where you specify such things as the list that will appear in a combo box and which cell will contain the output from a selection on the form control.

Each Control tab displays properties unique to each form control. Figure 20.3 shows the Control tab for the combo box. On this tab, specify the range containing the contents for the drop-down list, the output cell that will contain the result of a selection, and the number of items shown in the drop-down list when it displays.

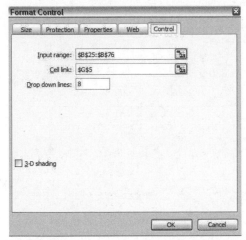

Figure 20.3: On the Control tab, you specify the input and output locations for a form control.

Selecting Data with a Combo Box or List

Scrolling lists and combo boxes are an excellent way to select one item from a long list. Selecting from a list reduces data entry errors and enables users to see all alternatives instead of just what they remember. Scrolling lists enable you to make a short object onscreen containing a long list of possible selections. Combo boxes are single-word high, but when selected they open to show a scrolling list. This saves considerable screen real estate.

TIP If you would like to work with the examples in this book, check the Introduction for information on how to download the sample data and example worksheets. Additional resources and examples are available at the author's web site at www.torconsulting.com.

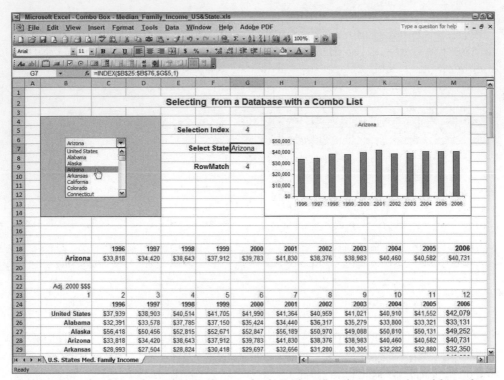

Figure 20.4: The row selected from the combo box identifies the row retrieved from the database.

Figure 20.4 shows a combo box on a simple dashboard that enables users to select one U.S. state, retrieve that state's median family income from 1996 to 2006, and display that income on a chart.

To add the combo box and formulas that identify the selection:

1. Click on the combo box in the Forms toolbar. In Excel 2007, select the combo box by clicking the Insert button in the Controls group on the Developers tab.

2. Drag in the worksheet where you want the combo box. Dragging will create the width and height of the combo box. If you click you will see just a large arrow. You can drag a corner of this arrow so the combo box displays appropriately.

3. Right click the combo box and select Format Control to display the Format Control dialog box.

4. In the Input Range box, enter the range containing the items you want to appear in the drop-down list. In this case the items are names of the states and the United States in range B25:B76.

5. In the Cell Link box, enter the cell where you want the number of the item select from the list to appear. This is cell G5.

6. In the Drop Down Lines box, enter the number of lines you want displayed when the list drops down.

7. Click OK.

When you click on the combo box, the drop-down list appears. Selecting an item from the list puts the number of that item's position in the list into cell G5. In some cases, you can use that position number directly to retrieve data; however, often you will need to convert it to text so that it can be used with VLOOKUP or MATCH as described in Chapter 18.

Here are the other formulas in the example that convert the selection, in G5, into the row of the database containing the selected state:

NAME	CELL	FORMULA	EXPLANATION
Select State	G7	=INDEX($B$25:$B$76,$G$5,1)	The INDEX finds the state name by looking down B25:B76 to the row returned in G5 by the combo box. Column 1 is specified in INDEX to look in the first and only column. An advantage to using INDEX over VLOOKUP is that you can look down any column in the table. It need not be just the first column.
Matching Row	G9	=MATCH($G$7,$B$25:$B$76,0)	MATCH uses the state's name in G7 to search down the first column of the database to find that state's corresponding row.

In this example, we've unnecessarily found the row for the selected state using MATCH when we already knew the row because it was the same as the G5. If you are doing a simple database retrieval, like this one, you can use G5 directly to retrieve data.

You need to use this system of matching with MATCH and INDEX if you are dealing with more complex situations in which:

- You need multiple drop-down lists to specify multiple criteria, as described in the section "Retrieving Data Given Multiple Key Words" in Chapter 18. (This is also explained in the following section.)

- You need one set of names displayed in the Combo list, but there are another set of longer or more technical names in the database. For example, a combo box might show English-language product names but the database contains products listed by a product identifier code.

Now that the row in the database is calculated, either from G5 for a simple situation, or by looking it up with MATCH, as in G9, you can retrieve the data from the database. The section in Chapter 18 titled "Adding a Drop-Down Selection List to Make Retrieval Easier" describes how to build this database and the retrieval formulas.

Basically, an INDEX function uses the row from G9 to retrieve a row of data from the database into the range B19:M19, where it displays in a chart. The functions that do this are:

NAME	CELL	FORMULA	EXPLANATION
Range Name	B24:M76	Db_MedianIncome	Range name containing the data.
Name of state retrieved from database	B19	=INDEX(db_ MedianIncome,$G$9+1,B$23)	INDEX retrieves the contents from the database at the intersection of the row G9+1 (plus one for the date header) and the column number in B23.
1996 data	C19	=INDEX(db_ MedianIncome,$G$9+1,C$23)	INDEX retrieves the contents from the database at the intersection of the row G9+1 (plus one for the date header) and the column number in C23.
Other data	D19:M19	Copy C19 across.	

Note that the row found in G9 had to have 1 added to it to correspond to the database rows, because the database range, B24:M76, had an additional row at the top for the date headers. Row 23, above the database, has numbers entered for each column in the database. This makes it easy to copy the formula in C19 across to D19:M19. C$23 in the INDEX formula makes a relative reference adjustment as it is copied, so each copy refers to the correct column in the database.

Note: List and Combo Box Are Similar but Different

The list box is like a combo box that is always open. Users can scroll down the list to select the item they want. The Control tab for the list box has two additional options, Multi and Extend. These are only available for use through Visual Basic for Applications.

Selecting Data with Multiple Criteria Using Multiple Combo Boxes

You can select from a database using multiple criteria by using multiple combo boxes, lists, or other controls and then matching against a key column in your database created by concatenating key words. This technique is often needed when your user must retrieve data from an Excel-based file that has hundreds or thousands of rows of information separated into categories.

In Figure 20.5, two combo boxes are used to retrieve a specific row from a database of 48 rows. Although this example database is small, I've used the same technique to retrieve data from Excel-based lists with thousands of rows and multiple combo boxes.

In Figure 20.5 the Product combo box receives its list from B17:B20. The number of the Product selected goes to cell F6. Cell F7 then converts this to text with the formula

```
=INDEX($B$17:$B$20,$F$6,1)
```

The Region combo box receives its list from C17:C20. The number of the Region selected goes to cell F9. Cell F10 then converts this to text with the formula

```
=INDEX($C$17:$C$20,$F$9,1)
```

Cell F12 then concatenates, or joins, these two words to create a new "key" word that will be matched against the contents in column 1 of the database. The concatenation formula in cell F12 is

```
=$F$7&$F$10
```

As explained in Chapter 18, you can use the concatenation function, &, to join together words in the database so that each row has a unique identifier or key. In this case, the formula in B28,

```
=C28&D28
```

has been copied down column B to create a unique key for each row in the database. The MATCH function in cell F14,

```
=MATCH($F$12,$B$27:$B$75,0)
```

can then be used to find the unique row in the database by matching the concatenation of your combo box selections against the concatenation in column B of the database.

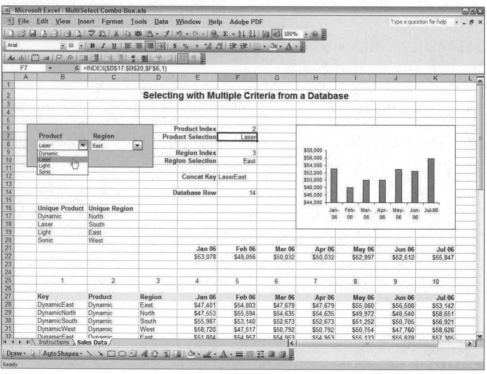

Figure 20.5: By using multiple combo boxes and a concatenated key, you can select data using multiple criteria.

When to Use a Data Validation List or Combo Box?

The Data Validation list, described in Chapter 18, allows you to create a cell that displays a list of choices when clicked. You also can type into the cell. In a data entry worksheet, I might use a Data Validation list, but in scorecards and dashboards I use a list or combo list. Here are the differences between Data Validation and the combo box.

Advantages to Data Validation

- User can type if desired, instead of selecting from a drop-down list.
- You can create an Error message that warns if an entry is invalid.
- The result is text rather than an index number. (Depending upon what you want to do, this can be an advantage or disadvantage.)

Disadvantages to Data Validation

- Unless you give it special formatting, the Data Validation cell looks like a normal cell. Dashboard users may not know to click in the cell.
- Because the data entry box is a cell, it must be aligned with other cells.

Advantages to Combo Box

- It is obviously a drop-down list, and the user knows to click on the down arrow.
- The user is forced to select items from a drop-down list, thus preventing errors.
- You can position it anywhere, regardless of cell alignment.
- You can attach a macro that triggers when the combo box is used.

Disadvantages to Combo Box

- If you are just looking for the text of the selection, then a combo box requires a VLOOKUP or INDEX.
- No pop-up instructions or error messages display unless you write a function to display them when a match is not found.

Creating Dynamic Cascading Combo Boxes or Lists

Cascading combo boxes or lists are useful when you have a very large list. Breaking this list into categories and items gives you the ability to deliver a more usable system. In Figure 20.6, for example, a long list of hospital quality indicators has been separated into categories that appear in the Category list in the combo box at B6. Selecting from this Category combo box changes the contents of the Quality Metric combo box at F6. This is easier for users than scrolling through long lists.

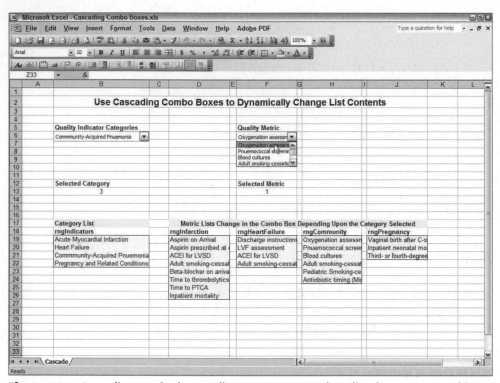

Figure 20.6: Cascading combo boxes allow you to present long lists by category and item within a category.

To create up to 29 cascading lists, use range names to name the lists that will appear in the combo box containing the list of items, not the Category combo box. In this example, there are four ranges used: rngInfarction, rngHeartFailure, rngCommunity, and rngPregnancy. An invisible dynamic range name is used to switch between these four range names depending upon the number in cell B13. The number in B13 is changed by selecting a category from the left Category List in B6.

To create the invisible dynamic range name:

1. Create range names for each list that will appear in the combo box whose contents will change.

2. Choose Insert, Name, Define Name to display the Define Name dialog box. In Excel 2007, on the Formulas tab in the Defined Name group, click the Define Name button. Figure 20.7 shows the dialog box when it has been completed.

3. Enter a name such as the name **rngComboList** in the Names In Workbook entry box. This will be the name for a named formula. The contents of that named formula will change depending upon the value in cell B13.

4. In the Refers To entry box, enter a CHOOSE formula that selects between the range names you have assigned to the lists. The formula in the example is

   ```
   =CHOOSE(Cascade!$B$13,rngInfarction,rngHeartFailure,rngCommunity,
   rngPregnancy)
   ```

5. Choose Add, then OK.

Figure 20.7: Use the Define Name dialog box to create a new dynamic range name that changes lists depending upon the category selection.

Within the Input Range for the combo box or list, you will enter the dynamic range instead of a cell reference. In this example, you would enter **rngComboList** in the Input Range for the Quality Metric Combo Box.

The CHOOSE function uses the value in B13 from the Quality Indicator Categories combo box to select from a list of choices which range to display in the Quality Metric combo box. CHOOSE can handle up to 29 choices.

Using Option Buttons

Option buttons, also known as radio buttons, are the round buttons that appear in groups. Option buttons are no different from combo boxes or list boxes in that you can only make one selection at a time. Use option buttons when there are only two or three choices, and use combo boxes or lists when there are more than three choices.

You can only select one option button from a group at a time. If you put two or more sets of option buttons on a worksheet you will find that they interfere with each other. To prevent groups from conflicting, put option buttons in groups by drawing a group box around each group of option buttons that you want to act as a single entity. The Group Box is on the Forms toolbar and looks like a small box with an XYZ title. Drag the outline of the box so it encloses all the option buttons in a group. Make sure option buttons and their text outline are completely enclosed. This keeps the groups distinct so that only one option in a group can be selected.

Title a group box by clicking in its title area and typing. You may need to add a few blank spaces after the title to ensure that the entire title displays.

Displaying or Hiding Data with a Check Box

It is easy to overwhelm a dashboard user with too much data. Initial requests for a dashboard have sometimes included four data lines, a forecast line, and a target or benchmark all on the same chart. Of course, presenting that much information on one chart makes for a confusing presentation. Instead, you should design your charts so they show just the information needed for decision-making. When additional data, such as trend lines, forecasts, or comparative data are needed, design your dashboards so that additional data series can be displayed on demand. Here's how to do that.

Figure 20.8 shows the chart of median family income by state that we've used earlier. This time, there is a straight-line trend line calculated in D19:M19. The FORECAST function in these cells references the data in D18:M18 so that the trend reflects the currently selected state.

The check box above the combo box returns a TRUE or FALSE to cell G12, depending upon whether the check box is selected or cleared. G12 is specified as the Cell Link in the Control Tab for the check box.

An IF function in cells B19:M19 controls whether the contents of row 19 appear or not. The formula in cell C19 is

```
=IF($G$12,FORECAST(C17,$C$18:$M$18,
$C$17:$M$17),"")
```

If G12 contains a TRUE, then the FORECAST function displays its results. If G12 is FALSE, then nothing displays. If you want to make individual data points disappear in a line, use the NA function instead of "".

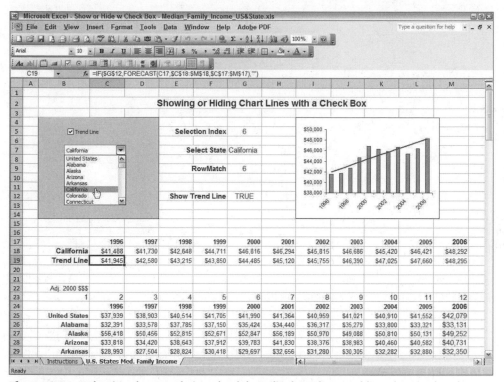

Figure 20.8: Selecting the Trend Line check box displays the trend line data in the chart.

Scrolling Charts through Time with a Slider Bar

Data series spanning many years may have your dashboard users wishing they could scroll through time so they can compare prior quarters and years. There is a way to do that—and to make it easy for users at the same time. Figure 20.9 shows the median family income dashboard we've used before. A horizontal scroll bar has been drawn below the chart. Dragging the "thumb" in the scroll bar animates the chart so that it scrolls through the time span from 1996 to 2006. For demonstration purposes, this example has a short timeframe, but the method is very handy when you have many years of data.

To draw a scroll bar in either the horizontal or vertical direction, click the Scroll Bar icon on the Form toolbar, then click and drag on the worksheet in the direction you want the scroll bar.

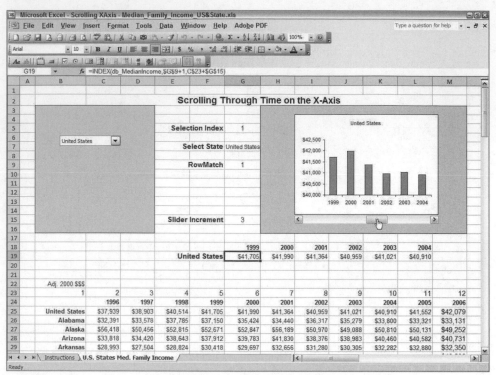

Figure 20.9: Use a horizontal scroll bar to scroll through a time series.

The scroll bar in Figure 20.9 has the following values on its Control tab.

Minimum Value	0
Maximum Value	5
Incremental Change	1
Page Change	5

Dragging the slider's thumb changes the value in cell G15. The dates in G18:M18 and the data in G19:M19 change as the value in G15 changes. The first year's formula in cell G18 is

```
=INDEX($C$24:$M$24,1,$G$15+1)
```

The first data's formula in cell G19 is

```
=INDEX(db_MedianIncome,$G$9+1,C$23+$G$15)
```

In the INDEX formula, G15, which is the slider value, is in the column parameter of INDEX. A change to G15 increments the column referenced by INDEX.

Scroll bars can be used in other ways. The vertical scroll bar in Figure 20.10 produces the effect of scrolling through a financial statement.

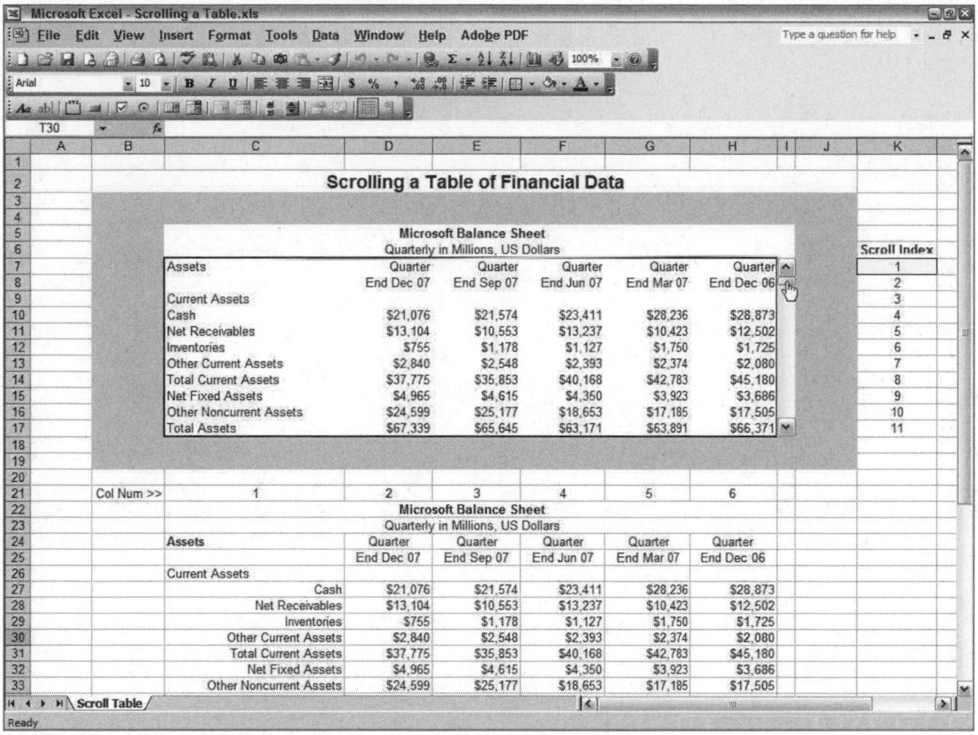

Figure 20.10: Here a vertical scroll bar enables users to scroll through a financial statement that is too large to appear in one screen.

For more tips on creating dashboards and scorecards in Excel, as well as for information on Balanced Scorecards and process mapping, go to www.torconsulting.com.

Summary

With the use of form controls and good formatting, you can create dashboards and scorecards that look good, are easy to use, and make it easier to make business decisions. The form controls are an excellent way of making your work professional-looking and easy to use.

CHAPTER 21

Working with PivotTables

What we see depends mainly on what we look for.
John Lubbock
Biologist and Politician, 1834–1913

It's not hard to argue that PivotTables are the most powerful feature in Excel. What is amazing is that they are also one of the least-used features. Most Excel users have heard of them, but have never used them.

If you have ever needed to analyze large amounts of data, such as building a summary table of sales by month, or doing statistical analysis on large lists, or finding the top 10 in a list, you would have benefited by knowing how to use PivotTables. All Excel users beyond novice level should at least learn the concept of a PivotTable so that they know when to use this powerful tool.

The power of PivotTables can bring accounting and finance people to tears. I used to teach a course at Sonoma State University on computers and spreadsheets for finance and accounting. About a week after going through an exercise on PivotTables I got a telephone call from a small company's internal accountant. Her voice sounded as if she was almost in tears. She told me how she used to spend a day and a half at the end of each month building and rebuilding tables in Excel so she could categorize revenue and expenses in different ways, "slice and dice," as well as doing some auditing. With what she now knew about PivotTables, she had reduced that day and a half to less than an hour of work. She could use the rest of that time in more productive areas for her company. She was ecstatic!

The data that a PivotTable analyzes can be stored in a list on a worksheet, in a small Access database, or in a large SQL server. The end result is that with a few minutes' work, your worksheets can import data and summarize (and then display) it the way you want.

Basic Concepts of PivotTables

PivotTables take lists and databases, analyze the data, and then return it into an Excel worksheet in the layout you specify. Figure 21.1 is a simple Excel list used in the examples in this chapter. It contains one header row and 624 rows of data covering product unit and dollar sales by region and date. To build a summary table from this, you would need to write complex SUMIF, COUNTIF, or any number of other statistical or financial formulas. And then, when you wanted a different view into the data, you would need to rewrite the formulas or conditions.

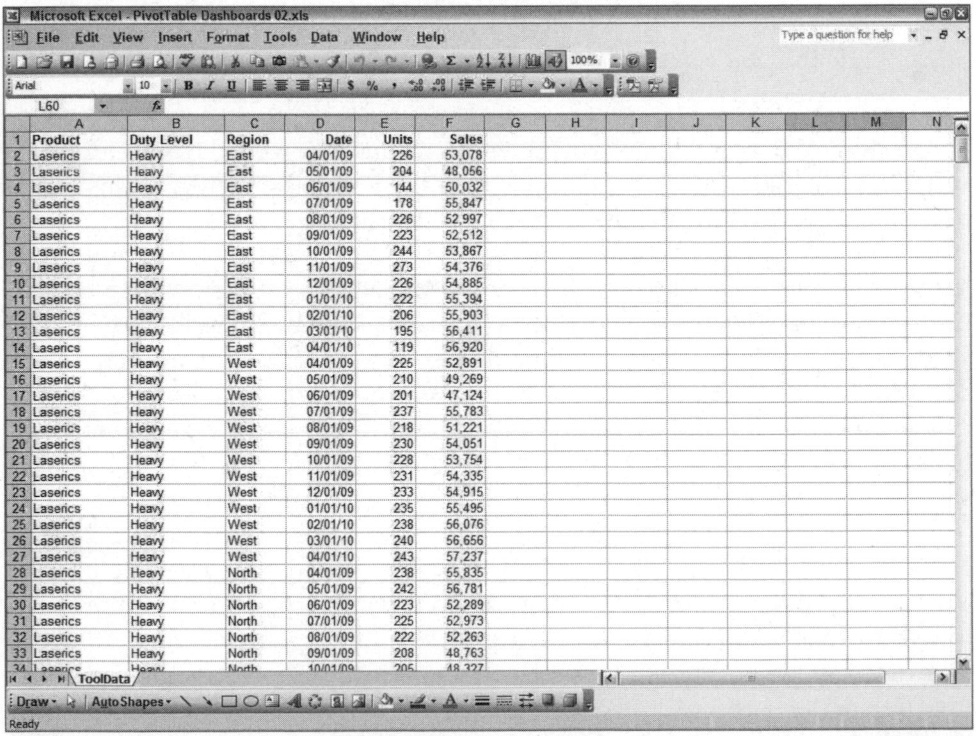

	A	B	C	D	E	F
1	Product	Duty Level	Region	Date	Units	Sales
2	Laserics	Heavy	East	04/01/09	226	53,078
3	Laserics	Heavy	East	05/01/09	204	48,056
4	Laserics	Heavy	East	06/01/09	144	50,032
5	Laserics	Heavy	East	07/01/09	178	55,847
6	Laserics	Heavy	East	08/01/09	226	52,997
7	Laserics	Heavy	East	09/01/09	223	52,512
8	Laserics	Heavy	East	10/01/09	244	53,867
9	Laserics	Heavy	East	11/01/09	273	54,376
10	Laserics	Heavy	East	12/01/09	226	54,885
11	Laserics	Heavy	East	01/01/10	222	55,394
12	Laserics	Heavy	East	02/01/10	206	55,903
13	Laserics	Heavy	East	03/01/10	195	56,411
14	Laserics	Heavy	East	04/01/10	119	56,920
15	Laserics	Heavy	West	04/01/09	225	52,891
16	Laserics	Heavy	West	05/01/09	210	49,269
17	Laserics	Heavy	West	06/01/09	201	47,124
18	Laserics	Heavy	West	07/01/09	237	55,783
19	Laserics	Heavy	West	08/01/09	218	51,221
20	Laserics	Heavy	West	09/01/09	230	54,051
21	Laserics	Heavy	West	10/01/09	228	53,754
22	Laserics	Heavy	West	11/01/09	231	54,335
23	Laserics	Heavy	West	12/01/09	233	54,915
24	Laserics	Heavy	West	01/01/10	235	55,495
25	Laserics	Heavy	West	02/01/10	238	56,076
26	Laserics	Heavy	West	03/01/10	240	56,656
27	Laserics	Heavy	West	04/01/10	243	57,237
28	Laserics	Heavy	North	04/01/09	238	55,835
29	Laserics	Heavy	North	05/01/09	242	56,781
30	Laserics	Heavy	North	06/01/09	223	52,289
31	Laserics	Heavy	North	07/01/09	225	52,973
32	Laserics	Heavy	North	08/01/09	222	52,263
33	Laserics	Heavy	North	09/01/09	208	48,763
34	Laserics	Heavy	North	10/01/09	205	48,327

Figure 21.1: PivotTables are a powerful tool that can be used on Excel lists, such as the one shown, or on external relational databases.

By using the Data, PivotTable command or, in Excel 2007, on the Insert tab, in the Tables group, by choosing PivotTable, you can create a formatted table from that list like the one shown in Figure 21.2. Building this table took no typing or formulas. It required 5 clicks and 5 drags for basic construction and layout. Another 8 clicks added the color and border formats and formatted the dates. What makes this even more powerful than using conditional consolidation formulas such as SUMIF and COUNTIF is that you can reorganize it and solve for different analyses with just a few clicks.

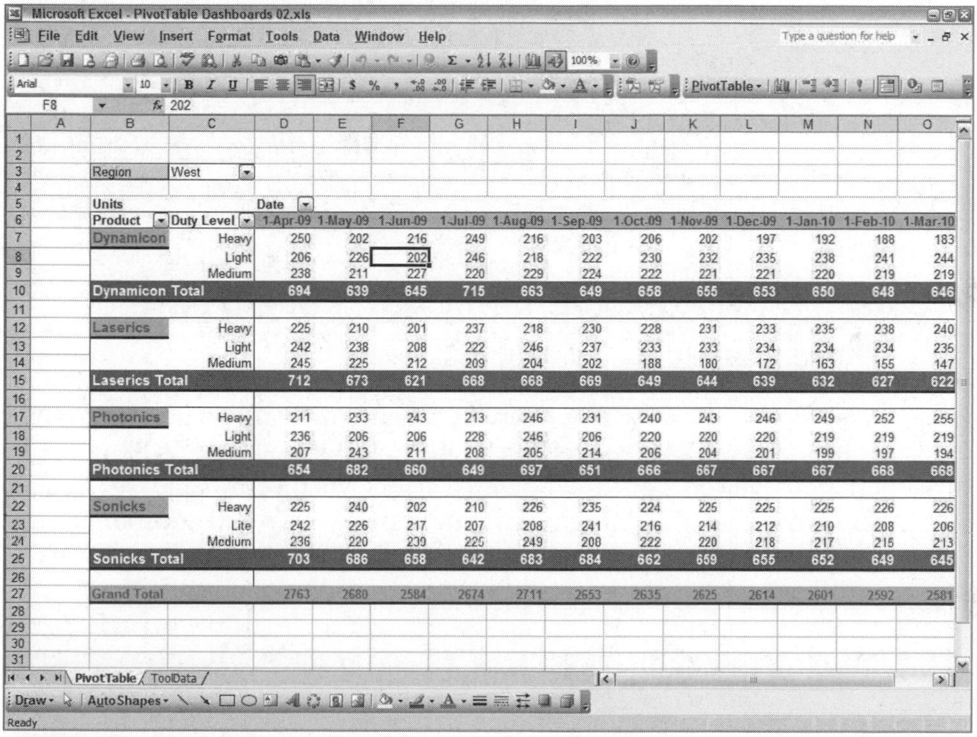

Region: West

Units		Date											
Product	Duty Level	1-Apr-09	1-May-09	1-Jun-09	1-Jul-09	1-Aug-09	1-Sep-09	1-Oct-09	1-Nov-09	1-Dec-09	1-Jan-10	1-Feb-10	1-Mar-10
Dynamicon	Heavy	250	202	216	249	216	203	206	202	197	192	188	183
	Light	206	226	202	246	218	222	230	232	235	238	241	244
	Medium	238	211	227	220	229	224	222	221	221	220	219	219
Dynamicon Total		694	639	645	715	663	649	658	655	653	650	648	646
Laserics	Heavy	225	210	201	237	218	230	228	231	233	235	238	240
	Light	242	238	208	222	246	237	233	233	234	234	234	235
	Medium	245	225	212	209	204	202	188	180	172	163	155	147
Laserics Total		712	673	621	668	668	669	649	644	639	632	627	622
Photonics	Heavy	211	233	243	213	246	231	240	243	246	249	252	255
	Light	236	206	206	228	246	206	220	220	220	219	219	219
	Medium	207	243	211	208	205	214	206	204	201	199	197	194
Photonics Total		654	682	660	649	697	651	666	667	667	667	668	668
Sonicks	Heavy	225	240	202	210	226	235	224	225	225	225	226	226
	Lite	242	226	217	207	208	241	216	214	212	210	208	206
	Medium	236	220	239	225	249	208	222	220	218	217	215	213
Sonicks Total		703	686	658	642	683	684	662	659	655	652	649	645
Grand Total		2763	2680	2584	2674	2711	2653	2635	2625	2614	2601	2592	2581

Figure 21.2: With 5 clicks and 5 drags, you can convert a list like that in Figure 21.1 into a dynamic table like this.

PivotTables can access data from lists within an Excel worksheet or from relational databases. To connect to a relational database, you will need to create an Office Data Connection to the database.

USING PIVOTTABLES WITH OLAP

If you want or need to use PivotTables with OLAP, check the Microsoft web site for support and whitepapers.

WHERE TO LEARN ABOUT BUILDING PIVOTTABLES

This chapter is not an introduction to creating PivotTables. PivotTables are covered in most introductory Excel books, and many free resources are available on the Web. For information about building and manipulating PivotTables, please refer to the informative books *Excel Advanced Report Development* (Wiley, 2005) or *Excel 2007 Advanced Report Development* (Wiley, 2007), by Timothy Zapawa). Other recommended books are *Beginning PivotTables in Excel 2007* and *Excel 2007 Excel Pivot Tables Recipes*, by Debra Dalgleish (Apress, 2007).

To learn more about PivotTables online, go to these sources:

- `http://Lacher.com` – **search for PivotTables.**
- `www.ozgrid.com` – **search for PivotTables.**
- `www.contextures.com` **is the web site of Debra Dalgleish, the author of multiple books on PivotTables.**

Creating an Auto-Expanding Database Name

If you are entering, retrieving, or storing data in Excel worksheets, then before you create a PivotTable you should create an automatically expanding range name for the database area referenced by the PivotTable. (You don't have to do this, but it will save you work and potential errors when your database changes size.) Using an auto-expanding range name allows you to add additional rows or columns of data, confident that they will be included in the PivotTable the next time it updates.

DOWNLOAD THE SAMPLE DATA AND EXAMPLE FILES

Check the Introduction of this book for instructions on how to download the sample data and example files to work along with the instructions in this book. The Introduction also contains links to additional resources for developing Balanced Scorecards and operational dashboards.

To create an auto-expanding range name for your data:

1. Enter your data on a new worksheet starting at cell A1. Enter headings in row 1. Enter only the database on this worksheet.

2. Choose Insert ➪ Name ➪ Define. In Excel 2007, on the Formula tab, in the Defined Names group, select Define Name. This will open the Define Name dialog box.

3. Define a calculated range name. Figure 21.3 shows the new range name of dbToolsData. The "db" prefix is a naming convention for identifying a database. The formula that calculates the range for this name is in the Refers To: entry box. The OFFSET formula syntax is

```
=OFFSET(reference,rows,cols,[height],[width])
```

An explanation of the OFFSET formula follows these steps.

4. Click Add, then OK.

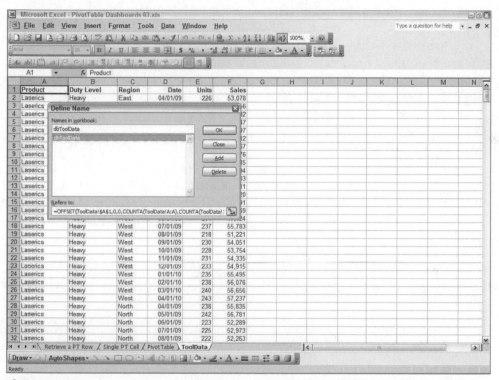

Figure 21.3: Create an auto-expanding range name for your database to ensure that new data is included in your PivotTable.

The "reference" is A1, the top-left corner of the data. There is no offset for rows or columns because the top-left reference for the defined name is the same as the top left of the database.

The height of the named database range is calculated by counting all filled cells in column A. The width of the database range is calculated by counting all filled cells in row 1.

```
COUNTA(A:A)
COUNTA(1:1)
```

The complete formula is

```
=OFFSET(ToolData!$A$1,0,0,
COUNTA(ToolData!A:A),COUNTA(ToolData!1:1))
```

where ToolData is the name of the worksheet tab.

CAUTION This formula only works correctly if all data is entered without leaving blank rows or columns. Calculations for the size of the database depend upon counting the filled cells in column A and row 1 so that one filled cell equals one row or column in the database. If there are blank cells in column A or row 1, the size of the database will calculate incorrectly.

You cannot use the name dbToolData in a function on the same worksheet where dbToolData resides, because the OFFSET formula covers all cells in the worksheet, and this will cause a circular reference. To prevent this you could restrict the range across which COUNTA counts. For example, instead of counting down all of column A with COUNTA(ToolData!A:A) the formula could have been written as COUNTA(ToolData!A1:A200) which would work as long as the database did not exceed row 200.

To test the name dbToolData to ensure that it is correct, move to another worksheet in this workbook and enter an INDEX formula to retrieve contents at the limits of the database. For example, the lower right corner of this database is

```
=INDEX(dbToolIndex,625,6)
```

This returns 44351, the last number in the Sales column.

To reference this auto-expanding database name for your PivotTable, enter the range name as your database reference in the second step of the PivotTable Wizard, as shown in Figure 21.4.

Figure 21.4: Enter the auto-expanding range name in the second step of the PivotTable Wizard.

Using PivotTable Results in Dashboards

In nearly all cases, you will want to keep the actual PivotTable as well as the data hidden from the Balanced Scorecard or dashboard users. PivotTables are one of those things that are easy once you understand their concept, but when multiple users share a dashboard, it only takes one untrained user to change the PivotTable layout so that it is unusable by the scorecard or dashboard. PivotTables are so powerful that you should still use them, but you should incorporate them safely into scorecards and dashboards.

I recommend you keep your PivotTable in a hidden worksheet and then extract and manipulate from it the data you want. With the following techniques, your users will have a lot of power with little danger—and you won't have to write any VBA macros.

Retrieving a Single Cell of Data from a PivotTable

There is one worksheet function that works with PivotTables:

```
GETPIVODATA(data_field,pivot_table,
[field1],[item1],[field2],[item2],…)
```

where data_field is the explicit text name in quotes of the data you want to retrieve. In most cases, these text names appear in the PivotTable titles to identify a result, such as "Sum of Sales." This is the field being calculated within the table. pivot_table is the name of the PivotTable, a cell within the PivotTable, or a named range in the PivotTable. This is used to identify the PivotTable from which data will be extracted. You can see and change the name of the PivotTable at the top of the PivotTable options box.

The associated pairs of [field1] and [item1] are the field names and an item within that field. The [field] and [item] enable you to identify which cell of data within the table you want. In Figure 21.2 (the finished table previously shown), an example would be a field name Product with an item of Dynamicon. You can have up to 14 of these sets of [field] and [item], and they do not need to match the order in the data or PivotTable.

Figure 21.5 shows a GETPIVOTDATA function retrieving a single cell's content from the PivotTable in Figure 21.2. The function is

```
=GETPIVOTDATA("Units",PivotTable!$B$5,
"Product","Dynamicon","Duty Level","Light","Date",DATE(2009,6,1))
```

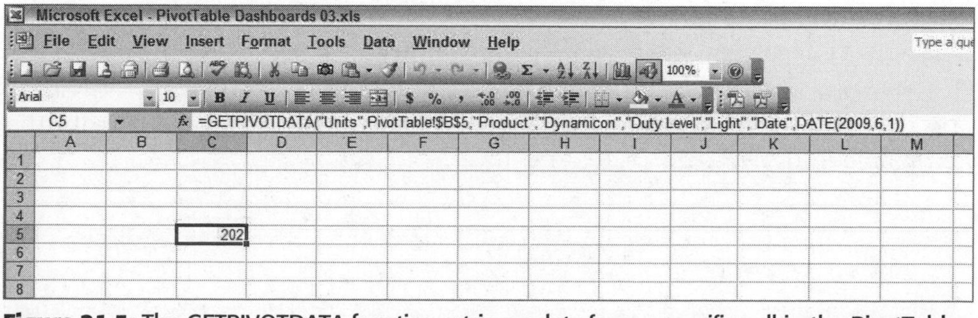

Figure 21.5: The GETPIVOTDATA function retrieves data from a specific cell in the PivotTable.

This function retrieves the result 202 from cell F8 in the PivotTable shown in Figure 21.2. Another way to look at this function is as a series of query requests, such as

```
Data = Units
Product = Dynamicon
Duty Level = Light
Date = Jun 1, 2009
```

Note that the current region selected in the PivotTable in Figure 21.2 is West. The result of 202 is for the West region only. Selecting a different Region in the PivotTable would change the value returned by GETPIVOTDATA. Later in this section, you will see how to control this.

The total for all products for April 1, 2009, can be retrieved with

```
=GETPIVOTDATA("Units",PivotTable!$B$5,
"Product","Dynamicon","Date",DATE(2009,4,1))
```

The total for all Products and all Duty Levels for April 1, 2009 can be retrieved with

```
=GETPIVOTDATA("Units",PivotTable!$B$5,
"Date",DATE(2009,4,1))
```

Note: An Easy Way to Create Complex GETPIVOTDATA Functions

Entry of GETPIVOTDATA functions would be very tedious and error-prone if you had to type it, but you can enter it easily by typing = in the worksheet where you want the PivotTable result and then clicking the appropriate cell within the data area of the PivotTable. Excel will write the full GETPIVOTDATA function for you.

Dynamically Retrieving Data from a PivotTable

The quoted text within the GETPIVOTDATA function might give you the idea that it can be replaced by text results from other worksheet functions. By following up on that idea, we will see how to extract data from a PivotTable using combo boxes or text entry fields.

Figure 21.6 shows a row of data retrieved from the PivotTable based on the Duty Level selected from the combo box. Selecting a Duty Level from the combo box in cell D4 changes the entire row of data in row 11 retrieved from the PivotTable in figure 21.2.

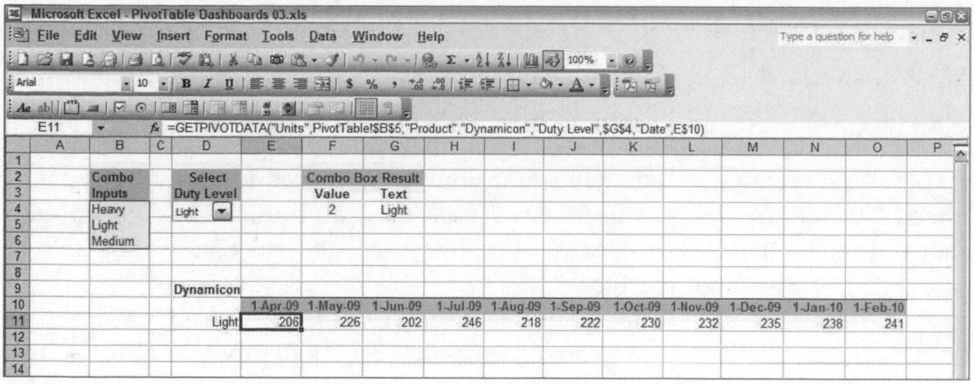

Figure 21.6: Replacing the parameters in the GETPIVOTDATA function with cell contents allows you to selectively retrieve whatever data you want from a PivotTable.

The combo box in D4 uses the list of names in B4:B6. Selecting the Duty Level from the combo box in D4 enters the item number selected in F4. Cell G4 then uses this number in an INDEX function to retrieve the text value of the selection from the range B4:B6. This may seem convoluted. Why not just type in the Duty Level name in G4? This would be fine for short lists with simple names, but if you have long lists, you will want your dashboard users to select from a combo box to prevent errors and to give them all possible choices. Using a combo box is explained in detail in Chapter 20, "Controlling Dashboards with Menus, Combo Boxes and Buttons."

The following GETPIVOTDATA function is in cell E11. It shows how the Item2 that matches "Duty Level" is the contents of cell G4, the result of the combo box.

The date used in the function is the date directly above the cell containing the GETPIVOTDATA function. When the function in E11 is copied across, it refers to the date in each column, but the same Duty Level.

```
=GETPIVOTDATA("Units",PivotTable!$B$5,"Product","Dynamicon",
"Duty Level",$G$4,"Date",E$10)
```

Again, the data retrieved will change depending upon the Region selected in the PivotTable's Page control. The following section shows you how to control all fields.

Once you understand how this works, you can use Chapter 20 to build tables that retrieve data from PivotTables based on selections from option buttons, combo boxes, and lists. It gives your users the ability to query the results of PivotTables, and it gives you control of the format while limiting potential mishaps.

Building a Safe User-Controlled PivotTable Display

Most dashboard users have a limited set of questions they need answered. Managers usually aren't out to probe every conceivable query using the PivotTable, and if a business analyst needs that capability you should teach him PivotTables. If, however, you have done your homework and know the types of queries and analytics your users need, then you can build sets of PivotTables that will answer a large majority of their questions, and you will be able to safely control the user interface.

To build a dashboard that gives users the answers they need, you need to know what fields they want to query, such as Product, Regions, and Dates. You also need to know which data they want analyzed (such as Units and Sales) and how they want it analyzed. In the example PivotTable layout in Figure 21.7, the Layout has been constructed to allow data retrieval by region, product, duty level, and date. (Note that in this example, the region is included on the left side and is not in the page field, as in the previous example.) The data being analyzed is the sum of units and the sum of sales. The result of this layout, from the same database as the rest of this chapter, is shown in Figure 21.8.

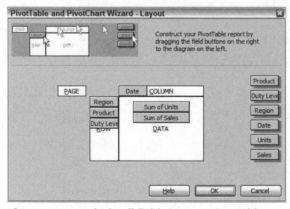

Figure 21.7: Include all fields in your PivotTable you want to access with GETPIVOTDATA.

Figure 21.9 shows how data can be retrieved from the PivotTable through the use of combo boxes. In this figure, cell C18 contains

```
=GETPIVOTDATA("Sum of Units",PivotTable!$B$5,
"Product",$G$10,"Duty Level",$B18,
"Region",$G$4,"Date",C$17)
```

The Product field refers to the contents of G10, the result of the combo box in C10. Region is specified in G4, the result of another combo box. Duty Level comes from the headings to the left in B18.

It is important to note that Sum of Units is specified uniquely as quoted text in the function. It does not reference a cell.

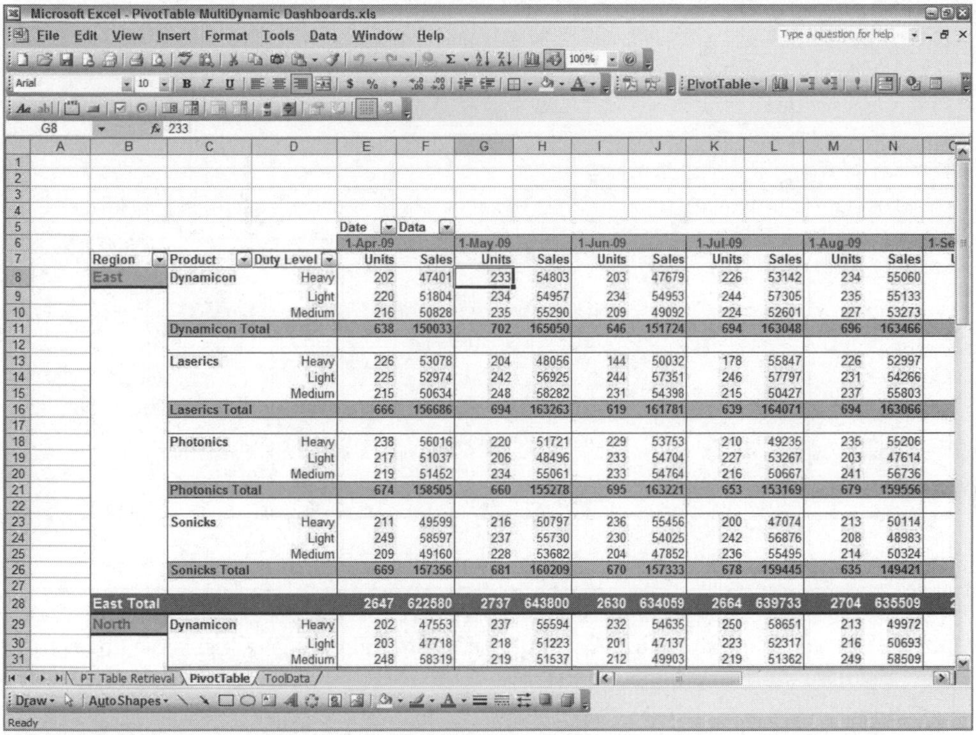

Figure 21.8: Including Region, Units, and Sales within the PivotTable area enables you to retrieve data dynamically on those fields.

TIP The example in Figure 21.9 shows two separate worksheet tables to display the Sum of Units or the Sum of Sales. You can give your users the ability to choose between Sum of Units or Sum of Sales by using an IF or CHOOSE function to select which quoted text will be used as the data_field in GETPIVOTDATA. The following formula changes the GETPIVOTDATA results between Sum of Units or Sum of Sales depending upon the value in C13. If C13 is 1, then Sum of Units displays. If C13 is 2, then Sum of Sales displays. The CHOOSE function chooses between "Sum of Units" or "Sum of Sales," depending upon the value in C13. Two option buttons that output to C13 would be a good way to give your users the choice of results.

```
=GETPIVOTDATA(CHOOSE($C$13,"Sum of Units","Sum of Sales"),
PivotTable!$B$5,"Product",$G$10,"Duty Level",$B18,"Region",
$G$4,"Date",C$17)
```

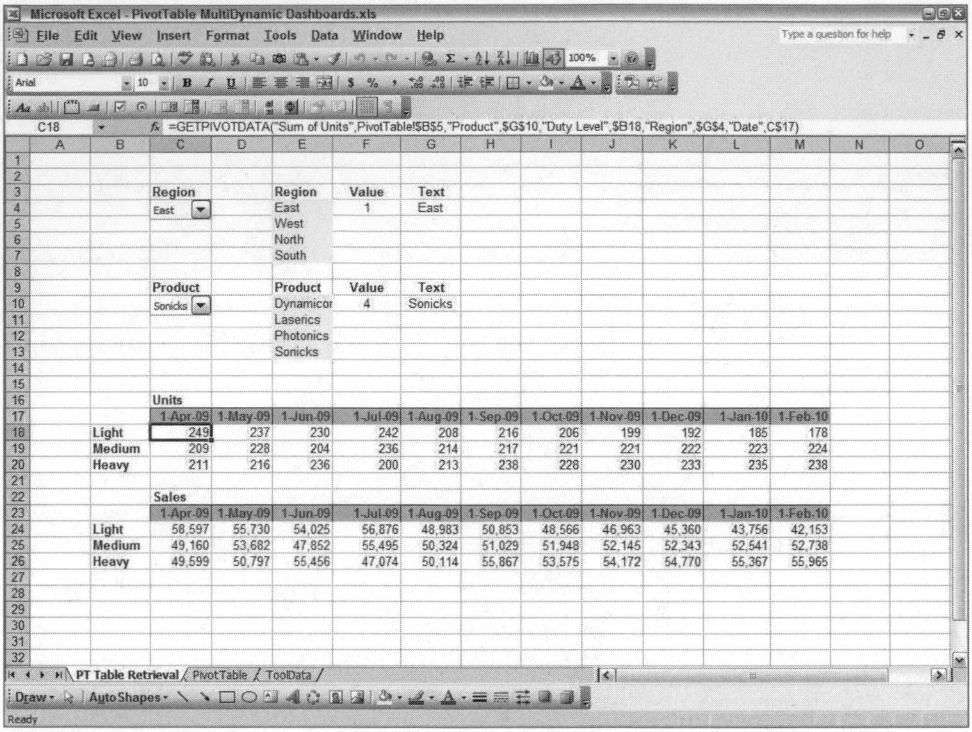

Figure 21.9: Combining a robust PivotTable with combo boxes gives users the ability to extract the data they need from a PivotTable.

Drilling Down to Detail with PivotTables

PivotTables include another powerful feature to aid in analysis. Double-clicking on a data cell within a PivotTable drills down to the data supporting that cell's result. Excel opens a new worksheet that displays the individual data elements analyzed. Figure 21.10 shows a worksheet displaying the raw data returned by double-clicking within the PivotTable we used in previous examples.

> **CAUTION** Inexperienced Excel users do not realize that when they double-click a cell in a PivotTable the new drill-down data is displayed in a new worksheet. When they want to close the sheet showing drill-down data, they have a habit of either closing the entire workbook or saving the workbook with the new worksheet. This eventually produces a workbook glutted with drill-down remnants.
>
> To turn off the drill-down feature on PivotTables, go to the PivotTable Options dialog box and clear the Enable Drill to Details check box. In Excel 2007, right-click in the PivotTable and choose PivotTable Options. On the Data tab, clear the Enable Show Details check box.

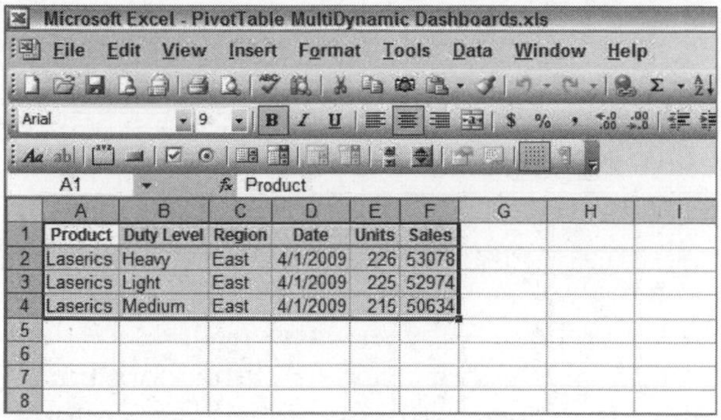

Figure 21.10: Double-clicking a data cell in a PivotTable opens a new worksheet showing the data used by that cell.

TIP PivotCharts are a nice feature of Excel when you are manually analyzing data. However, if you need to present bullet-proof charts that must keep their formatting as the PivotTable updates or changes, then I do not recommend their use. Instead, retrieve data from the PivotTable using the GETPIVOTDATA function, as described in this chapter, and base your chart on that data. Use the form controls described in Chapter 20 to enable users to easily change the table. This will give you more charting options, the formatting will be stable, and you can control user interaction. You and your users will be happier!

Updating the PivotTable Linked to Internal or External Data

Dashboard users are going to want the most up-to-date data. If they are viewing PivotTable results accessed dynamically from a database, they may need to update the PivotTable while the dashboard is open.

To update the PivotTable when it opens, right click in the PivotTable and open the PivotTable Option dialog box and then select the Refresh On Open check box. If your PivotTable is dynamically linked to a database, then you also can set in the PivotTable Option dialog box how frequently you want to refresh the PivotTable.

Summary

PivotTables are incredibly powerful and deserve to be the foundation behind any scorecard or dashboard linked to a database. They can retrieve selected data from a database, aggregate or do statistical analysis, group dates, group products, and more. However, with great power comes great responsibility that not all users have been trained to handle.

If your scorecards or dashboards will be used by inexperienced users, then I recommend learning what type of analysis your users need the most, building one or more PivotTables containing those analyses, and then hiding the PivotTables and retrieving the data using the form controls such as combo boxes from Chapter 20 and the GETPIVOTDATA function. This is a very powerful tool. Once you get the hang of this, your capability will expand greatly.

CHAPTER 22

Smoothing Data and Forecasting Trends

*I always avoid prophesying beforehand because it is much better
to prophesy after the event has already taken place.*

Winston Churchill
Statesman, 1874–1965

Humans have been forecasting ever since the first shaman squatted by a fire
and cast bones to divine the future. We forecast how long it will take us to get
to work based on the latest traffic jam, and when we get to work, we forecast
product sales, marketing response rates, or budget variance.

Now we cast bones with the aid of complex algorithms built into statistical
analysis programs such as SPSS. Even though few of us have consistent access
to SPSS or the skills to us it, we can get our everyday forecasting needs met with
Microsoft Excel. Most of what we need for simple forecasting and analysis is
built into Microsoft Excel and is very straightforward to use.

In this chapter you will learn how to smooth erratic data so you can see and
use the patterns hidden in the data. You will learn how to write your own formulas that work in any Excel worksheet and how to use the wizard in the Analysis
ToolPak. If you need to forecast data that may have a linear or curving trend,
you will also learn how to use Excel's TREND and GROWTH functions.

There is as much art to analyzing data and developing forecasts as there
is mathematical science. You must understand which mathematical method
is appropriate and which parameters to use to smooth or forecast data. The
qualitative art comes in knowing how far into the future you can acceptably
forecast, how much you can smooth data without losing what you want to see,
and how external factors such as population changes and competitive product
introductions may affect your forecast.

TIP As enjoyable as you may find it to sit in your office, sip coffee, and forecast amazing profit growth, to do so can be dangerous unless you get out in the real world and apply a realistic viewpoint to your forecasts. One CEO for a technology startup used a "hockey stick" curve to forecast the subscription-based revenue for his company. There was no evaluation of production capacity, distribution channels, or competitive pressure. After a few million dollars in angel and private investor funds were squandered based on outrageous forecasts, the business was closed. Every forecast should come with a red title that says, "Does this look realistic?"

Smoothing Erratic Data

Business data are rarely consistent and smooth; they are erratic. Business data reflect the peaks and valleys of randomness and the whims of people's emotions in the marketplace. Whether you are a giant corporation or a small- to mid-sized business, you need a way to smooth erratic data so you can see underlying patterns.

Moving averages are used to smooth erratic data so we can see underlying patterns. They work by taking an average of the data over a time period. That average smoothes erratic spikes or dips, but also "flattens" the data, causing rapid changes to be lost or delayed.

Most businesses look at data that are sampled monthly, such as sales, product turnover, and so forth. Data like these usually use a 3-month or 6-month moving average. By averaging the data over a shorter period of time, you see more of the data's erratic nature. This also lets you see rapid shifts in movement more quickly. Averaging over a longer time period smoothes erratic moves but delays the appearance of changes.

There is an art to knowing how much to smooth moving averages. If you smooth them too much, you may miss rapid shifts. If you don't smooth them enough, you may not be able to see an underlying pattern. Try different weighting or smoothing factors and try using different smoothing methods. This chapter will give you a couple of different approaches.

Smoothing Data with Simple Moving Averages

The simplest way to smooth a data series is with a simple moving average. In moving averages, a data value is "smoothed" by averaging the current data value with a set number of preceding data values. It is averaged over time.

For example, to average data over three periods, you would use a formula like this,

```
Forecast(t) = Average(Data(t) + Data(t-1) + Data(t-2))
```

where t is the time period for the forecast data, Data(t) is the data for the current period, Data($t-1$) is the data for the previous period, and Data($t-2$) is the data for two previous periods.

The time period over which you average the data is dependent upon how much you want the data smoothed. For most monthly data, 3 or 6 months of smoothing are useful.

> **CAUTION** If you need to complete a series with a linear or growth projection quickly, you can select the data series, then use the right mouse button to drag the fill handle to fill the empty cells with a linear or growth projection. Although this is handy for manual work, it doesn't help in dashboards. The data created by Excel with this method are static and do not update when you change or add additional source data.

Moving Averages with Formulas

Simple smoothing is easy to do with Excel formulas. You can also use Excel's Analysis ToolPak to create simple smoothing; however, it is so easy to do yourself that there is little need to use the Analysis ToolPak.

In Figure 22.1, the erratic data is in the range C5:C31. A smoothing formula is used in D7:D31 to create a smoother set of values. You can see the difference in the chart.

Cell D7 contains the formula

```
=AVERAGE(C5:C7)
```

This formula uses relative references to average the current data with the prior 2 months of data. Copying the formula through the range D7:D31 will produce data that are smoothed over 3-month periods.

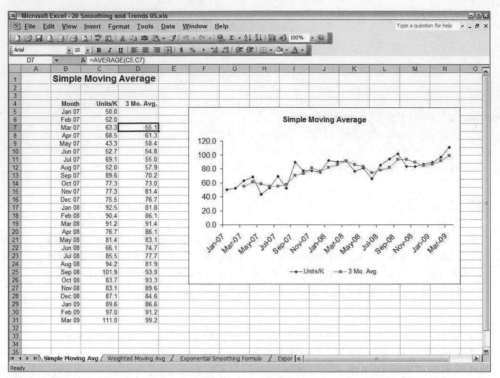

Figure 22.1: Simple smoothing can be done with AVERAGE and relative references.

Problems with Simple Moving Averages

Although easy to use, simple smoothing can be easy to misinterpret. Some issues it causes are these:

- There are no data points until the first average has been calculated. Notice in Figure 22.1 that cells D5 and D6 are blank.

- Old and recent data have the same weighting in the average. That means you won't see trends coming until they've been moving for at least half of the averaging period.

- If there are cycles in the data, the cycle in the smoothed data will lag reality by half the smoothing period.

- More erratic data may require smoothing over a longer period, but this will cause changes or cycles to be delayed and flattened.

Two other weighted average methods can resolve some of these problems.

Smoothing with Weighted Moving Averages

You can compensate for some of the problems in simple moving averages by using a weighted moving average. This assigns more weight to recent data and less weight to older data. All the weights must total 100 percent.

The equation looks like this:

```
Forecast(t) = Wt(t)*Data(t) + Wt(t-1)*Data(t-1)
+ Wt(t-2)*Data(t-2)
```

The weight applied to data for each of the prior periods is $Wt(t)$ for the current period, $Wt(t-1)$ for the prior period, and $Wt(t-2)$ for two prior periods. In order to smooth data while still seeing rapid shifts in data movement, you will want to apply greater weight to current data and less weight to older: for example, $Wt(t)=50\%$ for the current month, $Wt(t-1)=30\%$ for the prior month, and $Wt(t-2)=20\%$ for the second oldest month. Putting these three weighting values in separate cells enables you to change the weighting so you can try weights that produce the best smoothing while allowing you to see trends.

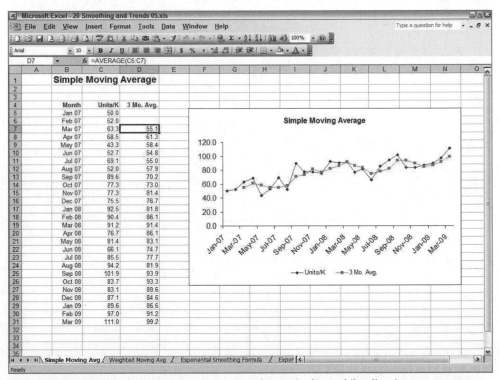

Figure 22.2: Weighted moving averages smooth erratic data while allowing you to see recent changes in movement.

Figure 22.2 shows three weighted values in these cells:

C4	.50
C5	.30
C6	.20

Cell D11 contains the weighted average smoothing formula

```
=($C$4*C11+$C$5*C10+$C$6*C9)
```

Copying this formula down the range D11:D32 produces a weighted average. Increasing the value in cell C4 gives more weight to current data. The total of cells C4, C5, and C6 must equal 100 percent.

Exponential Weighted Moving Average

Exponential smoothing is another method of compensating for the problems inherent in simple smoothing. Use exponential smoothing on erratic data that are not cyclical or seasonal. Exponential smoothing smoothes data by including an adjustment for error in the previous forecast. To do this, it uses a "smoothing factor," α.

The smoothing factor α specifies how much adjustment is made in the current forecast for prior error. The larger α is, the more the current forecast will respond to rapid changes.

The formula for exponential smoothing is

```
SmoothData(t) = α * ActualData(t-1) + (1 - α) * SmoothedData(t-1).
```

The value of α determines the amount of smoothing and responsiveness to data movement. The appropriate value for α is based on the analyst's judgment. Usual values for α are in the range of 0.01 to 0.3, but normally from 0.2 to 0.3. In this formula ActualData is multiplied times the smoothing factor and added to 1 minus the smoothing factor times the previous result of smoothing.

Exponential Smoothing with Formulas

Figure 22.3 shows data in C7:C33 being smoothed by the formulas in D8:D33. Cell D4 contains the smoothing factor α. Begin the first cell or cells in the forecast with actual data or an average of the first few data values. Cell D7 does this with

```
=C7
```

Cell D8 contains the first exponential smoothing formula,

```
=$D$4*C8+(1-$D$4)*D7
```

This formula is copied down the range D8:D33. Experiment by changing the smoothing factor in D4 to see how it smoothes erratic data.

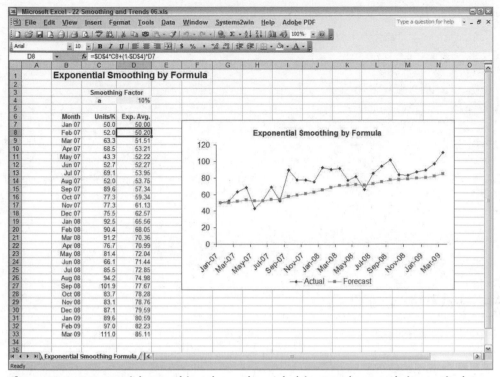

Figure 22.3: Exponential smoothing shows the underlying trend or trends in erratic data while still revealing rapid changes.

Adding the Analysis ToolPak to Excel

Excel has hundreds of built-in worksheet functions. There are additional functions that can help with statistics and forecasting, but they must be added to Excel with the Analysis ToolPak. The Analysis ToolPak is a free add-in that comes with Excel. In it you will get tools to guide you through complex analysis.

Be aware that you may not want to use the Analysis ToolPak. Many of the analyses produced by the ToolPak embed static values in the formulas. This means you will probably have to manually update your dashboard when data or assumptions change. Another consideration is that any interactive dashboard you create will require the end user to have the Analysis ToolPak installed as well.

The Analysis ToolPak is an add-in that comes with Excel, but you must install it. It contains additional statistical functions for use in Excel. One of these additional functions is the Moving Average tool.

To install the Analysis ToolPak in Microsoft Excel 2003,

1. Choose Tools, Add-Ins to display the Add-Ins dialog box shown in Figure 22.4.

Figure 22.4: The Add-Ins dialog box enables you to add additional analytical tools to Excel.

2. Select the Analysis ToolPak check box.

3. Choose OK.

If you are using Excel 2007, install the Analysis ToolPak by clicking the Microsoft Office button and then choose Excel Options. Select Add-Ins, and then in the Manage box, select Excel Add-Ins and Go. From the Add-Ins available box, select the Analysis ToolPak check box and then choose OK.

Once you have loaded the Analysis ToolPak, you will have numerous new statistical and forecasting tools available. To access the new functions, choose Tools, Data Analysis. In Excel 2007 the Data Analysis command will be available in the Analysis group on the Data tab.

Exponential Smoothing with the Analysis ToolPak

Excel has a built-in tool to guide you through creating exponential smoothing. To use the Exponential Smoothing tool, you must have the Analysis ToolPak installed as described in the previous section.

To create exponentially smoothed data using the Analysis ToolPak, follow these steps:

1. Choose Tools, Data Analysis. If the Data Analysis command is not visible, install Excel's Data Analysis ToolPak as described earlier in this chapter.

2. In the Data Analysis dialog box, select Exponential Smoothing and choose OK. Excel displays the Exponential Smoothing dialog box, as shown in Figure 22.5.

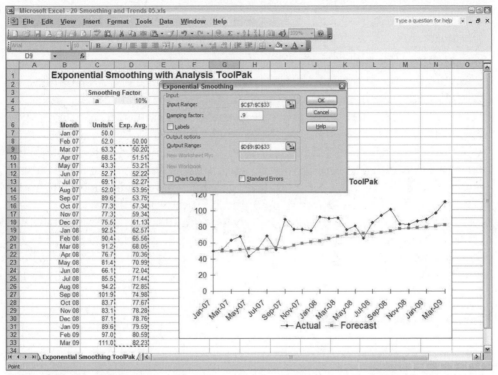

Figure 22.5: The Exponential Smoothing tool produces the same result as the manual process, but it gives you guidance.

3. Enter the range of the data in the Input Range box. In the figure, the data range is C7:C33.

4. Enter the damping factor in the Damping Factor box. Note that you cannot reference a cell; you must type it. Do not confuse the damping factor used in the ToolPak with the smoothing factor used earlier. They are not the same thing. The damping factor is $(1-\alpha)$. The smoothing factor, α, is normally between .01 and .3, so the damping factor will be between .99 and .7.

CAUTION In mathematics, the term α is referred to as the smoothing factor. It is normally in the range of .01 to .3. However, Excel's Exponential Smoothing dialog box asks for a Damping Factor as shown in Figure 22.5. The damping factor is one minus the smoothing factor, $(1-\alpha)$, so it ranges from .99 to .7.

5. If the data in your Input Range included a heading or label at the top, then select the Labels check box.

6. In the Output Range, select the cells where you want the smoothed data to appear. Usually this is adjacent to the Input Range.

7. Select the Chart Output check box if you want a chart embedded in the worksheet. The chart will not include the Category (X) Axis labels, so I usually create the chart myself.

The beginning of the output range will start with one #N/A error because Excel will not have data to calculate the first smoothed data value.

One reason you may want to create your own formulas to calculate exponential smoothing rather than using the Analysis ToolPak is so you can put the smoothing factor in a cell and reference it from the smoothing formulas. This makes it easy to test different smoothing factors. When you use the Analysis ToolPak, the numeric value for the damping factor is hard-coded in each formula making it difficult to try different smoothing, or damping, factors.

Another reason for using manually created formulas is you can use OFFSET and COUNTA as described in Chapter 17, "Working with Data That Changes Size," to create smoothing formulas that automatically adjust as the amount of data changes.

Forecasting Trends

All businesspeople wish they could see the future for their businesses. Although we can't see the exact future, Excel has functions that enable us to make probable estimates.

Forecasting with Worksheet Functions

Excel has a number of worksheet functions designed to help with forecasting. These functions are listed in Table 22.1.

Table 22.1: Worksheet Functions for Forecasting

FUNCTION	USE
FORECAST	Calculate projected future values
TREND	Calculate projected future values for straight-line trend
GROWTH	Calculate projected future values for exponential growth
LINEST	Calculate the formula of a straight line from data
LOGEST	Calculate the formula for an exponential curve from data

A discussion of the most commonly used functions follows. Once you understand how to use a couple of them, you will understand the others.

Forecasting Linear Trends with TREND

Humans innately make linear, or straight-line, forecasts. That is probably because it has been selectively programmed into our genes over the last 500 million years of evolution. Linear forecasts reflect what we expect in the physical world. If a ball is rolling in a straight line, it will probably keep rolling in that direction if nothing else intervenes. If a deer runs into the brush, we look for it appear in a straight line from where it entered.

Be aware of how easy it is to fall into the trap of relying on linear forecasts. Psychological research shows that humans tend to expect things to continue as they have in the recent past. That explains why people do exactly the opposite of what they should—buy into the top of economic bubbles and sell at the bottom of downturns. It takes the emotional intelligence of a Warren Buffet to divorce ourselves from the emotional drive that causes us to forecast in a straight line and expect more of the same.

Even with that proviso in mind, it is probably safe to use linear forecasting for many short-term forecasts, but be aware that this is only true for the short term. Every stock and index fund prospectus contains the proviso that past performance is not a predictor of future performance. That applies to the analysis of our own businesses as well.

Excel's TREND function uses the least squares method of finding the straight line that passes through a set of data with the minimum error. Forecasting with the TREND function is straightforward. The TREND function uses the syntax

```
TREND(known_y's, known_x's, new_x's, const)
```

Known_y's are the known data values for dependent data, usually shown on the Y or vertical axis of charts. *Known_x's* are the independent variables, usually shown on the X or horizontal axis of charts. If you do not enter *new_x's*, then Excel uses the existing *known_x's*. If *const* is TRUE, then TREND calculates a linear forecast where the forecast must be 0 when the x value is 0. You will usually make *const* blank or FALSE.

Figure 22.6 shows a TREND function calculating the best fit for the data in C7:C29. The TREND function is in D7:D29 and extends with forecasted results out to D33. Cell D7 contains the TREND formula

```
=TREND($C$7:$C$29,$B$7:$B$29,B7)
```

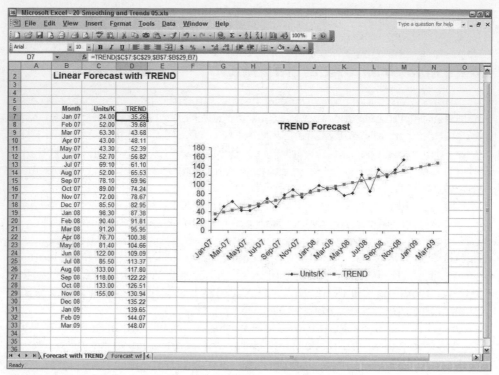

Figure 22.6: TREND calculates a straight-line forecast.

If you want to find the slope, intersect, and regression statistics, use the LINEST function or the Regression tool in the Analysis ToolPak.

Forecasting Trends with GROWTH

If you are working with systems that are similar to those that occur in nature, such as population changes, expanding sales of new products into a fertile market, and so forth, you may want to use Excel's GROWTH and LOGEST functions instead of TREND, FORECAST, and LINEST. GROWTH projects the values for exponential growth, like those common to population growth. LOGEST calculates the exponential growth formula and regression statistics.

Figure 22.7 shows the same data as used in Figure 22.6, but a GROWTH function has been used in cells D7:D33 to project future values.

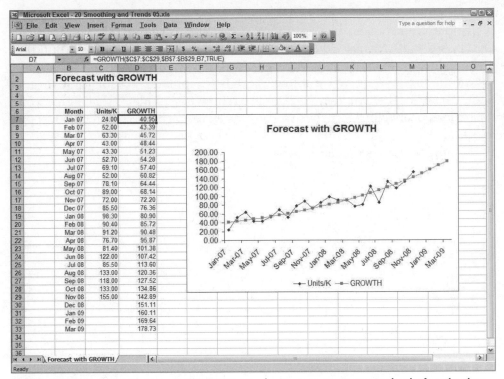

Figure 22.7: In some instances, GROWTH may be a more accurate method of projecting than TREND.

The GROWTH formula in cell D7 is

```
=GROWTH($C$7:$C$29,$B$7:$B$29,B7,TRUE)
```

GROWTH uses the same syntax and method of entering as does TREND. If you want to calculate the exponential best fit formula and regression statistics, use LOGEST.

Summary

Smoothing data and adding trend lines to your scorecards and dashboards can make forecasting and decision-making easier. In using them, you must be aware of how easy it is to misuse trends and forecasts. Only make forecasts for short time periods and understand that a forecast may only be valid if all conditions remain the same.

Adding trends and smoothed data to charts often creates an overloaded and visually messy chart. One way of resolving this is to give your dashboard's users the ability to show just the data, forecast, or smoothed series they want to see.

This is actually very easy to do. All it takes is the proper application of a check box and an IF function. To learn more about this see Chapter 20, "Controlling Dashboards with Menus, Combo Boxes, and Buttons," and Chapter 24, "Building Powerful Charts for Decision Making."

Another area you may want to explore is Chapter 23, "Displaying Targets and Alerts." In that chapter, you can learn how to add alerts that signal your dashboard users when target values have been reached or when they fall short. Alerts and targets are another very useful way of helping managers and executives make better and faster decisions.

Identifying Targets and Displaying Alerts

However beautiful the strategy, you should occasionally look at the results.
Sir Winston Churchill
Statesman, 1874–1965

Well-built Balanced Scorecards and operational dashboards make it easier to make good decisions. One way they do this is by putting the actual and target values in direct comparison, but this still forces the user to do the comparison. A good dashboard designer makes decisions even easier by highlighting or pinpointing the area that needs attention and focus. For example, in a column chart, if data fail to reach 80 percent of the target value, the column shows as red, which will then attract the attention of the decision-maker.

Also, when a decision is made, you want someone to take action. So you should design your scorecards and dashboards so the viewer can generate an e-mail right from within the chart. This chapter shows you how to do this in Excel.

Charting Target Values

Intermediate target values help you track your progress toward a long-range goal. Instead of measuring against a target value 6 months or a year away, you get better motivation and better control by tracking progress with intermediate targets. Figure 23.1 shows a simple combination chart that enables you to see monthly actual results versus target values. The actual values are columns, and the target values are markers from a line chart.

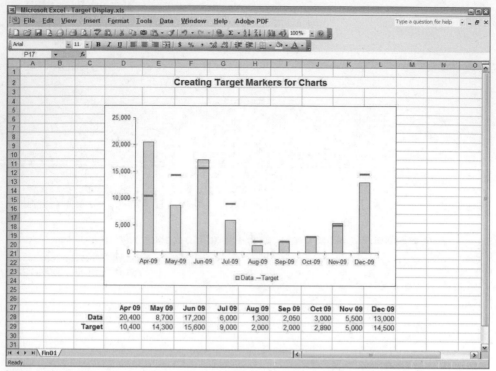

Figure 23.1: Use a combination chart to make an actual versus target chart.

To quickly create a chart like the one in Figure 23.1, begin with a column chart like that in Figure 23.2. This column chart uses actual values for one series and target values for the second series. Figure 23.1 is nothing more than a column chart with an overlapping line chart. The target line is invisible, and the line's marker has been increased in size.

To create target markers, follow these steps:

1. Right-click on a target column and choose Chart Type. In Excel 2007 choose Change Series Chart Type.

2. In the Chart Type dialog box, select the Line Type with Markers at each data value. Choose Ok. This produces a line chart of target values overlapping a column chart of actual values.

3. Right-click on the line and select Format Data Series.

4. From the Patterns tab, select a Line pattern of None. In Excel 2007 select Line Color, No Line. This makes the target line invisible. From the Marker pattern, select Custom and a wide line marker with a color visible over the column color. In Excel 2007 select Marker Options, Built In. Make the marker size greater than 10. Choose Ok.

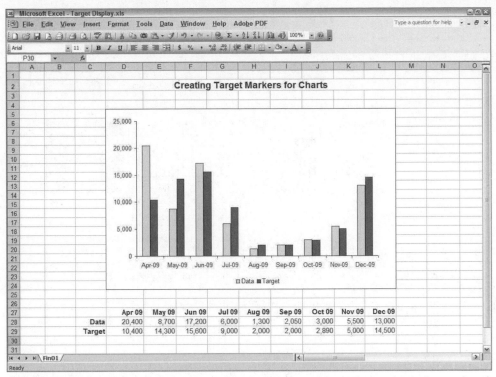

Figure 23.2: Create target markers in a chart by starting with a column chart of actual and target values and then changing the target's chart type to line.

Note: Combo Charts Are the Tricksters of Excel Charting

Most Excel tricks in charting and for creating complex charts are accomplished through combination charts, special formatting, and selectively displayed data. To see and learn from more examples of scorecards and dashboards, go to www.torconsulting.com.

Charting Alerts with Conditional Colors

Column charts, like the ones in Figure 23.1 and 23.2, force managers to "eyeball" whether actual values are within the set criteria for their target. Figure 23.3 shows the same type of column chart, but the columns in the chart change color depending upon what conditional criteria they have met. For example, if an actual value is within 90 percent or more of the target value, then the column is green. If the actual value is between 80 percent and 90 percent of the target value, then the column is yellow. If the actual value is less than 80 percent of the target value, the column is red. Conditional chart colors make it very quick and easy to identify where attention should be focused.

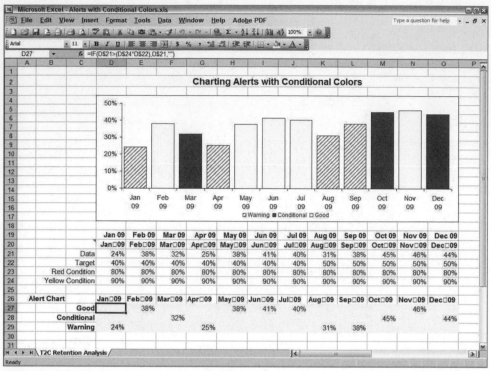

Figure 23.3: Decision-making is much easier with charts that use conditional color coding.

Conditional charts use a data series for each condition. Each of these series is given a different color or marker. Then, all the data series are displayed and adjusted so they appear to be a single data series.

Table 23.1 shows the ranges for data, targets, and conditional criteria that appear in Figure 23.4.

Table 23.1: Definition of the Cells and Criteria Shown in Fig. 23.4

VALUE	RANGE	COMMENT
Data	D21:O21	Actual values by month
Target	D22:O22	Target values by month
Red Condition	D23:O23	Upper red criteria level. If actual value is less than (Red condition * Target), then the actual is colored red.
Yellow Condition	D24:O24	Upper yellow criteria level. If actual value is between red and yellow condition of target, then actual column is yellow. Actual values above this condition are green.

The formulas in the range D27:O29 create three new data series that are used to create the colored column chart. The data in D27:O27 match the green condition, the data in D28:O28 match the yellow condition, and the data in D29:O29 match the red condition. The formulas in D27:D29 are copied to the right to the O column. The conditional formulas are shown in Table 23.2.

Table 23.2: Formulas Used to Create Colored Alerts in Column Charts

ACTUAL COLUMN COLOR	CONDITION	FORMULA IN COLUMN D
Green	If Data is greater than (Target * Yellow %)	D27=IF(D$21>(D$24*D$22),D$21,"")
Yellow	If Data is greater than (Target * Red %) and Data is less than or equal to (Target * Yellow %)	D28=IF(AND(D$21>(D$23*D$22), D$21<=(D$24*D$22)),D$21,"")
Red	If Data is less than or equal to (Target * Red %)	D29=IF(D$21<=(D$23*D$22),D$21,"")

Creating a column chart from the range C26:O29 produces the chart shown in Figure 23.4. This chart shows the same data values as the actual data, but each series has a different color. What needs to be corrected now is the wide spacing between columns. By adjusting spacing between columns, we can make these three data series appear to be the same data series.

To adjust Figure 23.4 so the columns fill in the interstitial spacing and look like a single series, follow these steps:

1. Right-click on any of the data series to display the Format Data Series dialog box.

2. Select the Options tab. In Excel 2007 select Series Options.

3. Change the Overlap value to 100 percent. Change the Gap Width to 20 percent. Choose Ok.

This trick of dividing a single data series into multiple series of columns, bars, or lines, each with its own color, is an effective way to apply color alerts on many types of charts. Although you can make as many conditions and colors as you want, going beyond three may become confusing for the dashboard users.

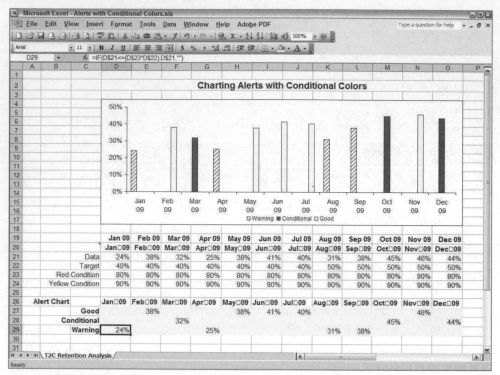

Figure 23.4: Conditional color charts actually use a different data series for each condition and its associated color.

Note: Multiline X-Axis Labels

Notice in Figure 23.4 that the X-axis has a double row of labels. There are a couple of methods for creating multiline X-axis labels depending on the version of Excel and the situation. In Figures 23.3 and 23.4, cell D20 contains the formula

```
=TEXT(D$19,"mmm")&CHAR(13)&TEXT(D$19,"yy")
```

This formula converts the date in D19 to a text, three-letter month abbreviation; joins that with a line break, CHAR(13); and finally appends a two-letter abbreviation for the year. Using the CHAR(13) in concatenated text is a useful trick in many text situations. Chapter 15, "Text Based Dashboards," provides more examples of how to concatenate (join) text, numbers, or dates.

Charting Alerts for the Top/Bottom *n*, Quartiles, and Percentiles

A frequent request I get when creating Balanced Scorecards and dashboards for marketing, sales, and manufacturing is to show the Top *n* or Bottom *n* for some set of data. For example, someone may need to identify the top five production issues, or the top quartile of salespeople, or the geographic regions producing the top 20 percent of results from a marketing campaign. (A related topic is the Pareto or 80/20 chart described in Chapter 24, "Building Powerful Charts for Decision Making.")

The example below uses the functions for top *n* and bottom *n* items, but you can use the same methods for

- Minimum and maximum values
- Top or bottom quartile
- Top or bottom percentile

Figure 23.5 shows a simple column chart where the top three and bottom three data values are identified with different colors or patterns. Entering a different value, such as 5, in cells D6 or E6, will identify the top and bottom five data values in the chart. Entering this value through the use of a combo box as described in Chapter 20, "Controlling Dashboards with Menus, Combo Boxes, and Buttons," is a functional feature that allows users to select their own Top/Bottom *n* range.

The months and data are in cells B10:C27. Cell D7 calculates the breakpoint where the bottom three data values begin. Cell E7 calculates the breakpoint where the top three data values begin. The formula in D7 is

```
=SMALL($C$10:$C$27,$D$6)
```

The formula in E7 is

```
=LARGE($C$10:$C$27,$E$6)
```

You could find other ranges just as easily by using other functions such as these:

```
MIN()
MAX()
QUARTILE()
PERCENTILE()
```

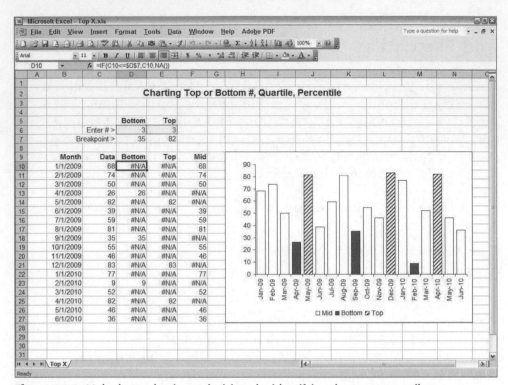

Figure 23.5: Make better business decisions by identifying the top *n*, quartile, or percentile to find where you are getting the greatest impact or where you need to focus the most attention.

You can also use a custom formula to create another statistical function or criterion.

The formulas in D7 and E7 use the values in D6 and E6 respectively to determine how many top *n* or bottom *n* are to be included. The breakpoint for top *n* and bottom *n* is then used by formulas in D10:F27 to determine whether a data value is in the top *n*, in the bottom *n*, or in between. These conditional formulas are shown in Table 23.3.

Table 23.3: Formulas to Calculate Conditional Columns

CALCULATION	RANGE	FORMULA
Bottom *n*	D10	=IF(C10<=$D$7,C10,NA())
Top *n*	E10	=IF(C10>=$E$7,C10,NA())
Mid	F10	=IF(AND(C10>$D$7,C10<$E$7),C10,NA())

The formulas in D10, E10, and F10 are copied down to row 27. This produces numeric values in a column when the condition is satisfied and #NA when they aren't satisfied. #NA is not plotted in Excel charts.

Now, using the technique described in the previous section, create a chart from the Month, Bottom, Mid, and Top columns. Right-click on one of the data series in the chart and choose Format ➪ Data Series. Select the Options tab and adjust Overlap to 100 percent and Gap Width to 20 percent. In Excel 2007 right-click the data series and choose Format Data Series, and then select Series Options to change the Overlap and Gap Width.

Charting Alerts with Line and XY Scatter Diagrams

Some data, such as clinical or manufacturing production data, are best charted with line or XY scatter diagrams. With these, you also can use a method similar to those described above to create conditional charts. To do so, however, you will need an additional formatting technique. Figure 23.6 shows a line chart with distinctive top and bottom markers. Especially when there are lots of data points, as in clinical or manufacturing scatter diagrams, you may find it hard to notice the difference between markers. If you need a better visual identifier in line and XY scatter diagrams, check the next example that shows how to attach a visual indicator to conditional data points.

The previous examples explain the formulas in the Top, Mid, and Bottom columns. In the previous example, a column chart, you didn't include the data values in the chart. For this chart, you will be plotting the Data values. Follow these steps to create a conditional line chart:

1. Select cells B9:F27 and use the Chart Wizard to create a column chart. This will produce a chart with four columns.

   In the following steps, you will change each column into a line chart. For the Data line series, you will remove the line markers but leave the line. For the Top, Mid, and Bottom line series, you will remove the line but leave the markers. You will want to make the Top, Mid, and Bottom markers distinct from each other.

2. Use the legend to identify each data series. Right-click the Data series and choose Chart Type. In Excel 2007 choose Change Series Chart Type. Select the Line with Markers and choose Ok.

3. Right-click the Data line and choose Format Data Series.

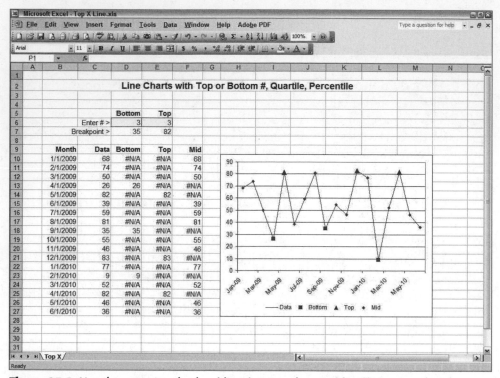

Figure 23.6: Use the same methods with unique markers to identify top *n* or bottom *n* items in a line or scatter diagram.

4. From the Patterns tab, select the color and weight you want for Line and select None for the marker. In Excel 2007 select Marker Options and None for the Marker Type. (The markers will be shown with distinctive markers by Top, Mid, and Bottom.)

5. Return to Step 2 and repeat this sequence, but now work on each of the Top, Mid, and Bottom series in turn. Change each to a line, then format these lines with None so the line disappears, but use a distinctive marker for Top, Mid, and Bottom series.

If you need greater visual differentiation for your top and bottom markers, then you may want to include the technique described in the following section.

Adding a Visual Indicator to Top/Bottom *n*, Quartile, and Percentile Charts

Microsoft Excel is a powerful and versatile charting engine. It includes the little-known ability to replace data points with pictures. You can use this ability to make your Top *n* or Bottom *n* data points stand out by replacing those data markers with pictures. Figure 23.7 shows an example where the top and bottom data points use large red circles with dots at midpoint. In this example, since it is easy to distinguish the top and bottom data points, both markers can be the same. You could make the picture used by each marker different. The picture could just as easily be an arrow or even a text identifier that was captured graphically.

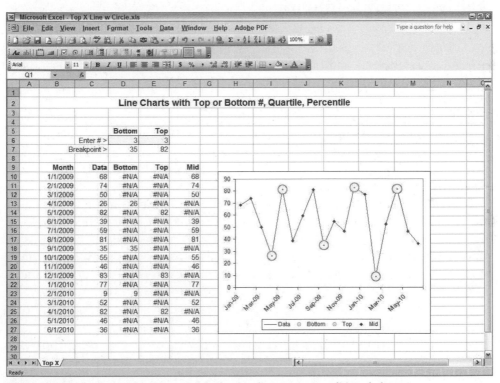

Figure 23.7: You can add any type of visual indicators to conditional charts.

First, you need to create the picture that will replace the line marker. For simple icons you can use Microsoft Paint found in Windows under Start ➪ Programs ➪ Accessories. Excel recognizes most major picture formats, so you can use any editor you are comfortable with.

Here's a warning: Once you replace a line marker with a picture, you can't resize the picture, although you can paste another picture over it. So, first create a couple of different-sized pictures and then select the size that works best.

To replace a marker with a picture in versions of Excel prior to 2007,

1. Select the line on which you want to paste a picture. The picture will replace the markers on the line.

2. Choose Insert ➪ Picture ➪ From File.

3. Find the picture in the folder where it is saved, select the picture file, and choose Ok.

The picture will replace the markers for that data series.

Alerting with E-mailing

Some high-end Business Intelligence systems include the ability to send an e-mail when an alert condition is met. These systems cost tens of thousands to hundreds of thousands of dollars for the software license fees, and then even more for consulting.

Although you can't replicate that capability using an Excel worksheet, you can make it easy to send an e-mail when an alert condition has been met. It takes just a few minutes to add alert-driven e-mail buttons. (With the addition of some non-trivial VBA code, it is possible to add the ability to send alert-driven e-mails from dashboards.)

To create an alert-driven e-mail system, you will combine a conditional test, the HYPERLINK function, and conditional formats. The simple example in Figure 23.8 shows a condition that tests whether the actual value in D8 is greater than 90 percent of the target value in D9. In this example, the textual "buttons" only appear when the actual value is less than 90 percent of the target value.

In actual use, you would probably use a conditional IF function with AND or OR to test target conditions. When an alert condition is met, then the buttons would display as shown in Figure 23.8.

The "text" button in E14 uses a formula that creates a hyperlink to my web site:

```
=IF($D$11=1,HYPERLINK("http://www.torconsulting.com",
"Executing Strategy and Operations"),"")
```

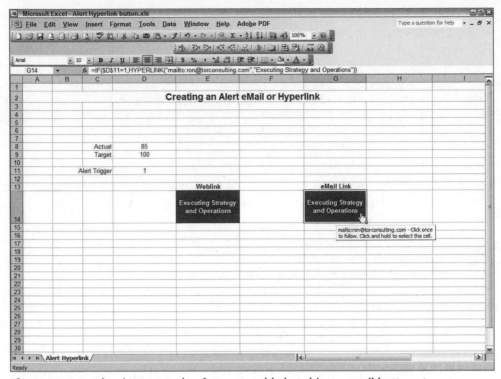

Figure 23.8: It takes just a couple of steps to add alert-driven e-mail buttons to your dashboard.

When the trigger value in D11 is 1, then the cell becomes a hyperlink to my web site, where there are more resources and a description of consulting services on executing strategy and operations. When cell D11 is 0, then the same cell becomes a blank cell.

The "text" button in G14 uses the formula that opens an e-mail message addressed to me:

```
=IF($D$11=1,HYPERLINK("mailto:ron@torconsulting.com",
"Executing Strategy and Operations"),"")
```

If you test this, please go ahead and send me an e-mail to let me know which parts of this book have been most valuable to you.

In this case, when the trigger value in D11 is 1, then the cell becomes a hyperlink that opens an e-mail to my personal e-mail address. When cell D11 is 0, then the same cell becomes a blank cell.

These two cells appear as normal blank cells when D11 is 0 and appear as textual buttons when D11 is 1. This is done with the Format Conditional Formatting command. To set these conditional formats, select the cells and then choose the

Format, Conditional Format command. In the first drop-down, select Formula Is, then enter the formula

```
=$D$11=0
```

as the condition to test for the format when the cell will have a normal format. Assign a normal format to that cell. Do the same for the second condition using the formula

```
=$D$11=1
```

to test when the format should appear as a textual button with a background pattern, border, and font that make the cell appear like a button. The finished Conditional Formatting dialog box should appear like that in Figure 23.9.

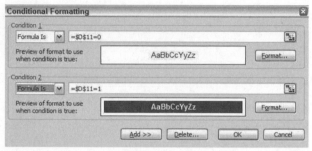

Figure 23.9: Use conditional formatting to make textual buttons appear when an alert condition is met.

Summary

As a dashboard designer and developer, your purpose is to help executives and managers make better decisions faster. That involves displaying the information they need for decision-making so it is quickly accessible and memorable. But that is only part of what is needed. Your dashboards should use Excel's analytical and conditional functions to identify when a decision is needed, and then use the alerts described in this chapter to identify where attention should be focused.

CHAPTER 24

Building Powerful Decision Making Charts

Effective leaders help others to understand the necessity of change and to accept a common vision of the desired outcome.

John Kotter
Harvard Business School Professor

Your dashboard users want better decisions faster. Selecting the right type of analytics and visual presentation will help give them what they want.

An important part of your job is understanding the business decisions that need to be made and the analysis and visual presentation that will aid the decision making process. The charts and graphs in this chapter are some of the more powerful charting types for business decisions.

TIP To gain full control over Excel's powerful charting engine, you need to learn how to handle combination charts. Combination charts enable you to have two Y axes on a chart. You also can have more than one chart type in a chart—combining column charts and line charts, for example.

In versions of Excel earlier than 2007, combination charts are found on the Custom Types tab of the first step in the Chart Wizard. Two useful combination charts are Line–Column on 2 Axes and Lines on 2 Axes. If you want to change how a data series charts, such as by changing a line to a column, select the data series and then choose Chart, Chart Type and select the chart type for that data series. Any number of chart types can exist on the same chart.

Seeing a Full Statistical Picture with a Box-and-Whisker Plot

The box-and-whisker plot, also known as a boxplot, is a statistical carry-all. In one chart it shows the minimum value, the lower quartile (Q1 or 25th percentile), the median, the upper quartile (Q3 or 75th percentile), and the maximum value.

Figure 24.1 shows a box-and-whisker plot. Each of these box-and-whisker plots refers to a set of data, shown in the range L8:N32. The bottom and top of the box are the 25th and 75th percentiles. The band in the middle of the box is the 50th percentile, the median. The triangle marker is the mean.

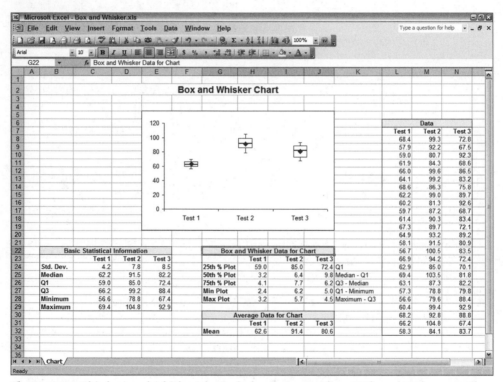

Figure 24.1: This box-and-whisker plot includes mean, median, 25th and 75th percentiles, maximum, and minimum values for a data set.

The tops and bottoms of the "whiskers" in this example show the maximum and minimum values, but they can also be used to show other percentile limits, top and bottom outliers, and still more. The mean, or average, is often shown as a dot or marker that overlays the box.

Although very useful, the box-and-whisker plot is not one of Excel's pre-defined charts. It is not difficult to create, but it is a little involved. There are a number of ways of creating a box-and-whisker plot in Excel.

To create a box-and-whisker plot showing the median, 25th and 75th percentiles, and minimum and maximum, follow these steps:

1. Create a table of the statistical values

CELL	FORMULA
C24	=STDEV(L8:L32)
C25	=MEDIAN(L8:L32)
C26	=PERCENTILE(L8:L32,0.25)
C27	=PERCENTILE(L8:L32,0.75)
C28	=MIN(L8:L32)
C29	=MAX(L8:L32)

2. Copy C24:C29 to fill D24:E29. This replicates the statistical values for Test 2 and Test 3 data.

3. Create a table of values used to plot the chart. Notice that only two of these charted values are actual statistical values; the other chart values are lengths of different stacked segments or error bar lengths. Create the following data tables for the chart values:

CELL	FORMULA	DESCRIPTION
H24	=C26	Q1; 25th percentile
H25	=C25-C26	Median—Q1; height of 50th percentile column segment
H26	=C27-C25	Q3 - Median; height of 75th percentile column segment
H27	=C26-C28	Q1—Minimum; lower error bar length
H28	=C29-C27	Maximum—Q3; upper error bar length
H32	=AVERAGE(L8:L32)	Average

4. Copy H24:H28 to fill I24:J28. Copy H32 to fill I32:J32.

5. Create a stacked column chart by selecting G23:J26. Make sure you use the Stacked Column. (Do not select the 100% column.)

6. Delete the gray chart background, the gridlines, and the legend. Format the column segments so that they have no fill color. Your chart should now look somewhat like Figure 24.2.

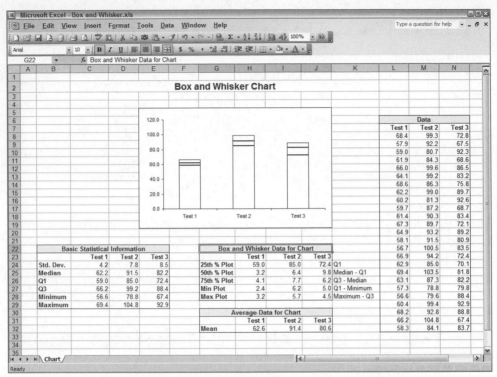

Figure 24.2: The basic stacked column chart, with 25th, 50th, and 75th percentiles.

7. Add the top whisker for the max value by right-clicking on the top segment, choosing Format Data Series, and selecting the Y Error Bars tab shown in Figure 24.3. In the Error Amount group, select Custom, and in the + (plus) reference box, enter the Max Plot data in H28:J28.

In Excel 2007, select the top segment. In the Chart Tools, select the Layout tab. In the Analysis group, click the down arrow next to Error Bars Options. In the drop-down list, select the More Error Bars Option to display the Format Error Bars dialog box. Select Display Direction Plus to make an error bar that goes up from the top of the segment. In Error Amount, select Custom, and then click the Specify Value button. Enter the reference H28:J28 as the Positive Error Value. Clear the Negative Error Value.

In any version of Excel, you should now see an error bar, the whisker, sprouting up from the top of the topmost segment.

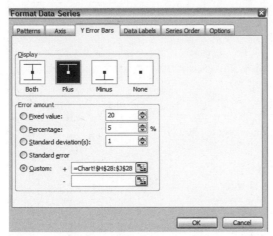

Figure 24.3: The Y Error Bars tab enables you to add the upper and lower bars to segments.

8. Add the bottom whisker for the minimum value by right-clicking on the segment touching the X axis, choosing Format Data Series and selecting the Y Error Bars tab. In the Error Amount group, select Custom, and in the – (minus) reference box, enter the Min Plot data in H27:J27.

In Excel 2007, repeat the process described in step 7, but select the column segment touching the X axis. Select from the Vertical Error Bars a bar in the Minus direction. In the Error Amount clear the positive Error Value box and enter H27:J27.

In any version of Excel, you should now see an error bar hanging down from the top of the lowest segment.

9. Right-click the Y-axis, choose Format Axis and adjust the Y axis scale. Your chart should now look like Figure 24.4.

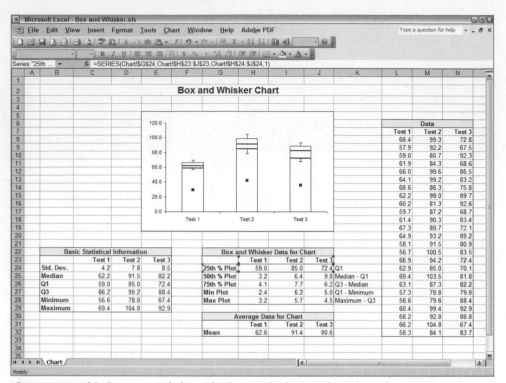

Figure 24.4: This figure reveals how the box-and-whisker plot is based on a stacked column chart.

10. Make the lower segment invisible. Right-click on the lowest segment and choose Format Data Series. Format the lowest segment with no border and no color so that it is invisible. Your chart should now look like the box-and-whisker plot in Figure 24.5.

If the box appears too wide, right-click on the box and choose Format Data Series; then select the Options tab. In Excel 2007, select Series Options. Increase the Gap Width until the boxes are narrow.

To add the average as a marker on the box-and-whisker plot, follow these steps:

1. Copy the average data: H32:J32.

2. Right-click on the chart background and choose Paste.

3. A new segment will be added to the chart. Right-click this new segment and choose Chart Type. In Excel 2007, choose Change Series Chart Type.

4. Select Line with Markers as the chart type for the new data, and choose OK.

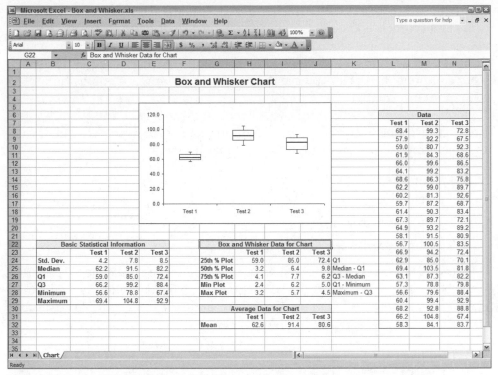

Figure 24.5: The finished box-and-whisker plot, before adding average markers.

5. Format the line so that it is invisible, and the marker is visible with a marker shape, color, and size that works for you. Figure 24.5 shows a finished box-and-whisker plot, including 25th and 75th percentiles, median and average, and max and min.

These same steps can be used to display other data, such as outliers, alert levels, or other percentile markers.

Bullet Charts—A Better Alternative to Gauges

Business Intelligence vendors seem to love to show dashboards with fancy colorful gauges. Some of these dashboards look like they have been freshly torn from the dashboard of an expensive Italian race car. Somewhere in the past, vendors took the term "dashboard" too literally.

I must admit that at first executives and managers like to see these round and colorful gauges. They look "cool." But you don't have to use a dashboard full of gauges too many times before you realize that all those large, colorful gauges are a waste. It is very difficult to see the relationships between different values when each appears in a gauge. Gauges use large-scale increments, so you can't see small changes. They waste space—one gauge shows one value, a target, and perhaps the alert limits. In that same space, you can fit five or six other components that let you see the relationships between values, as well as even more information.

Stephen Few, the author of the excellent book, *Information Dashboard Design*, took on this problem and developed an information visualization object he calls a "bullet graph." In a small space a bullet graph shows

- Data value
- Target value
- Easily readable scale
- Two or more easily readable alert limits

Figure 24.6 shows a bullet graph with its component parts labeled. The bullet graph in the figure is vertical, but bullet graphs can be horizontal as well. Bullet graphs are not a predesigned format in Excel and take some work to create, but once you've created one, you can plug in new data, and you're done.

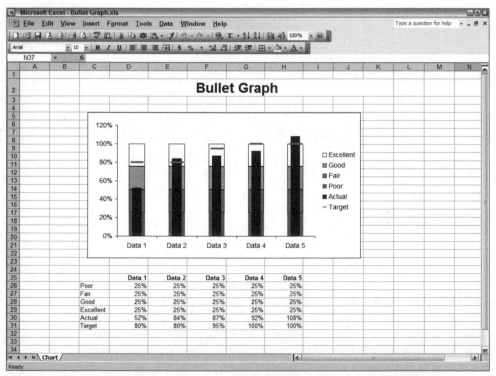

Figure 24.6: Bullet graphs display a great deal of information in a small space.

Bullet graphs are created by building a stacked column chart with the target, actual, and alert values as segments. (If you want a horizontal bullet chart, create a stacked bar chart.) The target value is then formatted to move independently and to appear as a dash marker. The actual value is also formatted to move independently and is thinned so that it appears over the alert value columns.

CAUTION Data *must* be arranged in the order shown in the figure to follow the steps to creating a bullet graph. If data are in a different order, the column segments may be difficult to select.

To build a bullet graph in versions of Excel before 2007, first create a stacked column chart of all values:

1. Enter only the data shown in Figure 24.6 in range C25:D31. More data will be added later to create additional bullet graphs. (You can have as many alert levels as you wish. This example shows four.)

2. Select the data and labels, C25:D31, and open the Chart Wizard.

3. Select the second column type, Stacked Column, and choose Next.

4. In Step 2 of 4 of the Chart Wizard, select the Series In Rows option on the Data Range tab. The Chart Wizard will show the column stacked as in Figure 24.7. Choose Finish.

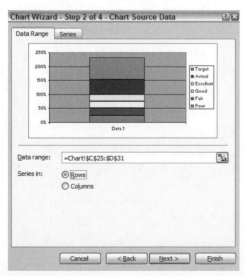

Figure 24.7: Selecting Series In Rows places the columns on top of one another.

5. Position the stacked column chart on the worksheet and delete the gray background and the gridlines.

To build a bullet graph in Excel 2007, start by building a stacked column chart:

1. Select C25:D31.

2. Insert a Stacked Column chart.

3. Select the chart, and in the Chart Tools ribbon, on the Design Tab, in the Data group, click the Switch Row/Column button. Your chart should now look similar to Figure 24.7.

Now format the target value segment so that it will appear as the independently floating marker shown in Figure 24.6. The target marker is the floating dash in Figure 24.6. To format this:

1. Right click on the target value, the top segment, and choose Format Data Series. In versions of Excel before 2007, on the Axis tab, select Secondary Axis and choose OK. In Excel 2007, in the Series Options, select Secondary Axis and choose OK. This moves the target value to the new Y axis on the right. The chart should look similar to Figure 24.8. The secondary axis appears on the right, and the target segment covers most of the other stacked columns.

   Do not delete the legend. It will help you discriminate between the different segments.

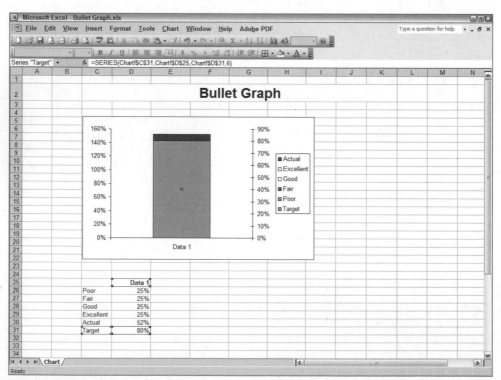

Figure 24.8: Moving the target value to a secondary axis enables it to move independently of the other segments.

2. Delete the secondary axis on the right by selecting it and pressing Delete. The target segment remains centered over the column.

3. Change the target segment so that it appears as a marker. Right-click the target segment and choose Chart Type. In Excel 2007, choose Change Series Chart Type. Select Line with Marker and choose OK. The target segment that was a column segment becomes a marker. There is no line, because there is only one point.

4. Right-click on the marker and choose Format Data Series.

5. Format the line so that it is invisible. Format the marker so that it is a heavy dash, as shown as shown in Figure 24.9. This formats the target marker as a heavy dash floating over the stacked columns. Choose OK.

Figure 24.9: Format the target marker as a heavy bar.

The target marker now appears as a heavy red dash floating over the stacked column chart, as shown in Figure 24.10.

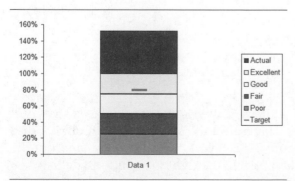

Figure 24.10: The red target value marker now floats over the alert and actual segments.

In the next steps, you will format the segment for Actual data as a column that is centered over the other columns. It will move independently of the four stacked alert column segments.

First, you must make the Actual data segment narrow so that the alert segments can be seen behind it. To do this

1. Right-click on the actual value segment and choose Format Data Series.

2. Select the Axis tab and select Secondary Axis. In Excel 2007, choose Series Options and Secondary Axis. Choose OK. This makes the actual value segment independent of the left axis. If you deleted the right Y axis previously, it will not be visible. If you did not delete it, select the right Y axis and press Delete.

3. Right-click on the actual value segment, which is now the same color, but touching the horizontal axis, and choose Format Data Series.

4. Select the Options tab (in Excel 2007 select Series Options), and change the Gap Width to 350. This reduces the width of the actual segment so that the alert segments can be seen. Choose OK.

The basic bullet graph is complete and appears as shown in Figure 24.11. At this point, you can right-click on each segment and select colors to differentiate each alert level. Alert colors are normally darker at the bottom and lighter toward the top. The actual value is usually black, and the target marker uses a color that stands out, like yellow or red.

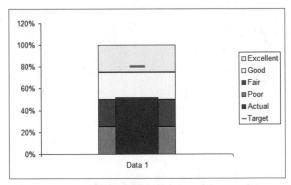

Figure 24.11: With a little additional formatting, your bullet graph will be an information-rich asset to your dashboards.

Add data by entering additional data to the right of the data, as shown in the range C25:H31 in Figure 24.6. Then select the chart. This will put handles around the data, as shown in Figure 24.12. Select the data series handle at the bottom of D31 in Figure 24.12, and drag it to the right to include all data. When you release the handle, all the data series will be charted as bullet graphs, as shown in Figure 24.13.

	Data 1	Data 2	Data 3	Data 4	Data 5
Poor	25%	25%	25%	25%	25%
Fair	25%	25%	25%	25%	25%
Good	25%	25%	25%	25%	25%
Excellent	25%	25%	25%	25%	25%
Actual	52%	84%	87%	92%	108%
Target	80%	80%	95%	100%	100%

Figure 24.12: Drag the data series handle to include additional data series.

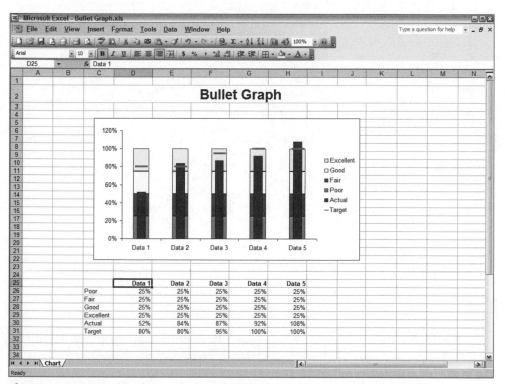

Figure 24.13: Once you have a bullet graph template, you can add additional data and include it in the bullet graph.

Once you have this basic bullet graph completed, you can use it as a template for other bullet graphs by changing the data.

Pareto Charts Show What Is Most Important

Although line and column charts are used most frequently in scorecards and dashboards, it's the Pareto chart that is really one of my favorites for helping decision makers. The name comes from Vilfredo Pareto, the 19th century economist and sociologist who gave us the 80/20 rule, often stated using examples such as "20% of your customers bring you 80% of your revenue."

Pareto charts are a great way to help business decision makers decide where to focus resources for the greatest impact. My clients have used Pareto charts to identify:

- Where to focus support and quality control
- Which clients should have greater focus
- Which product features are most desirable
- Which issues cause the greatest dissatisfaction

Figure 24.14 shows a Pareto chart that calculates which 20% of customers generate 80% of revenue. In this chart, it's easy to see that the first four customers contribute 80% of the revenue. In organizations with a large customer base, this type of analysis can help you identify where to focus your relationships, your quality control, your product features, and so forth.

To create a Pareto chart

1. Enter data as shown in B7:C16 of Figure 24.14. Notice that the data is sorted in descending order by Revenue.

2. Create a grand total for all data, as shown in C18:

   `=SUM(C7:C17)`

3. Calculate the percent of total for each item with the formula in D7,

   `=C7/$C$18`

   by copying it through the range D7:D16.

4. Calculate the cumulative percentage by entering the formula

   `=SUM($D$7:D7)`

   in E7 and copying it through E7:E16.

5. Enter the static 80% line values in F7:F16.

   In versions of Excel before 2007, create the Pareto chart from this table by

1. Selecting B6:C16 and then holding the Ctrl key down as you select the dis-contiguous range E6:F16. This leaves D6:D16 unselected.

2. Open the Chart Wizard and select the Custom Types tab. Select Line—Column on 2 Axis. Choose Finish.

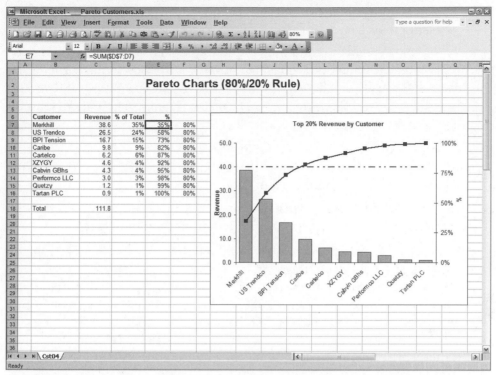

Figure 24.14: Pareto charts help you identify the 20% that has 80% of the impact.

This creates a double-axis chart with two column charts and one 80% line. All you have left to do is move the shorter of the column charts to the second axis and reformat it as a line.

1. Right-click the blue column segment representing cumulative % and choose Format Data Series. On the Axis tab, select Secondary Axis and choose OK. The cumulative % line is now associated with the right axis and takes on the appearance of the Pareto curve.

2. Right-click the blue column segment representing cumulative % and choose Chart Type. On the Standard Types tab, select Line with Markers and choose OK.

In Excel 2007, create a Pareto chart by

1. Selecting B6:C16 and then holding the Ctrl key down as you select the dis-contiguous range E6:F16. This leaves D6:D16 unselected.

2. Insert a Clustered Column chart, the first column chart in the gallery. (The columns representing percentages may be too small to see.)

3. Select the percentage columns by clicking on a Revenue column and then pressing the up or down arrow key to select the Percentage column.

4. Move the Percentage column to a secondary axis by right-clicking on the Percentage columns and choosing Format Data Series. In the Format Data Series dialog box, in Series Options, select Secondary Axis and then OK.

   At this point, the chart may look confusing. It should look like a stacked column chart with two axis.

5. Change the Percentage segment into a line with markers. Right-click on the Percentage column segment and choose Change Series Chart Type. Select the line with markers and choose OK.

   Your chart should now look like a Pareto chart without the 80% horizontal line. To add the 80% line, copy F7:F16 and paste it into the chart.

Your chart will now appear almost like the Pareto chart in Figure 24.14. All that remains is a little formatting.

Pareto charts depend upon the data being sorted in descending order. If you are doing a query from an external data source through MS Query or from a SQL generated file you can request that the data be returned in descending sort order. If you are retrieving unsorted data from an internal Excel worksheet, then use the autosorting formulas techniques described in the section "Sorting Lists by Formula" in Chapter 18, "Working with Lists and Tables of Data."

TIP I've been using Excel since before its public release in the mid-1980s, but there is still a book I keep handy on my bookshelf: John Walkenbach's *Excel Charts.* It has methods and tips that will help you create good-looking, powerful charts.

Variance Charts Make a Difference

If one of your objectives is to reduce variance from budget, then you should be charting variance, not actual and budget values. If you chart actual and budget values as two lines or two columns, you force your reader's mind to calculate the variance.

Figure 24.15 shows an HR variance chart where the variance calculation is done in the worksheet rather than the reader's mind. In this case, the reader can immediately see where staffing levels are ahead or behind.

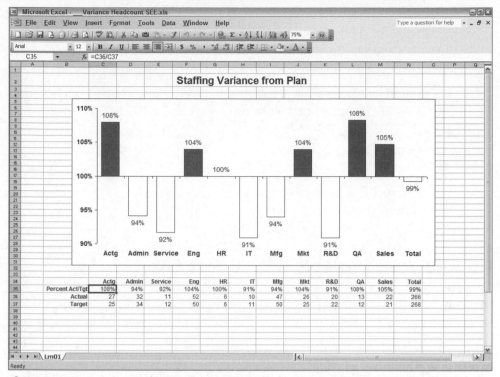

Figure 24.15: A variance chart makes variance from plan more apparent than simply charting both actual and target values.

In Figure 24.15, instead of charting actual and budget values, only the variance is charted, making the variance obvious. A few formatting techniques are used to make the chart more readable. The chart is based on values in row 35. The variance in cell C35 is calculated with the formula

```
=C36/C37
```

which is copied across.

To create this chart

1. Select B34:N35 and open the Chart Wizard.

2. Select the Clustered Column type and choose Finish.

3. Right click on the Y axis and choose Format Axis.

   - On the Scale tab, clear the Category (X) Axis check box, and enter 1 in the Crosses At box. This makes the horizontal axis cross the Y axis at the 100% mark, putting positive variance on top and negative variance underneath.

   - On the Scale tab, enter Minimum of .9 and Maximum of 1.1 for scale height. Choose OK.

4. Right-click on the X axis and choose Format Axis. On the Patterns tab, select Low for the Tick Mark Labels. This moves the department headings to the bottom of the chart. Choose OK.

5. Right-click on the columns and choose Format Data Series.

   - On the Data Labels tab, select the Value check box to display numeric values at the end of each column.

   - On the Options tab, adjust the Overlap and Gap Width to widen and position the columns.

   - On the Patterns tab, select a color for the positive variance and select the Invert If Negative check box for an opposite color for negative variance. Choose OK.

Project Your Projects with Gantt Charts

If you are creating dashboards for managers and project managers, they want to see project, task, and resource data on their dashboards. However, if you are building a Balanced Scorecard and want to show completion estimates for Strategic Initiatives, it can be better to just show executives the variance-from-forecast. This requires two different types of project management charts. A simplified Gantt chart is shown in this section, and the following section shows a project variance chart more appropriate for senior managers.

To create a Gantt chart like the one in Figure 24.16:

1. Enter the dates as shown. The end dates are the sum of the start date and duration. If a start date is dependent upon another end date, link the dependent start date to the end date.

2. Select B10:D22 and open Chart Wizard.

3. Select the Stacked Bar chart and choose Finish.

4. Right-click the X axis (showing project names), and choose Format Axis. Select the Scale tab and select Categories in Reverse Order to put Project 1 at top. Select Value (Y) Axis Crosses at Maximum Category to move the horizontal axis to the bottom.

5. If you want dates along the bottom, right-click the Y axis (showing dates) and choose Format Axis. Select the Patterns tab and select High in the Tick Mark Labels.

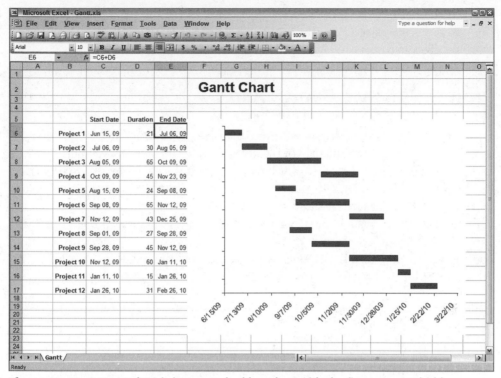

Figure 24.16: A Gantt chart is just a stacked bar chart with the first segment hidden.

6. Right-click the Start Date column segment, the leftmost segment, and choose Format Data Series. On the Patterns tab, select Border None and Area None so that the first segment is hidden and the duration appears to float.

7. Right-click the Y axis (showing dates) and choose Format Axis. Select the Scale tab. Set the dates so that only dates every other week display. Also set a start and end date. You can see the numeric value for the start date by reformatting the first date in cell C6 with a number format. The scale formats for this chart to show dates every four weeks are

Minimum	39979
Maximum	40260
Major Unit	28
Minor Unit	1

Finally, the chart is formatted for appearance and the project names along the category axis are formatted to be invisible, because they appear on the worksheet.

Project Variance Gantt Charts

Executives care about results—whether a project is on time, on budget, and on scope. One way to present this big picture is with a project variance chart. It shows where projects are ahead or behind. Using the same technique learned in Chapter 23, "Displaying Targets and Alerts," you can set different alert colors to identify variance farther out of limits.

Figure 24.17 shows a project variance Gantt chart. It uses a bar chart and shows just the difference between actual and target dates. Alert limits have been used so that different levels of variance appear in different colors. The target completion date for a project is the 0 point for the axis.

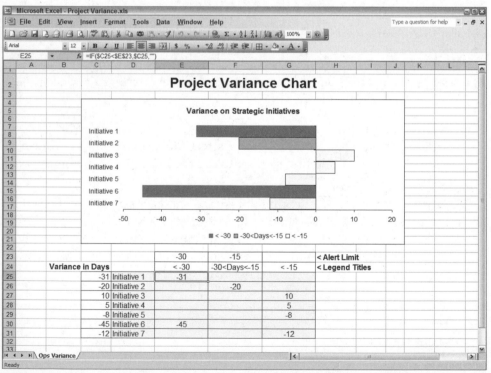

Figure 24.17: Project variance charts quickly identify projects that are not on time, on budget, or on scope.

To create a project variance Gantt chart

1. Select D24:G31 and open the Chart Wizard.

2. Select the Clustered Bar (the first bar chart) and choose Finish.

3. Remove the background and grid lines.

4. Right-click a bar and choose Format Data Series. On the Options tab, set Overlap to 100 and Gap Width to 0. This will make the three data series in columns E, F, and G appear as one series. Choose OK.

5. Right-click the Category (X) Axis, displaying initiative names, and choose Format Axis. On the Patterns tab, select Low for Tick Mark Labels. This moves all the Initiative titles to the left. Choose OK.

Apply color and border formats to the bars of each data series, and you have a variance project Gantt chart with conditional alert levels.

Control Charts

Six Sigma is the science of reducing variation in business processes to increase quality, reduce waste, and satisfy customers. There are many tools in a Six Sigma Black Belt's kit, but the one most frequently used to monitor and control variation is the control chart, also known as the Shewart chart. The control chart shows three things:

■ A centerline, usually the average of the data

■ An upper limit and lower limit within which the process should stay

■ Actual data

By using a control chart on any process, whether manufacturing, emergency room admission times, or bank processing times, it becomes visibly obvious when a process begins to go out of control. There are predefined events on a control chart that indicate to a Six Sigma professional that the process is probably, statistically speaking, going out of control. For the uninitiated, these predefined events can sound as if they are conjured out of thin air, but they have a sound statistical basis. Detection of these events can be automated in Excel, but only the basic control chart is shown here. These events that indicate that processes are probably out of control are

■ 1 data point outside the upper or lower control limit

■ 6 or more sequential data points steadily increasing or decreasing

■ 8 or more data points on one side of the centerline

■ 14 or more points alternating on either side of the centerline

The following steps show how to create a simple control chart like the one in Figure 24.18. Adding different types of alerts and identifiers is covered elsewhere in this book.

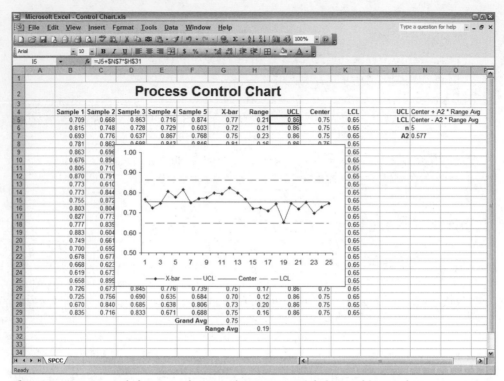

Figure 24.18: Control charts or Shewart charts are straightforward in Excel.

To create a simple process control chart like the one in Figure 24.18

1. Enter the sample data in B5:F29. This demonstration has five sets of sample measurements.

2. Calculate the sample averages in G5 with

    =AVERAGE(B5:F5)

    and copy them down.

3. Calculate the sample ranges in H5 with

    =MAX(B5:F5)-MIN(B5:F5)

    and copy them down.

4. Calculate the Grand Average and the Range Average in cells G30 and H31.

   The Control Limit formulas are

   ```
   UCL = Center + A2 * Range Avg.
   LCL = Center - A2 * Range Avg.
   ```

   For a sample of size n=5, the control chart constant for A2 is 0.577.

5. Enter the following formulas and copy them down.

NAME	CELL	FORMULA
UCL	I5	=J5+$N$7*$H$31
Center	J5	=$G$30
LCL	K5	=J5-$N$7*$H$31

6. Create the chart by selecting G4:G29, then hold the Ctrl key down as you also select I4:K29. You should have four columns selected—but skip I4:I29.

7. Open the Chart Wizard and select a Line Chart with Markers. Choose Finish.

You've created the control chart. All you need to do now is format it. You may want to apply the following formatting:

- Delete gray chart background and grid lines.
- Reformat the UCL, Center, and LCL lines with dashed line, without markers, and with a darker color.
- Adjust the Y axis scale size.
- Move the legend to the bottom.

Summary

A good dashboard developer needs to understand not just the software tools but the entire business process that is being controlled. Selecting the correct analytics and visual displays is important for fast, accurate business decisions.

If you have not read in Sections I and II how to interview executives and managers and define the critical few metrics, it is important that you do so. Chapter 12, "Creating Dashboards for Decision Making," covers tips on how to think about users' needs.

CHAPTER 25

Drilling to Detail

Never neglect details. When everyone's mind is dulled or distracted the leader must be doubly vigilant.

Colin Powell
Statesman, General

Scorecards and dashboards display summary results of large amounts of information. Inevitably, this forces two needs: a concise and obvious method for navigating through the data and the ability to drill down from summaries and results into the original data.

In this chapter you'll learn a couple of methods of creating simple navigation systems. Some are obvious, such as hyperlinks, but take a lot of display space. One of the other means of navigation uses a simple combo box to enable your users to jump to any named location in the workbook.

It's inevitable with Balanced Scorecards and operational dashboards that someone will find an item in the summary level that he wishes to examine in more detail. Doing so requires drilling down into the detailed data that generated the summary. There are many ways of doing this in Excel, but the methods depend upon how the data is accessed by Excel. This book is written for mid- to advanced-level Excel users who are usually retrieving data in the workbook. For that reason, this chapter covers methods of drilling down into data within the workbook. These usually limit drill-down to going one level deeper into data. More advanced methods, and almost unlimited levels and views in drilling, are possible when Excel is linked to a relational database.

Navigating

It's not uncommon for Balanced Scorecards to have 40 to 50 different displays and for operational dashboards to have 3 to 5. Then there are the operational reports you may want to link to from within dashboards. You want to give your users a clean and simple way to navigate between this information. They need to be able to quickly move between views of data so that they can understand relationships and make strategic and operational decisions.

Balanced Scorecards created in Excel are usually presented to the executive level by encapsulating the Excel charts and tables within a Microsoft PowerPoint presentation or an Adobe PDF document, as described in Chapter 29, "Publishing Balanced Scorecards and Operational Dashboards." If you publish to PowerPoint, you will need to create a new navigation system. But if you design your Excel navigation system correctly, it will work in the Adobe PDF file you send to executives.

If you stay within Excel for your scorecards and dashboards, then you have many options for navigation. In addition to normal Excel methods of navigation, I've shown a way to make a simple drop-down menu that enables you to jump to any named location in your workbook. This makes navigation almost foolproof, even for inexperienced Excel users.

Navigating with Simple Hyperlinks

You use hyperlinks to navigate between pages on the Web. Hyperlinks such as these are easy to create in Excel workbooks for navigation between worksheets, cells, and ranges. Your hyperlinks can be attached to text in a cell or to objects drawn with the Drawing toolbar. (Hyperlinks cannot be attached to charts.)

Figure 25.1 shows a hyperlink button at the top left of a briefing book page. Clicking this hyperlink button takes the user back to the Home page, the first page of the Balanced Scorecard.

Hyperlinks within cells are easy to create, and you can format them so they look like buttons. Before creating a hyperlink, name a cell or range to which you want the hyperlink to jump. (You cannot name a chart, but you can name a cell or range next to the chart so that the chart will display.)

To name a cell or range, select the cell or range. Choose the Insert ⇨ Name ⇨ Define command. In Excel 2007, on the Insert tab, in the Defined Name group, select Define Name. The Define Name dialog box displays. In it, type the name you want for the cell or range. Use upper- and lowercase text with no spaces.

CAUTION Make sure you name tabs using their final names before you create hyperlinks. Hyperlinks do not automatically update when a tab name changes. If you rename a tab, existing hyperlinks to that tab will produce errors.

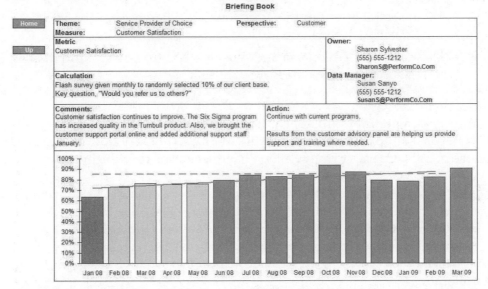

Figure 25.1: Clicking a hyperlink button or text takes the user to the location you specify.

If you want a text hyperlink in a cell, then type the text you want in a cell. If you want a hyperlink on an object, draw the object using the tools on the Drawing toolbar. Text hyperlinks in cells will convert and work in a PDF file if you use Adobe Acrobat to publish a Balanced Scorecard. Excel hyperlinks attached to a drawing object will not consistently convert in Adobe Acrobat 8.

To create the hyperlink

1. Select the cell containing text, or select the object you have drawn.

2. Choose Insert ➪ Hyperlink or press Ctrl+K to display the Insert Hyperlink dialog box shown in Figure 25.2. In Excel 2007, on the Insert tab, in the Links group, select Hyperlink.

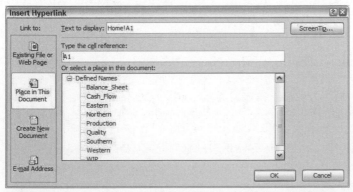

Figure 25.2: Use the Insert Hyperlink dialog box to add links to places within the same workbook or to other documents, or to open an e-mail window.

3. Click the Place in This Document icon on the left.

4. Type the cell location in the Type the Cell Reference Box or select the named range from the Place in This Document list.

5. Click the Screen Tip button and type any text tip you want to display when the user rolls the mouse over the link.

6. Choose OK.

Your text hyperlinks will appear underlined with a unique color. Objects with hyperlinks appear the same as without a hyperlink. For both of them, the mouse pointer changes to the selection hand when it is over the hyperlink.

TIP Hyperlinks cannot be attached to charts, but you can cover a chart with a drawing object, attach a hyperlink to the drawing object, and then double-click the object and set its Fill Transparency to 100% and its line to none. Hyperlinks on objects in Excel dashboards work well, but there are issues with them when converting using Adobe Acrobat 8 to publish a Balanced Scorecard.

Text hyperlinks and followed hyperlinks (hyperlinks that have been previously used), use formatting defined by an Excel formatting style. A "style" is a named collection of formatting properties. You can set these formats so that text hyperlinks appear like buttons by adding borders and a fill color behind the hyperlink. To set the formatting for a text hyperlink,

1. Choose Format Style to display the Style box shown in Figure 25.3.

2. Select Hyperlink from the Style Name list.

3. Select the Style Includes box you want to be included. To make text in cells look like buttons, this will include Font, Border, and Patterns.

4. Click Modify to display the Format Cells dialog box and change the formats for how you want all hyperlinks in the workbook to appear. To make links look like a button, you may want to add a border, a pattern different from the background, and bold Arial text.

5. Choose OK and click Add.

6. Repeat for the Followed Hyperlink style.

7. Click Close.

In Excel 2007, on the Home tab, in the Styles group, select Cell Styles. In the styles gallery that displays, right-click on either Hyperlink or Followed Hyperlink and choose Modify. Use this Style dialog box to modify the Hyperlink or Followed Hyperlink style so that the text box containing the hyperlink looks like a button.

Figure 25.3: Use the Format Style dialog box to make hyperlinks and followed hyperlinks look like buttons.

You may want to use drawing objects such as rectangles, rounded rectangles, and arrows as buttons with attached hyperlinks. Format the object either before or after you've attached a hyperlink. If you've already attached a hyperlink, you may find it difficult to select the object. The easiest way to select an object containing a hyperlink is to Ctrl+click the object. Double-click the edge of a selected drawing object to display its formatting dialog box.

Drawing objects used as buttons allow you to add some flair with the use of drop-shadows. To add a drop shadow to an object, select it and then click the Shadow Style icon at the far right side of the Drawing toolbar. You can directly select a shadow angle; by selecting Shadow Settings, you can change the shadow depth.

CAUTION   Chapter 29, "Publishing Balanced Scorecards and Operational Dashboards," describes how to publish your Excel scorecards using presentation software other than Excel. One of these methods is to publish to Adobe PDF documents. If you are publishing in PowerPoint or Adobe PDF, be sure to read Chapter 29 before creating a lot of hyperlinks in Excel.

TIP   If you are not publishing your scorecards and dashboards to another application, but are staying within Excel, then there are some fast methods of navigation built into Excel that your users may be able to use.

To jump between locations, press F5 and double-click on a range name to jump to that name. (The following section, "Navigating with a Drop-Down Menu," shows a more user-friendly method of doing this.)

Click the down arrow to the left of the cell reference box that is to the right of the function bar. From the drop-down list, you can select any named range to which you want to jump.

Press Ctrl+PgUp/PgDown to skip between tabs.

At the bottom of the Excel screen, right-click on the arrows used to scroll between tabs. A list of all tabs appears. Click the tab you want to jump to.

Navigating with a Drop-Down Menu

The simple hyperlinks just described are an easy way to create a menu button or a bank of buttons. They need no explanation, but they take a lot of screen real estate. They are also static, and they can't be manipulated using formulas. If you have had the misfortune of renaming worksheet tabs after you've created hyperlinks, you will find that links are broken.

There is another alternative that takes up little screen space, and that is something that users are familiar with from using web browsers. You can create a list of places to go to; clicking a name in the list jumps to the corresponding location.

Figure 25.4 shows a combo box that allows users to scroll through a long list of hyperlinks. This approach works well in displays where users are not navigating between two or three pages, but between many reports, charts, or data entry areas.

This method of navigation presents users with a combo box containing a list of locations. Users select a location from the drop-down list and then click the Go To >> text to jump to the selected location.

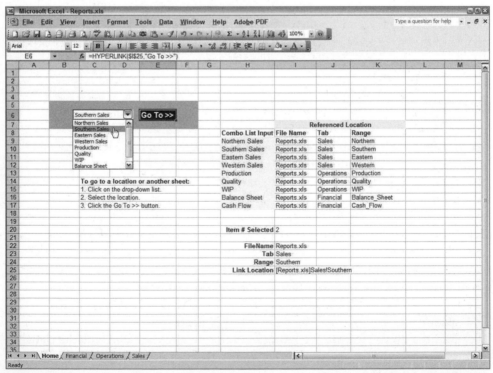

Figure 25.4: Using a drop-down list for navigation gives users easy access to cells, ranges, charts, and reports throughout a workbook.

This navigation system is built using a HYPERTEXT function in cell E6 under the Go To >> text. Selecting a name from the drop-down list builds a hyperlink address from the list in I9:K17. The hyperlink address built from the selection, shown in I25, is used by the HYPERLINK function in E6.

The function in E6 is

```
=HYPERLINK($I$25,"Go To >>")
```

Chapter 20, "Controlling Dashboards with Menus, Combo Boxes, and Buttons," describes how to use the combo box. This combo box gets its list from the cell contents in H9:H17. The output from your selection goes to cell I20 as the number of the item selected.

The file name, tab name, and range associated with the selection from the drop-down list are then calculated in cells I22:I24. An INDEX function in each of these cells uses the item number in I20 to look up the appropriate text for the file name, tab, and range. The formulas are

NAME	ADDRESS	FUNCTION
File Name	I22	=INDEX($I$9:$I$17,$I$20)
Tab	I23	=INDEX($J$9:$J$17,$I$20)
Range	I24	=INDEX($K$9:$K$17,$I$20)
Link Location	I25	="["&$I$22&"]"&I23&"!"&$I$24

Drilling Down to Detail

Balanced Scorecards and operational dashboards are important not just for monitoring progress and for alerting you to issues, but also for helping you identify where to look for solutions. This almost always requires drilling down to detailed data.

The following techniques do not allow the multiple levels of drill-down possible in very expensive business intelligence systems, but they do enable the display of another level of detail. The following methods assume that Excel is using data stored within a workbook. More advanced techniques are possible when Excel accesses data in relational databases or OLAP cubes.

Note: Download Sample Files for this Book

Sample data files and examples used in the book, as well as many more resources for Balanced Scorecards and operational dashboards, are available for free download. For information on how to download this information, please see the Introduction.

Creating Pseudo Drill-Downs with Hyperlinks

In Balanced Scorecards and many operational dashboards, drill-downs are used to move from the top-level summary screen to pre-defined detail screens. Figure 25.5 shows a summary level chart that appears after users click on a metric link on the Balanced Scorecard home page.

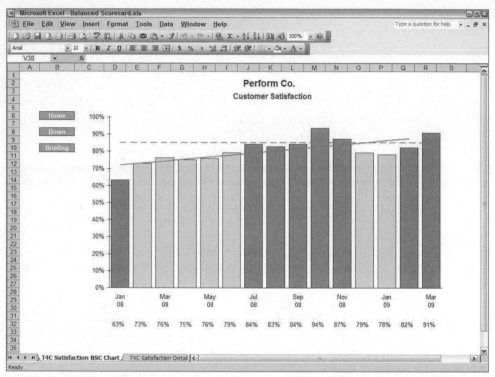

Figure 25.5: After clicking on a link in the Balanced Scorecard's home page users see the summary level chart shown here. Clicking the Down button takes them to predefined detail charts in Figure 25.6.

Clicking on the hyperlinked Down button in Figure 25.5 takes the user to Figure 25.6, a screen with pre-defined detail charts. These predefined detail charts are usually straightforward charts or analysis composed of the first-level categories under the summary, such as division summaries, product line, sales region, and so forth.

Note: Always Interview Users for Their Decision Making Needs

Before every touching the keyboard, interview the intended audience of your dashboard. Determine what data they need to make business decisions, what data is available, what data analysis they need, and what visual presentation will best help them.

In either display, if users click on the Briefing hyperlink, they are taken to the Briefing Book shown in Figure 25.7. The Briefing Book enables executives and managers to see at a glance what issues have already been identified and what actions are being taken. This can save time in strategy and operational review meetings.

If there are questions about the issue, actions, or data, clicking on the e-mail addresses at the upper right in Figure 25.7 opens a pre-addressed e-mail form to the appropriate individual. The e-mail link is created with Excel's Insert ⇨ Hyperlink command.

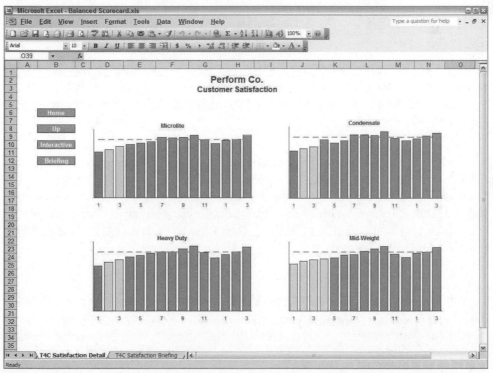

Figure 25.6: This first level of drill-down shows details for pre-defined categories.

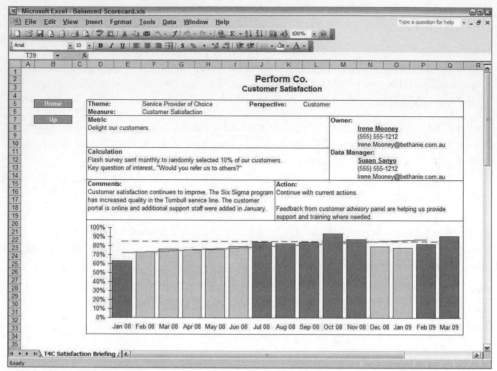

Figure 25.7: Clicking the Briefing Button displays a briefing book with definitions of the metric, comments, next steps, and contact information. Clicking an e-mail address opens a pre-addressed e-mail form.

The Interactive button in Figure 25.6 jumps to a worksheet where users can directly query specific data and analysis. It is important that you work with the business owner of the dashboard to give them the data and analysis in the presentation they need. Figure 25.8 shows one such interactive sheet. When you build interactive sheets that allow query and analysis, you will use a combination of techniques from the following chapters:

- Chapter 17, "Working with Data That Changes Size"
- Chapter 18, "Working with Lists and Tables of Data"
- Chapter 20, "Controlling Dashboards with Menus, Combo Boxes, and Buttons"
- Chapter 22, "Smoothing Data and Forecasting Trends"
- Chapter 24, "Building Powerful Charts for Decision Making"

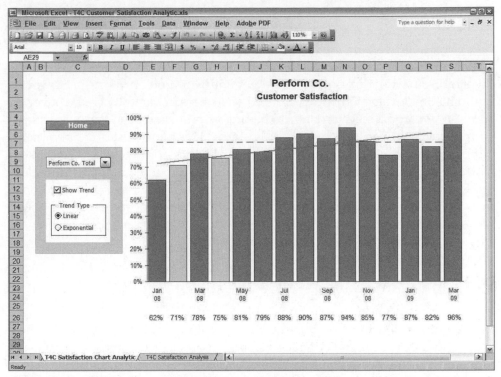

Figure 25.8: Clicking the Interactive button in the Balanced Scorecard jumps users to an Excel worksheet where they can analyze data in detail.

Drill-Downs in PivotTables

PivotTables are one of the most valuable data analysis tools Excel has. However, most Excel users do not understand how to use them, and infrequent Excel users are completely baffled by them.

With that proviso in mind, you can use PivotTables to truly drill down from a summary into detailed data. Chapter 21, "Feeding Dashboards from PivotTables," describes using PivotTables. To drill down in a PivotTable just double-click on a cell in the PivotTable. The detail that composes the summary will appear in a new sheet. For example, if you double-click on a cell containing the total sales by product for the month of June, then a new sheet will open showing you the detailed data that went into that total: all the sales, by individual product, in June.

Inexperienced Excel users get confused by this drill-down and by the new sheet of details that opens. It is common for them to close the entire workbook because they don't realize that a new worksheet has opened, not a new workbook.

But you can turn off the ability to drill-down in PivotTables. Right-click in the PivotTable and choose PivotTable Options. Clear the Enable Drill to Details check box to prevent drilling down by double-clicking.

Another issue that occurs when using PivotTables in dashboards is that PivotTables will not work with the sheet and workbook protected. However, without some protection, inexperienced users can accidentally create havoc in your dashboards. One alternative to having unprotected dashboards is to save your Excel dashboards with Read Only status. This allows users to open them, but prompts them to not save the dashboard by its original name. To make a worksheet read only, choose Tools ➪ Options and select the Security tab. Select the Read-Only Recommended check box and click OK. Save the workbook. In Excel 2007, click the Microsoft Office button, then choose Save As. Choose Tools, then General Options. Select the Read-Only Recommended check box, click OK, and click Save.

Drilling into a Data List by Clicking on a Row

In some cases you can't use a PivotTable to drill down into a database. Users may be untrained in PivotTables, or you want to control exactly what they see without extensive and complex macros. In other situations, you may want to keep the sheets completely protected, something that prevents the use of PivotTables. This method works even when the sheet is protected, so long as you allow cells to be selected on the protected sheet.

The following example gives users near click-to-drill capability with the use of a few formulas and a simple macro that anyone can create. Figure 25.9 shows the example. In this example, clicking anywhere in the Product Line Totals range, E6:L14, and then pressing Ctrl+d will display the data by region for that product line. The Product Line Totals could have been created with SUMIF formulas or with a PivotTable. The product details appear in the range F20:L24.

This works with a simple macro, shown in Figure 25.10, that retrieves the active row and active column when you press Ctrl+d. These row and column values are stored in the range names ActiveRow and ActiveCol.

After checking to make sure the selected cell is within the clickable area, the formulas calculate the name of the product line selected. That name is then used to retrieve its East, West, North, and South data from the database.

Note: An Alternative Method

An alternative to the INDEX method of retrieving data shown here is to use GETPIVOTDATA as described in Chapter 21, "Feeding Dashboards from PivotTables." If you create your summary table with a PivotTable, you can then use the method in this section to find the row and column names and use them to retrieve the appropriate data from the PivotTable using GETPIVOTDATA.

Microsoft Excel - Drill-Down in List.xls

File Edit View Insert Format Tools Data Window Help Adobe PDF

H6 = 898

	A	B	C	D	E	F	G	H	I	J	K	L
1					Drill Into A Data List by Clicking							
2												
3		Table Boundaries				1. Click a total. 2. Press Ctrl+d to see detail by region.						
4		TopRow	6		Summary		Product Line Totals					
5		LftCol	5		Product Line		Jan	Feb	Mar	Apr	May	Jun
6		BtmRow	14		Dynamic Heavy		892	898	875	875	881	866
7		RtCol	12		Dynamic Light		872	915	839	839	893	923
8					Dynamic Medium		952	906	884	884	954	910
9		Active Cell Location			Laser Heavy		932	863	865	865	900	889
10		SelectedRow	6		Laser Light		925	896	877	877	901	891
11		SelectedCol	8		Laser Medium		939	894	898	898	888	912
12		Boundary Test	FALSE		Light Angstrom		094	031	069	069	070	063
13					Light Micron		876	909	899	899	871	895
14					Light Milli		921	921	949	949	933	910
15		Active Cell										
16		Content	898									
17		Product Line	Dynamic Heavy			db column >>	4	5	6	7	8	9
18					Detail for:		Product Line Regional Detail					
19		Row Match in Database			Dynamic Heavy		Jan	Feb	Mar	Apr	May	Jun
20		Product Line	Region	Row		East	202	233	203	203	234	240
21		Dynamic Heavy	East	2		West	250	202	216	216	216	203
22		Dynamic Heavy	West	5		North	202	237	232	232	213	207
23		Dynamic Heavy	North	3		South	238	226	224	224	218	216
24		Dynamic Heavy	South	4								
25												
26			1		2		3	4	5	6	7	8	9
27							Product Line Database					
28			Key		Product Line	Region	Jan	Feb	Mar	Apr	May	Jun
29			Dynamic HeavyEast		Dynamic Heavy	East	202	233	203	203	234	240
30			Dynamic HeavyNorth		Dynamic Heavy	North	202	237	232	232	213	207

Sheet1

Figure 25.9: Click in a row of the Product Line Totals table, then press Ctrl+d to see details in the Product Line Regional Detail table.

The formulas to calculate the clickable area and whether the selected cell is within the boundaries are shown in Table 25.1:

Table 25.1 Formulas to Calculate the "Clickable" Range

LABEL OR RANGE	CELL	FORMULA
dbTotals	E6:L14	Range name
Top Row	C4	=ROW(dbTotals)
LftCol	C5	=COLUMN(dbTotals)
BtmRow	C6	=ROW(dbTotals) +ROWS(dbTotals)-1
RtCol	C7	=COLUMN(dbTotals) +COLUMNS(dbTotals)-1
SelectedRow	C10	=ActiveRow
SelectedCol	C11	=ActiveCol
Boundary Test	C12	=IF(AND(AND(ActiveRow>TopRow,ActiveRow<=BtmRow) ,AND(ActiveCol>=LftCol,ActiveCol<=RtCol)),TRUE,FALSE)

Notice that cells C10 and C11 contain the variable names ActiveRow and ActiveCol. These names are created by the simple macro below. The values of the active row and active column are stored in these names. These formulas return the values from the variables in the macro and place it in cells where spreadsheet formulas can use it.

The content of the selected cell in the Totals is retrieved in cell C16 with

```
=INDEX(dbTotals,ActiveRow-TopRow+1,
      ActiveCol-LftCol+1)
```

This formula looks in the clickable range, dbTotals, and retrieves the cell content at the row and column clicked. If the use of INDEX is unfamiliar to you, review its use in Chapter 18, "Working with Lists and Tables of Data."

The product name of the row containing the selected cell is retrieved in cell C17 with

```
=INDEX(dbTotals,ActiveRow-TopRow+1,1)
```

This is exactly the same as the formula retrieving the content of the selected cell, but here the content of the cell in the first column of the selected row is retrieved.

Now, find the rows in the database, dbProductLine, that match the product line and regions. These are calculated in D21:D24. Cell D21, for example, contains

```
=MATCH(B21&C21,$D$28:$D$64,0)
```

If the use of MATCH is unfamiliar to you, review its use in Chapter 18.

As Chapter 18 explains, MATCH searches down the first column of the database, $D$28:$D$64, for the row that has a match for B21&C21. B21&C21 is the concatenation of the product line name and one of the regions, for example, DynamicHeavyEast. The name of the product line changes, but the region values East, West, North, and South are fixed.

Finally, the data matching the product line and four regions is retrieved in cells G20:L23 using an INDEX function. Cell G20 for example contains

```
=INDEX(dbProductLine,$D21,G$17)
```

This looks in the dbProductLine database and retrieves the cell contents at row D21, which is 2 in the figure, and at column 4.

The macro that makes this possible is the simple two-line macro shown in Figure 25.10. Even if you aren't familiar with macros, you can make this work.

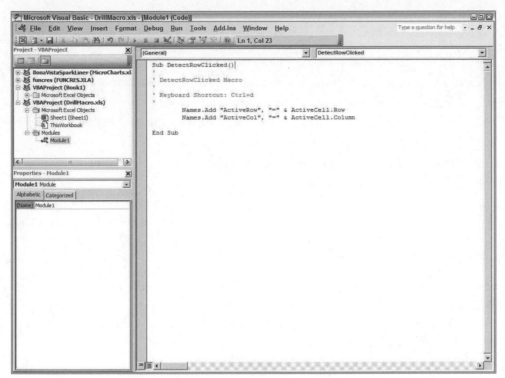

Figure 25.10: Type this simple macro into the VBA Editor to select data from tables.

For information on creating macros in Excel 2007, please refer to the Microsoft support web site, which contains detailed instructions. Go to http://office .microsoft.com, select the Products tab, and select Excel. In the search box, enter "create a macro" and click Search.

To create this macro in versions of Excel prior to 2007

1. Open the workbook you want to contain the macro and save it with a name.

2. Choose Tools ➪ Macro ➪ Record New Macro.

3. Enter the name DetectRowClicked without spaces in the Macro Name box.

4. Type a lower-case "d" in the shortcut key box and click OK.

5. Click on any cell in the worksheet to record an action, then click the square Stop Macro button on the floating toolbar.

Now add the Visual Basic for Applications code to the macro "shell" you have created:

1. Choose Tools ⇨ Macro ⇨ Macros to display the Macro dialog box.

2. Select the name you gave your macro and click Edit to open the VBA Editor.

3. Delete the black text between the Sub line and the End Sub line. This is the code for the cell you selected.

4. Type the following code between the Sub and End Sub lines.

```
Names.Add "ActiveRow", "=" & ActiveCell.Row
Names.Add "ActiveCol", "=" & ActiveCell.Column
```

5. Choose File, Save and close the VBA Editor.

To test your macro, type into separate cells

```
=ActiveRow
=ActiveCol
```

then press Ctrl+d. The cells containing these names should show the row and column number of the selected cell.

Summary

Giving your dashboard users the ability to drill down and see the detailed data they need to solve their problems is a huge part of why you are creating dashboards. In most cases, Balanced Scorecards will need one or two levels of drill-down from the business unit summary level. Because these levels of summary are predefined summaries, such as division data or regional data, you can create pre-defined detail views. Operational dashboards require more interactivity to help resolve issues. For these, you may need hyperlink menus that retrieve dashboards allowing interactive queries like the Interactive button in Figure 25.6 that opens Figure 25.8. The worksheet in Figure 25.8 gives the user interactive queries. Some chapters that will help you build interactive dashboards are Chapter 18, "Working with Lists and Tables of Data," Chapter 20, "Controlling Dashboards with Menus, Combo Boxes, and Buttons," and Chapter 21, "Feeding Dashboards from PivotTables." For dashboards that allow greater interaction with larger data sets, read Chapter 28, "Integrating Dashboards and External Data."

CHAPTER 26

Using Excel Add-Ins for Extra Capabilities

The thing is, continuity of strategic direction and continuous improvement in how you do things are absolutely consistent with each other. In fact, they're mutually reinforcing.

Michael Porter
Harvard Business School Professor

Microsoft Excel is easily the world's most used numeric analysis tool. It has analytical and charting capabilities that lend power to business analysis, but there are niche areas where it could use additional capability. This chapter describes two tools that work with Excel to create more powerful scorecards and dashboards.

MicroCharts is an Excel add-in that gives you the power to create miniature charts that fit within worksheet cells. This makes it possible to create information-rich tables containing both rows of numeric data and charts. The ability to see many charts at one time, without extraneous charting clutter, makes it easier to see relationships. With MicroCharts WebEdition, you can create dynamic dashboards that access OLAP cubes and relational databases.

Xcelsius uses Excel as a data modeling tool. You draw a dashboard by dragging chart and selector components onto a canvas and then linking the components to Excel. When you are ready to publish your dashboard, Xcelsius exports the dashboard as a stand-alone Flash file that runs in any web browser. Using a higher-level version of Xcelsius enables you to connect the dashboard dynamically to almost any database.

Adding MicroCharts for an Information-Rich Display

MicroCharts enables you to insert miniature charts into worksheet cells. These charts are created with a custom font so they fit into cells and can be formatted as text, but they have the high-resolution appearance of a chart. Figure 26.1 and 26.2 illustrate a number of the different miniature charts available with MicroCharts.

MicroCharts subscribes to the charting philosophy voiced by Edward Tufte and Stephen Few: don't distract from information with unnecessary chart elements and "ink." This "keep it simple and clear" philosophy enables you to fit a lot of charts into a small area. By placing these charts adjacent to their data, you can immediately see where data are trending or if performance limits are exceeded. As Figure 26.2 illustrates, using MicroCharts is also an excellent way to show detailed information that backs up a summary chart.

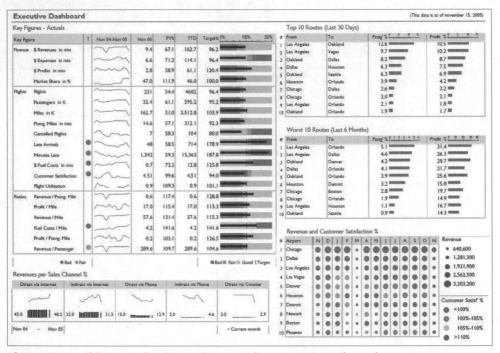

Figure 26.1: This example of reporting on airline operations shows how you can use MicroCharts to create an information-rich, but easily analyzed dashboard or report.

MicroCharts makes it easy and productive to use Stephen Few's bullet charts and Edward Tufte's Sparkline charts. With just a few clicks, you can embed these minimalist charts into a cell. Without MicroCharts, you can create bullet charts in Excel using the techniques described in Chapter 24, "Building Powerful Charts for Decision Making," and you can create Sparklines as described in Chapter 19, "Creating Miniature Charts and Tables," but it takes a lot more work, and the Excel versions are larger.

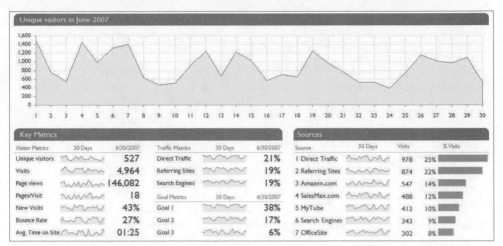

Figure 26.2: The Web Analytics example illustrates how MicroCharts makes analysis easier by showing summary data along with detail components.

MicroCharts enables you to insert cell-sized charts in a wide variety of chart styles. Figure 26.3 shows the numerous chart types available with MicroCharts. Examples of the chart types available are:

- **Sparklines:** Sparklines was invented by Edward Tufte to minimize extraneous information. It allows you to create line and point charts showing trends without needing additional information from axis, grid lines, legends, and elements. All you need is the source data in a table next to the Sparkline.

- **Horizontal and vertical bullet graphs:** Bullet graphs, invented by Stephen Few, show the same reference information found in gauges, but they use significantly less screen real estate. Because the display is on a linear scale, it is easier to see relative positions than on the curve scale of a gauge.

- **Column charts:** These charts show relative changes in discrete values.

- **Horizontal and vertical bar graphs:** These graphs show relative sizes between related items.

- **Pie charts:** These show relative proportions to a total.

- **Win/Lose charts:** These show a binary state of positive or negative (win/lose).

MicroCharts is from BonaVista, an XLCubed Technology company. They are the producers of XLCubed, software that makes linking Excel dashboards to OLAP cubes and relational databases more accessible to Excel users.

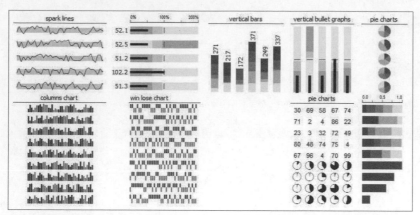

Figure 26.3: This gallery shows a few of the MicroCharts that can be inserted into Excel cells.

The MicroCharts Professional Edition for Excel is an inexpensive add-in that any individual or business can afford. You can download a free, 30-day trial copy of MicroCharts and learn more about XLCubed by going to www .bonavistasystems.com. Installing the trial version of MicroCharts also installs tutorials and sample worksheets showing impressive results.

MicroChart Demonstration

You can create MicroCharts by clicking on the Insert MicroChart button on the MicroCharts toolbar, or by inserting a custom worksheet function just as you would any Excel function. The following example shows how easy it is to insert and format a series of MicroCharts to show trends in a hospital's clinical data.

Creating a MicroChart

MicroCharts works within normal Excel worksheets. In this example, a short list containing clinical data has been opened; it includes 18 clinical quality indicators tracked over 15 months. If you want to follow this example, you can download the data file from the Internet locations listed in the Introduction and obtain a free, 30-day trial copy of MicroCharts from www.bonavistasystems.com.

If the MicroCharts toolbar does not display in your worksheet after you have installed it, then choose View ⇨ Toolbars and select MicroCharts.

To create a MicroChart,

1. Open the worksheet Clinical Quality 00 MicroCharts and select the data D9:L26.

2. Click the Insert MicroChart button, and the Chart Type dialog box will display as shown in Figure 26.4.

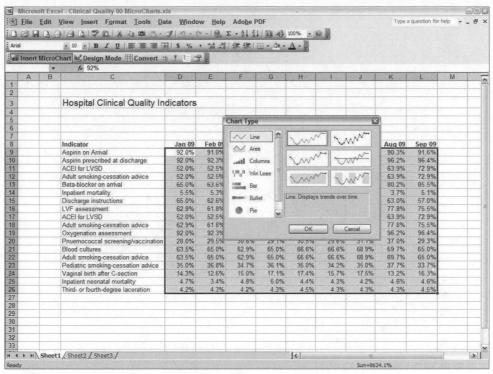

Figure 26.4: The Chart Type dialog box enables you to select from seven different chart styles with numerous preformatted settings.

3. Select the top left Sparkline that uses minimal formatting. You will add custom formatting later.

4. Click OK, and the Source Data and Chart Location dialog box will appear as shown in Figure 26.5. By preselecting the data area and not including the data headings, the dialog box will appear with the source data range already selected.

5. The box, "Where do you want to put the chart?" has the range M9:M26 preselected because charts that show trends normally appear to the right of the data. The box, "Where do you want to put the formula?" has M8 preselected. MicroCharts' custom function will be placed in this cell, but later you will be able to replace it with a visible title. You can select the cells you want for any of these ranges.

6. Click OK to complete the MicroCharts. In this example, the chart for each row of data will appear to the right of those data. The MicroCharts function is visible in the cell above the charts and in the formula bar shown in Figure 26.6. You can later make this appear as a text title.

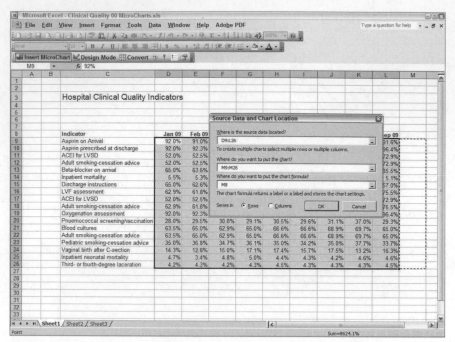

Figure 26.5: In the Source Data and Chart Location dialog box, select where the data are located, where you want the chart(s), and where you want the MicroChart formula.

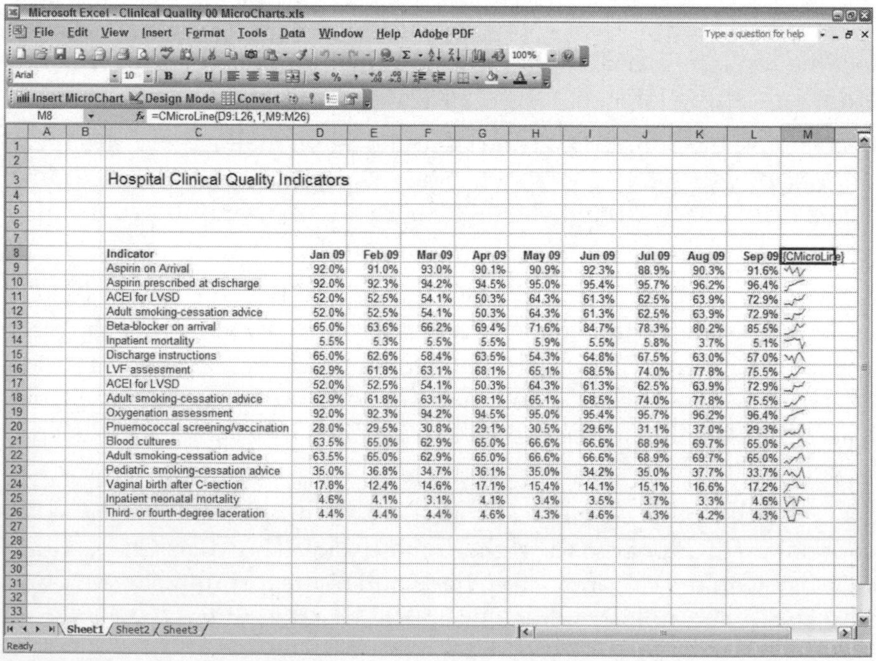

Figure 26.6: MicroCharts are inserted in the cells you have specified. The custom function is visible in the cell above the charts and in the formula bar.

Formatting a MicroChart

MicroCharts are easy to insert and useful in showing trends. You can make these charts easier to read and more attractive with a little formatting.

MicroCharts uses a set of custom fonts to create the chart in a cell, so you can increase the font's point size at any time. Excel treats MicroCharts like text, so any text formatting will work. To make the charts larger,

1. Select the range containing the MicroCharts, M9:M26.

2. Use a font-formatting procedure to change the font's point size for this range from 10 points to 12 points. Notice that the MicroCharts that are created increase in size.

There are many other formatting changes you can make to MicroCharts using the Format Chart command. To modify the chart's display of lines, points, and colors

1. Right-click any cell containing a MicroChart.

2. Select the Format Chart command to display the Format Chart dialog box shown in Figure 26.7.

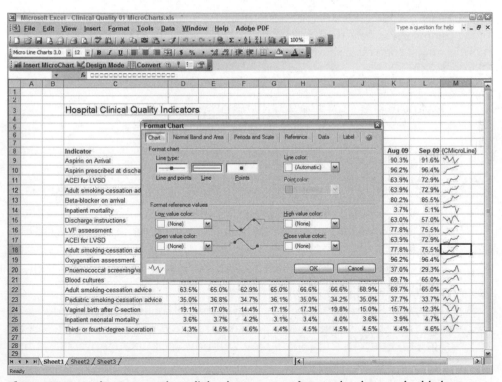

Figure 26.7: In the Format Chart dialog box, you can format the chart and add chart features such as Normal distribution area, baseline, and more.

3. In the Chart tab, select Line and Points from the Line type option.

4. In Line Color, select Light Blue Color 33.

5. In Point Color, select Bright Dark Blue Color 5. Notice that in the lower left corner of the dialog box, a display shows how the MicroCharts will look with this formatting. Figure 26.8 shows the Chart dialog box completed.

6. Click OK to see the results.

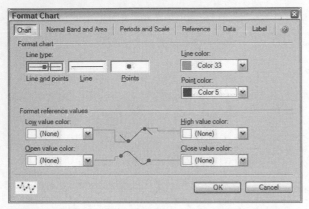

Figure 26.8: Use the Chart tab to format the features for the chart type you have chosen. Notice the display in the lower left corner that shows the results of your selections.

If you want to show the Normal distribution band on the chart or create a shaded area chart,

1. Right-click any cell containing a MicroChart and select the Format Chart command.

2. In the Format Chart dialog box, select the Normal Band and Area tab.

3. Select the Normal Band on the right. This creates a shaded area on the chart that is either a specified number of standard deviations or a custom width you specify.

4. Select a Normal Band Color of Light Grey Color 15. Notice the sample chart at the lower left of the dialog box.

5. Change the Standard Deviation to 1.5. This will make the grey shaded area range from the average + or - 1.5 standard deviations. The Chart Format dialog box and its sample display will now look like Figure 26.9. Click OK to see the results on the worksheet.

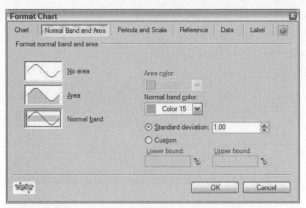

Figure 26.9: Use the Normal Band and Area tab to add a shaded band showing the standard deviation or a band width you calculate.

Finally, let's double the MicroChart's width, make sure that it does not plot blank cells as zeros, and replace the MicroChart function in cell M8 with a title.

1. Right-click any cell containing a MicroChart and select the Format Chart command.

2. In the Format Chart dialog box, select the Periods and Scale tab. Make sure the Aspect Ratio check box is selected. This controls the width to height ratio.

3. Change the Aspect Ratio to 2 and notice that the sample display width changes.

4. Click the Data tab, and for Missing Value Handling, select the Not Plotted (Leave Gap) option.

5. Select the Label tab and in the Chart Label box type **Charts**. This is the title that will display over the MicroChart function in cell M8.

6. Click OK.

7. The chart is wider, so double-click the column heading on the right side of the Charts column to adjust the column width for wider charts.

Your completed MicroCharts for hospital clinical indicators should look similar to Figure 26.10.

Distributing a Spreadsheet with MicroCharts

MicroCharts are created with a custom font set, which makes it easy to share Excel worksheets created with MicroCharts. Before sending the worksheet containing MicroCharts to another Excel user, click on the Convert button on the MicroCharts toolbar. This displays a dialog box that gives you two choices:

- Attach the custom font set to the worksheet so other users can see the high-resolution MicroCharts
- Convert the charts into graphics that are still good, but do not have a high resolution

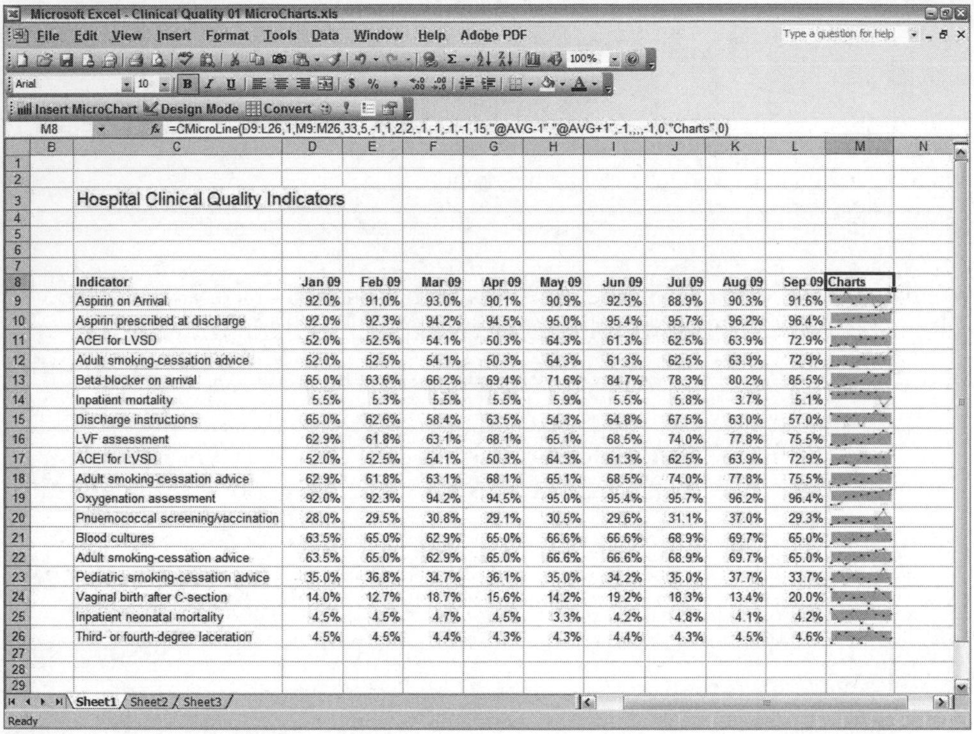

Hospital Clinical Quality Indicators

Indicator	Jan 09	Feb 09	Mar 09	Apr 09	May 09	Jun 09	Jul 09	Aug 09	Sep 09	Charts
Aspirin on Arrival	92.0%	91.0%	93.0%	90.1%	90.9%	92.3%	88.9%	90.3%	91.6%	
Aspirin prescribed at discharge	92.0%	92.3%	94.2%	94.5%	95.0%	95.4%	95.7%	96.2%	96.4%	
ACEI for LVSD	52.0%	52.5%	54.1%	50.3%	64.3%	61.3%	62.5%	63.9%	72.9%	
Adult smoking-cessation advice	52.0%	52.5%	54.1%	50.3%	64.3%	61.3%	62.5%	63.9%	72.9%	
Beta-blocker on arrival	65.0%	63.6%	66.2%	69.4%	71.6%	84.7%	78.3%	80.2%	85.5%	
Inpatient mortality	5.5%	5.3%	5.5%	5.5%	5.9%	5.5%	5.8%	3.7%	5.1%	
Discharge instructions	65.0%	62.6%	58.4%	63.5%	54.3%	64.8%	67.5%	63.0%	57.0%	
LVF assessment	62.9%	61.8%	63.1%	68.1%	65.1%	68.5%	74.0%	77.8%	75.5%	
ACEI for LVSD	52.0%	52.5%	54.1%	50.3%	64.3%	61.3%	62.5%	63.9%	72.9%	
Adult smoking-cessation advice	62.9%	61.8%	63.1%	68.1%	65.1%	68.5%	74.0%	77.8%	75.5%	
Oxygenation assessment	92.0%	92.3%	94.2%	94.5%	95.0%	95.4%	95.7%	96.2%	96.4%	
Pnuemococcal screening/vaccination	28.0%	29.5%	30.8%	29.1%	30.5%	29.6%	31.1%	37.0%	29.3%	
Blood cultures	63.5%	65.0%	62.9%	65.0%	66.6%	66.6%	68.9%	69.7%	65.0%	
Adult smoking-cessation advice	63.5%	65.0%	62.9%	65.0%	66.6%	66.6%	68.9%	69.7%	65.0%	
Pediatric smoking-cessation advice	35.0%	36.8%	34.7%	36.1%	35.0%	34.2%	35.0%	37.7%	33.7%	
Vaginal birth after C-section	14.0%	12.7%	18.7%	15.6%	14.2%	19.2%	18.3%	13.4%	20.0%	
Inpatient neonatal mortality	4.5%	4.5%	4.7%	4.5%	3.3%	4.2%	4.8%	4.1%	4.2%	
Third- or fourth-degree laceration	4.5%	4.5%	4.4%	4.3%	4.3%	4.4%	4.3%	4.5%	4.6%	

Figure 26.10: It takes little work to create and format MicroCharts that add valuable insight to information-rich dashboards or reports.

Before converting your worksheet for distribution, save the worksheet to be distributed with a new name and then convert it. Keep the production and distribution versions separate. Converting the worksheet permanently removes the MicroChart functions from the worksheet.

An additional alternative for distributing your work from MicroCharts is to create a PDF of the worksheet. This creates a high-quality file that users can read without having the MicroCharts custom font set. Also, if you have users at distributed locations, you can use the MicroCharts WebEdition. With this edition, you can create a multi-user report shared over the Internet.

Creating Flashy Interactive Dashboards with Xcelsius Engage

Xcelsius dashboards will visually grab people every time. I have seen senior executives literally come out of their chairs when they see a demo using their own corporate data displayed in an interactive Xcelsius dashboard. Figures 26.11 and 26.12 illustrate two operational dashboards that were created as a "proof of concept" for clients before final development. Although these dashboards are not as information-rich and dense as those created with MicroCharts, the Xcelsius dashboards make it very easy and engaging to drill down into detail and compare different data sets.

Xcelsius Engage is a powerful tool that is excellent for creating operational dashboards containing fewer than 500 rows of data, or with the connectivity version for creating dashboards linked to a database or data warehouse. Developing dashboards in Xcelsius is easy for simple dashboards, but it becomes increasingly more complex as the dashboards become more complex. Creating Balanced Scorecards containing tens of embedded daughter dashboards is possible but daunting, and may be difficult to support. Part of the difficulty in working with complex dashboards in Xcelsius is that there are so many visualization components and visual effects available that users and designers continually want to add more. It's a real magnet for "feature creep."

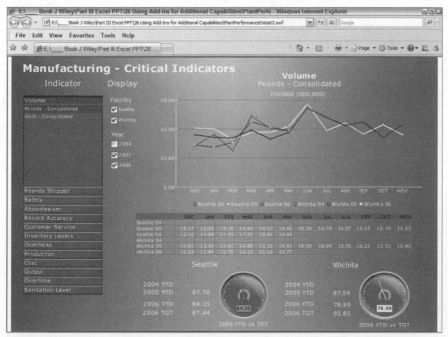

Figure 26.11: By using this dashboard, managers in a manufacturing plant can display and compare 85 performance indicators for two plants over a 3-year period.

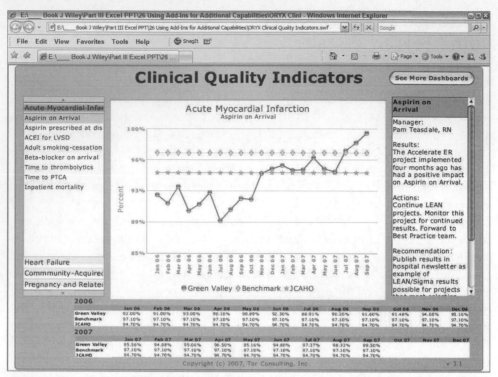

Figure 26.12: This chart displays hospital data, a benchmark, and the Joint Commission's recommended standards for 21 clinical quality metrics. Data can be updated from Excel or by linking directly to a database.

Figures 26.13 and 26.14 show some of the interactive capability of Xcelsius. In Figure 26.13, a List Builder dialog box displays that prompts you for multiple selections from the list on the left. The list you build is on the right. After you build your list and click the Update button, the chart updates as in Figure 26.14 to show a comparison between the list items you have selected. On the left in Figure 26.14, you can see the check boxes and combo boxes available for further modifications.

A dashboard like the one shown in Figures 26.13 and 26.14 is not elementary to create. The advantages to creating it in Xcelsius Engage is that it can be easily embedded within a web page so that anyone can access it and it is easy and straightforward to use.

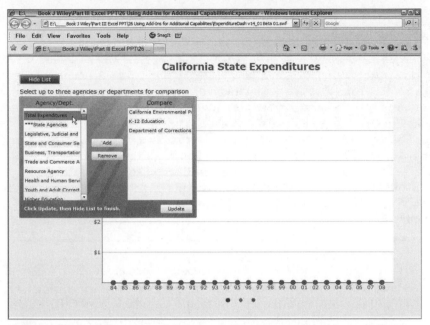

Figure 26.13: Analysts examining the California government's expenditures select from the List Builder those agencies or departments they want to analyze or compare. The chart behind the List Builder displays multiple sets of data.

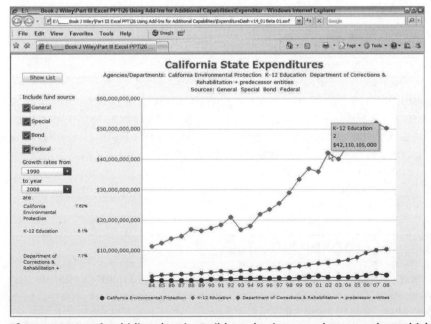

Figure 26.14: After hiding the List Builder, a business analyst can select which funding sources to include and the time frame over which to measure growth. All data are stored in Excel and published with the dashboard.

XCELSIUS AND MICROCHARTS ARE ALMOST ANTITHETICAL

MicroCharts, shown earlier in this chapter, is a perfect tool for creating infor-mation-rich, concise displays that show only the data needed and no more. These charts are not flashy; they just show what you need to make a decision. Although easy to create, they are not interactive unless you add some of the interactive formulas and functions I've presented in this book. MicroCharts can be linked to OLAP cubes and relational databases for dynamic updates.

Xcelsius is about making data look good and interactive, but sometimes at the expense of too much color and pizzazz. Charts and gauges cover a lot of screen area. Often, users want so many sliders, combo boxes, and gauges that the dashboard exceeds easy utility. All versions of Xcelsius are very scalable and secure, and the advanced Xcelsius has a wide range of database connectivity.

Xcelsius is very scalable and distributable. Dashboards created in Xcelsius include the data and formulas from the Excel model, but they are completely separate from Excel once the dashboard is published in Flash. The Flash dashboard can display data embedded within it or link to multiple data sources. Full role-level security is maintained by the dashboard so that users can log in with full security through any secure network they normally use.

Xcelsius uses Excel to hold static data, formulas, and values referenced by graphical components such as charts, sliders, combo boxes, and lists. When a dashboard is published from Xcelsius, the dashboard becomes a stand-alone Adobe Flash file that runs in any web browser: Excel is no longer connected to the dashboard. This removes the complaint some IT departments have about Excel's lack of scalability and security.

Xcelsius works with a subset of Excel functions. Xcelsius has limits in its analytic capability so it can't handle all of Excel's analytical functionality. It is designed as a "data visualization engine" not as an analytical tool. Once you go beyond basic dashboard displays, you will need to understand the nuanced differences between how Xcelsius and Excel interpret formulas and function errors. I've found with my clients that to use Xcelsius at a high level, a proficient, mid-level Excel user needs one or two days of hands-on training to learn these nuances as well as a different data layout.

Note: Beware of VLOOKUP in Xcelsius

VLOOKUP is a standard among intermediate Excel users for looking up infor-mation from a list. In Xcelsius, there are situations where it will not return what you expect. Instead of using VLOOKUP in Xcelsius, use a combination of INDEX and MATCH functions to retrieve data from a list. Examples of INDEX and MATCH are in multiple chapters in this book, especially those chapters dealing with tables of data and creating interactive charts.

There are multiple versions of Xcelsius, and each has progressively greater database capabilities. With Xcelsius you can link to simple ODBC and Crystal Reports, or to almost any database.

Xcelsius works best as the data visualization component for data retrieved from a database. That means creating a query in Xcelsius, sending the query out to a database or data warehouse, and retrieving a limited set of data. Xcelsius then charts or displays that limited set of data. It is also designed to work as a data visualization tool with Business Intelligence systems from Business Objects.

A Demonstration of Xcelsius Engage

Xcelsius builds visually striking dashboards, and it can do so easily with little need for extensive formulas in Excel. In the example shown in Figure 26.15, a drop-down or combo list is used to select from 18 hospital quality indicators with data from January to September. The data for the selected indicator is shown in the chart. The dashboard in Figure 26.15 is the end product of this demonstration.

If you want to work through this demonstration, you can download a trial version of Xcelsius at `http://www.businessobjects.com`. For information on downloading the sample files for this demonstration, please refer to the Introduction.

An Xcelsius component automatically calculates the trend for the selected data; however, the trend data is only displayed in the chart if a check box is selected. An Excel IF function is used to show or hide the trend data depending on the value returned by the check box.

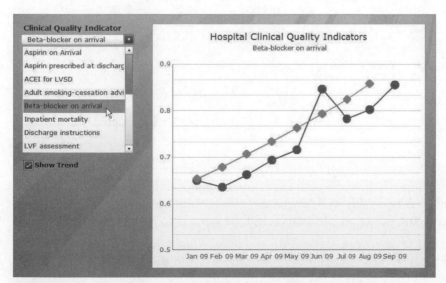

Figure 26.15: Selecting an indicator from the combo list displays the data in the chart. Selecting the check box displays the trend line for the data.

Creating a Model to Select and Chart Data

Begin using Xcelsius dashboards by creating a structure in Excel for data, formulas, titles, and triggers that control Xcelsius features. Figure 26.16 shows the Excel worksheet used for this example. Data are in C15:L32. The labels for the combo or drop-down list are the titles for the data rows in C15:C32.

Range C12:L12 will later contain trend analysis data derived by Xcelsius. The range C10:K10 contains a formula that transfers the trend analysis data from row 12 to row 10 when the check box value in D5 is 1. The Xcelsius dashboard will contain a check box that changes the value in D5.

	A	B	C	D	E	F	G	H	I	J	K	L	M
1													
2													
3			Title>	Hospital Clinical Quality Indicators									
4													
5			Forecast Check Box>	1									
6													
7													
8				Jan 09	Feb 09	Mar 09	Apr 09	May 09	Jun 09	Jul 09	Aug 09	Sep 09	
9		Chart>											
10	Forecast Chart>		0	0	0	0	0	0	0	0	0		
11													
12		Forecast>											
13													
14			Indicator	Jan 09	Feb 09	Mar 09	Apr 09	May 09	Jun 09	Jul 09	Aug 09	Sep 09	
15			Aspirin on Arrival	92.0%	91.0%	93.0%	90.1%	90.9%	92.3%	88.9%	90.3%	91.6%	
16			Aspirin prescribed at discharge	92.0%	92.3%	94.2%	94.5%	95.0%	95.4%	95.7%	96.2%	96.4%	
17			ACEI for LVSD	52.0%	52.5%	54.1%	50.3%	64.3%	61.3%	62.5%	63.9%	72.9%	
18			Adult smoking-cessation advice	52.0%	52.5%	54.1%	50.3%	64.3%	61.3%	62.5%	63.9%	72.9%	
19			Beta-blocker on arrival	65.0%	63.6%	66.2%	69.4%	71.6%	84.7%	78.3%	80.2%	85.5%	
20			Inpatient mortality	5.5%	5.3%	5.5%	5.5%	5.9%	5.5%	5.8%	3.7%	5.1%	
21			Discharge instructions	65.0%	62.6%	58.4%	63.5%	54.3%	64.8%	67.5%	63.0%	57.0%	
22			LVF assessment	62.9%	61.8%	63.1%	68.1%	65.1%	68.5%	74.0%	77.8%	75.5%	
23			ACEI for LVSD	52.0%	52.5%	54.1%	50.3%	64.3%	61.3%	62.5%	63.9%	72.9%	
24			Adult smoking-cessation advice	62.9%	61.8%	63.1%	68.1%	65.1%	68.5%	74.0%	77.8%	75.5%	
25			Oxygenation assessment	92.0%	92.3%	94.2%	94.5%	95.0%	95.4%	95.7%	96.2%	96.4%	
26			Pnuemococcal screening/vaccination	28.0%	29.5%	30.8%	29.1%	30.5%	29.6%	31.1%	37.0%	29.3%	
27			Blood cultures	63.5%	65.0%	62.9%	65.0%	66.6%	66.6%	68.9%	69.7%	65.0%	
28			Adult smoking-cessation advice	63.5%	65.0%	62.9%	65.0%	66.6%	66.6%	68.9%	69.7%	65.0%	
29			Pediatric smoking-cessation advice	35.0%	36.8%	34.7%	36.1%	35.0%	34.2%	35.0%	37.7%	33.7%	
30			Vaginal birth after C-section	16.6%	17.6%	17.7%	14.6%	12.5%	14.4%	15.1%	15.6%	19.8%	
31			Inpatient neonatal mortality	3.2%	4.4%	4.4%	3.1%	3.9%	4.5%	3.8%	3.1%	3.8%	
32			Third- or fourth-degree laceration	4.3%	4.4%	4.4%	4.4%	4.4%	4.3%	4.3%	4.3%	4.4%	
33													
34													
35													

Figure 26.16: Range C15:L32 contains Excel's list of data. The area charted is C8:L10.

1. Load the sample Excel file into Xcelsius by starting Xcelsius and choosing Data, Import; then open the Excel worksheet used in this example, Clinical Quality 00 Xcelsius.XLS. This file is available at the web sites listed in this book's Introduction. Xcelsius will look similar to Figure 26.17.

2. Put a line chart component on the blank dashboard "canvas" by clicking Charts in the component list at the left and then clicking Line Chart. Click in the canvas at the top of the page. A blank line chart will appear on the canvas.

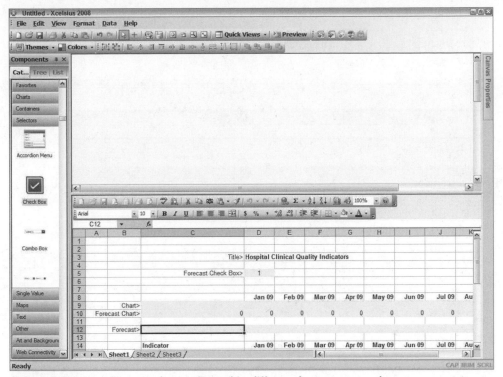

Figure 26.17: Xcelsius can be configured in different layouts. Here, chart components are on the left, the top area shows the dashboard canvas, and the lower area shows the Excel worksheet.

3. Add a combo box from which users can make a selection by clicking Selectors in the component list at the left and then clicking Combo Box. Click in the canvas to the left of the chart. A drop-down combo list will appear.

4. Add a check box from the Selectors at the left by clicking on Check Box and then clicking in the canvas well below the combo list. Your canvas should now look similar to that in Figure 26.18.

5. Connect the combo box to the worksheet so the combo box knows where to find the list of items for its menu. To do that, select the Combo Box by clicking on it. At the right side of the screen, a tab will change from Properties to Combo Box 1.

6. Now you will show the combo box where the menu items are located in the worksheet. With the Combo Box selected, click the Combo Box 1 Property tab on the right side of the screen. Clicking on this tab will display properties for the Combo Box, such as appearance and worksheet references. Click the General tab. The screen should look similar to Figure 26.19. Click the Excel indicator to the right of the Labels box (labels are the values that

display in a combo box drop-down list). Select the range C15:C32 on the Excel worksheet in the lower part of the screen. The names at the left edge of the data will now show in the drop-down list.

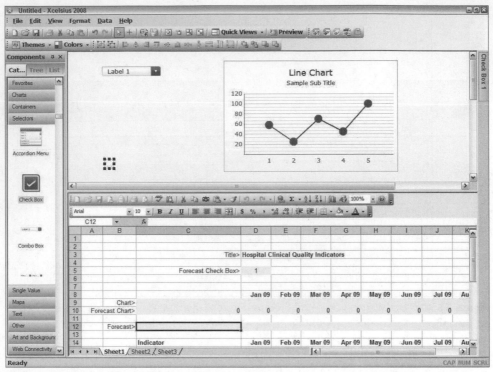

Figure 26.18: Dashboard components are selected from the list of components on the left and dropped onto the dashboard canvas where needed.

At this point, you are about to see an example of the major difference between Xcelsius and Excel. In most cases in Excel, you need to create formulas to move or analyze data. In Xcelsius this is done for you by the actions you specify in the property box. With the following steps, you will set up Xcelsius so that when you select an item from the Combo Box, the corresponding row of data is copied by Xcelsius into a chart range.

7. Tell Xcelsius what to do when an item is selected from the drop-down list by selecting Row from Insert Type. Clicking the small "I" icon will show you an animation of what Xcelsius will do with this action.

8. Specify where the database is in the Excel worksheet by selecting C15:L32 in the Source Data.

9. Specify where Xcelsius should make a copy of the data that matches your selection from the menu. Select C9:L9 in the Destination. The Combo List property box should now look like that shown in Figure 26.19.

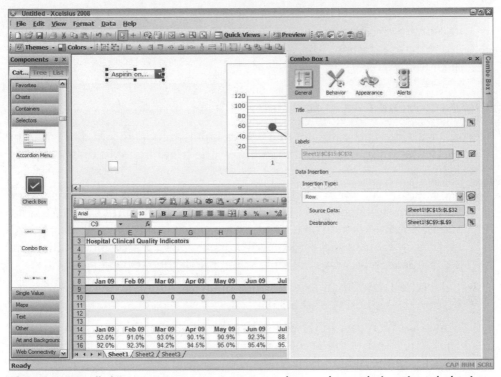

Figure 26.19: All chart components use a property box to change their actions, behaviors, and appearance.

When the data destination is entered correctly, a selection from the drop-down list in the combo box will copy the corresponding row out of the database range and into the destination row. This destination row will be linked to an Xcelsius line chart.

10. Your next step is to link the chart to where data will be copied. Click on the chart and then click the Line Chart 1 property tab on the right of the screen. This will display the chart's properties.

11. On the Line Chart 1 properties tab, you will want to specify where the line chart will look for data. Select the By Range option under the Data group, then click the worksheet selector to the right. Select the range C8:L10. The X-axis dates are in row 8. The data being moved from the database are in row 9, and a trend line data will be moved later in this exercise into row 10. Your chart will now display the data in C8:L10but there are no data there yet.

12. Remove the legend from the chart by selecting the Appearance tab in Line Chart 1 properties, and then the Text tab. Clear the Legend check box.

13. To see your combo list and chart work, click the Preview button at the top of the screen. This will generate and display a preview version of the Flash-based dashboard. Click the Preview button again to return to the design view.

Adding a Trend Line to the Chart

Xcelsius has a Trend component that will calculate trends, so you don't need to do the calculation in Excel. In this example, the trend line will display in the chart when the check box is selected.

1. Add the Trend Analyzer component to the dashboard by clicking Other in the chart components at the left, scrolling down until you see Trend Analyzer, and clicking on it. Then click on any blank area of the dashboard canvas. A Trend Analyzer icon will appear. Don't worry about hiding the icon: this icon becomes invisible when the dashboard is published.

2. Select the Trend Analyzer icon, then open the Trend Analyzer 1 property box on the right side of the screen.

3. Specify which data in the worksheet you want analyzed for trends. On the General tab of the Trend Analyzer 1 property tab, click the worksheet selector to the right of Data, then select D9:L9. This is the range in which the data the user selects are copied from the database. These are also the data you want to analyze for trends.

4. Select the type of trend analysis from the Trend Analyzer property box by selecting Use Best Fit.

5. Specify where the results of the analysis, the new trend line, will be put on the worksheet by clicking the worksheet selector to the right of Analyzed Data Destination, then selecting C12:L12.

The process you have just completed uses Xcelsius's built-in trend analyzer to find the best fit curve for the data in row 9. Xcelsius puts the trend analysis back into the worksheet in row 12.

It's a good idea to make trend lines so they can be turned on or off. You'll use the check box to do that. For the trend analysis data to move into the chart area, the check box value in cell D5 must be 1. The cells in C10:L10 contain a simple IF formula that retrieves data from C12:L12 when D5 contains 1. So if the check box is selected and D5 is 1, the trend values appear in C10:L10 and are charted.

To prepare the check box,

1. Select the check box, then open its property box.

2. On the General tab, specify the title for the check box by typing Show Trend.

3. Indicate what values the check box will have when it is clear or selected. Check boxes are predefined to have a Source Data value of 0 for unchecked and 1 for checked, so we don't need to change the Source Data property.

4. Tell the check box where on the worksheet to put the Source Data value when the check box is clicked. Click the worksheet selector to the right of the Destination box and select cell D5.

When you select the check box, Xcelsius will put a 1 in cell D5. When D5 is 1, the values from the trend analysis in row 12 will be transferred to row 10 by the IF functions in row 10 and then displayed in the chart.

Click the Preview button at the top and test your dashboard. Figure 26.20 shows how this simple dashboard appears with a little additional formatting and the use of backgrounds, themes, and color schemes.

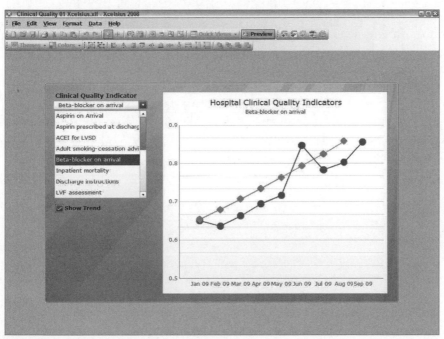

Figure 26.20: Xcelsius helps you create good-looking dashboards with backgrounds, graphics, design themes, and color schemes.

Publishing the Dashboard for Distribution

Xcelsius generates dashboards in Flash, the drawing and animation medium commonly used in web pages. Once generated, the dashboards are no longer associated with the Excel worksheet that was used as the data model.

Xcelsius dashboards, because they are Flash, can be published and distributed in many "envelopes." You can publish your dashboards to appear within native Flash, HTML pages, PDF files, Microsoft Outlook, Microsoft PowerPoint slides, Microsoft Word documents, and of course within Business Objects enterprise software.

Summary

Two of the premiere tools for extending Excel's scorecard and dashboard capability are MicroCharts and Xcelsius. If you want to create dashboards or reports that are rich in information and may need to link to a database, then opt for MicroCharts and distribute within Excel worksheets. If you face an environment where you cannot distribute Excel worksheets, your audience demands highly attractive solutions, or you need highly secure dashboards dynamically linked to databases, then choose Xcelsius.

For more information on MicroCharts and Xcelsius search for them on the Web. To download and review the examples shown here, go to the web sites listed in the Introduction.

With the Excel concepts you learn in this book, and with these two tools, you have the power to create powerful, interactive dashboards capable of helping business users monitor performance and take action. Remember to begin gradually with a scorecard or dashboard project and don't take on too many features, so that both you and the user will win.

Finishing Touches

God is in the details.
**Ludwig Mies van der Rohe
Architect, 1886–1969**

Creating a bulletproof system that shines with small finishing touches will make you look like a professional. This chapter provides you with a few useful tips.

Adding Context and Comments with Briefing Books

The Briefing Book, Figure 27.1, should be behind every Balanced Scorecard objective and every operational dashboard. It gives the contextual, historical, and action information that won't appear in a chart or table. It shows the dashboard's purpose, status, actions that have been taken, ownership of objectives, and data and contact details.

You can create a Briefing Book on a worksheet by copying and pasting the chart and then using the Alignment tab on the Format Cells dialog box to format cells so they hold paragraphs of text. To create large, contiguous blocks of cells that contain word-wrapped paragraphs, select all the cells you want to appear as a block, then choose Format ➪ Cells and select the Alignment tab. In the Alignment tab, select ➪ Horizontal (Left Indent) ➪ Vertical (Top) ➪ Word Wrap ➪ Merge Cells.

To do the same thing in Excel 2007, select the cells you want to act as a block. Right mouse click and choose Format Cells. On the Alignment tab, select Horizontal (Left Indent), Vertical (Top), Wrap Text, and Merge Cells.

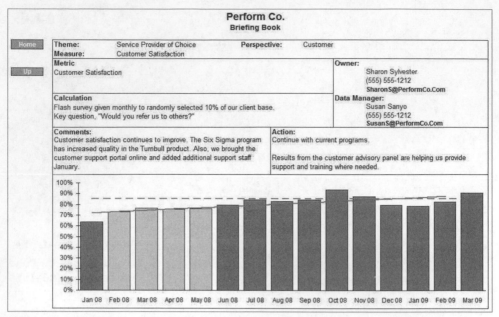

Figure 27.1: A Briefing Book gives the context, actions, and owners related to a dashboard's objective and metrics.

Protect your Briefing Book: have objective and data owners enter their text comments on a separate sheet that links to the word-wrapped cells in the Briefing Book.

Displaying Pop-Up Content and Dynamic Help

There are many ways to create in-context comments, analysis, or help in Excel dashboards, but one of the easiest and most attractive is to modify the in-cell comment box. The only detriment to this method is that content must be updated manually or via VBA. Figure 27.2 shows a comment that pops up with a custom shape, font, and background color.

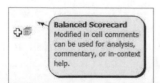

Figure 27.2: Modified in-cell comment boxes can be used as pop-ups that contain comments, analysis, and in-context help.

Before you create your first comments, you will probably want to change the User Name that appears at the top of a comment. You will want to change it to something appropriate such as Help, Analysis, or Commentary. To set the default title, choose Tools ⇨ Options and select the General tab. In the User Name box, enter the title you want. In Excel 2007, click the Office button, select Excel Options, then Popular, and then change the User Name.

Changing the User Name will not change the title of existing comment boxes. You can manually edit or delete the title in any comment box when the comment box is open for editing.

To insert a cell comment, choose Insert ⇨ Comment. In Excel 2007, click Review, then select New Comment. With the comment open in editing mode, you can type and edit in it as well as change the title. You can edit the comment by right-clicking on the cell and choosing Edit Comment.

To modify the comment box so it pops up with a distinctive appearance, right-click on a cell containing a comment and chose Edit Comment. When the comment box displays, right-click on its edge and choose Format Comment. You can modify the font, text alignment, colors, and lines.

Modifying the shape of the comment box takes a little more work. In versions of Excel prior to Excel 2007, make sure the Drawing toolbar is displayed so you have access to the Draw, Change Auto Shape command. In Excel 2007, you will need to add the Change Shape button to the Quick Access toolbar at the top left of the screen.

To add the Change Shape button in Excel 2007, click the Office button, select Excel Options, then Customize. In the Choose Commands from list, select Smart Art Tools/Format. Add the Change Shape tool, located in the left list, to the Quick Access toolbar list. Click OK. The Change Shape tool will now appear at the top left of Excel.

Now that you have access to a shape-changing tool, right-click on the cell containing the comment, then choose Edit Comment. Click the edge of the comment box. In pre–Excel 2007 versions, then select Draw, Change Auto Shape from the Drawing toolbar and select a new shape. In Excel 2007, select the Shape Change tool and then select a new shape.

To make the location of your pop-up information boxes stand out, put a symbol in the cell that will indicate more information. The small icon showing multiple pages in Figure 27.2 is a WingDing 2 symbol.

If you have many pop-up comments on a dashboard, create one and customize it, then copy and paste it into other locations with Paste Special ⇨ Comment. Change the text in each with the Edit Comment command.

Controlling Dashboard Display

In most cases, you will want your Balanced Scorecard or dashboard to show a clean background without row and column headers, scroll bars, and so forth. To turn off items you may not want to show:

1. Choose Tools, Options and select the View tab in the Options dialog box

2. In the Show group, clear all the check boxes:

   - Startup Task Pane
   - Formula Bar
   - Status Bar
   - Windows in Taskbar

3. In the Window Options group, clear all the check boxes of items you do not want to display:

   - Page breaks
   - Formulas
   - Gridlines
   - Row and column headers
   - Outline symbols
   - Zero values
   - Horizontal scroll bars
   - Vertical scroll bars
   - Sheet tabs

4. Choose OK

The display options are available in Excel 2007 by clicking the Microsoft Office button and selecting Excel Options, Advanced. Scroll down to see the Display options. Additional options to control sheet appearance are available in View, Show/Hide.

Note that you can still switch between hidden tabs using Ctrl+Page Up/Down.

Hiding Worksheets

Worksheets that contain all your formulas and analytics should be hidden from user view and tampering. (You did separate your charts, tables, formulas, and data into separate worksheets didn't you? To learn more about creating a good

Excel worksheet architecture see Chapter 29, "Publishing Balanced Scorecards and Operational Dashboards.")

To hide worksheets so a user can't see them, but to still have them available for formula use, choose Format ⇨ Sheet ⇨ Hide. To display a hidden worksheet, choose Format ⇨ Sheet ⇨ Unhide, select the sheet from the list of hidden sheets, and then click OK. In Excel 2007, right-click a worksheet tab and select Hide or Unhide.

TIP When you have lots of worksheets, clicking through all the tabs gets tedious. To quickly see a tab's name and jump to it, right-click on the scrolling buttons to the left of the tabs and select the worksheet you want from the list that displays.

Sending Conditional E-mails from Dashboards

The purpose of scorecards and dashboards is to change behavior and actions. A productive enhancement for getting the action started is to send an e-mail from within your dashboard to the person who can make a change in performance. You can even make an e-mail button that appears when a target value is met.

The HYPERLINK function in Excel creates a hyperlink and displays a text name in a cell. The HYPERLINK syntax is

```
=HYPERLINK(link_location,[friendly_name]).
```

Normally, the link location is a URL with the `http:prefix.com`, like the examples shown in Excel Help. However, you can make the function send e-mail with a syntax that looks like this:

```
=HYPERLINK(
   "mailto:ron@torconsulting.com",
   "Balanced Scorecard Consulting").
```

Typing this syntax into a cell produces a hyperlink that, when clicked, opens an e-mail window in Outlook. (You will need to test this for your e-mail system.) To make this into an e-mail button that only appears when a condition is met, follow these steps that explain the example in Figure 27.3.

1. In cell C8, enter an e-mail address with the mailto: prefix — for example,

   mailto:ron@torconsulting.com.

   When you press Enter, this cell will become a hyperlink that sends an e-mail. Notice that it has hyperlink formatting.

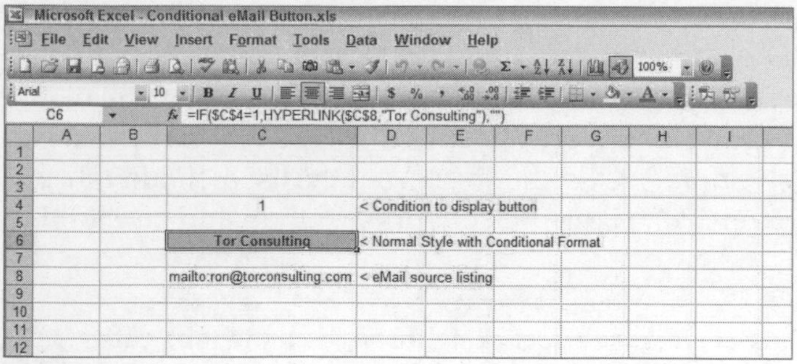

Figure 27.3: An e-mail button that displays when an alert condition is met makes it even easier to take action from within a dashboard.

2. Remove the hyperlink format from cell C8 by selecting C8, choosing Format, Style, selecting Normal from the Style Name list, and clicking OK.

3. Enter 1 in cell C4. This will be a sample condition. We could test for many different alert conditions as described elsewhere in the book.

4. In cell C6 enter the formula

```
=IF($C$4=1,HYPERLINK($C$8,
   "Tor Consulting"),"").
```

This formula displays the HYPERLINK function when C4 contains 1, but displays nothing otherwise.

Test this by typing 1 or 0 in cell C4 and watching the e-mail link appear or disappear. Notice that when the e-mail link is not visible, the mouse pointer still changes when over the cell, but it will not send an e-mail.

To make a button effect that appears or disappears with the e-mail link,

1. Select the hyperlink cell, C6.

2. Choose Format ➪ Style, select Normal from the Style Name list, and then click OK.

3. Choose Format ➪ Conditional Formatting. In the Conditional Formatting dialog box that appears, enter the formula that appears in Figure 27.4. Select the Format button and format the e-mail cell with patterns and borders to make it appear like a button when C4 contains a 1. Do not create a second conditional format. Choose OK.

TIP   Combine the e-mail function you've learned here with form controls like the combo list and concatenating text, both described elsewhere in this book, to create drop-down lists of multiple e-mail recipients.

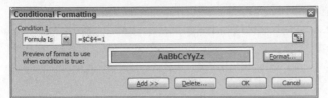

Figure 27.4: Use Conditional Formatting to make the e-mail button formatting appear or disappear.

Adding Headers and Footers

Headers and footers are critical for knowing which data is most current in printed reports or screen shots of dashboards. Believe me, this can prevent confusion. For dashboards that update daily or even hourly, this is essential for understanding differences between dashboard or report results. In addition, your header or footer might include a proprietary or company confidential message.

Locating and Removing Phantom Links

There will come a time when you open a workbook and Excel will pop up a dialog box asking if you want to refresh or open linked workbooks. But you can't find any links. If you are the only user of the workbook, it is an annoyance. But if this is a Balanced Scorecard or dashboard for executives and managers, it must be fixed. Here is how to fix it.

First, check for links by choosing the Edit ➪ Links command, which opens the Edit Links dialog box. In Excel 2007, on the Data tab in the Connections group, select Edit Links. In the dialog box, you can see workbooks that are linked to the active workbook. Click on any linked worksheets shown in the Edit Links dialog box and look at the workbook the link references.

One reference that is easy to forget is when chart data series link to external worksheets. If this happens, click on the data series within a chart to see if the chart formula shows an external link. If the formula contains an external link, rewrite the formula so it has a valid reference.

If you want to remove a link that no longer links to a workbook, select it in the Edit Links box, click the Change Source button, and link it to the active sheet itself. Re-save the workbook with a new name. If you reopen the workbook and it still asks if you want to update the link, then you probably have a link within a named range.

To find a link within a named range, choose Insert ⇨ Name ⇨ Define. In Excel 2007, on the Formulas tab, in the Defined Name group, select Name Manager. In the Define Name dialog box, click on each named range in turn and watch the Refers To box at the bottom. If you find a name with an external reference or #REF! error, then delete it or rewrite it.

Protecting Content, Worksheets, and Workbooks

Some of the scorecards, dashboards, and templates I have built have hundreds of hours of development in them. That adds up to a lot of money and intellectual property. Your work is just as valuable to you and to your organization, and you don't want untrained users accidentally mucking with the inner workings.

Here's how to protect your Balanced Scorecard and dashboards from accidental changes or from changes by untrained developers. Protecting your workbooks will also set them up so they retain the restricted areas and display settings you have chosen.

CAUTION Excel and Microsoft Office product protection methods are designed to protect the contents and display settings from inexperienced users. Do not use them to protect company confidential data. If you want to protect proprietary information in a Balanced Scorecard, then encapsulate your scorecard within a securely encrypted PDF file as described in Chapter 29.

Excel has multiple layers of protection. Cells, worksheets, and workbooks (files) each have their own protection. Each layer of protection can have different attributes; for example, protecting structure but allowing data entry.

One frequent misunderstanding is how worksheet protection works. First, you must specify which cells you want unprotected, and then you must turn on worksheet protection. Initially, all cells in a worksheet are formatted to be protected when worksheet protection is turned on. Once worksheet protection is turned on, cells you have not formatted as unprotected will become protected.

If you want cells to be unprotected, you must select them and then choose the Format, Cells command to display the Protection tab in the Format Cells dialog box. In Excel 2007, select the cells you want to be unprotected, and then in the Home tab in the Cells group, select Format. In the drop-down list, select Format Cells to display the dialog box. In the Format Cells dialog box, select the Protection tab and clear the Locked check box.

Locking or unlocking cells does not take effect until worksheet protection is enabled. Enable worksheet protection with the Tools ⇨ Protection ⇨ Worksheet command. In Excel 2007, on the Home tab in the Cells group, select Format. In the drop-down list, select Protect Sheet. Select the check boxes that describe which worksheet properties you want protected.

There is a lot written about protection. It is covered in the Excel help files as well as in books and on the Internet. All these sources include tips that will help you with protection for dashboards.

When you set protection for the worksheet, in most cases you will want to clear all check boxes in the Protect Sheet dialog box except the Select Unlocked Cells check box.

Unprotect cells that contain hyperlinks or they won't work. Unprotect cells that receive input from a Form Control, such as a slider or combo box, or you will receive an error.

When you protect the workbook, always protect the structure. If you want to prevent your dashboard from being reduced to a resizable window, then also select the Window check box.

Restricting the User's Range

For a professional appearance you will want your dashboards to look as much as possible as if they are stand-alone applications and not Excel worksheets. In addition to turning off gridlines and row and column headers, described elsewhere in this chapter, you should limit the user's ability to move outside a range you prescribe. In most cases, you will want to limit users' cursor movement so they can only see the tables, text, and charts in the active worksheet.

It's actually very easy to do. Adjust your dashboard's formatting so it fills the screen as you want users to see it, and then hide all columns to the right, and all rows below. The user will not be able to scroll or select beyond what he or she sees. If you have protected the worksheets, users will not be able to unhide the rows and columns.

To hide rows, select the full row below the last row you want to see. Press Shift+Ctrl+Down Arrow to select that row and all lower rows. Now choose Format ➪ Row ➪ Hide. To hide the columns on the right, select the column to the right of the last column you want visible. Press Shift+Ctrl+Right Arrow to select that column and all columns to the right. Now choose Format ➪ Column ➪ Hide. You will be left with a small worksheet area of visible cells. Users can neither select nor scroll outside this area.

If you are using Excel 2007, select the outer rows or columns as described above, then on the Home tab in the Cells group, select Format. In the drop-down list, select Hide & Unhide and then Hide Rows/Columns.

Oops! I almost forgot to tell you how to get those areas back. Select the last row or column that is visible and drag toward the hidden rows or columns. Now choose Format ➪ Row/Column ➪ Unhide. They will reappear. This works the same in Excel 2007.

Summary

When it comes to scorecards and dashboards, the most important purpose you have is communicating information that aids decision-making. Your second most important purpose is to make your scorecards and dashboards easy to use and attractive.

With a few finishing touches, such as those described in this chapter, you can make your dashboards look like polished, stand-alone applications rather than Excel worksheets. And it doesn't hurt to set up your scorecard or dashboard so users can't accidentally destroy your hard work.

CHAPTER 28

Data Integration Methods

If 98% of the metrics are right, why worry about the other 3%?

Anonymous

At every conference or workshop on Balanced Scorecards or operational and performance dashboards I hear stories of organizations that have wasted large sums of money by purchasing a large Business Intelligence system before they fully understand the needs and scope of the information they need to harvest, analyze, and distribute.

The consensus among Balanced Scorecard consultants is to start simply, by entering data manually or linking worksheets to text files or simple relational databases. Operational and performance dashboards that have static requirements, with data that is not being refreshed continuously, can also use simple data integration methods to produce great results.

Small- to mid-sized businesses or departments of large corporations usually do not have the hundreds of thousands of dollars and extensive IT resources necessary to implement a Business Intelligence system. In those cases, using Excel with data integration is a very cost-effective solution. When expansion is needed, many mid-sized corporations do a great job with SQL relational databases or OLAP cubes combined with well-designed Excel dashboards.

Manual Data Entry or Automated Data Integration?

Surveys of large corporations with Business Intelligence systems show that most scorecards or operational dashboards use six to seven different data sources.

These are organizations with enterprise wide ERP and CRM systems. My experience with small- and mid-sized organizations is that they have data in even more disparate sources.

There seems to be a consensus among Balanced Scorecard consultants that Balanced Scorecard software should begin with manual data entry or text file integration. Balanced Scorecard data is usually at a summary level, so it is available in summary reports that can be typed in monthly or that can be stored and integrated as text files.

One of the serious problems with using a manual data entry system, even with a Balanced Scorecard that has only 12 to 24 metrics, is that those metrics require a geometrically larger amount of raw data for calculation. Within six months to a year, the data owners become weary of collecting, calculating, and entering data. Updates soon lag. This is just one more piece of organizational inertia that a Balanced Scorecard doesn't need. I recommend using manual data entry for a few months until the system is tested, and then creating a simple integrated data system like the ones described here so that data collection, calculations, and updates are automatic.

Operational dashboards face the same issues. They usually involve large amounts of data that are in someone's worksheet, but they are rarely in a form useful in a dashboard and thus they require reentry. This sucks up personnel time, introduces error, and slows the process. If this is an operational dashboard that is critical for performance, then creating a simple data integration method like the ones described here will save you time and errors.

TIP Entering or importing data, targets, and alert limits in one workbook separate from the analytics and charts makes the architecture of your system more secure and flexible. By putting data, targets, and alert limits in separate workbooks, the Strategic Theme sponsors can have access to their data, targets, and alerts without having access to the Balanced Scorecard analytics and charts.

As Chapter 29, "Publishing Balanced Scorecards and Operational Dashboards," describes, keeping data in a separate worksheet or workbook makes it easier to make changes to the entire system, because data is not structurally involved with the analytics. For example, you should design your system so that you can point the analytics to a new data source just by changing a range name.

Keeping data in a workbook separate from the analytics and charts enables the data owner or Strategic Theme sponsor to open the data workbook and make corrections without touching the analytics and charts. If you keep data in a separate workbook, you may want to keep the related user-updated targets and alert limits in that same workbook.

A downside to having data in separate workbooks is that you will need to update links in the analytic workbooks to make sure they use the most current data. This is easily done with the Edit, Links command.

RESOURCES FOR ADDITIONAL INFORMATION ON DATA INTEGRATION

For additional information on integrating Excel with external data sources please check *Excel Advanced Report Development* (Wiley, 2005) and *Excel 2007 Advanced Report Development* (Wiley, 2007), by Timothy Zapawa, and *Excel & Access Integration with Office 2007*, by Michael Alexander and Geoffrey Clark (Wiley, 2007).

Manual Data Entry for Dashboards

Manual data entry worksheets are little more than tables created to allow users to enter data. You also should create user-entered tables for targets and alert levels that so users can update them.

There are a number of advantages to manual data entry tables for Balanced Scorecard and dashboards:

- They are quick to implement.
- They don't require IT support.
- Manual data entry is perfect for new metrics requiring small calculations and those that aren't in a system, such as Employee Engagement survey results.
- Theme sponsors can delegate someone to update data.
- Data worksheets can be constructed for each Strategic Theme sponsor with unique passwords and data layout.
- Each data workbook can contain data, targets, and alert levels so that managers can update them easily.

But there are disadvantages to manual data entry tables for Balanced Scorecard and operational dashboards, too:

- Initial creation can involve a painful amount of data entry.
- Operational dashboards may require large amounts of ongoing data entry to track daily operations.
- Not keeping data refreshed can lead to the failure of a Balanced Scorecard.
- There is no data integrity.
- Manual data entry introduces errors.
- There is no audit trail.

For a better user interface in your data entry worksheets, use light shading in alternating rows. Keep the top and left-side headings in view during data entry by using the Windows, Freeze Panes command to allow the data area to scroll while keeping the top and left headings in view. Apply conditional formatting to data areas so that data that is out of limits appears as red.

Automating Data Retrieval with Text Files

One of the easiest ways of automating and upgrading from the labor-intensive method of manually entering data is to import text files containing data into Excel. This works well when there are many data owners with data kept in many different systems, ranging from Excel sheets to small databases to large enterprise systems. All the data can be exported from each of these different systems into text files in a common data folder. The Balanced Scorecard or dashboards can then import the data needed. Imported data can be refreshed manually or Excel can be set to refresh at timed intervals.

The text files created for this method may come from accounting systems, CRMs, ERPs, project management report utilities, or even Excel worksheets saved in text format.

Importing text files has some advantanges:

- Doing so is easy to implement.
- You can manage many disparate data sources.
- Each data owner is responsible for his individual data.
- Doing so reduces manual work.
- The amount of IT support required is minimal.

But, just like manual entry, it has its disadvantages:

- Extensive calculations or calculations involving multiple data sources may have to be done in Excel rather than at the data source.
- Some IT or report writer assistance may be needed to generate the reports (text files).
- Data integrity is limited, because data is not dynamically linked to the source but rather is exported.

Creating Text Data Files

Most software systems include a report-writing utility. In the majority of cases, this is an embedded minimalist version of Crystal Reports. A report-writing utility can create the text files you need. You may use an existing report that is printed in CSV, TXT, or PRN format. However, in most cases it is easier to create a new report in a simple columnar format containing just the data needed for the Balanced Scorecard or dashboards.

TIP Make sure you store dashboards, worksheets to be imported, and data source text files in the same folder. This reduces or eliminates complex links and makes it easier to find and manage files.

FILE TYPE	DELIMITER	DESCRIPTION
TXT	Tab delimited	Data are separated by a tab character.
CSV	Comma separated values	Data are separated by a comma. If the data includes a comma, such as currency value, then the value is enclosed in quotes.
PRN	Even width columns	Data are aligned in specific columns. If printed in a monospaced font, you will see data align in columns. Almost any software system can be set up to create a PRN file.

While in development you may want to create sample text files. You can create sample CSV, PRN, or TXT files from within Excel by creating an Excel list with the headers and data in columns. Format the data as you expect to receive it. When you save the data in Excel, select CSV, PRN, or TXT as the file format in the Save As dialog box.

To open these files in a word processor so that you can modify them, right-click on the file name in Windows Explorer, choose Edit With, and select a word processor such as Notepad. Note that the CSV file is represented in File Explorer with an Excel icon. Double-clicking a CSV file will automatically import it in Excel. However, for creating dashboards that automatically refresh, you will want to follow the text file import techniques described below.

Step-by-Step to Importing a Text Data File

When you work with IT or the report writer who will export data from a source system, it is best if you can export directly to an Excel or CSV file with headers. Excel will open either of these formats directly.

Although Excel will open these two file formats directly from File ⇨ Open, you may want to use the following procedure so that you can specify how frequently the worksheet should automatically update.

The Text Import Wizard takes slightly different paths for opening and parsing (separating) CSV, TXT, and PRN files. It will automatically parse a CSV file into appropriate cells. TXT files, which have data separated by tabs, are also recognized. If you import PRN files, you will be given the opportunity to drag markers left or right to mark where columns of data begin and end.

The following example walks you through the steps to import a tab-delimited text file with the extension TXT. You will be able to set the update frequency for importing at the end of the import process. This enables the worksheet to automatically update itself when new data is available.

To follow this example, create a TXT file or download the sample files as described in the Introduction. To open the text files into Excel

1. Open the worksheet into which you will import data.

2. Select the top left cell where you want data to be imported.

3. Choose Data, Import External Data, Import Data to display the Select Data Source dialog box shown in Figure 28.1 for versions of Excel before 2007. In Excel 2007, on the Data tab, in the Get External Data group, select From Text to display the Import Text File dialog box. (This command will not be available on a worksheet in which you already have imported data.)

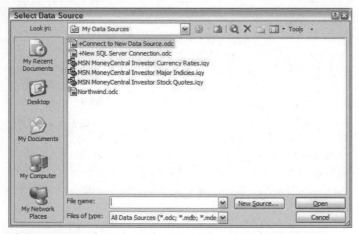

Figure 28.1: When the Select Data Source dialog box first opens, you will not see the option to connect to a text file.

4. In the Files of Type box, select Text Files (*.txt, *.prn, *.csv, . . .). If your text file is not visible, move to the folder containing it.

5. Select the text file. In this example, a tab-delimited TXT file has been selected. Click Open.

6. Step 1 of 3 of the Text Import Wizard opens as shown in Figure 28.2 for a TXT file. Excel makes a best guess at the text file format. You can see what the raw data looks like at the bottom of the dialog box. If you open a PRN file, the wizard will automatically select the Fixed Width option. Click Next.

7. Step 2 of 3 in the Text Import Wizard enables you to change how the data is parsed, or segmented into parts. In the lower portion of the dialog box, you can see how your selections will affect the data to be imported. Click Next.

Step 2 will look differently depending upon whether you are importing a CSV, TXT, or PRN file. CSV and TXT use the comma and tab characters, respectively, to separate data, so you will see the dialog box shown in Figure 28.3. PRN files separate data into columns using space characters. The wizard will select the Fixed Width option and display a Step 2 dialog box in which you can mark where columns should be separated.

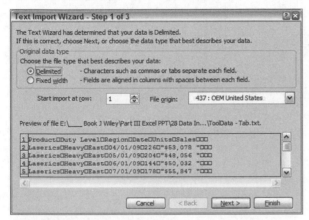

Figure 28.2: Step 1 of 3 in the Text Import Wizard dialog box enables you to select how to parse (segment) the text file.

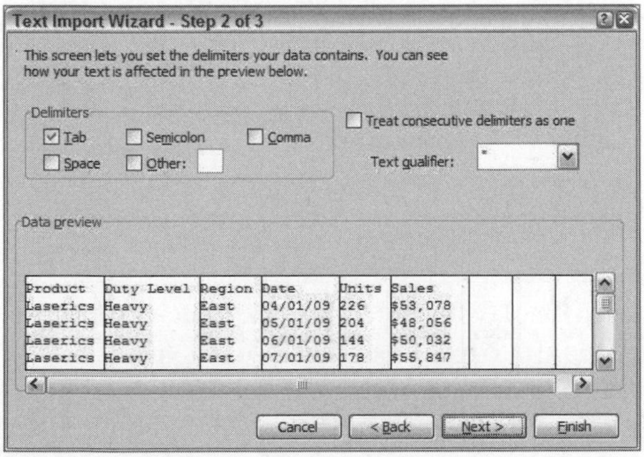

Figure 28.3: Excel usually makes the correct choices for Step 2 of 3 in the Text Import Wizard.

8. Step 3 of 3 in the Text Import Wizard, shown in Figure 28.4, allows you to mark which columns to ignore and to format columns in ways other than Excel estimated. Click Next.

Figure 28.4: Step 3 of 3 in the Text Import Wizard emables you to set column formats if Excel does not choose correctly.

9. In the Import Data box, shown in Figure 28.5, select where you want the new data to be inserted.

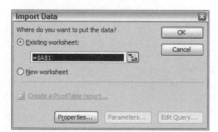

Figure 28.5: Select the upper left corner of where you want data to import on an existing worksheet.

10. Choose the Properties button to display the External Data Range Properties dialog box in figure 28.6. This dialog box enables you to specify how the import will refresh and how existing data will be affected by new data. These settings are described in the section titled "Refreshing Data Automatically."

11. Choose OK in the External Data Range Properties box and then OK in the Import Data box. Your data will import into the worksheet as shown in Figure 28.7.

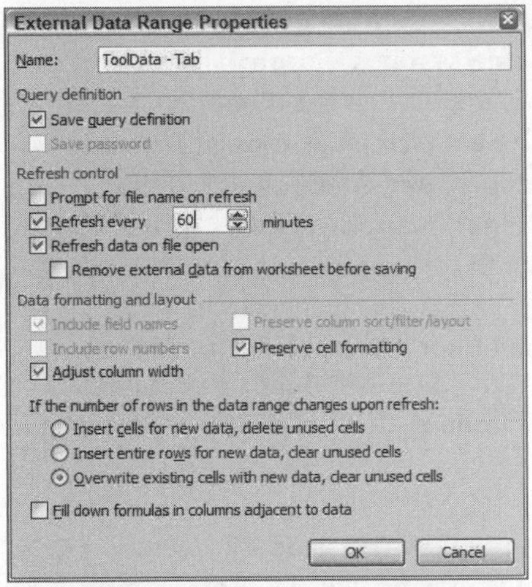

Figure 28.6: The External Data Range Properties box is where you specify how data will be refreshed.

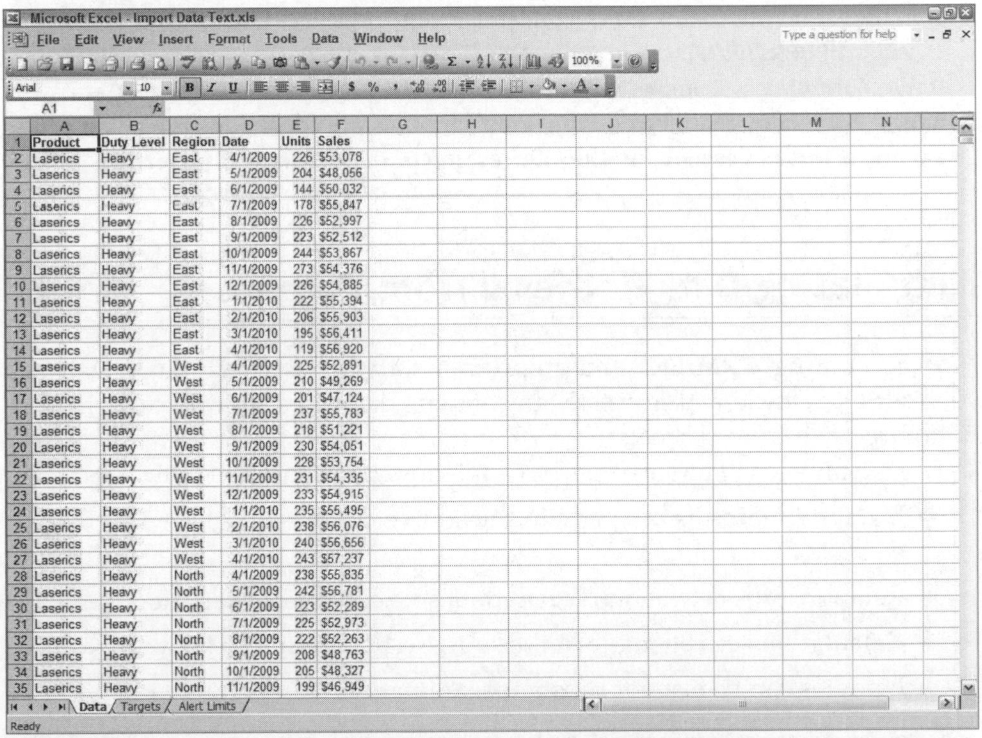

	Product	Duty Level	Region	Date	Units	Sales
2	Laserics	Heavy	East	4/1/2009	226	$53,078
3	Laserics	Heavy	East	5/1/2009	204	$48,056
4	Laserics	Heavy	East	6/1/2009	144	$50,032
5	Laserics	Heavy	East	7/1/2009	178	$55,847
6	Laserics	Heavy	East	8/1/2009	226	$52,997
7	Laserics	Heavy	East	9/1/2009	223	$52,512
8	Laserics	Heavy	East	10/1/2009	244	$53,867
9	Laserics	Heavy	East	11/1/2009	273	$54,376
10	Laserics	Heavy	East	12/1/2009	226	$54,885
11	Laserics	Heavy	East	1/1/2010	222	$55,394
12	Laserics	Heavy	East	2/1/2010	206	$55,903
13	Laserics	Heavy	East	3/1/2010	195	$56,411
14	Laserics	Heavy	East	4/1/2010	119	$56,920
15	Laserics	Heavy	West	4/1/2009	225	$52,891
16	Laserics	Heavy	West	5/1/2009	210	$49,269
17	Laserics	Heavy	West	6/1/2009	201	$47,124
18	Laserics	Heavy	West	7/1/2009	237	$55,783
19	Laserics	Heavy	West	8/1/2009	218	$51,221
20	Laserics	Heavy	West	9/1/2009	230	$54,051
21	Laserics	Heavy	West	10/1/2009	228	$53,754
22	Laserics	Heavy	West	11/1/2009	231	$54,335
23	Laserics	Heavy	West	12/1/2009	233	$54,915
24	Laserics	Heavy	West	1/1/2010	235	$55,495
25	Laserics	Heavy	West	2/1/2010	238	$56,076
26	Laserics	Heavy	West	3/1/2010	240	$56,656
27	Laserics	Heavy	West	4/1/2010	243	$57,237
28	Laserics	Heavy	North	4/1/2009	238	$55,835
29	Laserics	Heavy	North	5/1/2009	242	$56,781
30	Laserics	Heavy	North	6/1/2009	223	$52,289
31	Laserics	Heavy	North	7/1/2009	225	$52,973
32	Laserics	Heavy	North	8/1/2009	222	$52,263
33	Laserics	Heavy	North	9/1/2009	208	$48,763
34	Laserics	Heavy	North	10/1/2009	205	$48,327
35	Laserics	Heavy	North	11/1/2009	199	$46,949

Figure 28.7: Imported text data parses into cells and formats as you specify. It will update from the text file when you click the update icon, or automatically, at timed intervals.

CAUTION If you haven't run into this issue yet, you will, and it will drive you crazy, even when you are ready for it. Some systems — especially older accounting systems — export numeric data as text. When Excel imports a text file, the numeric data may remain text, but look onscreen as though it is numbers. This commonly occurs with UPCs, ZIP codes, and credit card numbers, but I have seen it in file exports from many older financial systems. These "numbers in text clothing" cause problems in Excel formulas, in PivotTables, during sorting, and in charts.

You can adjust for this problem in the Text Import Wizard by selecting the appropriate format in step 3 of the Wizard. If the data still does not act like a number, try creating a formula in another column, such as =D6*1, that forces the text in D6 to become a number.

TIP Data may come in looking differently than how you need it for your dashboards. For example, East Coast ZIP codes may be missing their leading zeros, or you may need the first initial and last name of salespersons but find that a file contains full names. If you aren't under a deadline, then figuring out formulas to modify the data can be fun. To create the new data, add a column to one side of the imported data and write formulas that manipulate the data. Functions that are useful are & (concatenation), TRIM, LEFT, RIGHT, MID, FIND, LOWER, UPPER, PROPER, and other text functions. Make sure you set the Fill Down Formulas in Columns Adjacent to Data check box in the External Data Range Properties check box so that your formulas are copied down as data expands. This is described in the "Refreshing Data Automatically" section.

Automating Data Retrieval from Databases

Most accounting, CRM, ERP, and proprietary software uses relational databases such as SQL, Oracle, and Access. Many of these databases allow Excel to import data directly into worksheets.

The advantages of importing from a relational database are that

- Data maintains its integrity in the source database — there is only one source of the truth.

- Relationships between different data sources can be examined.

- Calculations can be made in the source database rather than in Excel.

- Updates can be made for instant examination.

Some of the disadvantages of linking to relational databases are that

- It may require IT or consultants .

- Excessive data acquisition may slow system access.

Step-by-Step to Importing Data from a Relational Database

Importing data from a relational database follows similar steps for most databases. You will probably need assistance from IT to make your initial database connection if it is different from the Access demonstration that follows.

If you have Microsoft Access on your computer, you can follow this example of how to link an Excel worksheet to a relational database. If you do not have Microsoft Access, then you can download the same Microsoft Access file by going to the Microsoft web site and searching for the text:

```
Access Northwind database download
```

Download the sample Northwind.mdb file to a folder where you can access it for the following example. If you have Access installed, the following steps will tell you where to locate Northwind.mdb.

To link a data worksheet to the Northwind.mdb relational database

1. Open the worksheet into which you will import data. The example shows a workbook dedicated to data, targets, and alert limits.

2. Select the top left cell where you want data to be imported.

3. Choose Data ➪ Import External Data ➪ Import Data to display the Select Data Source dialog box shown in Figure 28.8. In Excel 2007, on the Data tab, in the Data from Other Sources group, select From Data Connection Wizard and skip to step 5. (This command will not be available on a worksheet in which you already have imported data.)

4. Select +Connect to New Data Source.odc and click New Source to display the Data Connection Wizard shown in Figure 28.9.

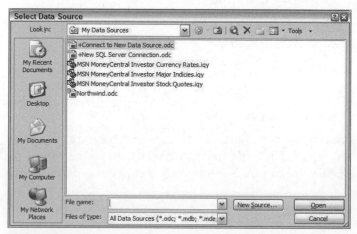

Figure 28.8: When the Select Data Source dialog box first opens, you will not see the option to connect to a text file.

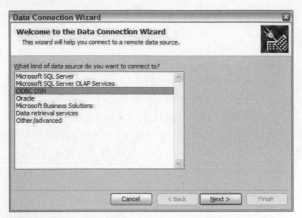

Figure 28.9: The Data Connection Wizard displays data sources to which you can connect.

5. Select the ODBC DSN (Data Source Name), as shown in Figure 28.10, and choose Next.

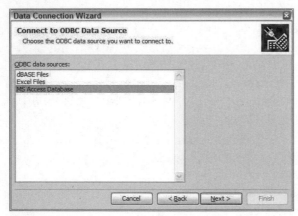

Figure 28.10: Select the ODBC source you need to connect to.

6. In the Data Connection Wizard, select MS Access Database as the data source you want to connect to. Click Next.

7. In the Select Database dialog box, select the Access Northwind.mdb database file. If you downloaded the file from Microsoft, go to the folder in which you saved it. If you have Access on your computer, you can find Northwind.mdb in

```
C:\Program Files\Microsoft Office\Office ##\Samples
```

After selecting Northwind.mdb, click Next.

8. In the Select Database and Table dialog shown in Figure 28.11, you must select the tables you want to link to. If IT has built a special table containing all the data you need, then select the Connect to a Specific Table check box. If you have more than one table you want to link to, clear the Connect to a Specific Table check box. Click Next.

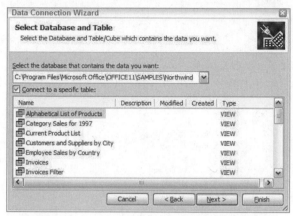

Figure 28.11: Select the tables from the database to which you want the Excel worksheet to have access.

9. In the Save Data Connection File and Finish box enter a new title for this connection and any descriptive information that is helpful. Click Finish and then Open to open the new connection for insertion.

Figure 28.12: In the Import Data dialog box, specify where in the worksheet you want the data. Click Properties to specify how frequently you want your dashboard updated.

10. Specify where in the existing worksheet you want the new data, as shown in Figure 28.12. Click the Properties button to specify how frequently you want your dashboard updated. Click OK. Data will appear in the worksheet similar to that in Figure 28.13.

ProductID	ProductName	SupplierID	CategoryID	QuantityPerUnit	UnitPrice	UnitsInStock	UnitsOnOrder	ReorderLevel	Discontinued
1	Chai	1	1	10 boxes x 20 bags	18	39	0	10	
2	Chang	1	1	24 - 12 oz bottles	19	17	40	25	
3	Aniseed Syrup	1	2	12 - 550 ml bottles	10	13	70	25	
4	Chef Anton's Cajun Seasoning	2	2	48 - 6 oz jars	22	53	0	0	
6	Grandma's Boysenberry Spread	3	2	12 - 8 oz jars	25	120	0	25	
7	Uncle Bob's Organic Dried Pears	3	7	12 - 1 lb pkgs.	30	15	0	10	
8	Northwoods Cranberry Sauce	3	2	12 - 12 oz jars	40	6	0	0	
10	Ikura	4	8	12 - 200 ml jars	31	31	0	0	
11	Queso Cabrales	5	4	1 kg pkg.	21	22	30	30	
12	Queso Manchego La Pastora	5	4	10 - 500 g pkgs.	38	86	0	0	
13	Konbu	6	8	2 kg box	6	24	0	5	
14	Tofu	6	7	40 - 100 g pkgs.	23.25	35	0	0	
15	Genen Shouyu	6	2	24 - 250 ml bottles	15.5	39	0	5	
16	Pavlova	7	3	32 - 500 g boxes	17.45	29	0	10	
18	Carnarvon Tigers	7	8	16 kg pkg.	62.5	42	0	0	
19	Teatime Chocolate Biscuits	8	3	10 boxes x 12 pieces	9.2	25	0	5	
20	Sir Rodney's Marmalade	8	3	30 gift boxes	81	40	0	0	
21	Sir Rodney's Scones	8	3	24 pkgs. x 4 pieces	10	3	40	5	
22	Gustaf's Knäckebröd	9	5	24 - 500 g pkgs.	21	104	0	25	
23	Tunnbröd	9	5	12 - 250 g pkgs.	9	61	0	25	
25	NuNuCa Nuß-Nougat-Creme	11	3	20 - 450 g glasses	14	76	0	30	
26	Gumbär Gummibärchen	11	3	100 - 250 g bags	31.23	15	0	0	
27	Schoggi Schokolade	11	3	100 - 100 g pieces	43.9	49	0	30	
30	Nord-Ost Matjeshering	13	8	10 - 200 g glasses	25.89	10	0	15	
31	Gorgonzola Telino	14	4	12 - 100 g pkgs	12.5	0	70	20	
32	Mascarpone Fabioli	14	4	24 - 200 g pkgs.	32	9	40	25	
33	Geitost	15	4	500 g	2.5	112	0	20	
34	Sasquatch Ale	16	1	24 - 12 oz bottles	14	111	0	15	
35	Steeleye Stout	16	1	24 - 12 oz bottles	18	20	0	15	
36	Inlagd Sill	17	8	24 - 250 g jars	19	112	0	20	
37	Gravad lax	17	8	12 - 500 g pkgs.	26	11	50	25	
38	Côte de Blaye	18	1	12 - 75 cl bottles	263.5	17	0	15	
39	Chartreuse verte	18	1	750 cc per bottle	18	69	0	5	
40	Boston Crab Meat	19	8	24 - 4 oz tins	18.4	123	0	30	

Figure 28.13: Relational database data inserted in a worksheet can be updated manually or automatically.

Selecting the Edit Query button in the Import Data dialog box enables you to modify the data query for this connection. You also can access and modify the query by right-clicking within the data in the Excel worksheet and choosing Edit Query. At the end of the Query Wizard, you have the opportunity to use MS Query, an easy-to-use tool to modify database queries.

Importing Data Using a PivotTable

The previous Step-by-Step examples resulted in flat files imported from text or relational databases. If you want to import data from a relational database and convert it to a categorized table with PivotTable type analysis, you can use Excel's PivotTable to directly import the data from an external database and then create a PivotTable that you can update from the database.

If you have done your homework as described in Sections I and II of this book, you will know exactly what information is needed so that your PivotTable can generate just the data your scorecard or dashboard needs. In some cases, you may want the database manager to create calculated fields in the database or create new joins between tables to give you the data you need in your dashboard.

To retrieve data into your scorecard or dashboard from the linked PivotTable, use the GETPIVOTDATA function and techniques described in Chapter 21, "Feeding Dashboards with PivotTables."

Step-by-Step to Importing Data to a PivotTable

To retrieve data from an external data source and create a PivotTable, follow these abbreviated steps:

1. Open the data worksheet and select the cell where you want the upper left corner of the PivotTable.

2. Choose the Data ⇨ PivotTable and PivotChart Report command.

3. In Step 1 in the PivotTable Wizard, select External Data Source, and click Next.

4. In Step 2 in the PivotTable Wizard, select Get Data.

5. In the Choose Data Source, select your database or the NWind sample MS Access Database you have. Choose OK.

6. In the Select Database window, open the folder containing your relational database file; select that file, and choose OK.

7. In the Query Wizard Choose Columns dialog box, shown in Figure 28.14, choose the tables you want to use in your PivotTable. Choose Next.

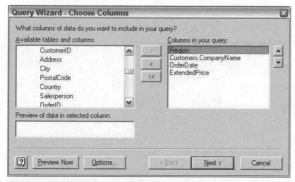

Figure 28.14: Select the tables and columns you want to use for a PivotTable.

8. The Query Wizard gives you the opportunity to filter and sort the data returned. Choose Next until you reach Query Wizard Finish.

9. Select Return Data to Microsoft Office Excel. Choose Finish.

10. In Step 2 of 3 of the PivotTable Wizard, choose Next.

11. In Step 3 of 3 of the PivotTable Wizard, you are able to create the layout for your PivotTable. Continue creating a PivotTable from this point onward using normal PivotTable methods.

To create a PivotTable connected to an external data source in Excel 2007, follow this example using the Nwind.mdb Access database:

1. In Excel 2007, on the Insert tab, in the Tables group, select PivotTable.

2. In the Create PivotTable dialog box, select Use an External Data Source and click Choose Connection.

3. In the Existing Connection dialog box, select a connection to a database if you previously created one.

4. If you have not previously created a connection to a database, click the Browse for More button in the Existing Connection dialog box. In the Select Data Source dialog box, choose from the list + Connect to New Data Source and choose Open. In the Data Connection Wizard, choose ODBC DSN and click Next. Choose MS Access Database and then browse for and select your database or the sample Nwind.mdb. Click Next. Select the tables from the database that you want to include in the PivotTable. Click Next and Finish to return to the Create PivotTable dialog box.

5. In the Create PivotTable dialog box, choose OK and design your Excel 2007 PivotTable in the layout box.

Figure 28.15 shows a completed PivotTable for the Northwind database. This PivotTable shows the sum of the total extended price for each customer for all regions by month. Although dates were entered individually in the database, months were created by grouping the Order Field by month.

Refreshing Data Automatically

Once you have imported your data from a text file or relational database, you will want to ensure that your dashboard reflects the most current data. You can manually update imported data or update data when the worksheet containing the data opens, or at set intervals while it is open.

To manually update any imported data, whether from a text file, relational database, or PivotTable, right-click inside the data and choose Refresh Data.

To automate the refresh of data in a PivotTable that is linked to a database, right-click within the table and choose Table Options. In the PivotTable Options dialog box, select the Refresh on Open and Refresh Every ___ Minutes check boxes.

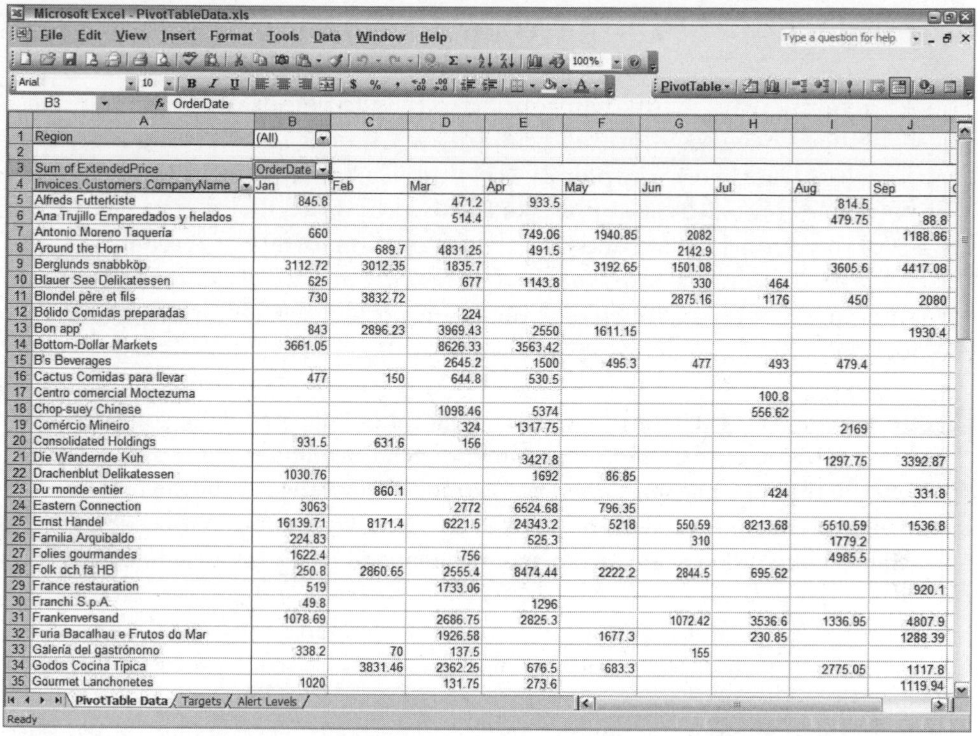

Region	(All)								
Sum of ExtendedPrice	OrderDate								
Invoices.Customers.CompanyName	Jan	Feb	Mar	Apr	May	Jun	Jul	Aug	Sep
Alfreds Futterkiste	845.8		471.2	933.5				814.5	
Ana Trujillo Emparedados y helados			514.4					479.75	88.8
Antonio Moreno Taquería	660			749.06	1940.85	2082			1188.86
Around the Horn		689.7	4831.25	491.5		2142.9			
Berglunds snabbköp	3112.72	3012.35	1835.7		3192.65	1501.08		3605.6	4417.08
Blauer See Delikatessen	625		677	1143.8		330	464		
Blondel père et fils	730	3832.72				2875.16	1176	450	2080
Bólido Comidas preparadas			224						
Bon app'	843	2896.23	3969.43	2550	1611.15				1930.4
Bottom-Dollar Markets	3661.05		8626.33	3563.42					
B's Beverages			2645.2	1500	495.3	477	493	479.4	
Cactus Comidas para llevar	477	150	644.8	530.5					
Centro comercial Moctezuma							100.8		
Chop-suey Chinese			1098.46	5374			556.62		
Comércio Mineiro			324	1317.75				2169	
Consolidated Holdings	931.5	631.6	156						
Die Wandernde Kuh				3427.8				1297.75	3392.87
Drachenblut Delikatessen	1030.76			1692	86.85				
Du monde entier		860.1					424		331.8
Eastern Connection	3063		2772	6524.68	796.35				
Ernst Handel	16139.71	8171.4	6221.5	24343.2	5218	550.59	8213.68	5510.59	1536.8
Familia Arquibaldo	224.83			525.3		310		1779.2	
Folies gourmandes	1622.4		756					4985.5	
Folk och fä HB	250.8	2860.65	2555.4	8474.44	2222.2	2844.5	695.62		
France restauration	519		1733.06						920.1
Franchi S.p.A.	49.8			1296					
Frankenversand	1078.69		2686.75	2825.3		1072.42	3536.6	1336.95	4807.9
Furia Bacalhau e Frutos do Mar			1926.58		1677.3		230.85		1288.39
Galería del gastrónomo	338.2	70	137.5			155			
Godos Cocina Típica		3831.46	2362.25	676.5	683.3			2775.05	1117.8
Gourmet Lanchonetes	1020		131.75	273.6					1119.94

Figure 28.15: A PivotTable such as this one linked to your relational database can give your dashboard up-to-the-minute results.

To automate the refresh of data imported from a text file or relational database, right-click in the data and choose Data Range Properties. In the External Data Range Properties dialog box that appears, use the following settings to control data refresh:

- Select Save Query Definition to keep the same query.
- Clear Prompt for File Name on Refresh, or you will be prompted for the filename each time the worksheet automatically refreshes.
- Select Refresh Data on File Open to refresh the data when the file opens.
- Select Refresh Every ___ Minutes to refresh the data at set intervals while the worksheet is open.

You need to consider how the new data will affect existing data in the worksheet. If the number of rows in the data range changes upon refresh, your options are

- Insert cells for new data, delete unused cells
- Insert entire rows for new data, clear used cells
- Overwrite existing cells with new data, clear unused cells

Linking Imported Data to Your Dashboard

There are many ways to link your imported data to your dashboard analytics. These methods have been covered primarily in Chapter 18, "Working with Lists and Tables of Data," and Chapter 21 "Feeding Dashboards from Pivot Tables."

If you have imported a flat file, like those in Chapter 18, insert a column to the left of the imported data and use a concatenation formula to create a unique key. Against this unique key you can use INDEX and MATCH to find data as explained in Chapter 18. When new data is imported, the key updates to match the new data.

> **TIP** If you insert columns of formulas adjacent to imported data, you want to make sure that the formulas expand to match the number of rows of data. To ensure that this happens, open the External Data Range Properties dialog box and select the Fill Down Formulas in Columns Adjacent to Data check box. Formulas will automatically fill adjacent columns to newly imported data.

Another method for linking your dashboard to an imported datalist is to use the imported list as the source for a PivotTable. Updating the PivotTable updates the data. Use the GETPIVOTDATA function as described in Chapter 21 to extract the data your dashboard needs.

Note: Creating an Auto-Expanding Database Name

The size of the data you import will probably change, but you need to refer to it consistently. To do this, use a dynamic range name to name your imported data. Chapter 21 includes a section titled "Creating An Auto-Expanding Database Name" that describes how to do this.

What is OLAP and When Should You Use It?

Relational and transactional databases work well enough when data is extracted in small amounts from smaller tables, when the databases are not under intense loads, and when data extraction does not require a lot of calculation and analysis. However, if your dashboards retrieve data from large data sets, if they require many calculations, if there are many transactions hitting the database from many users, or if the database is not optimized for your data requests, you may begin to see the following issues:

- Relational and transactional systems may be overloaded, which slows data transfer to your dashboards.
- Data requiring extensive calculations before export slows the system or the extraction.

- Users may lock each other out of files.

- You may need data multiple sources that merges with the appearance of a common *lingua franca*.

- Table and field names aren't understandable by business and Excel users.

- Data isn't normalized or calculated in the way expected by business and Excel users.

- Excel users are unable to develop their own queries.

The solution to these problems for many organizations is to use an Offline Analytical Processing (OLAP) cube. An OLAP cube will solve many of these problems and give you greater access and analytic ability, but there are trade-offs.

The data from an OLAP cube is not real-time — it is usually updated once a day. The OLAP cube is built from data in a relational or transaction database. This construction of the OLAP cube often occurs in the early hours of the morning. An advantage is that calculated data can be precalculated before it is needed. Another advantage is that table and field names can have names understandable to general business and Excel users. A detriment can be that OLAP cubes contain analytical summaries and calculations. They do not contain the original source data. That reduces or eliminates the ability to drill down multiple levels into data.

Even so, many organizations that have well-defined metrics and that understand their needs find that they are able to create highly productive dashboards and performance analyses using the more cost-effective OLAP cubes with Excel.

If you are interested in OLAP cubes that work with Excel, take a look at the products described in Table 28.1. These products cover a broad range of price points, IT involvement, and Excel accessibility.

Table 28.1: OLAP Cubes That Work with Excel

PRODUCT	VENDOR	COMMENT
TM1	Cognos (IBM)	The original OLAP product. It includes 25 Excel functions.
Analysis Services	Microsoft	Bundled with MS SQL Server. Requires significant IT involvement.
PowerOLAP	Palo	Well designed to work with Excel. Includes more than 60 functions for Excel users. Significant cost savings over Cognos and Microsoft versions. Recommended by ExcelUser.com.
XLCubed	XLCubed	This is an OLAP client that enhances Excel capabilities with OLAP Cubes. XLCubed is from the owners of MicroCharts, reviewed in Chapter 26, "Using Excel Add-ins for Extra Capabilities."

Summary

Having the most current data in your Balanced Scorecard or dashboard can be of paramount importance. At the same time, you don't want to create an administrative nightmare requiring extra labor just to maintain data. Using the tips from this chapter, you can integrate your dashboards with your data sources so that scorecards and dashboards update automatically. It is relatively easy to export text files from disparate systems to a common folder and then build dashboards that update automatically. Similarly, you can store dashboard data in an Access or SQL database and link directly to the data.

CHAPTER 29

Publishing Balanced Scorecards and Dashboards

*Knowing a great deal is not the same as being smart;
intelligence is not information alone but also judgment,
the manner in which information is collected and used.*

Dr. Carl Sagan
Astronomer, Scientist, Writer
1934–1996

Publishing your Balanced Scorecard or operational dashboards takes more thought than just sending out an e-mail or updating an Excel worksheet. Communicating your organization's performance gap requires a vehicle that can handle the analytics while being easy to develop and maintain, maintaining security on confidential data, producing portable content for traveling executives and managers, and having great presentation quality across multiple platforms.

There are many Business Intelligence (BI) tools and vendors, but the most widely used BI tool in corporate divisions and small- to mid-sized businesses continues to be Excel. Within this non-BI environment there are three main methods of distribution used for Balanced Scorecards and dashboards developed with Excel. Balanced Scorecards and dashboards can remain in Excel, with distribution through an e-mailed workbook, a shared folder on a network, or a portal such as Microsoft SharePoint. The two other methods of publishing and distribution are used for Balanced Scorecards. In these methods, Microsoft PowerPoint or Adobe Acrobat is used to publish a static version of a scorecard or dashboard. The pages of output are linked together by hyperlinks throughout PowerPoint slides or Adobe PDF pages. In either case, hyperlinks to external Excel workbooks can be used to open related interactive worksheets.

EXCEL, THE DEFAULT CLIENT TOOL OF BUSINESS INTELLIGENCE SOFTWARE

All large Business Intelligence software systems come with some form of query, reporting, and dashboard tool, but the vast majority of business people are devoted Excel users, not BI tool users. Not only do they have years of experience with Excel, they have worksheets they've spent years customizing for their specific needs. For this reason, many BI vendors include a data acquisition method so that Excel can access live data from the BI system. Some of the major vendor products that enable Excel to access BI data are Microsoft's PerformancePoint, Cognos's Business Intelligence Analysis for Microsoft Excel, and Business Objects' software.

Publishing Directly in Excel

Operational and performance dashboards created in Excel can often stay in Excel as long as users are trained in using the dashboard, or the dashboard is "bulletproofed." Chapter 27, "Finishing Touches," describes some methods of bulletproofing a dashboard and of giving it a professionally finished appearance.

Advantages of leaving a scorecard or dashboard in Excel and distributing it are that

- The business unit has an existing network or portal that can manage security for dashboard files.

- Many Excel users with one or two days' training such as the workshops we provide can develop a dashboard for their operational needs.

- Interactive dashboards that perform data queries or allow user interaction must be in Excel; such interactivity cannot be recreated in PowerPoint or Adobe PDF.

Disadvantages of using Excel as the distribution media are that

- Most dashboard developers cannot make scorecards or dashboards bulletproof, meaning that they should only be used by the developer and a small cohort.

- Widespread downloading of data without live links to a database can produce many versions of the truth — multiple dashboards, each showing a different result or slightly different data.

- Excel dashboards are difficult to scale and distribute widely throughout an organization. Many users may want their own private version of a dashboard, so they pirate it, causing havoc with version control and data integrity.

■ Dashboards look differently on different screens. If you have executives and managers using different versions of Excel on office computers and laptops and through VPNs from home, you will hear about the different appearances.

TIP Develop a naming convention and name worksheet tabs before you create hyperlinks in Excel. Hyperlinks reference the text of a tab name. The hyperlink does not automatically update when you change a tab's name, so changing a worksheet tab name may force you to recreate many hyperlinks.

Many of these disadvantages can be controlled with structure and discipline. Data integrity, or preventing "many versions of the truth," can be managed by creating Excel dashboards that use data links. And dashboards should always show the data source and time of data capture. Scalability is a larger issue. In large corporations, surveys have shown that some dashboards have more than 100 users. Such widespread use is difficult to control.

But Excel can be used very effectively, especially at the business unit level or in small- to mid-sized businesses that have an understanding of the contexts it works in and what problems it solves.

EXCEL IS AN EFFECTIVE TOOL FOR EXECUTIVE SCORECARDS

Throughout this book, the term scorecard has taken on the meaning of Balanced Scorecards, but Excel can also be used to create Executive Scorecards. Executive Scorecards are multi-dashboard systems similar to a Balanced Scorecard, but with metrics monitoring broad operational areas or aligning functionally rather than strategically.

Architecture

Workbook architecture is one of those topics that most people want to skip over in learning about Excel, but it will save you a lot of grief. I'll make this bulleted and quick, so please read these tips on best practices with Excel.

Most Excel users learn basic Excel in a one- or two-day class and then learn on the job thereafter. Consequently, few workbooks have an architecture that lends itself to easy maintenance. I doubt that there is one Excel user out there who hasn't created a worksheet and returned to it a year or even months later unable to immediately understand how it worked. Imagine what it is like when you inherit someone else's worksheets. For the preservation of your peace of mind, as well as the preservation of your business, use a standard architecture.

A few guiding rules:

- Use range names whenever possible to self-document your formulas.

- Use dynamic range names so that database and list names automatically expand. (Chapter 21, "Feeding Dashboards from PivotTables," includes a section titled "Creating An Auto-Expanding Database Name.")

- Keep all data, target values, and alert levels on a separate worksheet or workbook.

- Create each chart on its own worksheet.

- Keep the analytics for one dashboard on one worksheet.

- Lay out analytic worksheets in horizontal bands with labels naming the purpose of the band. For example, one band could be retrieval of queried data from the data worksheet, another band could be trend analysis, another band could be menu and form control settings, another band could be chart data, and so forth.

- Build tabular reports in a cascade of staggered rectangles from top left to bottom right on a worksheet. With this arrangement, inserting or changing the column width or row height through one report's table will not affect another table.

Publishing Multi-Dashboard Systems

If your dashboards require user interaction, such as querying new data or using combo boxes to change charts, you will need to distribute your dashboards in Excel. However, executive level dashboards that have 15 to 20 dashboards with pre-defined queries and static charts need a different method of distribution.

The most common method of publishing scorecards with multiple static dashboards is to encapsulate the views in a Microsoft PowerPoint presentation or in an Adobe Acrobat PDF. Encapsulating a fixed set of the most commonly viewed dashboards:

- Makes navigation easy

- Bulletproofs the system against untrained operators

- Creates a portable package that looks good on any display

- Keeps analysis at a strategic level rather than enabling detailed drill-down

- Keeps data highly secure when PDF files are used

- Enables collecting of comments and sticky notes on dashboards or score-cards when PDF files are used

Hierarchy of Views

Systems built for PowerPoint or PDF most commonly have one main page showing the Balanced Scorecard or the executive dashboard. This main page may be a simple text dashboard, as described in Chapter 15, "Text Based Dashboards," or it may be more robust, as shown in Figure 29.1. Pages like this are created in Excel, display live charts, show alert conditions, and can be published and distributed in either PowerPoint or PDF.

The advantage to using a main page such as this is that an executive can see the status of all metrics at a glance. Alert levels use a conditional color behind each chart. The miniature charts, from Chapter 19, "Creating Miniature Charts and Tables," actually reflect real data.

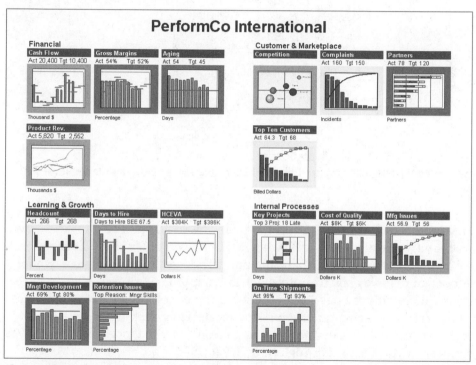

Figure 29.1: This Balanced Scorecard homepage was created in Excel and published for distribution as a PowerPoint slide or Adobe PDF page. Chart titles are hyperlinks to detailed information.

When the scorecard reader wants more detail, he can click the chart heading, a hyperlink, which takes him to the PowerPoint slide or PDF page that contains more detail. Figure 29.2 shows an example of a detailed view presented after clicking on a metrics title on the homepage of the Balanced Scorecard. Notice the navigation hyperlink buttons at the top left. Clicking one of these buttons takes the reader down to another level of detail or to a briefing book.

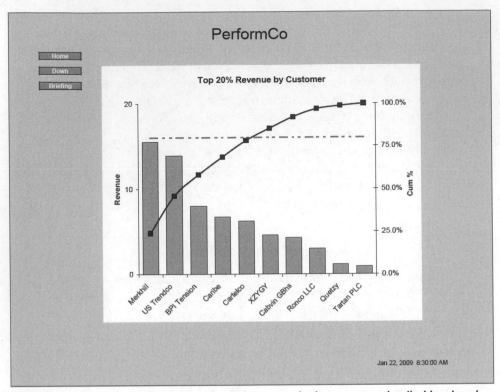

Figure 29.2: Clicking a title in the Balanced Scorecard takes you to a detailed level such as this.

Figure 29.3 shows a second level of drill-down. It is difficult to drill down more than two levels with Excel published in PowerPoint or PDF, because each layer adds a geometrically expanding number of static views. Here is where it is important to have done the interview and mapping work described in Parts I and II. Not only do you need to have the right metrics, you need to know what level of detail and viewpoint are needed for decision making.

In Figure 29.3, there is an Interactive button. This Balanced Scorecard was designed with a PDF containing all top-level charts and briefing books. At the lowest level, for some metrics, is an Interactive button. Clicking the Interactive button on a networked computer opens an Excel worksheet that enables users to do interactive queries on the source database.

Figure 29.4 shows the Briefing Book. A Briefing Book gives your readers access to the context, contacts, and actions for an operation or objective. Chapter 27, "Finishing Touches," describes how to add conditional e-mail links to Briefing Books.

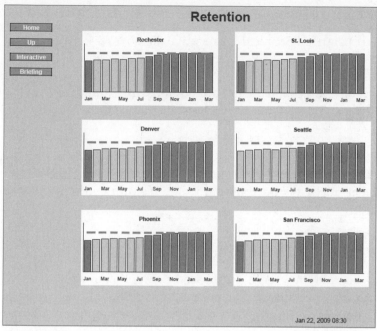

Figure 29.3: Although doing so increases complexity, you can create a drill-down to a second level of detail. The "Interactive" button in this figure is a hyperlink that opens an Excel workbook with interactive queries on this data.

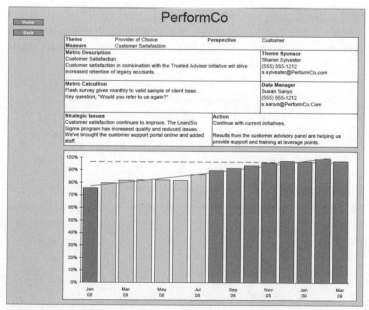

Figure 29.4: Always give your users a Briefing Book with the context, contacts, and current actions.

Deciding How to Publish Your Scorecard or Dashboard

You can publish your Balanced Scorecard, executive dashboard, or operational dashboards in Excel, PowerPoint, or PDF. Which of the three should you use? Here are a few criteria and alternatives.

If you are developing operational dashboards that require interactive operation, such as changing chart or data orientations, or that require links to live data, then:

- Use any version of Excel.
- Use one of the data acquisition methods described in Chapter 28, "Integrating Dashboards and External Data" if you need to automate data integration.

Balanced Scorecard in Excel 2007

If you are using Office 2007 to create a Balanced Scorecard or an Executive Scorecard with multiple operational dashboards, avoid the "issues" in links between Excel 2007 and PowerPoint 2007 by using one of the following two methods:

- Develop and maintain the system in Excel XP/2003 and publish in the matching version of PowerPoint XP/2003. If you need to distribute in PowerPoint 2007, import it to PowerPoint 2007 from the earlier version of PowerPoint, but do not change any links or refresh data in the PowerPoint slides.

or

- Develop and maintain in Excel 2007 or an earlier version and publish with Adobe Acrobat Professional v8.0 or newer. Do not publish with PowerPoint 2007.

TIP To learn more about the linkage issues between Excel 2007 and PowerPoint 2007, go to the Microsoft website and search for the error message "Some linked files were unavailable and can't be updated" or search for Article ID 927284.

Creating Less Complex Balanced Scorecards in PowerPoint

If you have only a few static dashboard views — perhaps 15 to 20 — without many layers of drill-down, and if high data security is not required, then:

- Develop and maintain in Excel XP/2003 and use Edit ⇨ Paste Link to transfer the charts and tables into PowerPoint XP/2003.
- Manually create and maintain hyperlink buttons on the PowerPoint slides to navigate between slides.

- When Excel data changes update PowerPoint slides with the Edit ⇨ Links command or by opening the PowerPoint presentation and all Excel files simultaneously, and then saving the PowerPoint file.

- Make PowerPoint slides that have hyperlink buttons that link "out" to an Excel workbook. Save the Excel workbook with the tab visible that you want to first see when the hyperlink is clicked.

Creating Complex or High-Security Balanced Scorecards in PDF

If you have a more complex Balanced Scorecards containing many slides with multiple layers, or requiring highly secure encryption, or you want to bind additional documents with the scorecard or dashboard, then:

- Develop and maintain in any version of Excel.

- Put all Balanced Scorecard worksheets you want to publish in one Excel workbook. As later diagrams show the workbook published in PDF may be fed by other analytic or data workbooks.

- Create text hyperlink buttons between worksheets in Excel to make navigation more structured. Text hyperlink buttons will be maintained when the PDF file is generated. This enables you to maintain all your construction and hyperlinks in one file.

- Publish your Balanced Scorecard from Excel to a PDF file with Adobe Acrobat, version 8.0 or newer. All text hyperlinks in the Excel source will be maintained. (Do not put hyperlinks on graphic objects in Excel as they may not publish in Adobe Acrobat.)

- Reopen the PDF file and add any other documents you want attached, enable comments and sticky notes for readers, and modify production settings.

Publishing in PowerPoint

Publishing Excel XP/2003 information in PowerPoint XP/2003 is straightforward. Whether you have many Excel workbooks or a single workbook, you will produce a single PowerPoint presentation that contains charts and tables linked to the original source in one or more Excel workbooks.

The result will be a PowerPoint presentation with slides that are a "snapshot" of a dashboard at one point in time. If the Excel data changes, you can refresh the PowerPoint file by updating the links in PowerPoint to the Excel charts and data.

Excel 2007 and PowerPoint 2007 have issues maintaining their links. The links between Excel 2007 and PowerPoint 2007 can be lost. A note in this chapter describes how to learn more at the Microsoft web site.

Microsoft Office applications, although they have a password protection feature, are not highly secure. The password in Office documents is to prevent settings and content from being modified by untrained users, not to prevent the theft of data. Utilities are available to break Microsoft Office passwords. If your dashboards contain highly confidential data, you should keep them inside a secure network or use the Adobe PDF method for publishing described later in this chapter.

Advantages and Disadvantages of Publishing in PowerPoint

The advantages of publishing in PowerPoint are that:

- Accurate screen reproduction is maintained on different monitors and resolutions.
- It is easy, but tedious, to create hyperlink buttons between PowerPoint slides.
- PowerPoint is bundled with Microsoft Office.
- It's easy to train someone to build and refresh the PowerPoint slides.
- A hyperlink on a slide can open an Excel dashboard.
- Executives and managers know how to operate PowerPoint.

The disadvantages of publishing in PowerPoint are that:

- All navigational hyperlinks must be manually drawn and linked.
- The number of hyperlinks can quickly become large and difficult to manage.
- Hyperlinks in Excel workbooks are not maintained when copied to PowerPoint.
- Excel 2007 and PowerPoint 2007 may not maintain links. When you attempt to refresh, you can receive the error message, "Some linked files were unavailable and can't be updated."

Architecture

Always separate data from analytics and charts as shown in Figure 29.5. Depending upon your situation, you may have the data in a separate worksheet or workbook from the analytics and charts. This gives you the ability to relink your analytics to other data sheets. It also enables users to enter data such as targets, alert levels, and briefing book commentary without working with the analytic and charts workbooks.

Analytics and charts may be in separate workbooks or a single larger workbook. The charts, tables, and briefing book comments that you want in the Balanced Scorecard are copied out of the source workbook and pasted with Paste Special into the PowerPoint presentation.

Navigational hyperlinks in the PowerPoint presentation must be created manually in the PowerPoint presentation. Keep all files in the same folder to reduce complexity and link failure.

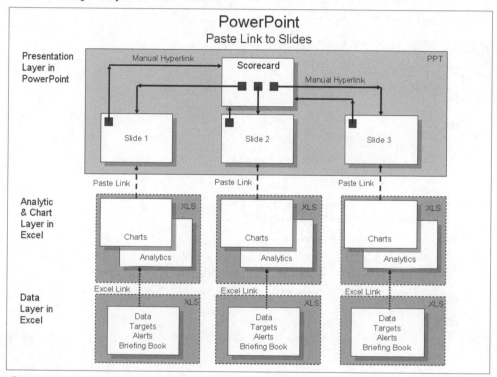

Figure 29.5: PowerPoint is frequently used to publish dynamically linked Excel charts and tables.

Step-by-Step to Creating the PowerPoint Presentation

Before you begin, make sure you have all Excel workbooks, data workbooks, and PowerPoint files in the same folder. This will reduce or eliminate link failure later.

Use the View ➪ Master ➪ Slide Master command to display the slide master. Format the slide master with common elements and formats you want in all slides, such as background, title, header, and footer.

To link a chart or table from Excel to a PowerPoint slide so that it can be refreshed when data changes:

1. Select the range of cells you want to show in the PowerPoint. If you are selecting a chart, select the range behind the chart.

2. Choose Edit ⇨ Copy.

3. Activate PowerPoint and display the blank slide that will contain this content.

4. Choose Edit ⇨ Paste Special to display the Paste Special dialog box shown in Figure 29.6.

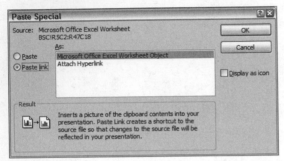

Figure 29.6: Copy the Excel range and then use Edit ⇨ Paste Link to create a linked PowerPoint slide.

5. Select Paste Link as Microsoft Office Excel Worksheet Object. This creates an object in PowerPoint that is linked back to the source Excel file. If the Excel range you selected contains hyperlinks, they are not copied.

6. Choose OK.

7. The Excel object will appear in the PowerPoint slide. Resize it by dragging the corner handles.

Create navigation buttons between slides by drawing buttons with the Drawing toolbar. Use the Insert ⇨ Hyperlink command, Ctrl+K, to link the button to another slide.

Once you have created PowerPoint slides with linked data, you can refresh slides when Excel files change by using the following steps:

1. Open the PowerPoint file.

2. Choose Edit ⇨ Links to display the Links dialog box.

3. Select the Excel workbooks containing new data. (You can use Ctrl+Click to select non-contiguous files or Shift+Click to select multiple contiguous files.)

4. Select Update Now or Open Source to update the slides.

5. Choose Close.

If you are working in a PowerPoint slide and need to open the source Excel workbook, double-click the Excel object in the PowerPoint slide. This opens Excel and loads the source workbook.

Publishing in Adobe Acrobat

Although most people who create Excel-based Balanced Scorecards publish them in PowerPoint, Adobe Acrobat has some distinct advantages. For one thing, if you are using Office 2007 on a network, publishing in a PDF is more stable than publishing in PowerPoint 2007. Furthermore, Acrobat is designed for high-quality production and presentation on any output device. All text hyperlinks in the Excel source are maintained in the PDF that is published. This means that if you can create and maintain the majority of the navigation system in Excel, it will automatically convert in PDF. When you are building a Balanced Scorecard that might have a homepage, 15 main pages, 8 drill-down detail pages, and 15 briefing books, with three or four hyperlinks on each page, it becomes much easier to maintain the links in the Excel source document.

> **CAUTION** Before you begin creating navigational hyperlinks in Excel, make sure worksheet tabs have their final names. Excel hyperlinks reference worksheet tabs as text names — the hyperlink does not automatically update if you change the tab name. If you change a tab name, you will have to manually update all hyperlinks pointing to it.
>
> Second, do not create graphical hyperlink buttons in Excel if you want to convert the file to PDF. Hyperlinks on graphics cause problems in Adobe Acrobat 8. Instead, create text hyperlinks in a cell that is formatted to look like a button. As Chapter 25, "Drilling to Details and Navigating to Locations," explains, text hyperlinks are very easy to create and copy between worksheets.

Advantages and Disadvantages of Publishing in PDF

There are many advantages to publishing a Balanced Scorecard in PDF:

- Text-based hyperlinks can be maintained in Excel and published to PDF.

- Adobe Acrobat has multiple types and levels of security, including public-key encryption and certificates. Certificates enable you to publish with different levels of access for different types of users.

- Readers with the free Adobe Reader can add comments and sticky notes that others can see, as shown in Figure 29.7.

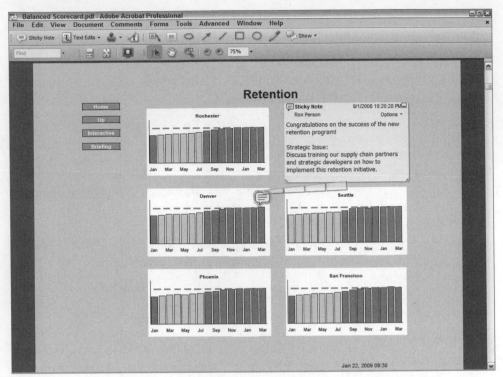

Figure 29.7: Balanced Scorecard readers using the free Adobe Reader can post comments and sticky notes on the PDF for others to read.

- Other document formats can be included in the PDF, enabling you to include and link to backup context and documentation originally sourced in Word, PDF, image files, AutoCad, and so on.

- The PDF file is refreshed by regenerating the PDF which reimports all source files you originally used. You can edit the list of source files before refreshing if you desire.

Additional advantages to publishing in PDF are that

- It displays consistently on any computer and screen resolution.

- A free PDF viewer, Adobe Reader, includes the ability to add comments and sticky notes.

- Links to external files can be created manually in the Acrobat document.

- Acrobat works with Excel 2007, bypassing the linkage issues with PowerPoint 2007.

- Output can be of the highest print or media quality.

- Hyperlinks can open files outside the PDF, such as an interactive Excel file.

The disadvantages of publishing Excel worksheets to a PDF are

■ The high purchase price of Adobe Acrobat Professional

■ Learning "yet another" piece of software

■ Teaching executives how to maximize the PDF to full screen (Ctrl+L for full screen and Esc to return) and how to add comments or sticky notes.

■ Developing the page setup settings for publication. (You need to discover the page setup settings in Excel that fit your PDF output.)

■ Developing the settings for customized headings, background colors, watermarks, and so on.

Architecture

This is repeating what has been said before, but put your data in a separate worksheet or workbook, as illustrated in Figure 29.8. Any worksheets in Excel that hyperlink to other Excel worksheets must be in the same workbook if you want the hyperlinks to continue working in the PDF.

Once the Excel workbook is converted to PDF, it will no longer have a connection or data link to the original Excel source document. However, you can easily update the PDF when Excel data changes by using Adobe Acrobat's File ➪ Combine Files ➪ Reuse Files command, as explained later in this chapter.

Step-by-Step to Publishing in Adobe PDF

The software you need for publishing a Balanced Scorecard in PDF format is Adobe Acrobat. The resulting PDF files can be read with the free Adobe Reader. You can get a trial version of Adobe Acrobat and a free copy of Adobe Reader at www.adobe.com.

TIP If there is a formatting, indexing, setup, or production capability you need, Adobe Acrobat has it. Adobe Acrobat has been used for years by commercial printers to prepare files for print production, so just about any production feature you can think of has been incorporated.

To publish your Excel-based Balanced Scorecard in PDF

1. Create your Balanced Scorecard as shown in the architecture schema in Figure 29.8. All hyperlinks in Excel must use text hyperlinks, and the links between worksheets must be within the same workbook for them to refer to the equivalent page in the PDF. Links in Excel to another Excel workbook will open the Excel workbook.

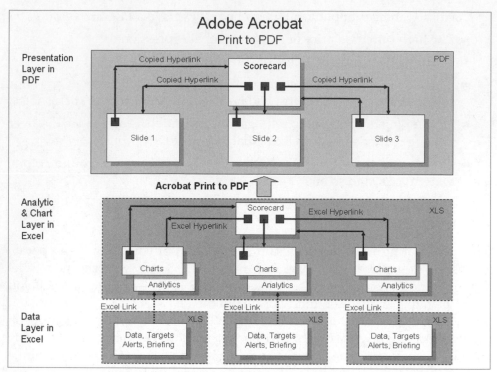

Figure 29.8: Publishing a Balanced Scorecard in PDF file format provides a secure file format that updates with a single click of the mouse in Adobe Acrobat Pro.

2. Create all Excel worksheets (tabs) with the page setup they will use when published to PDF. Set the print format in Excel as landscape with minimum margins and the page centering horizontally and vertically, and be consistent across all pages settings.

> **TIP** In Adobe Acrobat, after you select a workbook(s), select the worksheets you want to include in the PDF. The worksheets appear in the PDF exactly as they would if printed. A best practice is to format all worksheets to be printed with the same page setup so that they all have the same positioning and appearance in the PDF.

3. Put all files in one folder. Include in that folder any additional documents such as other Excel workbooks, Word documents, AutoCAD files, PDF documents, or graphics you want in the final PDF. The final PDF document can contain content from multiple documents, not just the Excel Balanced Scorecard.

4. Open Adobe Acrobat.

5. Choose File ⇨ Combine ⇨ From Multiple Files to display the Combine Files dialog box.

6. Choose the Add Files button and then select the file(s) containing your Balanced Scorecard and the other documents you want included in the Balanced Scorecard PDF. Choose Add Files. Figure 29.9 shows the Combine Files dialog box.

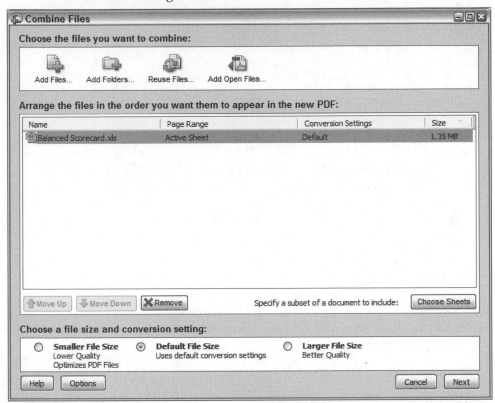

Figure 29.9: Select the workbooks and other files in the Combine Files dialog box.

7. Reorganize files in the order you want by selecting a file and clicking the Move Up button.

8. Select which worksheets in a workbook you want in the PDF by selecting the filename and choosing the Choose Sheets button.

9. In the Preview and Select Sheets dialog box, shown in Figure 29.10, select the sheets you want in the PDF. Organize the sheets in the order you want them to appear. You can preview a worksheet by selecting its tab in the preview window. Choose OK.

10. Choose Next and select Merge Files Into a Single PDF.

11. Choose Create.

12. Choose Save, and then Save again, to save the PDF file so it can be reused to remember the files merged, as well as any custom backgrounds or headers you add.

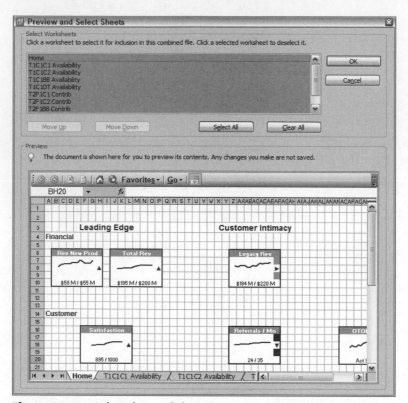

Figure 29.10: Select the worksheets you want printed using the Preview and Select Sheets dialog box.

The PDF you have created contains the worksheets you specified and any other document pages you included. Text hyperlinks in the Excel file are converted for use in the PDF.

Some modifications to the PDF file you may want to make are:

- Manually creating any hyperlinks in the PDF that were not created in the PDF. This might include buttons in the PDF that open Excel files, backup documentation, or videos.

- Formatting the PDF file to display titles common to each page, to use background colors to fill to the margins, and so forth.

- Giving readers the ability to add comments and markups by choosing the command Advanced ⇨ Enable Usage Rights in Adobe Reader.

- Adding the security and encryption levels you want.

- Making sure you resave the Adobe PDF file you have modified.

Once you have a created a PDF file that contains your Balanced Scorecard and any backup documentation, you can refresh when the Excel source files change. Make sure all source files are still in the same folders. To refresh the PDF file

1. Choose Files ➪ Combine.

2. In the Combine Files dialog box, choose the Reuse Files button.

3. Choose the PDF file you want to refresh from the Recently Combined Files list. The source workbooks and documents used in that PDF appear in the File Contents to Reuse list on the right.

4. Choose Add Files.

5. Choose Next.

6. Choose Create.

7. Choose Save.

8. Choose Save.

Summary

As a Balanced Scorecard and dashboard developer, you walk a tightrope between executive teams with a strategic, long-range view and operational teams with a detailed, up-to-the-minute view. The executive leadership team needs an easy-to-navigate, high-level view of the "critical few" strategic metrics and operational performance. They only need to see enough detail to be able to identify a general area of issues. Usually one or two levels of drill-down along pre-defined queries are sufficient. On the other hand, operational and performance management requires the ability to drill down to lower levels and to perform interactive queries to find the cause of issues. This requires a robust Excel dashboard that may link to a database.

Index